DRONES AND INTERNATIONAL LAW

Rebecca Mignot-Mahdavi explores the ways in which war, technology, and the law interact and reshape one another in the context of counter-terrorism. She demonstrates that drone programs are techno-legal machineries that facilitate and accelerate the emergence of a new kind of warfare. This new model of warfare is individualized and dematerialized in the sense that it focuses on threat anticipation and thus consists in identifying dangerous figures (individualized warfare) rather than responding to acts of hostilities (material warfare). Revolving around threat anticipation, drone wars endure over an extensive timeframe and geographical area, to the extent that the use of drones may even be seen, as appears to be the case for the United States, as part of the normal functioning of the state, with profound consequences for the international legal order.

REBECCA MIGNOT-MAHDAVI is Lecturer in International Law at the University of Manchester. She is a leading expert on issues of global security governance. Her work reflects on states' evolving legal and policy capacity to deal with security threats, where new forms of non-state transnational risk, counter-risk strategy, and technology are in play. She has also been a guest lecturer at Sciences Po since 2018, an associate fellow at the T.M.C. Asser Institute (University of Amsterdam), a research fellow at the International Center for Counter-Terrorism, and a member of the Board of Directors of the International Society for Military Law and the Law of War.

CAMBRIDGE STUDIES IN INTERNATIONAL AND COMPARATIVE LAW: 180

Established in 1946, this series produces high quality, reflective and innovative scholarship in the field of public international law. It publishes works on international law that are of a theoretical, historical, cross-disciplinary or doctrinal nature. The series also welcomes books providing insights from private international law, comparative law and transnational studies which inform international legal thought and practice more generally.

The series seeks to publish views from diverse legal traditions and perspectives, and of any geographical origin. In this respect it invites studies offering regional perspectives on core *problématiques* of international law, and in the same vein, it appreciates contrasts and debates between diverging approaches. Accordingly, books offering new or less orthodox perspectives are very much welcome. Works of a generalist character are greatly valued and the series is also open to studies on specific areas, institutions or problems. Translations of the most outstanding works published in other languages are also considered.

After seventy years, Cambridge Studies in International and Comparative Law sets the standard for international legal scholarship and will continue to define the discipline as it evolves in the years to come.

A list of books in the series can be found at the end of this volume.

DRONES AND INTERNATIONAL LAW

A Techno-Legal Machinery

REBECCA MIGNOT-MAHDAVI
University of Manchester

CAMBRIDGE
UNIVERSITY PRESS

CAMBRIDGE UNIVERSITY PRESS

Shaftesbury Road, Cambridge CB2 8EA, United Kingdom

One Liberty Plaza, 20th Floor, New York, NY 10006, USA

477 Williamstown Road, Port Melbourne, VIC 3207, Australia

314–321, 3rd Floor, Plot 3, Splendor Forum, Jasola District Centre, New Delhi – 110025, India

103 Penang Road, #05-06/07, Visioncrest Commercial, Singapore 238467

Cambridge University Press is part of Cambridge University Press & Assessment, a department of the University of Cambridge.

We share the University's mission to contribute to society through the pursuit of education, learning and research at the highest international levels of excellence.

www.cambridge.org
Information on this title: www.cambridge.org/9781009346559

DOI: 10.1017/9781009346603

First published 2023

A catalogue record for this publication is available from the British Library.

Library of Congress Cataloging-in-Publication Data
Names: Mignot-Mahdavi, Rebecca, 1992- author.
Title: Drones and international law : a techno-legal machinery / Rebecca Mignot-Mahdavi, University of Manchester.
Description: Cambridge, United Kingdom ; New York, NY : Cambridge University Press, 2023. | Series: Cambridge studies in international and comparative law | Includes bibliographical references and index.
Identifiers: LCCN 2022058740 (print) | LCCN 2022058741 (ebook) | ISBN 9781009346559 (hardback) | ISBN 9781009346597 (paperback) | ISBN 9781009346603 (epub)
Subjects: LCSH: Uninhabited combat aerial vehicles (International law) | Drone aircraft–Law and legislation.
Classification: LCC KZ6687 .M54 2023 (print) | LCC KZ6687 (ebook) | DDC 341.6/3–dc23/eng/20230105
LC record available at https://lccn.loc.gov/2022058740
LC ebook record available at https://lccn.loc.gov/2022058741

ISBN 978-1-009-34655-9 Hardback

To my mother, Sophie Mahdavi

CONTENTS

FOREWORD

As I write this Foreword, twenty-one years to the day since the terrorist attacks of September 11, 2001, one might reasonably ask, "Do we need another book on armed drones?" The expansion and proliferation of the use of the technology in the service of the targeted killings of suspected terrorists has engendered macabre fascination and outraged denunciation since the first, shadowy strike conducted by the US against Qa'id Salim Sinan Al-Harithi in November 2002. Previous Israeli uses of the tactic of targeted killing had been criticized by the US government as extrajudicial executions, but it has been widely documented that the US embraced targeted killing with both arms after it declared a global conflict with Al-Qaeda and "associated" non-state armed groups. As the conflict in Afghanistan dragged on, and a new and even more destructive conflict in Iraq was initiated by the US-led invasion, the global use of drone technology to conduct not only surveillance and intelligence operations ("finding" and "fixing") but also striking at targets ("finishing") has proliferated: in addition to Yemen, Afghanistan, Pakistan, and Iraq, Somalia, Mali, Syria, and Libya were places in which drone strikes took place against suspected non-stated armed groups. Most recently, Osama bin Laden's deputy Ayman al-Zawahiri was killed on the balcony of his safe house in Kabul on July 31, 2022, showing unequivocally that such strikes will continue even after – or perhaps because of – the end of "boots on the ground" in Afghanistan. Several other countries, including France and the UK, have in recent years adopted both the legal rationales and the technological instruments necessary to conduct drone strikes.

The evolution of the technology, bureaucracy, legal rationales, and institutional routines enabling this practice has been written about from a wide variety of angles over the last twenty years: journalistic, theoretical, legalistic, and more. Almost all studies have focused on the US program, overlooking the emerging adoption of the practice and technology by European states and others such as Australia. But Rebecca

Mignot-Mahdavi's account transcends these narrower approaches and offers instead a holistic vantage point on what she calls a "techno-legal machinery" that has become durable and continuous: an assemblage of legal rationales that stretch and reshape core legal concepts in the international law of self-defense and international laws of war; an extensive set of affordances enabled by multiple technological developments that have been assembled around and united through legal arguments and bureaucratic routines; a steadily growing infrastructure of airstrips, sensing equipment, data collection and processing, control rooms, satellite links, and computational power. Mignot-Mahdavi shows us that, taken as a whole, this assemblage has not only become highly stable and self-perpetuating, but it is now continuously future-oriented in its preoccupation with new and emerging threats.

The promise of an organized and permanent apparatus of surveillance, intelligence gathering, and data collection and processing is intensified and accelerated by innovations in machine learning and big data analytics. This is exemplified by the US Department of Defense's 2017 creation of the Algorithmic Warfare Cross-function Team, "Project Maven," to maximize the exploitation of 700,000 hours of drone footage and other data gathered during counterinsurgency drone operations.[1] The aim of this special taskforce was to bring artificial intelligence / machine learning techniques to bear on this vast data archive, in order to yield more actionable battlefield intelligence. Project Maven was recently transferred to the authority of the National Geo-Spatial Intelligence Agency in order to accelerate the development of "computer vision efforts that will deliver automated GEOINT detections to both intelligence analysts and warfighters. . . . These efforts will give us our millions of eyes to see the unseen."[2] The infamous Gorgon Stare[3] of the Predator drone is thus not just a piece of hardware. It is also a metaphor for a permanent state of

[1] Richard H. Schulz and Richard D. Clarke, "Big Data at War: Special Operations Forces, Project Maven, and Twenty-First-Century Warfare," August 25, 2020, Modern War Institute Blog, https://mwi.usma.edu/big-data-at-war-special-operations-forces-project-maven-and-twenty-first-century-warfare/.

[2] Vice Admiral Robert Sharp, then-director of the National Geospatial-Intelligence Agency, quoted in Theresa Hitchens, "Pentagon's Flagship AI Effort, Project Maven, Moves to NGA," April 27, 2022, *Breaking Defense*, https://breakingdefense.com/2022/04/pentagons-flagship-ai-effort-project-maven-moves-to-nga/.

[3] Arthur Holland Michel, *Eyes in the Sky: The Secret Rise of Gorgon Stare and How It Will Watch Us All* (Mariner Books, 2019).

anticipation and threat awareness afforded by the techno-legal machinery in which drones are a central actant.

Mignot-Mahdavi's book allows us to better grasp this state of affairs and see its implications more clearly. In the process she has assembled an indispensable archive of the present, piecing together factual and technical information, reportage, legal analysis, and theoretical constructs from a vast literature. The role of law is placed within this machinery not simply as rule or standard, permission or prohibition. Rather, it emerges as *the* indispensable medium for the construction and articulation of many moving parts – it authorizes, to be sure, but it also backstops the creation of new bureaucratic roles and institutional routines, and makes possible the continuity of the drone program across four different US administrations. The premises of the global battlefield, the continuous combatant, the unending *casus belli* provided by the continued *existence* of designated terrorist groups, the unwilling or unable state lacking effective sovereignty: all of these legal devices are soberly reconstructed and examined, not with the apoplexy of someone who believes that law can save us from institutionalized violence but with a coolly diagnostic eye of the analyst seeking to reverse engineer a system that now seems to run itself. Each of these legal arguments was individually controversial over the last twenty years; taken as a whole and operationalized into a standing bureaucracy of threat identification and lethal force application, they represent a revolution in the law governing the use of force by one state in the territory of another. The asymmetry in the application of these concepts should be self-evident: We find ourselves plausibly debating the legality of drone strikes over Misrata, but certainly not over Manchester or Munich. The intuitive hierarchy of sovereignty presupposed by this contrast is given legal form by the constellation of legal concepts that have been recalibrated in order to stabilize the techno-legal machinery of drone strikes. As Mignot-Mahdavi shows, this hierarchy of sovereignty brings with it a hierarchy of humanity: only some, such as denizens of Yemen or North-West Pakistan, will be compelled to bear the losses eventuating from the functioning of this vast apparatus.

The originality and insight yielded by the analysis and research found in this book answer the question I posed at the outset of this Foreword, "Do we need another book on armed drones?": Yes, we need this one.

Professor Nehal Bhuta
Chair of International Law, University of Edinburgh

ACKNOWLEDGMENTS

My unlimited thanks go to my mother, Sophie, and my father, André, for offering me the keys to explore what is visible to the eyes, but not always easy to fetch and cherish, and what is more imperceptible in the dark. Every day of my life, I have been lucky enough to get inspiration and unwavering support from two loving and free-spirited human beings who never stop learning, trying to understand the complexities of the world, and do it always with tolerance for the vulnerable, *esprit critique*, indignation but also playfulness and joy. *Merci, maman, de me porter à tout âge pour penser, oser et jouer – ce travail t'est dédié à toi, à ta force et à ta douceur, aux racines et aux ailes que tu t'es et m'as données, à ta liberté.* From a distance or close-up, my family's support and love gave me serenity and rootedness. I also wish to thank my friends, for being such inspiring, trustworthy, tolerant, strong, and loving women.

I would like to acknowledge the generosity, with their time and mind, of Nicola Hargreaves, Professor Sarah Cleveland, Professor Steve Ratner, Professor Avril Haines, Professor Jennifer Welsh, Professor Damien Scalia, Professor Dapo Akande, Professor Stéphanie Hennette-Vauchez, and Professor Bernard Harcourt. Discussions with colleagues of the Human Rights Institute of Columbia Law School, of the Individualization of War Project, of the European Forum on Armed Drones, and of the EUI International Law Working Group, and also with those whom I met at conferences and workshops, especially at the Lieber Institute of WestPoint and at the ESIL Conference in Athens, have been very constructive and inspiring. In the process of turning the thesis into a book, Sara Kendall, Loïc Azoulai, and Claus Kress have been the most generous readers and examiners I could have wished for. I will carry the memory of our discussion on December 11, 2020, forever with me. I also wish to thank the Asser community and in particular Janne Nijman, Christophe Paulussen, Sofia Stolk, Geoff Gordon, Rumyana van Ark, Berenice Boutin, and Klaudia Klonowska. I am finalizing this book in my new home, the Manchester International Law Center, where I have again met inspiring and kindhearted colleagues and friends.

I am also forever grateful to the students who followed my classes at the University of Nanterre, Sciences Po, the University of Amsterdam, and the University of Manchester. Thank you for embarking on the learning processes I invite you on with rigor, enthusiasm, and creativity. You, and the students I will meet in the future, give me the impetus to carry out these projects. The same goes for the inspiring teachers and professors I have met along the way, from a very young age; those who were passionate about sharing with us tools that would help us think independently and critically: from Mr. Chabanel in fourth grade, Mrs. Blasco and Mr. Morris in secondary school and high school, to Professor Goulven Boudic, Professor Charlotte Girard, Professor Vaurs-Chaumette, Marina Eudes, Professor Champeil-Desplats, Professor Julian Fernandez, and, of course, Professor Poncela (and through her, I dare say, Michel Foucault!).

Professor Bhuta, Nehal, your guidance has exceeded all expectations I had when entering this journey. Thank you for believing in this project and my ability to carry it out; for giving me the space to freely explore my intuitions even when they were at the stage of Foucauldian babbling. Thank you for helping me to navigate at the right pace, in the right direction, and for giving me the support and inspiration to turn seemingly tumultuous seas into friendly ones. My heartfelt thanks for making this exploration one that never ceased to be intellectually stimulating, but also one of mutual respect, recognition, and friendship. One that I ended with nostalgia and, above all, with lasting memories of discussions behind gigantic piles of books, from Schifanoia to Edinburgh.

1

Drone Programs Reconfiguring War, Law, and Societies around Threat Anticipation

This is a story about how war, drone technologies, and the law interact and reshape one another in the counterterrorism context.[1] This interaction between war, drone technologies, and the law constitutes what is called here a program. By conceptualizing this interaction as forming a program, this book shows how the elements surrounding and constituting these programs form a network of interrelated factors. The book draws together the technological, the military, and the legal, without centering on one of these elements as being isolated[2] or singular.[3] This attempt to explore drone uses as a program entails compiling their textual, bureaucratic, and material traces and thus avoids reducing the phenomena surrounding drone uses to drone strikes. The book is accordingly an act of making visible the multiple textures of the socio-techno-legal phenomena related to drone technologies, from surveillance to targeting. Ultimately, this book lays bare the ways in

[1] This study focuses on aerial drones that are used for military purposes, also called "combat drones," "military drones," Unmanned Combat Aerial Vehicles (UCAV), or Remotely Piloted Aircraft Systems (R.P.A.S). *Oxford Essential Dictionary of the US military*: A drone is "a vehicle designed to be remotely controlled during operations on land or sea or in the air." Human intervention is still at play. In this sense, drones have to be distinguished from autonomous weapons systems. Drone pilots, and not the drone itself, make the decision to kill. The case studies are mostly related to drones that are not only equipped with surveillance capabilities but also capable of conducting lethal strikes. This does not mean that the findings are only applicable to this type of drones. In fact, many findings apply to surveillance drones, especially when they are used in the same contexts as combat drones.

[2] John Law, *Aircraft Stories: Decentering the Object in Technoscience* (Duke University Press, 2002), 2: Law talks about fractional coherence as the way of "drawing things together without centering them"; "Knowing subjects, or so we've learned since the 1960s, are not coherent wholes. Instead they are multiple, assemblages. This has been said about subjects of action, of emotion, and of desire in many ways, and is often, to be sure, a poststructuralist claim. But I argue in this book that the same holds for objects too."

[3] Ibid., 3–4. Considering these elements or factors as singular, would entail assuming that they hold together coherently.

which drone programs extend warfare in time and space, while exacerbating state power.

How can and should one write a story about such multi-textured phenomena?[4] This book embraces and cultivates the idea that the purpose of (socio-)legal scholarship is not to clarify or simplify social phenomena, in our case, socio-techno-legal phenomena.[5] The book identifies as many textures and elements composing such phenomena as possible – a potentially endless exercise if not delineated by time, space, and subjectivity, as it is here. In doing so, the book intends to make some of drone programs' textures visible in a meticulous way. Simultaneously, by telling this story of drone programs, the book cannot avoid performing and producing them.

Interest in drone wars is unlikely to fade for many reasons. Drone wars that reached a peak in the United States (US) in the early 2010s[6] are now spreading. While most literature on drone wars has focused on the US drone wars, this study intends to grapple with the role that the technology plays in reshaping warfare and pushing gray legal areas to breaking points beyond the confines of US drone wars of the Obama era. It explores the UK and French case studies alongside the US drone wars under Presidents Bush, Obama, and Trump. Following the UK, which started using combat drones in 2014,[7] France started using its first armed Reapers from its Niamey base in Niger against jihadist groups in the Sahel region in late 2019[8] and is still involved in the Sahel region.[9] In addition, in February 2019, Australia announced the development of a locally designed combat drone, capable of both surveillance and

[4] This exercise in self-reflexivity about positionality when trying to make visible the different facets and elements of textured phenomena is encouraged by John Law, both in his *Aircraft Stories*, ibid. and in John Law, *After Method: Mess in Social Science Research* (Routledge, 2004).

[5] Law, *After Method.*

[6] See Database of The Bureau of Investigative Journalism on Drone Warfare, www.thebureauinvestigates.com/projects/drone-war.

[7] See statistics of Drone Wars UK, https://dronewars.net/uk-drone-strike-list-2/.

[8] Madame Florence Parly, Ministre des armées, Université d'été de la défense 2017, "Discours de clôture," Toulon, September 5, 2017, www.defense.gouv.fr/salle-de-presse/discours/discours-de-florence-parly/discours-de-cloture-de-florence-parly-universite-d-ete-de-la-defense-2017; Loi de programmation militaire 2019–2025, July 2018, see also the Annexed report; Nathalie Guibert, "La France entre dans l'ère des drones armés," *Le Monde*, March 21, 2019, www.lemonde.fr/international/article/2019/03/21/la-france-entre-dans-l-ere-des-drones-armes_5439209_3210.html.

[9] French Ministry of Armed Forces, Opération Barkhane, www.defense.gouv.fr/operations/bande-sahelo-saharienne/operation-barkhane.

targeting,[10] and the manufacturing by Boeing is being finalized at the time of writing in March 2022.

Even if this book focuses on the use of combat drones by states against non-state actors, it is interesting to note that non-state armed groups increasingly use commercial drone technology to manufacture their own home-made explosive systems of varying degrees of sophistication.[11] Still today, however, drones used by non-state armed groups do not share the technical capacities of state-used drones, not only in terms of strength and precision of the strikes they are capable to conduct, but also with regard to the surveillance apparatus that characterize state-used drones on which this study focuses.

The preoccupations of the book are organized around a series of questions. How do drone technologies (from surveillance to targeting capacities), legal narratives, and military strategy interact with and reshape one another? What reality does this interplay bring about? Is there anything specific to counterterrorism uses of drones and drone technologies that explains the intensification of the pressures put on the international norms regulating the use of force in the counterterrorism context?

1.1 Drone Programs as a Network of Interacting Factors: Law × Technology × Military Strategy × Enemy

Describing drone programs as a network of interacting and interdependent factors including the contemporary technological capacities of drones, law, and military strategy is one of the main aspects of this study. All chapters identify where and how these factors converge or diverge and examine the result of this interaction. This description shows that combat drone technologies facilitate anticipatory warfare – the scope of which is indefinite in time and space – and that the law is rearranged around anticipation.

[10] Minister for Defense, the Rt. Hon. Christopher Pyne MP, Joint Media Release, “Australian-Designed Unmanned ‘Loyal Wingman’ Aircraft to Be Developed with Industry,” February 27, 2019, www.minister.defence.gov.au/minister/steven-ciobo/media-releases/australian-designed-unmanned-loyal-wingman-aircraft-be.

[11] Ash Rossiter, “Drone Usage by Militant Groups: Exploring Variation in Adoption” (2018) 34 *Defense and Security Analysis* 2, 113–26; Linda Schlegel, “Interview: Rising Drone Capabilities of Non-state Actors,” *Global Risk Insights*, April 17, 2018, https://globalriskinsights.com/2018/04/interview-risk-non-state-actor-drone-capabilities/.

Anticipation in a war paradigm means that the decision to use force is based not on material circumstances of armed attack or participation in hostilities, depending on the framework we are interested in. Instead, the decision to use force is triggered by the behavior of the target and elements of context, taken to reveal that the individual belongs to a transnational terrorist group. The objective to anticipate threats dictates that if there is a capacity to kill an individual who has a hostile intent and belongs to a militant group before they conduct an attack, action is taken based on available behavioral and contextual elements. The military strategy and practice of anticipation at war in the counterterrorism context can be broken down and conceptualized in two ways: first, through what the book calls individualized warfare, and second, through its corollary, the dematerialized decision to use force. Drone surveillance and strikes consist in identifying dangerous figures (*individualized warfare*) rather than responding to witnessed acts of hostilities (*material warfare*).

The studied states have crafted legal narratives to justify this individualized and dematerialized kind of warfare facilitated by drones. These states have put the laws regulating the use of force against non-state armed groups at the heart of their justification and interpreted them to accommodate anticipatory warfare. These narratives have stepped up the pressure put on the norms, by exploiting legal uncertainties such as that regarding the temporal scope of conflicts, and by offering novel legal interpretations, such as direct participation in hostilities in the form of continuous combat function, or the right of self-defense as a paradigm to tackle threats posed by individuals with hostile intent rather than by armed attacks.

Further examining the socio-techno-legal phenomena produced by drone programs, the book explores the long-term effects of drone programs over populations living under drones in particular, and over the international legal order in general. While the literature provides a thorough discussion of the different legal interpretations suggested by the US and the UK to regulate drone operations, scholarly reflections have not focused on the broader socio-legal implications of drone programs as a whole. Because it was initially ruled out that drones might play a specific role in reshaping the military strategy and practice against non-state actors and in making new legal rationales emerge, the extra step of investigating the potential long-term effects of drone programs was not made. I give a concrete account of US power rituals through the analysis of the US drone program as it is the most stable and the one that has been the object of socio-legal investigations. In a granular manner, the book shows that once drone programs are institutionalized, they have a serious impact on state power, with an operating state that conducts rituals of sovereignty over the populations living under drones.

The book proposes an explanation for how and why states active in the war on terror use the law in more or less malleable ways depending on the actor concerned. On the one hand, third states, affected by this expansion of state power, are tamed through notions such as unwilling/unable. While such concepts derive from extensive legal interpretations, the norms so interpreted are still recognizable. On the other hand, jihadist groups – which in the last instance are the *raison d'être* of this expansion of a surveillance and targeting apparatus extraterritorially – are the object of legal rationales that push legal gray zones to breaking points to such an extent that some norms' contents and meanings are difficult to recognize, and the possibility of infinite warfare emerges.

Different theories about the law have emerged from the debate on the proposed legal rationales for drone programs. On the one hand, the US legal rationales articulated for the development of the US drone program – used to certain extents by France and the UK – have never consisted in pseudo-scientific discourses or truth claims about the law. They do not claim that there is only one possible interpretation (the one they support) of international legal norms. On the contrary, they rest on the idea that a norm can be interpreted in multiple ways as norms and their open texture provide possibilities for struggles and reasonable disagreements about the interpretation of norms. Furthermore, these legal rationales consider that such struggles and reasonable disagreements are necessarily embedded in specific contexts and depend on contemporary goals and tactics. Following this understanding of the law, the studied states propose norm interpretations in accordance with a specific context – the war against transnational jihadist groups – in accordance with a certain mode of warfare – data warfare, and precise targeted killings, through drones – and adapted to a related military strategy – anticipation of threats and individualization of war.

On the other hand, most legal scholarship against the use of drones tends to deny that the content(s) of norms have a historical trajectory and often frames absolute truth discourses about the content of the norms. They tend to neglect the room for reasonable disagreements and sound unrooted in front of states' legal rationales. This book suggests that states' legal rationales reflect a more powerful and refined theory about the law than the theory embraced by many scholars and NGOs who have argued against drone programs. As a result of weak counterarguments, the book shows that states active in the war on terror have exploited the semantic possibilities of the norms and their uncertainties in such a way that their rationales have reset some of the limits and reshaped the contents of key conceptual differentiations and oppositions (combatant/civilian, criminal/enemy, status/conduct, battlefield/non-battlefield).

Another flaw in existing debates, exceptions aside,[12] is that most of the literature on drone uses treats drones just like any other (discriminate) weapon.[13] Many studies on post-9/11 drone strikes against terrorists revolve around two points: first, that drones are not inherently problematic and should be treated like any other weapon; and second, for some (underexplored) reason, the way drones are used has posed an unprecedented challenge to the legal frameworks applicable to the use of force. In other words, these studies assume that there is nothing specific, or special, about drones. The report of the U.N. Special Rapporteur on extrajudicial, summary, or arbitrary executions Agnes Callamard of June 29, 2020 encapsulates this lasting hybridity, if not paradox, in how drones are studied:

> A reasonable argument can be made that to single out drones is misplaced, given that many targeted killings are carried out by conventional means – e.g. Special Operations Forces. Indeed, these also raise serious concerns. The present report thus contains findings applicable to all forms

12 See, on the contrary, studies or at least references to the potential consequences of drones' technological capacities: Mary Ellen O'Connell, "Seductive Drones: Learning from a Decade of Lethal Operations" (2011) *Journal of Law, Information & Science*, Notre Dame Legal Studies Paper No. 11–35; Laurie R. Blank, "After Top Gun: How Drone Strikes Impact the Law of War" (2012) 33 *University of Pennsylvania Journal of International Law* 3, 675; Grégoire Chamayou, *Drone Theory* (Broché, 2015); Eyal Benvenisti, "The Legal Battle to Define the Law on Transnational Asymmetric Warfare" (2010) 20 *Duke Journal of Comparative & International Law* 339–59.

13 Rosa Brooks, "Drones and the International Rule of Law" (2014) *28 Ethics & International Affairs* 1, 83–103; Michael N. Schmitt, "Drone Attacks under the *Jus ad Bellum* and *Jus in Bello*: Clearing the 'Fog of Law'," in M. N. Schmitt, Mike N. Schmitt, Louise Arimatsu, and Tim McCormack (eds.), *Yearbook of International Humanitarian Law*, Vol. 12 (T.M.C. Asser Press, 2010), 313: "The article concludes that there is little reason to treat drones as distinct from other weapons systems with regard to the legal consequences of their employment." Jean-Baptiste Jeangène Vilmer, "Légalité et légitimé des drones armés" (2013) 3 *Politique étrangère* 199–32; Stuart Casey-Malsen, "Pandora's Box? Drone Strikes under *jus ad bellum, jus in bello* and International Human Rights Law" (2012) 94 *International Review of the Red Cross* 886, 597–625; Christian Tams and James G. Devaney, "Jus ad Bellum: Crossing Borders to Wage War against Individuals," in Steven J. Barela (ed.), *Legitimacy and Drones* (Taylor & Francis, 2016), 46; Hugh Gusterson, *Drone: Remote Control Warfare* (The MIT Press, 2016); Sarah Kreps and John Kaag, *Drone Warfare* (Polity Press, 2014).

> of targeted killings, no matter their method. Nonetheless, understanding the particularities of armed drone technologies is crucial if we are to keep pace with current and expected developments impacting on the protection of the right to life.[14]

The intuition and persistence in considering, after nearly two decades of US drone program, that drones are not in themselves vectors of meaningful developments correspond to a vision of state actors as agents in full autonomy and control of the course of action. Yet, the perspective that only the decisions of state agents matter in understanding practice and legal change is misleading as it overlooks the power of other actors, including that of technology. State representatives, their decisions, and the legal evolutions they instigate, do not exist in a vacuum. While it is true that the legal and political discourses used to justify the way that drones are employed challenge the law, they are only some out of many components of the natural and manufactured world. State agents' choices are generated by an evolving environment within which they generate new habits and practices. The essence of a technology lies in how it encourages actors to re-perceive the world and their own practice within it.

When this book holds that the strategy of drone programs and individualized warfare would not exist as such were it not for their technological capacities, it does not mean that military drones are a brand-new tool or that their current capabilities were not sought after and progressively achieved. On the contrary, the idea of arming drones was contemplated from the onset of their development.[15] The Digital Revolution, from the late 1950s to the late 1970s, fostered the development of drones for surveillance purposes. Moving from technological development to practice, the US started to use military drones to collect intelligence during the Vietnam War.[16] They were followed by Russia, which

[14] Human Rights Council, "Report of the Special Rapporteur on Extrajudicial, Summary or Arbitrary Executions," U.N. Special Rapporteur Agnes Callamard, June 29, 2020, A/HRC/44/3, para. 3.

[15] William Arkin, *Unmanned: Drones, Data, and the Illusion of Perfect Warfare* (Little, Brown, 2015), chapter 5; Barry D. Watts, "The Evolution of Precision Strike" (2013) Center for Strategic and Budgetary Assessments, https://csbaonline.org/uploads/documents/Evolution-of-Precision-Strike-final-v15.pdf, 17–18.

[16] David Cenciotti, "The Dawn of the Robot Age: US Air Force Testing Air-Launched UCAVs Capable to Fire Maverick and Shrike Missiles in 1972," *The Aviationist*, March 14, 2012, http://theaviationist.com/2012/03/14/the-dawn-of-the-robot-age/; Ian G. R. Shaw, *Predator Empire: Drone Warfare and Full Spectrum Dominance* (University of Minnesota Press, 2016), 71.

deployed surveillance drones for military intelligence purposes in Ukraine, Belarus, and Latvia.[17] In 1973, Israel used surveillance drones during the Yom Kippur War, and again in 1982 when invading Lebanon.[18] During the first Gulf War and during the Kosovo War, military drones were used for intelligence, surveillance, and reconnaissance purposes.[19] Yet it was between the Kosovo War and military intervention in Afghanistan that their use morphed from surveillance to surveillance *and* combat drones.[20] In February 2001, the US Air Force carried out the first successful experimental strike in the Nellis Air Force Base where a Predator drone successfully deployed a Hellfire missile against its target.[21] From a fictional situation with a fictional target, combat drones were first used in real situations against real targets later the same year. US drone operators stationed in the Nevada Desert started to conduct drone strikes extraterritorially in several zones across the globe. The US was followed by the UK and Israel,[22] and more recently by France.[23] From 2001 onward, drone strikes were officially conducted in Afghanistan, Yemen, Pakistan, Somalia, Libya, Syria, Iraq, and the Occupied Palestinian Territories.

While drones are not new, contemporary drones possess unprecedented capabilities. Aerial military drones are used to kill but they also have surveillance capacities. Recent technological advances have multiplied drones' operational efficiency by refining and accelerating each step of the decision-making process: orientation, observation, selection,

[17] Yefim Gordon, *Soviet/Russian Unmanned Aerial Vehicles* (Midland Publishing, 2005); Océane Zubeldia, *Histoire des drones* (Perrin Editions, 2012), chapter 1.

[18] Ben Hartman, "Ya'alon: IDF Cuts Revolutionary, Will Recreate Army," *The Jerusalem Post*, July 11, 2013, www.jpost.com/defense/yaalon-idf-cuts-revolutionary-will-produce-new-army-319510.

[19] "Predator Drones and Unmanned Aerial Vehicles (UAVs)," *The New York Times*, updated March 5, 2012, http://topics.nytimes.com/top/reference/timestopics/subjects/u/unmanned_aerial_vehicles/index.html.

[20] Arkin, *Unmanned: Drones, Data*, chapter 9: "The Machine Builds."

[21] Steve Coll, *Ghost Wars: The Secret History of the CIA, Afghanistan, and bin Laden, from the Soviet Invasion to September 10, 2001* (Penguin Books, 2004).

[22] UK Drone Strikes List, Drone Wars UK, https://dronewars.net/uk-drone-strike-list-2/.

[23] Speech of the French Minister of the Armed Forces, Madame Florence Parly, "Discours de clôture"; Statute, LOI no. 2018-607 du 13 juillet 2018 relative à la programmation militaire pour les années 2019 à 2025 et portant diverses dispositions intéressant la défense, www.legifrance.gouv.fr/eli/loi/2018/7/13/ARMX1800503L/jo/texte, and Annexed report; Guibert, "La France entre dans l'ère des drones armés."

surveillance, engagement, and targeting.[24] In other words, armed drones are equipped to "find, fix, and finish" targets.[25] The enhancement of the military operational process is achieved because drone's current technological capabilities have two core objectives: precision and ubiquity. The objective of precision (and related technological tools) concerns not only surveillance and intelligence collection but also the selection of the target and the lethal strike. The objective of ubiquity requires the capacity to be permanently everywhere in order to control, select, and terminate a target.

1.2 Compiling the Textual, Bureaucratic, and Material Traces of Drone Programs as Techno-Legal Machineries

As mentioned, this book can be thought of as an act of compiling the textual, bureaucratic, and material traces of these programs in order to lay bare the infrastructure that is extending warfare in time and space and exacerbating state power. The extraterritorial use of combat drones against non-state actors is not easy to study because of the lack of available information as, among other factors, much of it is classified. For this reason, when drones are used to target people on the territory of failing states, as in the case of Somalia, the affected state, and others, can remain unaware of the use of drones for a long time, or even forever. Besides, by the time suspicions arise that drones have been used, the evidence may well have disappeared. Therefore, it is difficult to obtain exact data on the number of drone strikes and the number of casualties of the strikes.

Some of the best aggregate databases on drone strikes currently available to the public has been put together by The Bureau of Investigative Journalism (TBIJ) and Drone Wars UK, independent journalist organizations, which report on US and UK drone strikes, respectively, and their related civilian casualties.[26] Some major think tanks, such as New America, have also reported on drone strikes.[27] These databases are also

[24] Arkin, *Unmanned: Drones, Data*; Charlie Savage, *Power Wars: The Relentless Rise of Presidential Authority and Secrecy* (Little, Brown, 2015), 240, 273.

[25] The Intercept, The Drone Papers, September 2015, https://theintercept.com/drone-papers/the-assassination-complex/.

[26] The Bureau of Investigative Journalism (TBIJ), www.thebureauinvestigates.com/; Drone Wars UK, https://dronewars.net/.

[27] New America, www.newamerica.org/.

used and fed by law clinics in order to build their own reports.[28] Another precious investigative and research project has been led by Forensic Architecture in collaboration with TBIJ. They set up a colossal project with an interactive cartographic web platform that presents the distribution of drone strikes, the context and composition of the area where they took place, the number of people reported killed, and the types of targets reported hit was instrumental in identifying patterns and connections between drone strikes scenarios.[29] Other reports, such as "The Uncounted" conducted by Azmat Khan and Anand Gopal published by *the New York Times* provide a detailed account of a drone strike in Iraq that was very helpful in tracking and confirming these patterns and connections.[30] Some investigations and reports also come from international organizations, such as organs of the United Nations, especially in the aftermath of a strike contested for having caused civilian casualties.[31] Information can also be found in reports and resolutions issued by the Human Rights Council that are thematic or country-specific.[32] In 2015, confidential documents of the US government and military were

[28] See, for example, International Human Rights and Conflict Resolution Clinic (Stanford Law School) and Global Justice Clinic (NYU School of Law), "Living Under Drones: Death, Injury, and Trauma to Civilians from US Drone Practices in Pakistan," September 2012, www-cdn.law.stanford.edu/wp-content/uploads/2015/07/Stanford-NYU-Living-Under-Drones.pdf, vi.

[29] Forensic Architecture, The Drone Strikes Platform, https://forensic-architecture.org/investigation/the-drone-strikes-platform.

[30] Azmat Khan and Anand Gopal, "The Uncounted," *The New York Times*, November 16, 2017, www.nytimes.com/interactive/2017/11/16/magazine/uncounted-civilian-casualties-iraq-airstrikes.html?_r=0.

[31] United Nations Multidimensional Integrated Stabilization Mission in Mali (MINUSMA), "Rapport sur l'incident de Bounty du 3 janvier 2021," March 2021, https://minusma.unmissions.org/sites/default/files/rapport_final_bounty_bounty9.pdf. This report followed the strike conducted by the French Barkhane forces in the village of Bounty, in Mali, in January 2021, on people who were attending a wedding at the time of the strike.

[32] For a thematic report, see Philip Alston, "Report of the Special Rapporteur on Extrajudicial, Summary or Arbitrary Executions," May 28, 2010, Human Rights Council, A/HRC/14/24/Add6; see also Human Rights Council, "Ensuring Use of Remotely Piloted Aircraft or Armed Drones in Counter-Terrorism and Military Operations in Accordance with International Law, Including International Human Rights and Humanitarian Law," Resolution A/HRC/25/L.32, March 24, 2014; Christof Heyns, "Report of the Special Rapporteur on Extrajudicial, Summary or Arbitrary Executions," April 24, 2015, Human Rights Council, A/HRC/29/37; for a country report, see "Report of the United Nations High Commissioner for Human Rights on the Situation of Human Rights in Afghanistan and on the Achievements of Technical Assistance in the Field of Human Rights in 2013," January 10, 2014, A/HRC/25/41, §21.

leaked by The Intercept.[33] Finally, drone operators themselves can be a source of information on the military strategy implemented through drone surveillance and drone strikes.[34]

Evidence of drone strikes provided in testimonies, reports by journalists, NGOs, international organizations but also by official statements or legislative documents at national level has allowed me to distinguish and study two different types of drone strikes: *targeted killings* and *signature strikes*. A targeted killing is "the intentional, premeditated and deliberate use of lethal force, by States or their agents acting under color of law, or by an organized armed group in armed conflict, against a specific individual who is not in the physical custody of the perpetrator."[35] Therefore, an individual who is subject to a targeted killing is identified beforehand. By contrast, *signature strikes* consist of drone operators "fir[ing] on people whose identities they do not know based on evidence of suspicious behavior."[36] In other words, signature strikes aim to target individuals, groups of individuals, vehicles, buildings, and so forth where it is possible to report suspicious behavior or signs of a significant threat of harmful behavior. State practice of signature strikes is the most obscure and difficult to study as major information about what criteria trigger suspicion and what elements compose the profile of an individual who is considered a legitimate target is lacking. In order to fill this gap, all available narratives on drone strikes, published and related in informal discussions, were used in order to identify a set of criteria that seemed to systematically play a role in the decision to kill. Reflections that follow are made on the basis of primary and secondary sources, and discussions with a broad range of actors from governmental officials to NGO members and journalists – discussions facilitated by my involvement as observer member of the European Forum on Armed Drones, my former

[33] The Drone Papers, The Assassination Complex, The Intercept, October 2015, https://theintercept.com/drone-papers/the-assassination-complex/.

[34] M. Drevet, L. Mieusset, R. Mignot-Mahdavi, C. Pinel, and A. Yehiel, "Testimony of a French Drone Operator: Anticipatory Strikes in the Sahel," *European Forum on Armed Drones (EFAD)*, February 16, 2022, www.efadrones.org/testimony-of-a-french-drone-operator-anticipatory-strikes-in-the-sahel/. The testimony can be found here: www.irsem.fr/le-collimateur/dans-le-viseur-27-frappe-de-drone-dans-le-desert-malien-09-04-2021.html and its translation into English here: www.efadrones.org/wp-content/uploads/2022/02/Drone-strike-in-the-Malian-desert_interview-in-English-2.pdf.

[35] Alston, "Report of the Special Rapporteur on Extrajudicial, Summary or Arbitrary Executions," A/HRC/14/24/Add.6, para. 1.

[36] Cora Currier and Justin Elliott, "Drone Warfare 'Signature Strikes'," *Global Research*, February 27, 2013, www.globalresearch.ca/drone-warfare-signature-strikes/5324491.

affiliation to the French Ministry of Defense's research center in 2015, and my time in New York at Columbia Law School as a Research Fellow of the Human Rights Institute in 2018. These discussions helped me corroborate and test hypotheses, but all errors remain my own.

Assembling empirical evidence to make visible the different procedures, elements, and textures of drone programs is necessary but not sufficient. While the literature is already rich with doctrinal analysis of the legal issues raised by the use of force, including through drones, doctrinal analysis had to play a role in this book, and one that is essential to the argument about the interplay between law, military strategy, and technology. Adopting the internal point of view was crucial in order to identify which available options within each legal concept have been mobilized to push for a specific use of drones. In other words, deciphering the legal narratives from within was critical in order to be precise about the features of the war they support. Without doctrinal analysis, the book would not manage to identify with depth what shape warfare is taking or how law and technology intimately affect one another. Besides, to decompose and recompose the legal narratives in all their complexity was key to showing that law is not receding in the face of transnational terrorist threats but almost at the epitome of its strength and power; to showing, more specifically, that law is rearranged around anticipatory warfare. Adopting the external point of view in the book complements this method and allows me to make sense of the institutional transformations that take place in order for drone programs' specific structures to emerge, to make sense of the new reality that drone programs bring about and of the techno-legal possibilities available in this counterterrorism space, including the new possibilities for international legal norms.

The concepts of legal gray zones and uncertainties are recurring in this book. The book adopts the viewpoint that such gray areas are inherent to legal norms. Just as it is banally human to ignore what the future holds, it is logical that behavior is regulated according to general standards alone. Such standards are then applied to particular cases that were not, and could not have been envisaged when the norm was initially created.[37]

[37] While this feature of the law is commonly attributed to legal realism or critical legal studies (see Jean D'Aspremont, *Formalism and the Sources of International Law* (Oxford University Press, 2011), 138: "Legal realism had long ago proved that law is beset by indeterminacy and that its language is insufficient to provide a determinate answer to problems which it is purported to apply to, thereby endowing law-applying authorities

In order to take place, this application involves that the relevant actors of a system – in the international legal order, these actors are more often states than judges – interpret the general standard. This interpretation can remain constant and submitted to limited controversies as long as the circumstances remain unchanged. During this period of time, the norm may well appear clear and certain. Yet, when circumstances change, the norm's inherent gray areas and indeterminacies – which had hitherto remained invisible – will be salient again and trigger discussions about any proposed new interpretation. In such circumstances, legal uncertainty leads to (reasonable) disagreement in the sense that some plausible arguments can be formulated in support of each interpretative theory. Hence, norms present a certain degree of uncertainty but also of constraint: there are only so many interpretative options and reasons for action available in a legal norm. This is precisely why the positivist idea that because we can give a norm content, we can know the "truth" about what the law exactly requires, is simplistic and inaccurate. The fact that we can give content to the norm means that the structure of concepts may *limit* the set of reasons that are available to justify action, but not that it gives us only *one* meaning on the basis of which we can criticize conduct as clearly falling within or outside the concept. What often prevents the legal debate from being fruitful is precisely when its participants do not accept that there is not only one possible interpretation of the norm and that additional reasons in support of a given interpretative theory must be mobilized for it to prevail.

In the light of the above, this study rests on the idea that despite inherent gray areas and uncertainties, international legal norms can perform constraint, albeit modest, on how states articulate their reasons

with a leeway that allows them to make decisions according to their understanding of justice"), even famous legal positivists asserted the indeterminate nature of the law (see H. L. A. Hart, *The Concept of Law*, 2nd ed. (Clarendon Press, 1997 [1961]). Hart wrote entire chapters respectively on discussing the open-textured feature of law, the inevitability of exercising discretion for applying the law and on the rule-creating powers of judges. In the same vein, Kelsen highlighted that all law is partly determinate and partly indeterminate, and that applying the law involves a cognitive and a willful act. In a similar line, Raz notes that legal authorities do not necessarily or always apply the law of a given system/legally valid rules). See for a very helpful analysis of law's open texture and determinacy, Robert Brandom, "A Hegelian Model of Legal Concept Determination," in Graham Hubbs and Douglas Lind (eds.), *Pragmatism, Law, and Language* (Routledge, 2014), 19–39.

for what they do.[38] However, another phenomenon – related to law's content and limited determinacy – pertains to the fact that the logical determinacy of norms rests on specific concrete presuppositions and scenarios. When the norms are applied to different scenarios than those on which they were initially premised, this book argues that states make extreme propositions about legal concepts that ultimately change their very object or make them lose any constraining function. As a consequence, it becomes very difficult to determine what the norm content is: this is what is meant by "exacerbating the pressures put on the norms regulating the use of force" or "push to breaking points uncertainties in the law." In other words, the book suggests that while the semantic indeterminacy of a norm is not unlimited, the way in which such a semantic frame of certain legal concepts is exploited can lead to a disturbing situation where it is very hard (if not impossible) to use it in order to regulate conduct.

1.3 A Techno-Legal Machinery

A machinery is the assemblage of multiple machines, forces, and factors that altogether produce an activity, practice, or phenomena that would not have existed were it not for this assemblage and the interaction of forces set in motion.[39] Naming drone programs – the assemblage of a human, social, and technological elements – a "machinery" is an

[38] On the contrary, a legal realist or a critical legal scholar would almost always argue that the law can never perform a constraining function, and that if it does, it does not have anything to do with the norm's semantics but rather with power relationships and political choices. See, for example, Karl N. Llewellyn, *Jurisprudence: Realism in Theory and Practice* (Transaction Publishers, 2008 [1962]): Llewellyn considers that court decisions can almost never be explained by reference to legal reasons, which are assumed to always be indeterminate, but rather by reference to the political or ideological beliefs of judges.

[39] My definition builds on the conceptual work done by Michel Foucault around the concept of machinery that he uses on several occasions without ever clearly defining it and sometimes as a synonym for "dispositif" or "apparatus." See, for instance, in Michel Foucault, *Surveiller et Punir: Naissance de la Prison* (Gallimard, 1975), 67, 139, 158, 165, 175, 179, 203, 205, 212, etc. See also Michel Foucault, *Les Anormaux. Cours au Collège de France. 1974–1975* (Gallimard, 1999), 34. Although he does not define the concept in a rigid manner, Foucault describes various machineries (of disciplinary power, of the justice system, or of the prison system, for instance) in a way that has accompanied and informed the description made in this book of drone programs as a set of forces and factors giving birth, through their assemblage and interaction, to infinite warfare and exacerbating state power.

invitation to trace the genealogy of this interaction of factors and what it produces. The products of the machine lie outside and within the machine. They lie in the procedures, modes, and types of interactions between these forces (here, law, drone technologies, and military strategy) and between these forces and other elements beyond the said machinery. Machineries are performative as they infiltrate, capture, or conduct human bodies, behaviors, and institutions, and shape social interactions.[40]

The argument of the book that drone programs in international law are a techno-legal machinery extending warfare and exacerbating state power unfolds as follows. After going through all contexts of uses of drones by the three studied states, the US, the UK and France, in Chapter 2, Chapter 3 demonstrates how drone strikes can be progressively embedded in an institution, thereby substantiating the shared intuition that they deserve to be referred to as part of a "machinery" or a "program." I show that the use of drones appears as an institution through the formation of a bureaucracy, the stabilizing force of the technology itself, and normalizing power of legal rationales. In Chapters 4, 5, and 6, I use both doctrinal and empirical methods to analyze the type of war that emerges from drones' techno-legal machinery. I show how, through narratives about the law and imaginaries about drones' technology crafted by states active in the war on terror, war is rearranged around threat anticipation to target hostile individuals (Chapter 4), how war is thus designed to combat ever-proliferating enemies/ever-expanding enmity (Chapter 5), and how war, finally, is devised to take place anywhere (Chapter 6). Finally, Chapter 7 warns about the less visible effects of an infinite warfare conducted through surveillance technologies and building on extensive legal interpretations, both for the populations living under drones and for other states in the international legal order. I argue that, beyond the extension of warfare in time and space, drone programs as a techno-legal machinery establish rituals of sovereignty over the populations living under drones. Analyzing this extension of state power and the use of legal rhetoric to make the disruption of sovereignty acceptable allows me to differentiate between malleable uses of the law and its uncertainties to tame the "other inside," that is, states, on the one hand, and deformalization of norms to annihilate the "other outside," that is, jihadist groups, on the other hand.

[40] Michel Foucault, *Surveiller et Punir*, 139.

The epilogue retraces the explanations, inchoate in the book, of *why* this exacerbation of state power resting on enhanced technological capacities and de-/reconstructed legal frameworks is taking place.[41] It suggests that this socio-techno-legal phenomenon of extensive warfare and state power has developed because of the infinite enmity that characterizes the relationship between states and transnational jihadist groups and networks.

[41] See Epilogue.

2

Contexts

This book's scope of analysis includes the US but also the UK drone program and the use of drones by France. When I started to work on this book, combat drones were officially used for lethal purposes by three states, namely, the US, the UK, and Israel, and my intuition, after having spent a year as a Researcher at the French Ministry of Defense's research center, was that France would arm its drones, which prompted me to closely follow parliamentary discussions and the design of counterterrorism legislation and strategy in France. Israel was swiftly excluded from the scope of this research project since drones appear to be used in a different framework, one that does not exactly aim at the "anywhere war" against individuals pertaining to transnational terrorist networks beyond regional reach. Instead, Israeli drones have mainly been used in Gaza for the surveillance and targeting of individuals identified as Hamas members and members of other groups such as Islamic Jihad.[1] On the contrary, including in the scope of study the UK and France proved very instructive for understanding the reach and breadth of the sophisticated legal rationales crafted by the Obama administration to regulate the indefinite extraterritorial use of drones against non-state actors in time and space.

Overall, this book finds that the influence of these US rationales is more important than anyone would like to admit. While the UK does not explicitly embrace the idea of expanding warfare to wherever terrorist groups emerge, it appears from discussions on their first drone strikes in Syria and their refusal to disclose information on the location of current drone operations,[2] that the temporal and spatial limitation of their war

[1] Jack Khoury and Yaniv Kubovich, "Gaza-Based Islamic Jihad Drops Claim of Israeli Drone Strike," *Haaretz*, December 12, 2017, www.haaretz.com/israel-news/gaza-based-islamic-jihad-drops-claim-of-israeli-drone-strike-1.5628454.

[2] Rosalind Comyn, "Rights Watch (UK) Taking UK Government to Court over Refusal to Disclose Legal Basis for Targeted Killings," *Rights Watch UK*, July 20, 2017, www.rwuk.org/rights-watch-uk-taking-uk-government-to-court-over-refusal-to-disclose-legal-basis-for-targeted-killings/.

on terror is uncertain and can be explained more by the intense parliamentary scrutiny than by any actual characteristic of the government's counterterrorism strategy.[3] Where the UK seems to join the US most is in individualizing the use of force against members of transnational terrorist networks. The transformative framework used by the UK to claim a right of individual self-defense is similar to that of the US and is also in line with the dematerialization of the decision to use force in self-defense.[4] As regards France, even in the absence of officially and clearly articulated legal rationale, the terminology used in official statements and legally binding documents suggests that France considers being at war against "jihadist groups," and will pursue its military efforts against them for as long as and wherever these groups exist, reemerge, and recompose themselves.[5] The French operational and legal logic not only resembles the US rationale and practice but goes beyond it.

Before developing the argument of this book, it is important to have a good overview of the contexts where combat drones have been deployed as this will serve as a basis for the study. The description of the contexts in which drone operations have been conducted extraterritorially against non-state actors by the US, the UK, and France follows a chronological sequence, and draws some common and diverging features of the different legal rationales crafted by these states.

2.1 Afghanistan: US Drone Operations

Afghanistan is the first country in which combat drones were used by the US. By the end of 2001, President George W. Bush had put the CIA in charge of a global manhunt against Al Qaeda, the Taliban, and associated forces, starting in Afghanistan.[6] The order gave the CIA the power to kill as part of the "war on terror." This was officially waived under Obama who, instead, gave the final command to the US Air France Central

[3] Chapter 6.

[4] Chapter 4.

[5] Chapter 5, Sections 5.1 and 5.2. Chapter 6, Section 6.1. Rebecca Mignot-Mahdavi, "Le Silence des Agneaux: France's War against 'Jihadist Groups' and Associated Legal Rationale" (2020) *ICCT Journal*, https://icct.nl/publication/le-silence-des-agneaux-frances-war-against-jihadist-groups-and-associated-legal-rationale/.

[6] Mark Mazzetti, *The Way of the Knife: The CIA, a Secret Army, and a War at the Ends of the Earth* (Penguin Books, 2014), 12; J. Cofer Black, CIA Director of the Counterterrorist Center from 1999 to 2002, argued in favor of the CIA's use of the armed Predator in Afghanistan to hunt and kill the Taliban, and members of Al Qaeda, starting with Bin Laden.

Command for the strikes in Afghanistan.[7] Since 2001, drone strikes have been continually conducted in the region with various peaks of intensity,[8] most recently in September 2019 with 1,113 confirmed strikes in the space of a month.[9] The past nineteen years of conflict between Afghanistan and the US can be divided into three phases. The first phase started on October 7, 2001, and came to an end on June 18, 2002. It is marked by the US's aim to remove the Taliban from power.[10] The second phase started on June 19, 2002, when the new Afghani government of Hamid Karzai came to office with the support of the international coalition formed by the International Security Assistance Force and the *Operation Enduring Freedom*.[11] The operation ended on December 28, 2014, (thereby starting the third phase) when the North Atlantic Treaty

[7] The Bureau of Investigative Journalism (TBIJ), "Afghanistan: US Air and Drone Strikes, 2015 to Present," www.thebureauinvestigates.com/projects/drone-war/afghanistan. Nonetheless, it is highly likely that the CIA was still present in Afghanistan even if command of the drone program was given to the US Air Force. See Greg Miller, "White House Mistakenly Identifies CIA Chief in Afghanistan," *The Washington Post*, May 25, 2014, www.washingtonpost.com/world/national-security/white-house-mistakenly-identifies-cia-chief-in-afghanistan/2014/05/25/ac8e80cc-e444-11e3-8f90-73e071f3d637_story.html.

[8] TBIJ reports that Afghanistan has been hit by more drone strikes than any other country. When finalizing this text in May 2020, the last confirmed strikes date back to March 24, 2020, see TBIJ, "Drone Strikes in Afghanistan," www.thebureauinvestigates.com/projects/drone-war/afghanistan. For details on this last strike, see TBIJ, Case no. AFG4236Ci, March 24, 2020, www.thebureauinvestigates.com/drone-war/data/afghanistan-reported-us-covert-actions-2020#strike-47179. See Jack Serle, "Comment: If Drone Strikes Continue in Afghanistan, the Lack of Transparency Must Not," October 16, 2014, www.thebureauinvestigates.com/2014/10/16/comment-if-drone-strikes-continue-in-afghanistan-the-lack-of-transparency-must-not/.

[9] See TBIJ, "Afghanistan: US Air and Drone Strikes," and see also, for a chart representing the peaks, www.thebureauinvestigates.com/projects/drone-war/charts?show_casualties=1&show_injuries=1&show_strikes=1&location=afghanistan&from=2015-1-1&to=now. One of these September 2019 drone strikes was the object of media coverage. See "U.S. Drone Strike Kills 30 Pine Nut Farm Workers in Afghanistan," *Reuters*, September 20, 2019, www.reuters.com/article/us-afghanistan-attack-drones-idUSKBN1W40NW.

[10] George W. Bush, Presidential Address to the Nation, October 7, 2001, https://georgewbush-whitehouse.archives.gov/news/releases/2001/10/20011007-8.html. For a critical assessment of the war in Afghanistan, see Michael John Williams, *The Good War: NATO and the Liberal Conscience in Afghanistan* (Palgrave Macmillan, 2011); and more particularly on the use of drones in Afghanistan, see Matt J. Martin and Charles W. Sasser, *Predator: The Remote Control Air War over Iraq and Afghanistan: A Pilot's Story* (Zenith Press, 2010).

[11] See, for a timeline of the Operation Enduring Freedom in Afghanistan, CNN, "Operation Enduring Freedom Fast Facts," Regularly Updated until September 30, 2015, http://edition.cnn.com/2013/10/28/world/operation-enduring-freedom-fast-facts/.

Organization (NATO) formally ended combat operations in Afghanistan and transferred full security responsibility to the Afghan government.[12] The US has nonetheless maintained its involvement in particular from the air, as almost all boots have been removed from the ground.[13] A fourth phase might eventually be identified with the agreement of February 29, 2020, between the US and the Taliban in Doha, with the planned departure of US troops from Afghanistan within a year,[14] even though the most recent strikes were conducted after the agreement was signed.[15]

2.2 Yemen: US Drone Operations

Al Qaeda's presence in Yemen dates back to the early 1990s. From Yemen, it has launched attacks on foreign targets, for example, when it organized the bombing of the USS *Cole* in the Gulf of Aden in 2000. In November 2001, two months after the 9/11 attacks and after Yemen's President Saleh visited Washington, Yemen stepped up its counterterrorism cooperation efforts with the US and became a key site for the US campaign against Al Qaeda. The first known US drone strike outside Afghanistan hit Yemen in 2002, killing six people,[16] including Qaid Salim Sinan al Harithi, the leader of Al Qaeda in Yemen and a key planner in the attack on the USS *Cole*. Following this, the US interrupted its military

[12] NATO, "NATO and Afghanistan," www.nato.int/cps/en/natohq/topics_8189.htm; US Department of Defense, "Obama, Hagel Mark End of Operation Enduring Freedom," DoD News, Defense Media Activity, Washington, DC, December 28, 2014, www.defense.gov/News-Article-View/Article/603860/obama-hagel-mark-end-of-operation-enduring-freedom.

[13] TBIJ, "Afghanistan: Reported US Covert Actions 2019," www.thebureauinvestigates.com/drone-war/data/afghanistan-reported-us-covert-actions-2019.

[14] Agreement for Bringing Peace to Afghanistan between the Islamic Emirate of Afghanistan, which is not recognized by the United States as a state and is known as the Taliban, and the United States of America, February 29, 2020, www.state.gov/wp-content/uploads/2020/02/Agreement-For-Bringing-Peace-to-Afghanistan-02.29.20.pdf; Joint Statement on the Signing of the US–Taliban Agreement, by Special Envoys and Special Representatives of the European Union, France, Germany, Italy, Norway, the United Kingdom, the United Nations and the United States of America on the Occasion of the Signing of the US–Taliban Agreement on February 29 in Qatar, March 9, 2020, www.state.gov/joint-statement-on-the-signing-of-the-u-s-taliban-agreement-2/.

[15] For details on this last strike, see TBIJ, Case no. AFG4236Ci.

[16] TBIJ, "US Strikes in Yemen, 2002 to Present," www.thebureauinvestigates.com/projects/drone-war/charts?show_casualties=1&show_injuries=1&show_strikes=1&location=yemen&from=2002-1-1&to=now.

operations in Yemen for seven years. However, in 2009 when Al Qaeda in Yemen merged with the Saudi Arabian branch of Al Qaeda to form Al Qaeda in the Arabia Peninsula (AQAP), the group arguably became stronger with attacks launched within and beyond Yemen's border and sustained a media presence directed at Yemenites and translated into English for Western audiences.[17] The US restarted drone strikes in 2011.[18]

Reportedly, it is both the US Joint Special Operations Command (JSOC) as well as the CIA that have been running drone airstrike operations in Yemen.[19] Under the command of General David Petraeus since 2011, the CIA accelerated its transition from a spy agency into a military agency, similar to a permanent clandestine version of the Pentagon, particularly in Yemen.[20] General Petraeus insisted that the White House help finance the CIA's expansion of its drone fleet and ordered an unprecedented operation: the targeted killing of an American citizen, Anwar al-Awlaki.[21] In Yemen, President Abdrabbo Mansour Hadi has said that he personally approved each strike as well.[22] Although the Obama administration acknowledged providing weapons to the Yemeni government to fight AQAP, it never claimed to

[17] "Al Qaeda in the Arabian Peninsula," Stanford Center for International Security and Cooperation, https://cisac.fsi.stanford.edu/mappingmilitants/profiles/al-qaeda-arabian-peninsula#text_block_18748.

[18] TBIJ, "US Strikes in Yemen, 2002 to Present." From January 2011, inspired by movements in Tunisia and Egypt, pro-democracy protesters demanded President Saleh's resignation. These events set in motion a confrontation between the international security force, followed by the regular army against the demonstrators, which were themselves joined by other groups of Saleh's opponents, including the Houthis, tribal military groups, and AQAP. This confrontation was destined to escalate. In May 2011, fighting broke out in Sana'a and the violence spread beyond the city. In February 2012, the new president Hadi was elected and this was followed by a drop in violence, although a series of AQAP attacks were reported.

[19] The Intercept, The Drone Papers, "The Kill Chain," https://theintercept.com/drone-papers/the-kill-chain/, based on a slide from a May 2013 Pentagon presentation showing the chain of command for ordering drone strikes and other operations carried out by JSOC in Yemen and Somalia. See, for the full document, https://theintercept.com/document/2015/10/14/small-footprint-operations-5-13/#page-2.

[20] Mazzetti, *The Way of the Knife*, 299–302.

[21] Ibid., 302.

[22] Greg Miller, "In Interview, Yemeni President Acknowledges Approving U.S. Drone Strikes," *The Washington Post*, September 29, 2012, www.washingtonpost.com/world/national-security/yemeni-president-acknowledges-approving-us-drone-strikes/2012/09/29/09bec2ac-0a56-11e2-afff-d6c7f20a83bf_story.html.

bring support to the Yemeni government as an official ally in the Yemen–AQAP conflict.[23] Obama explained, however, that the US individually carries out attacks against individuals in Yemen when they pose a direct threat to the US or its interests,[24] and more recent data shows that a similar practice was conducted under the Trump administration.[25] In March and April 2017 alone the US carried out eighty air attacks with jets and drones,[26] and at the time of finalizing this text in May 2020 the last confirmed US strike dates to November 1, 2019,[27] and two strikes conducted in 2020 could also potentially be US strikes.[28] The attacks are mostly directed against individual non-state actors ahead of a potential attack.[29]

23 Speech by John Brennan to the Council on Foreign Relations, Washington, DC, August 9, 2012, www.lawfareblog.com/2012/08/transcript-of-john-brennans-speech-at-the-council-on-foreign-relations/: "So while we [the US] have aided Yemen, the Yemeni government, in building their capacity to deal with an AQAP insurgency that exists on the ground there, we're not involved in working with the Yemeni government in terms of direct action or lethal action as part of that insurgency."

24 President Obama made this statement in his War Powers Resolution 6-Month Reports of June 15, 2012, December 14, 2012, and June 14, 2013, www.whitehouse.gov/the-press-office/2012/06/15/presidential-letter-2012-war-powers-resolution-6-month-report; www.whitehouse.gov/the-press-office/2012/12/14/letter-president-war-powers-resolution; and www.whitehouse.gov/the-press-office/2013/06/14/letter-president-regarding-war-powers-resolution.

25 Jack Serle, "Trump's 100 Days: US Air Campaign Hammers Yemen with Almost a Strike a Day," TBIJ, April 27, 2017, www.thebureauinvestigates.com/stories/2017-04-27/us-air-campaign-hammers-yemen-with-almost-a-strike-a-day.

26 TBIJ, "US Strikes in Yemen, 2002 to Present."

27 See TBIJ, "Drone Strikes in Yemen," www.thebureauinvestigates.com/projects/drone-war/yemen.

28 See TBIJ, "US Strikes in Yemen, 2002 to Present."

29 In the expectation that this point is developed in another chapter, here are a few initial explanations. First, the administration asserts that it is only responding to a threat to the US, suggesting it does not consider itself a party to the Yemen–AQAP conflict. According to this rationale, the US government should be applying a war model to its actions only if there is a genuine armed conflict between the US and AQAP, which is not evident. Otherwise, the US needs to act in accordance with the higher threshold for the use of force under applicable law enforcement standards found in international human rights law. The International Court of Justice first affirmed the applicability of international human rights law even during armed conflicts in Nuclear Weapons (1996). See ICJ, Legality of the Threat or Use of Nuclear Weapons, Advisory Opinion, July 8, 1996, ICJ Reports 1996, 226, §25: "The Court observes that the protection of the International Covenant of Civil and Political Rights does not cease in times of war, except by operation of Article 4 of the Covenant whereby certain provisions may be derogated from in a time of national emergency." Similarly, in *The Wall* (2004), the Court confirmed the applicability of international human rights law to situations of military occupation, ICJ, Legal Consequences of the Construction of a Wall in the Occupied Palestinian Territory, Advisory Opinion, July 9, 2004, ICJ Reports 2004, 136.

2.3 Pakistan: US Drone Operations

After the 9/11 attacks, President Musharraf decided to assist the US in its fight against Al Qaeda,[30] largely based on its origins in Pakistan.[31] The US has conducted drone strikes in Pakistan since 2004 under the command of the CIA.[32] These strikes increased markedly in 2008, after George W. Bush signed a secret order to escalate the CIA's covert war in Pakistan,[33] and further increased again after Obama's accession to the White House in 2009.[34]

It is interesting to note that, contrary to what NGOs, journalists, and human rights law university clinics report on the many civilian casualties in Pakistan,[35] the Obama administration has declared that there were no civilian casualties in the country.[36] This study explores how this discrepancy lies in the difference between the loose conditions under which US

[30] "Musharraf Makes His Case for Helping U.S.," *CNN World*, September 19, 2001, https://edition.cnn.com/2001/WORLD/asiapcf/south/09/19/pakistan.address/index.html; Mazzetti, *The Way of the Knife*, 171.

[31] "Al Qaeda," Stanford Center for International Security and Cooperation, https://cisac.fsi.stanford.edu/mappingmilitants/profiles/al-qaeda#text_block_18733.

[32] TBIJ, "Pakistan 2004 onwards CIA Drone Strikes," www.thebureauinvestigates.com/projects/drone-war/charts?show_casualties=1&show_injuries=1&show_strikes=1&location=pakistan&from=2004-1-1&to=now: The US has been carrying out drone strikes in Pakistan since June 2004. There have been more strikes on the country than on any other beyond Afghanistan.

[33] Mazzetti, *The Way of the Knife*, 173.

[34] TBIJ, "CIA and US Military Drone Strikes in Pakistan, 2004 to Present," www.thebureauinvestigates.com/projects/drone-war/charts?show_casualties=1&show_injuries=1&show_strikes=1&location=pakistan&from=2004-1-1&to=now.

[35] TBIJ, "Civilians Killed," https://docs.google.com/spreadsheets/d/1NAfjFonM-Tn7fziqiv33HlGt09wgLZDSCP-BQaux51w/edit#gid=1976356146; Open Society Foundations, "After the Dead Are Counted: U.S. and Pakistani Responsibilities to Victims of Drone Strikes," November 2014, www.opensocietyfoundations.org/publications/after-dead-are-counted-us-and-pakistani-responsibilities-victims-drone-strikes; Amnesty International, "'Will I Be Next?' US Drone Strikes in Pakistan," 2013, www.amnesty.org/download/Documents/12000/asa330132013en.pdf; International Human Rights and Conflict Resolution Clinic (Stanford Law School) and Global Justice Clinic (NYU School of Law), "Living Under Drones: Death, Injury, and Trauma to Civilians from US Drone Practices in Pakistan," 2012, www-cdn.law.stanford.edu/wp-content/uploads/2015/07/Stanford-NYU-Living-Under-Drones.pdf.

[36] See John Brennan, White House Homeland Security and Counterterrorism Adviser, Obama Administration Counterterrorism Strategy (C-Span Television Broadcast June 29, 2011), www.c-spanvideo.org/program/AdministrationCo.

officials consider targets to be legitimate, on the one hand, and the higher thresholds used by NGOs and most legal scholars, on the other hand.[37]

The Bureau of Investigative Journalism reports that drone strikes were still probably carried out after the Obama administration in Pakistan even if fewer strikes have been launched under the Trump administration,[38] whose last confirmed strike dates back to July 4, 2018.[39]

2.4 Somalia: US Drone Operations

In 2007, following the Somali civil war, the United Nations mandated a peacekeeping force, the "African Union Mission in Somalia" (AMISOM), with an initial six-month mandate. However, it was only from August 2017 that AMISOM's security responsibility would be gradually handed over to Somali security forces.[40] During its mandate, AMISOM planned and worked to push the armed group, al-Shabaab out of Mogadishu and other locations.[41] The US simultaneously started to carry out strikes in 2007, but combat drones were only used for that purpose from 2011 onward as part of the Pentagon's Joint Special Operations Command. It is reported that a spike in the extraterritorial use of combat drones by the US in Yemen occurred in 2016 under the Obama administration,[42] but reported numbers went higher still when Trump took office.[43]

[37] The Intercept, The Drone Papers, The Assassination Complex (2015), https://theintercept.com/drone-papers/the-assassination-complex/.

[38] TBIJ, "US Drone Strikes in Pakistan," www.thebureauinvestigates.com/projects/drone-war/charts?show_casualties=1&show_injuries=1&show_strikes=1&location=pakistan&from=2004-1-1&to=now.

[39] TBIJ, "Pakistan: Reported US Strikes 2018," www.thebureauinvestigates.com/drone-war/data/pakistan-reported-us-strikes-2018#strike-19510.

[40] UN Security Council Resolution 2372 (2017), August 30, 2017, SC/12972, www.un.org/press/en/2017/sc12972.doc.htm.

[41] "Al-Shabaab Joining al Qaeda, Monitor Group Says," February 9, 2012, *CNN*: al Shabaab pledged allegiance to Al Qaeda in 2012. However, its relationship with Al Qaeda remains uncertain.

[42] TBIJ, "US Strikes in Somalia, 2007 to Present," https://docs.google.com/spreadsheets/d/1-LT5TVBMy1Rj2WH30xQG9nqr8-RXFVvzJE_47NlpeSY/edit#gid=1110953463; Robert Chesney, "Airstrikes outside Areas of Active Hostilities: Attacks in Somalia and Questions about the Current Shape of the Policy," *Lawfare*, March 7, 2016, www.lawfareblog.com/airstrikes-outside-areas-active-hostilities-attacks-somalia-and-questions-about-current-shape-policy.

[43] There were fourteen reported air strikes (including drone strikes, knowing that all were potentially drone strikes) in Somalia in 2016 and had reached forty-seven in August 2019. See TBIJ, "US Strikes in Somalia, 2007 to Present," https://docs.google.com/spreadsheets/

Initially, drone strikes in Yemen were justified by the need to protect American lives from threats posed by members of al-Shabaab and Al Qaeda working together.[44] In early 2016, however, the US started to conduct operations aiming to defend AMISOM members from threats posed by al-Shabaab members who were not related to Al Qaeda. The Pentagon Press Secretary, Peter Cook stated that,

> The strike was conducted using manned and unmanned aircraft. The fighters who were scheduled to depart the camp posed an imminent threat to U.S. and African Union Mission in Somalia (AMISOM) forces in Somalia. The removal of these fighters degrades al-Shabaab's ability to meet the group's objectives in Somalia, including recruiting new members, establishing bases, and planning attacks on U.S. and AMISOM forces.[45]

The US justifies drone strikes according to a mixed rationale: in self-defense to protect US citizens against the continuing imminent threat posed by al-Shabaab, and in self-defense to protect American and AMISOM forces on the ground (the threat being respectively abstract and anticipated, on the one hand, and probably more tangible and actual, on the other hand). It has been argued that in this case, the US argument goes beyond the announcement made by the Obama administration in 2013[46] that it will follow a policy of sharply limiting the use of lethal force to the conditions that lethal force respects the principle of self-defense interpreted as the use of force aimed at "prevent[ing] or stop[ping]

d/1-LT5TVBMy1Rj2WH30xQG9nqr8-RXFVvzJE_47NlpeSY/edit#gid=1110953463, see the year-by-year summary.

44 Letter from the President, "Six Month Consolidated War Powers Resolution Report," June 11, 2015, https://obamawhitehouse.archives.gov/the-press-office/2015/06/11/letter-president-six-month-consolidated-war-powers-resolution-report.

45 US Department of Defense, "Statement from Pentagon Press Secretary Peter Cook on Airstrike in Somalia," Press Operations, Release No. NR-076-16, March 7, 2016, www.defense.gov/News/News-Releases/News-Release-View/Article/687305/statement-from-pentagon-press-secretary-peter-cook-on-airstrike-in-somalia?source=GovDelivery.

46 "Remarks by the President at the National Defense University," National Defense University, Fort McNair, Washington, DC, The White House, May 23, 2013, www.whitehouse.gov/the-press-office/2013/05/23/remarks-president-national-defense-university; "Fact Sheet: The President's May 23 Speech on Counterterrorism," www.whitehouse.gov/the-press-office/2013/05/23/fact-sheet-president-s-may-23-speech-counterterrorism; "Fact Sheet: U.S. Policy Standards and Procedures for the Use of Force in Counterterrorism Operations Outside the United States and Areas of Active Hostilities," May 23, 2013, www.whitehouse.gov/the-press-office/2013/05/23/fact-sheet-us-policy-standards-and-procedures-use-force-counterterrorism.

attacks against U.S. persons" and "against a target that poses a continuing, imminent threat to U.S. persons."[47]

2.5 Iraq and Syria: US and UK Drone Operations

On August 7, 2014 President Barack Obama ordered what he called "limited strikes" against ISIL in order to protect US personnel in Iraq. US airstrikes began the next day and initiated another US military intervention in Iraq that was subsequently named Operation Inherent Resolve.[48] One month later, on the eve of the commemorations for 9/11, Obama announced that he was broadening the military campaign, both in geographical scope and purpose. Airstrikes would also be expanded to take place in Syria. In addition, not only would airstrikes be undertaken to directly protect Americans in Iraq but also to "destroy ISIL."[49] Obama said that the US "will hunt down terrorists who threaten [their] country, wherever they are," meaning that they "will not hesitate to take action against ISIL in Syria, as well as Iraq."

It is worth remembering that there has been no UN Security Council resolution on the military action by the US and its partners. The Security Council only adopted a resolution compelling states to prevent their nationals from joining jihadists in Iraq and Syria but it did not authorize military attacks.[50] The US has not made any explicit claim that the Coalition was acting in self-defense under Article 51 of the Charter, although Obama's reference to the need to respond to the threat for American lives posed by ISIL members might be read as meaning that the legal rationale for the extraterritorial use of force against non-state actors in Iraq and Syria draws on the principle of self-defense. Finally,

[47] This argument has been formulated by Chesney, "Airstrikes Outside Areas of Active Hostilities."

[48] Chris Cole, "Drone in Iraq and Syria: What We Know and What We Don't," Drone Wars, November 7, 2014, https://dronewars.net/2014/11/07/drones-in-iraq-and-syria-what-we-know-and-what-we-dont/.

[49] Barack Obama, "Statement by the President on ISIL," The White House, September 10, 2014, www.whitehouse.gov/the-press-office/2014/09/10/statement-president-isil-1: "America will lead a broad coalition to roll back this terrorist threat. Our objective is clear: We will degrade, and ultimately destroy, ISIL through a comprehensive and sustained counterterrorism strategy . . . we will expand our efforts beyond protecting our own people and humanitarian missions, so that we're hitting ISIL targets as Iraqi forces go on offense."

[50] UN Security Council, Resolution 2178 (2014), September 24, 2014, S/RES/2178 (2014), www.un.org/en/sc/ctc/docs/2015/SCR%202178_2014_EN.pdf.

some insist that the new government in Iraq has consented to military assistance, therefore providing a legal justification for the strikes.[51] As for Syria, the Iraqi conflict has spilled over into Syrian territory, as has the justification for the use of force in Iraq. The American administration for its part uses an admixture of *jus in bello* and *jus ad bellum* rationale to justify the use of force in Syria.[52]

On September 25, 2014, the British Parliament granted authorization for the use of force in Iraq as part of the International Coalition against ISIS.[53] Since then, the UK has been in a non-international armed conflict with ISIS,[54] as part of a collective self-defense action on behalf of the Iraqi government.[55] A few weeks later, the UK confirmed that it was deploying

[51] Louise Arimatsu and Michael Schmitt, "The Legal Basis for the War against ISIS Remains Contentious," October 6, 2014, *The Guardian*, www.theguardian.com/commentisfree/2014/oct/06/legal-basis-war-isis-syria-islamic-state.

[52] Nehal Bhuta, "On Preventive Killing," *EJIL Talk!*, September 17, 2015, www.ejiltalk.org/on-preventive-killing/#more-13651.

[53] UK Parliament, "Commons Recalled to Debate Iraq: Coalition against ISIL," September 26, 2014, www.parliament.uk/business/news/2014/september/house-of-commons-debate-uk-government-response-to-isil/. MPs voted 524 to 43 to approve the Government motion on Iraq: Coalition against ISIL. The motion reads as follows:

> further acknowledges the request of the Government of Iraq for international support to defend itself against the threat ISIL poses to Iraq and its citizens and the clear legal basis that this provides for action in Iraq; notes that this motion does not endorse UK air strikes in Syria as part of this campaign and any proposal to do so would be subject to a separate vote in Parliament; accordingly supports Her Majesty's Government, working with allies, in supporting the Government of Iraq in protecting civilians and restoring its territorial integrity, including the use of UK air strikes to support Iraqi, including Kurdish, security forces' efforts against ISIL in Iraq; notes that Her Majesty's Government will not deploy UK troops in ground combat operations; and offers its wholehearted support to the men and women of Her Majesty's armed forces.

[54] On the conflict characterization, see Chapters 5 and 6, and for now, note that this characterization is derived from Article 3 Common to the Four Geneva Conventions of 1949 and Article 1 of the Additional Protocol to the Geneva Conventions of August 12, 1949, and relating to the Protection of Victims of Non-International Armed Conflicts (Protocol II), June 8, 1977. Conflicts are defined on the basis of the status of the parties to the conflict (state versus state or state(s) versus non-state armed groups) and not on the basis of the geography of the conflict (cross-border or delineated within the boundaries of a state).

[55] At the time of writing, in May 2020, the UK is still conducting airstrikes against Daesh in Iraq. See for governmental reports, UK Ministry of Defence and the Rt. Hon. Ben Wallace MP, "Update: Air Strikes against Daesh," May 29, 2020, www.gov.uk/government/news/update-air-strikes-against-daesh.

combat drones from Afghanistan for operations in Iraq.[56] On November 5, 2014, the Defense Secretary Michael Fallon announced that the UK was sending more drones to Iraq.[57]

In spring 2015, the National Security Council – the main governmental forum for addressing national security and intelligence matters in the United Kingdom – held a meeting to decide how to face the current activities of several British nationals described as "ISIS fighters" in third countries.[58] The government decided to conduct drone strikes to target these British nationals, even in Syria if necessary. It is in this context, and without having obtained parliamentary authorization to extend UK operations to Syria, that Reyaad Khan and Ruhul Amin, along with a third ISIS militant were targeted on August 21, 2015 in Syria. This means that these strikes were not part of the already established International Coalition against ISIS in Syria, as the UK had not joined it when they were conducted.[59] On September 7, 2015, Prime Minister David Cameron informed the UN Security Council that it had conducted this strike in the exercise of the UK's "inherent right of individual and collective self-defense."[60] Their argument, albeit ambiguous in certain aspects and reformulated several times, as will be seen below, was grounded in the language of Article 51 of the UN Charter and tainted with *jus in bello* elements.

[56] UK Ministry of Defence, "Update: Air Strikes in Iraq," October 6, 2014, www.gov.uk/government/news/latest-iraq-air-strikes.

[57] UK Defense Secretary Michael Fallon, "UK to Provide Further Support to Forces Fighting ISIL," November 5, 2014, www.gov.uk/government/news/uk-to-provide-further-support-to-forces-fighting-isil; Cole, "Drone in Iraq and Syria."

[58] Ewen MacAskill and Richard Norton-Taylor, "How UK Government Decided to Kill Reyaad Khan," *The Guardian*, September 8, 2015, www.theguardian.com/world/2015/sep/08/how-did-britain-decide-to-assassinate-uk-isis-fighter-reyaad-khan-drone-strike.

[59] David Cameron's Oral Statement to Parliament, "Syria: Refugees and Counter-Terrorism – Prime Minister's Statement," September 7, 2015, www.gov.uk/government/speeches/syria-refugees-and-counter-terrorism-prime-ministers-statement:

> Mr Speaker, I want to be clear that this strike was not part of coalition military action against ISIL in Syria – it was a targeted strike to deal with a clear, credible and specific terrorist threats to our country at home … I have been absolutely clear that the government will return to this House for a separate vote if we propose to join coalition strikes in Syria.

[60] United Kingdom Mission to the United Nations, September 7, 2015, Letter on Drone Strike, www.justsecurity.org/wp-content/uploads/2015/09/UK_UNSC_Letter_on_Drone_Strike_7Sept2015.pdf.

2.6 Libya: US Drone Operations

In Libya, US strikes were initially conducted against Colonel Gaddafi's forces and thus, as targeting state agents, fell outside the scope of this study on the use of drones against non-state actors. However, in February 2011, inspired by the movements in Tunisia and Egypt, demonstrations in support of democratic reform took place in Libya.[61] These were followed by large-scale repression of the population. The security forces used live ammunition to preempt the spread of the protests, killing demonstrators and giving rise to further protests and demonstrations.[62] Violence escalated on both sides.[63] On February 22, 2011, the High Commissioner for Human Rights condemned the reported use of "machine guns, snipers and military planes" against the demonstrators.[64] The UN Security Council adopted Resolution 1970 and urged the Libyan authorities to respect human rights and international humanitarian law.[65] On March 17, 2011 this first resolution was followed by Resolution 1973 authorizing a no-fly zone over Libya and obliging states to use "all necessary measures" to protect civilians.[66] It is on this note that the US intervened, with the eventual aim of driving Gaddafi from power.[67] To this end, the US relied on CIA drone strikes, which escalated markedly after an attack was made on the American diplomatic compound in Libya in September 2012.[68] In June 2018, it was reported that

61 Report of the International Commission of Inquiry on Libya to Investigate All Alleged Violations of International Human Rights Law in the Libyan Arab Jamahiriya, June 1, 2011, A/HRC/17/44, para. 37.

62 "Libya Security Forces Kill 84 over Three Days," Human Rights Watch, February 19, 2011, www.hrw.org/en/news/2011/02/18/libya-security-forces-kill-84-over-three-days.

63 "Popular Protest in North African and the Middle East (V): Making Sense of Libya," International Crisis Group Middle East/North Africa Report No. 107, June 6, 2011.

64 "Pillay Calls for International Inquiry into Libyan Violence and Justice for Victims," Office of the High Commissioner for Human Rights, February 22, 2011, www.ohchr.org/en/NewsEvents/Pages/DisplayNews.aspx?NewsID=10743&LangID=E.

65 UN Security Council, Resolution 1970 (2011), February 26, 2011, S/RES/1970, www.undocs.org/S/RES/1970%20(2011).

66 UN Security Council, Resolution 1973 (2011), March 17, 2011, S/RES/1973, www.undocs.org/S/RES/1973%20(2011).

67 Mazzetti, *The Way of the Knife*, 316.

68 David D. Kirkpatrick and Steven Lee Myers, "Libya Attack Brings Challenges for U.S.," *The New York Times*, September 12, 2012, www.nytimes.com/2012/09/13/world/middleeast/us-envoy-to-libya-is-reported-killed.html; Mazzetti, *The Way of the Knife*, 321: "[T]he skies above Benghazi filled with the buzzing sound of American drones."

approximately 550 drone strikes had been conducted in the country by the US since 2011.[69]

In this post-2011 insurgency context, operations in Libya expanded to non-state armed groups, and in particular the Islamic State in Libya, thus transforming it into a case that falls within the scope of this study.[70] It is interesting to note that in January 2016, the US and Italy signed an agreement in which Italy allowed the US to use an air base in Sicily to conduct drone operations against the Islamic State in Libya and elsewhere in northern Africa.[71] The agreement obliges the US to secure permission from the Italian government every time it wants to release a combat drone and limits the authorization to defensive operations. Although it will be studied later in this book, this limitation can already be nuanced in the light of the extension of what is considered as defensive actions and the US's extensive interpretation of its right of self-defense.

2.7 G5 Sahel: French Drone Operations

France has been involved in Burkina Faso, Chad, Mali, Mauritania, and Niger since 2014, as part of the French-led Barkhane military mission aiming to counter terrorism and eradicate jihadist groups in the region.[72] Terrorist threats in the Sahel include the influential Boko Haram, Al Qaeda in the Islamic Maghreb, Ansaru, and the Al-Mulathamun Battalion. From late-2019, early-2020, the Barkhane Operation has benefited from French armed drones.[73] Before arming its drones, France had

[69] Mazzetti, *The Way of the Knife*, 321.

[70] Nick Turse, Henrik Moltke, and Alice Speri, "Secret War: The US Has Conducted 550 Drone Strikes in Libya Since 2011 – More Than in Somalia, Yemen, or Pakistan," The Intercept in partnership with *La Repubblica*, June 21, 2018, https://theintercept.com/2018/06/20/libya-us-drone-strikes/.

[71] Gordon Lubold and Julian E. Barnes, "Italy Quietly Agrees to Armed US Drone Missions over Libya," February 22, 2016, www.wsj.com/articles/italy-quietly-agrees-to-armed-u-s-drone-missions-over-libya-1456163730.

[72] "Fin de Serval au Mali, lancement de l'opération 'Barkhane' au Sahel," *France 24*, July 13, 2014, www.france24.com/fr/20140713-operation-serval-mali-france-barkhane-le-drian-defense-militaire-terroriste: on the announcement by French Minister of Defense Jean-Yves le Drian of the launch of Operation Barkhane to replace the Operation Serval that was limited to Mali.

[73] French Minister of the Armed Forces, Madame Florence Parly, "Discours de clôture de Florence Parly – Ministre des armées, Université d'été de la Défense 2017," September 5, 2017, www.defense.gouv.fr/salle-de-presse/discours/discours-de-florence-parly/discours-de-cloture-de-florence-parly-universite-d-ete-de-la-defense-2017.

already started to conduct surveillance operations and had made several important strikes in the Sahel region, also in coordination with local troops and allies.

It is to be expected that the French military presence in the region will last. Indeed, the objective of pursuing the mission until jihadist groups have been eradicated – an objective that appears in several official statements and parliamentary discussions – [74] is at the heart of the military strategy. The current law on military programming for 2019–2025 revolves around the strategy to combat "jihadist terrorism," but also refers to a "terrorist threat inspired by the Jihadist movement," or uses the simple umbrella term, "jihadist groups." Since President Hollande's administration, French state officials have invariably declared being at war against jihadist terrorism, from President François Hollande,[75] Prime Minister Manuel Valls,[76] and Minister of Defense Jean-Yves Le Drian[77] to President Emmanuel Macron[78] and Minister of the Armed Forces Florence Parly.[79] Rather than defining those different groups as constituting separate armed conflicts, jihadist groups from Al Qaeda,

[74] Among other sources that will be mentioned below, official views can be found in the reported parliamentary discussions initiated in 2015 on the measures implemented by the French governement to fight against terrorism, Commission d'enquête relative aux moyens mis en œuvre par l'État pour lutter contre le terrorisme depuis le 7 janvier 2015, Reports, Comptes rendus, www2.assemblee-nationale.fr/14/autres-commissions/commissions-d-enquete/moyens-pour-lutter-contre-le-terrorisme/(block)/ComptesRendusCommission/(instance_leg)/14/(init)/0-14.

[75] President François Hollande, Discours du président de la République devant le Parlement réuni en Congrès (Speech in front of Parliament), November 16, 2015, www.diplomatie.gouv.fr/fr/politique-etrangere-de-la-france/defense-et-securite/actualites-et-evenements-lies-a-la-defense-et-la-securite/attentatsparis-serie-d-attaques-terroristes-a-paris-novembre-2015/article/discours-du-president-de-la-republique-devant-le-parlement-reuni-en-congres-16.

[76] Discours de Manuel VALLS, Premier ministre à l'Assemblée nationale – Engagement des forces en Syrie, November 25, 2015, www.gouvernement.fr/sites/default/files/document/document/2016/01/20151125_discours_de_manuel_valls_premier_ministre_-_engagement_forces_en_syrie_relu.pdf.

[77] Jean-Yves Le Drian, Ministre de la défense, "Qui est l'ennemi?" [Who Is the Enemy], Discours d'ouverture des Assises nationales 2015 de la Recherche stratégique, Paris, décembre 1, 2015, www.asafrance.fr/item/officiel-discours-d-ouverture-des-assises-nationales-2015-de-la-recherche-strategique-de-m-jean-yves-le-drian-ministre-de-la-defense-a-paris-le-1er-decembre-2015-extrait.html.

[78] Interview of President Macron, "Macron, un an après: le grand entretien en intégralité," Mediapart, YouTube, April 15, 2018, www.youtube.com/watch?v=mt0as7x-kfs&t=964s.

[79] Florence Parly, "L'EI est d'ores et déjà en train de redéployer son action," *France 24*, November 15, 2017, www.france24.com/fr/20171511-entretien-florence-parly-etat-islamique-terrorisme-barkhane-g5-sahel.

ISIS, Jabhat al-Nosra or Boko Haram seem to have been treated as part of the same conflict as far back as the presidency of François Hollande.[80] It is in this context of warfare against undifferentiated jihadist groups that the arming of drones took place. Already, surveillance drones and then, combat drones have been presented as perfectly adapted instruments for the strategic aims of French counterterrorism. The Minister of the Armed Forces, Florence Parly, praised the benefits of combining surveillance and targeting capacities in the same machine when announcing the arming of drones in September 2017.[81] She explained that combat drones add multiple values to modern warfare, from "imperceptibility" to "capacity to hover over areas of operation" to, above all, "permanent surveillance combined with sustained and discrete targeting capacity."[82] Although the French drone fleet is not large, combat drones have become a weapon of choice in the French fight against terrorism in the Sahel and they are used, at least on some occasions, as a way to anticipate threats outside moments of ongoing hostilities.

On January 3, 2021, the Barkhane forces conducted a strike on a group of individuals located in the village of Bounty, in Mali.[83] In the aftermath

[80] Commission d'enquête relative aux moyens mis en œuvre par l'État pour lutter contre le terrorisme depuis le 7 janvier 2015, Session of May 9, 2016, Report no. 20, www.assemblee-nationale.fr/14/cr-cemoyter/15-16/c1516020.asp#P324_120754: "Nous ne faisons pas la guerre à un terrorisme désincarné; nous faisons la guerre à des groupes djihadistes." See more generally parliamentary discussions on the measures implemented by the French government to fight against terrorism initiated in 2015, Commission d'enquête relative aux moyens mis en œuvre par l'État pour lutter contre le terrorisme depuis le 7 janvier 2015.

[81] French Minister of the Armed Forces, Madame Florence Parly, "Discours de clôture de Florence Parly."

[82] Ibid.,

> Mais dès lors qu'il s'agit de traiter ces cibles, il faut aujourd'hui faire appel à d'autres moyens, avions ou hélicoptères de combat, dont les frappes sont d'ailleurs parfois guidées par nos drones de surveillance. Le succès de l'opération repose donc sur la disponibilité et la parfaite coordination de plusieurs moyens, avec des temps de déploiement sur zones importants, alors même que l'opportunité de traiter la cible est souvent fugace. … À l'avenir, avec la décision que j'annonce aujourd'hui, les drones armés permettront d'allier en permanence la surveillance, l'endurance dans la discrétion et la capacité de frappe, au moment le plus opportun.

[83] "Mali: le doute subsiste après une intervention de l'armée française," TV5Monde, January 6, 2021, https://information.tv5monde.com/afrique/mali-le-doute-subsiste-apres-une-intervention-de-l-armee-francaise-390514.

of the strike, locals and journalists reported that the operation resulted in numerous civilian casualties. France, for its part, declared in a press release that its troops had targeted "members of a terrorist armed group" in full compliance with international humanitarian law.[84] This event, and the divergent views on how to characterize what happened, led the MINUSMA to open an investigation, which resulted in a report published on Tuesday March 30, 2020.[85] The report concludes that twenty-two casualties resulted from the strike, among which were nineteen civilian deaths and three members of the terrorist group Katiba Serma, a semi-autonomous arm of the jihadist group Macina Liberation Front.[86] Out of the nineteen civilian deaths, sixteen died directly from the strike and the others died from their wounds. The casualties, including those identified as civilians by the MINUSMA, were the intended targets of the strike. France, both before[87] and after the report,[88] insists that only legitimate targets were hit. On January 7, 2021, the Ministry shared the following detailed information on what triggered the decision to strike: (*translated from French*)

> On Sunday January 3, in the afternoon, after several days of intelligence gathering, the Barkhane force conducted an operation in the Douentza region, area characterized by the presence and action of terrorist armed groups such as the Katiba Serma. . . .
> In this area, more than an hour before the strike, a REAPER drone had identified a motorcycle with two individuals at the north of RN16. The vehicle joined a group of about forty adult men in an isolated zone. All the

[84] Minister of the Armed Forces, Press release, Barkhane Operation, "Frappe contre un rassemblement de membres d'un groupe armé terroriste dans la région de Douentza," January 7, 2021, https://archives.defense.gouv.fr/salle-de-presse/communiques/communique-de-presse_operation-barkhane_frappe-contre-un-rassemblement-de-membres-d-un-groupe-arme-terroriste-dans-la-region-de-douentza.

[85] United Nations, Multidimensional Integrated Stabilization Mission in Mali, "Report on the Bounty Strike" ["Rapport sur l'incident de Bounty du 3 janvier 2021"], March 2021, https://minusma.unmissions.org/sites/default/files/rapport_final_bounty_bounty9.pdf.

[86] "Making Sense of the Sahel in Recent Years, the Region Has Become a Base for Violent Extremists and Those Fighting Them," *ADF*, July 7, 2020, https://adf-magazine.com/2020/05/making-sense-of-the-sahel/.

[87] Minister of the Armed Forces, Press release, Barkhane Operation, "Frappe contre un rassemblement de membres."

[88] Minister of the Armed Forces, Press release, Barkhane Operation, "Réaction au rapport de la Minusma sur les frappes de janvier au Mali," March 30, 2021, www.asafrance.fr/item/communique-de-presse-du-ministere-des-armees-reaction-au-rapport-de-la-minusma-sur-les-frappes-de-janvier-au-mali.html.

> intelligence gathered, including real time information, allowed us to identify this group as belonging to an armed terrorist group. The observation of the zone for more than an hour and a half also allowed to exclude the presence of women and children. Considering the behavior of the individuals, of the tools identified, and combining all collected intelligence, the strike was ordered.[89]

The MINUSMA report gets into interesting detail about the local tradition of having men and women spend part of the wedding celebrations in separate groups and concludes that only three of those men were presumably part of a violent non-state armed groups. Although the targets were not engaged in hostilities at the moment of the strike, their behavior, age, sex, and location were taken to reveal their role as part of the military arm of a terrorist group. The press releases from the French Ministry of the Armed Forces and the MINUSMA report might diverge on some elements but they all agree on one thing: Barkhane forces found the targets legitimate based on evidence other than witnessed participation in hostilities, among which, the facts that all individuals were men, apparently military-aged, unusually gathered, in a region known for terrorist groups' presence, and that some of them carried weapons.

A drone strike story, told by a French operator lieutenant-colonel in charge of leading a drone strike in an interview conducted for the podcast Le Collimateur (podcast of the Strategic Research Institute of the French Military School (IRSEM)), on April 9, 2021 confirms the hypothesis that France has been conducting signature strikes in the Sahel, and more generally a war by "risk analysis" or by anticipation.[90] In the interview, the lieutenant-colonel describes a mode of target selection that identifies individuals as belonging to a terrorist group based on elements that can include, for example, the apparent age and sex of the targets, their behavior, geolocation, and their carrying of weapons.

[89] Minister of the Armed Forces, Press release, Barkhane Operation, "Frappe contre un rassemblement de membres."

[90] M. Drevet, L. Mieusset, R. Mignot-Mahdavi, C. Pinel, and A. Yehiel, "Testimony of a French Drone Operator: Anticipatory Strikes in the Sahel," European Forum on Armed Drones (EFAD), February 16, 2022, www.efadrones.org/testimony-of-a-french-drone-operator-anticipatory-strikes-in-the-sahel/. The testimony can be found here: www.irsem.fr/le-collimateur/dans-le-viseur-27-frappe-de-drone-dans-le-desert-malien-09-04-2021.html and its translation into English here: www.efadrones.org/wp-content/uploads/2022/02/Drone-strike-in-the-Malian-desert_interview-in-English-2.pdf.

2.8 Common Patterns of Legal Rationale

A general and more or less explicit legal rationale emerges for the three states studied. When case specificities are excluded, we can identify two patterns in the argument developed by states to justify the extraterritorial use of drones against non-state actors. First, they all assert that their drone program is in full accordance with domestic and international law.[91] While most of the time refusing to provide details on the methods used to implement the policy, on the process of selecting targets, or on how legality of drone strikes is ensured,[92] the governments insist on the legality of extraterritorial drone strikes and their compliance with

[91] See, for example, Jeh Johnson, Dean's Lecture at Yale Law School, "National Security Law, Lawyers and Lawyering in the Obama Administration," Yale Law School, February 22, 2012, www.cfr.org/national-security-and-defense/jeh-johnsons-speech-national-security-law-lawyers-lawyering-obama-administration/p27448: "We must apply, and we have applied, the law of armed conflict, including applicable provisions of the Geneva Conventions and customary international law, core principles of distinction and proportionality, historic precedent, and traditional principles of statutory construction." See French Minister of the Armed Forces Florence Parly, Déclaration de Mme Florence Parly, ministre des armées, "Speech on the Ethics of Air Power and Controlling the Air Space," October 19, 2021, www.vie-publique.fr/discours/282081-florence-parly-19102021-ethique-de-la-puissance-aerienne. Finally, for the UK, see Rt. Hon. Jeremy Wright QC MP, Attorney General's Speech at the International Institute for Strategic Studies, January 11, 2017, www.gov.uk/government/speeches/attorney-generals-speech-at-the-international-institute-for-strategic-studies.

[92] TBIJ, Covert War on Terror, The Data, www.thebureauinvestigates.com/2011/08/10/the-bush-years-2004-2009/. Obama acknowledged that the US was using drones to target suspected terrorists in FATA in an online video chat on January 31, 2012. See President Obama's Google+ Hangout, WHITEHOUSE.GOV, January 30, 2012, www.whitehouse.gov/photos-andvideo/video/2012/01/30/president-obama-s-googlehangout. See John O. Brennan, Assistant to the President for Homeland Security and Counterterrorism, "The Efficacy and Ethics of US Counterterrorism Strategy," Remarks at the Woodrow Wilson International Center for Scholars, April 30, 2012, www.wilsoncenter.org/event/the-efficacy-and-ethics-uscounterterrorism-strategy; Letter from Amnesty International et al. to Barack Obama, President of the United States, May 31, 2012, www.justforeignpolicy.org/node/1242(requesting that information be released to Congress concerning US drone use). For France, see French Minister of the Armed Forces, Madame Florence Parly, "Discours de clôture de Florence Parly":

> Je veux par avance réfuter de possibles amalgames et dissiper d'éventuelles craintes. Non, un drone armé n'est pas un robot tueur. Ce sont deux systèmes qui n'ont rien de semblable. Cette décision ne change rien aux règles d'usage de la force, au respect du droit des conflits armés et je reste plus que jamais attachée au respect du droit international et de nos engagements relatifs à la maîtrise des armements et à la préservation des populations civiles dans les conflits.

international law.[93] Even though the US, UK, and French governments do not systematically provide details on the way they conduct their policy, the US under the Obama administration and the United Kingdom and France at the occasion of contested strikes have publicly developed legal arguments to justify drone strikes against non-state actors in foreign territories. They do so in slightly different ways: the US in a more straightforward and detailed manner, the UK in a direct and detailed way when asked by Parliament, and France in more general terms.

Second, they all include references to both *jus in bello* and *jus ad bellum* when framing their war on terror and, more specifically, when justifying drone operations in this context. Regarding the *jus in bello* framework, it is interesting to note that even when arguing for extensive presidential war powers, the Bush administration always used the armed conflict paradigm to talk about the war on terror.[94] The legal justification of the Obama administration for using armed drones against Al Qaeda, the Taliban, and associated forces is at the core of this study, and can be described as consisting of a hybrid paradigm composed of both *jus in bello* and *jus ad bellum* arguments.[95] On the one hand, there was still the

[93] Cameron, Oral Statement to Parliament, "Syria: Refugees and Counter-Terrorism": "The action we took was entirely lawful. The Attorney General was consulted and was clear there would be a clear legal basis for action in international law. We were exercising the UK's inherent right to self-defence."

[94] President G. W. Bush Addresses the Nation, September 20, 2001, Transcript available in *The Washington Post*, www.washingtonpost.com/wp-srv/nation/specials/attacked/transcripts/bushaddress_092001.html: "On September the 11th, enemies of freedom committed an act of war against our country . . . Our war on terror begins with Al Qaeda, but it does not end there. It will not end until every terrorist group of global reach has been found, stopped and defeated." Some even consider that Bush did not per se claim a zone of authority outside of armed conflict governed by IHL. In this sense, see, Kenneth Anderson, "Targeted Killing in U.S. Counterterrorism Strategy and Law: A Working Paper of the Series on Counterterrorism and American Statutory Law" (2009) Digital Commons of the American University Washington College of Law, Working Papers https://digitalcommons.wcl.american.edu/cgi/viewcontent.cgi?referer=&httpsredir=1&article=1007&context=fac_works_papers, 3: "Even the Bush Administration, with its unrivaled enthusiasm for executive power, always sought to cast its killing targets as the killing of combatants in what it legally characterized as armed conflicts, governed by the laws of war on the conduct of hostilities, known as 'international humanitarian law' (IHL)."

[95] Harold Koh, Legal Adviser, US Department of State, "The Obama Administration and International Law," Speech at the Annual Meeting of the American Society of International Law, Washington, DC, March 25, 2010, www.state.gov/s/l/releases/remarks/139119.htm: "As I have explained, as a matter of international law, the United

idea of an armed conflict with Al Qaeda, the Taliban, and associated forces in the aftermath of the 9/11 attacks.[96] On the other hand, the extraterritorial use of force would be justified by the imminent threat posed by an individual under a revised version of the right of self-defense.[97] The mix also includes elements of domestic law, in particular the unmodified 2001 Authorization for the Use of Military Force (AUMF) that Congress passed in the wake of the September 11 attacks.[98]

In 2013, the US implied that it would focus almost exclusively on the right to self-defense to conduct drone operations using the May 2013 Presidential Policy Guidance (hereafter, PPG), but this message has to be read in the light of the diplomatic ambitions of the PPG. It was developed in a context in which drone strikes were becoming increasingly frequent and increasingly identified by the public. There was concern among the allies and of various members of Congress and civil society groups, and also within the US government itself (in particular in the State Department) regarding compliance with international law. As a consequence of the hard work done by Obama's Legal Advisers to clarify their legal framework for the use of drones, and in an (eventually successful) attempt to reassure allies, the PPG was formulated as a matter of policy to try and bring the US practice as close as possible to the legal understanding of US allies regarding when force could be used. Mainly, the latter seemed to be of the view that lethal force could not be used in an extraterritorial location, where and when no active hostilities were ongoing but based purely and simply on an IHL theory that the person was a participant in some transnational armed conflict. Instead, allies were comfortable with a *jus ad bellum* justification that that person

States is in an armed conflict with al-Qaeda, as well as the Taliban and associated forces, in response to the horrific 9/11 attacks, and may use force consistent with its inherent right to self-defense under international law."

[96] The US has defined AQAP as an organized armed group that is "either part of, or an associate of, al Qa'ida." See Nasser al-Aulaqi vs. Leon Panetta, US Motion to Dismiss, US District Court for the District of Columbia, December 14, 2012, www.aclu.org/files/assets/tk_govt_motion_to_dismiss.pdf.

[97] Koh, "The Obama Administration and International Law": "Of course, whether a particular individual will be targeted in a particular location will depend upon considerations specific to each case, including those related to the imminence of the threat, the sovereignty of the other states involved, and the willingness and ability of those states to suppress the threat the target poses."

[98] See, for example, Johnson, General Counsel, US Defense Department, "National Security Law, Lawyers and Lawyering in the Obama Administration"; Attorney General Eric Holder, "Remarks at Northwestern University School of Law," March 5, 2012, www.justice.gov/iso/opa/ag/speeches/2012/ag-speech-1203051.html.

had to pose an imminent threat under a self-defense theory for the use of lethal force. The PPG thus entrenched a mixed *jus ad bellum/jus in bello* legal narrative for the extraterritorial use of drones against non-state actors. This features some requirements that clearly would not be required under IHL, such as the preference for "capture" over "kill", the near certainty of the absence of civilian casualties, and above all the requirement that the individual poses a continuing imminent threat.

The above-mentioned contextual elements are absolutely vital when it comes to understanding that the PPG does not exclude the *jus in bello* framework from the US legal theory on the use of drones. On the contrary, one could convincingly argue that the US has always considered itself to be in an armed conflict against Al Qaeda and associated forces and that framing operations occurring outside moments and/or areas of ongoing active hostilities as *jus ad bellum* was more of a rhetorical and diplomatic move. Supporting this view is the *jus ad bellum* element of *continuing* imminent threat articulated by the PPG, which transforms the right of self-defense into a paradigm to target individuals continuously having a hostile intent, and could have just as well be targeted under an IHL theory according to which: (i) there is no geographical criterion set by the law to constrain the scope of conflicts; and (ii) members of non-state armed groups can be targeted as direct participants in hostilities holding a continuous combat function even when and where they are not currently actively participating in hostilities. As is shown in Chapter 3, this mixed legal framework formulated by the Obama administration remains in force under the Trump administration.

Public parliamentary debates and official statements on the UK drone program were triggered by the Reyaad Khan strike. Although the government struggled to justify the strike in the first place, an admixture of *jus in bello* and *jus ad bellum* could be identified even in early justifications. When discussing the August 2015 UK strikes in Syria, neither Michael Fallon in his hearing,[99] nor David Cameron in his oral statement,[100] nor any other UK official clearly identified these strikes as exclusively conducted in the exercise of self-defense. On the contrary,

[99] Rt. Hon. Michael Fallon, "Oral Evidence: The UK Government's Policy on the Use of Drones for Targeted Killing," 2015, http://data.parliament.uk/writtenevidence/committeeevidence.svc/evidencedocument/human-rights-committee/the-uk-governments-policy-on-the-use-of-drones-for-targeted-killing/oral/27633.html.

[100] David Cameron, "Syria: Refugees and Counter-Terrorism."

the idea that was put forward was that the conflict in Syria was an extension of the conflict against ISIS in Iraq. A mix of *jus in bello* and *jus ad bellum* similar to that of the US appeared even more clearly after the government was invited by the Parliamentary Joint Committee on Human Rights and later on by the Intelligence and Security Committee of Parliament, to explain their legal justification for their use of drones. As this book will discuss in detail, the two Parliamentary reports clarified the legal rationale for the UK drone program[101] and showed that UK drone operations in Syria rest on a mixture of *ad bellum* and *in bello* reasoning. The argumentative elements that are contentions for the US are justified in similar ways by UK officials, such as by the Attorney General Jeremy Wright who, in his 2017 speech at the International Institute for Strategic Studies, referred to the Bethlehem Principles and in particular to his loose conception of imminence, defined as continuous intent, to argue that a state has a right to use force in self-defense.[102]

The same *jus in bello/jus ad bellum* combination appears to be used by France to frame its so-called war against jihadist groups. Overall, France appears to use the framework of non-international armed conflict against non-state armed groups to regulate its extraterritorial counterterrorism efforts, and this does not appear to be limited to the Sahel region, since neither the Strategic Review[103] nor the Law on Military Programming restrain the military strategy to the situation in the Sahel.[104] These documents also mention the necessary anticipation of threats wherever these emerge.[105] On other occasions, particularly regarding the strikes in Syria against ISIS, French officials relied upon the right to self-defense for

[101] UK Parliament Joint Committee on Human Rights (JCHR), Report on the Government's Policy on the Use of Drones for Targeted Killings, May 10, 2016; UK Parliament Intelligence and Security Committee, Report on UK Lethal Drone Strikes in Syria, April 26, 2017.

[102] The Rt. Hon. Jeremy Wright QC MP, Attorney General's Speech at the International Institute for Strategic Studies.

[103] Strategic Defense Review, Revue stratégique de défense et de sécurité nationale, 2017, www.defense.gouv.fr/dgris/presentation/evenements/revue-strategique-de-defense-et-desecurite-nationale-2017.

[104] Statute reference is : Loi no. 2018-607 du 13 juillet 2018 relative à la programmation militaire pour les années 2019 à 2025 et portant diverses dispositions intéressant la défense, www.legifrance.gouv.fr/eli/loi/2018/7/13/ARMX1800503L/jo/texte; Annexed Report to the Law on Military Programming (it should be noted that it also has legislative value), Rapport annexé, (appears at the end of the legislation), www.legifrance.gouv.fr/affichTexte.do?cidTexte=JORFTEXT000037192797&dateTexte=20181122.

[105] Mignot-Mahdavi, "Le Silence des Agneaux."

the strikes in Syria, and an extensive interpretation thereof, similar to that of the US and the UK.[106] They argued that France is acting legitimately under the right to self-defense when conducting strikes in Syria because of the attacks that are organized and perpetrated by ISIS members from Syria "against France and other countries."[107] What emerges, therefore, is the use of a mixed framework, with, on the one hand, *jus in bello* appearing through the multiple references to the existence of a conflict against jihadist groups in general, that were mentioned above. On the other hand, the *jus ad bellum* framework and an extensive version of the right of self-defense emerge from references to threats and anticipating those threats wherever they may surface.

[106] Speech of Former French Prime Minister, Discours de Manuel Valls devant l'Assemblée Nationale, September 15, 2015, www.gouvernement.fr/syrie-la-france-est-en-guerre-contre-le-terrorisme-le-djihadisme-l-islamisme-radical-ce-sera-long-2873: "Il s'agit ainsi d'identifier et de localiser le dispositif de Daech pour être en mesure de le frapper sur le sol syrien et d'exercer ainsi notre droit à la légitime défense, comme le prévoit l'article 51 de la Charte des Nations unies." Déclaration de M. Jean-Yves Le Drian, Ministre de la Défense, en réponse à une question sur les frappes aériennes françaises en Syrie, à l'Assemblée nationale le 30 septembre 2015, Questions d'actualité à l'Assemblée nationale, September 30, 2015.

[107] Sixth Conference of the French President on the Challenges and Priorities of the Executive Policy, Sixième Conférence du Président de la République François Hollande, September 7, 2015, Palais de l'Élysée, www.vie-publique.fr/discours/196108-conference-de-presse-de-m-francois-hollande-president-de-la-republique.

3

The Institutionalization of Drone Programs

How did the new kind of deterritorialized, dematerialized, and individualized warfare – extensive in both time and space – become durable? To what extent can it be considered as part of the normal functioning of the states using drones? This chapter finds that the development of the use of drones in the US, in comparison with its British and French counterparts, is best described as one of institutionalization, thereby substantiating the shared intuition that they deserve to be referred to as part of a "machinery" or a "program."[1] I illustrate that this process derives from a combination of factors, including: (i) narratives about the threat posed by polymorphous transnational terrorist networks; (ii) the formation of a bureaucracy dedicated to the use of drones – bureaucracy that I define as the structured, harmonized, and depersonalized interaction of agents; and (iii) the elaboration of sophisticated legal rationales to support the use of drones. These factors that I identify in the elaboration of the US drone program are vectors of durability and legitimacy. Durability is found in the existence of habits and the recognition of certain activities as such, but also as the economy of effort required once the activity is routinized, "habitualized."[2] Legitimacy refers to the implementation of the durable activity in a "normative fabric" of a community of actors.[3] I define the normative fabric as the set of justifications and mechanisms, legal and political, designed to make a practice acceptable, both inside the institution (state agents believe in the merits of drone use against jihadist groups) and outside of it (the population believes that such a practice is acceptable in a democratic society in order to deal with a given context).

[1] For instance, in The Drone Papers (2015), the team of The Intercept uses the terms "bureaucracy" and "assassination complex" to describe the structures, procedures, and practices related to the use of drones.

[2] Peter L. Berger and Thomas Luckmann, *The Social Construction of Reality: A Treatise in the Sociology of Knowledge* (Penguin, 1991).

[3] Paul S. Goodman, *Change in Organizations* (Jossey-Bass, 1982).

These two features of durability and legitimacy are interconnected: a strong legitimation exercise will maintain the stability of the institution over time and deter individual temptations to redefine or deconstruct the institution and the rationales sustaining it.[4] As a result of this process, the use of drones in the US has been integrated into the normal functioning of the state and has become an organized and permanent solution, and not a temporary or prompt solution, to the existence of jihadist terrorism. The Obama administration was aware and actively embraced the normalizing effect of establishing special decision-making processes and legal rationales for the use of drones. In fact, Charlie Savage reports that the Obama administration placed "great faith in process, believing that the interagency decision-making frameworks it crafted could constrain powers such as targeted killing operations and hoping that these frameworks would seem so self-evidently rational that they would outlive the administration's tenure."[5] This reveals both an objective to establish constraint through these mechanisms, but also the willingness to create a drone program that would stand the test of time.

However, as will be further developed in Chapters 4, 5, and 6, state representatives, their decisions, and the legal evolutions they instigate are only some of the powerful factors shaping the reality, alongside which technological tools play a similarly performing function. Indeed, drones, as any cutting-edge technology, are in themselves vectors of meaningful developments. Changes in legal interpretations and military strategy are generated by an evolving human–nonhuman environment within which human agents acquire new habits and practices. We have also seen that the sustained use of force in foreign territories against terrorist groups since 9/11 does not imply that populations live in a permanent and uninterrupted state of exception, or are governed in a continuous legal vacuum, contrary to what was witnessed early on in the war on terror.[6] Far from it, the law played a central role in the development of drone programs.[7] What this chapter shows is that far from suspending the

[4] Berger and Luckmann, *The Social Construction of Reality*, 80; Ludwig Wittgenstein, *Philosophical Investigations* (4th ed., Wiley-Blackwell, 2009 [trans. and ed. by P. M. S. Hacker and Joachim Schulte]).

[5] Charlie Savage, *Power Wars: The Relentless Rise of Presidential Authority and Secrecy* (Little, Brown, 2017), 293.

[6] Giorgio Agamben, *State of Exception* (University of Chicago Press, 2005).

[7] Finally, and this is an element of institutionalization that will not be explored due to time and place constraints, the distinction between the different powers – executive, legislative, and judicial – remains. Accountability mechanisms activated by parliament, although

usual functioning of institutions and the regulation of institutional practices, drones can trigger and consolidate the creation of a bureaucracy when it is introduced as the most adequate technological tool to conduct a chosen military strategy. The central case study of this chapter is the US drone program, as it was stabilized through the creation of structures and bureaucratic interactions, a highly legalistic mode of justification, and narratives about drones being tailor-made to fight a transnational and polymorphous enemy.

3.1 Transnational Terrorist Networks: Calling for a Systemic Individualization of War

Drone programs emerged to face an enemy reputed to call for a new form of hostilities, focused on anticipating threats posed by individuals. While contemporary jihadist groups have unique characteristics that differentiate them from non-state armed groups in traditional civil wars, the belief that they deserve a special treatment is shaped by discourses about jihadist groups formulated not only by other actors, but also by jihadist groups themselves. This rhetoric portrayal from both sides effectively forged the military strategy against non-state actors, and drones' technological capacities were presented as making ends meet by holding out the promise of unprecedented precision and enhanced anticipatory capacities. It eventually supports the idea that the individualized conduct of warfare facilitated by drones' technological features may make permissive legal interpretations more acceptable on the grounds that it is strategically and technically sound.

In some respects, contemporary transnational terrorist networks can be distinguished from traditional non-state armed groups. I should stress that I use the term "traditional" for clarity purposes; but such groups still exist today and are still the protagonists of some non-international armed conflicts even if instances of contemporary warfare largely consist of conflicts between states and non-state armed groups of a transnational

limited, are still exercised and even serve, in some instances, to further stabilize the drone program. It should be noted here that Agamben's argument is somewhat confusing and imprecise, linking the state of exception with the state of necessity. On the one hand, he argues that the state of exception is characterized by the suspension of the usual distinction and balance between the executive, the legislative, and the judicial. On the other hand, though, when this distinction remains, Agamben does not mean that there is no potential for a state of exception. Indeed, he seems to say that any presidential regime is a platform for the state of exception, considering the very limited extent of parliamentary power.

character.[8] I refer alternatively to transnational terrorist networks and transnational jihadist groups – the second terminology pointing to these groups' project to establish a global caliphate – and focus on the two transnational jihadist groups that states have identified as their main enemies in the war on terror, namely, Al Qaeda and ISIS. Although ISIS positioned itself as the pioneer of the global jihadist movement, both groups have a project of establishing a caliphate and compete with each other to that end.[9] If at first the priority of ISIS was to reterritorialize the jihad and create local political entities (contrary to the global nature of Al Qaeda's project from the start), ISIS ended up joining the project of global jihadism in two ways: first, through the creation of an international jihadist legion, and second, through the rejection of the concepts of the nation-state and state borders.[10] Thus, ISIS's project for a caliphate as well as Al Qaeda's plans for a global jihad cultivate the fantasy of perpetual territorial expansion.[11] Because their transnational ambition is

[8] Uppsala Conflict Data Program, http://ucdp.uu.se/#/encyclopedia. The most recent reports of the US National Counterterrorism Center clearly show that national/separatist terrorism still exists (India, Philippines, Sri Lanka). Two-thirds of the terrorist attacks carried out in India in 2015 (67 percent) were attributed to the Communist Party of India-Maoist or Maoist perpetrators not specifically identified as belonging to a particular organization. In the Philippines, the Moro Islamic Liberation Front, based in Mindanao, fights for the acquisition of an autonomous region of the Moro people from the central government. The Communist Party of the Philippines/New People's Army (CPP/NPA) perpetrates attacks to overthrow the Philippine government. See Bureau of Counterterrorism and Countering Violent Extremism, Country Reports on Terrorism 2016, Released July 2017, www.state.gov/documents/organization/272488.pdf; Office of the Coordinator for the Counterterrorism, National Consortium for the Study of Terrorism and Responses to Terrorism: Annex of Statistical Information, June 2016, www.state.gov/j/ct/rls/crt/2015/257526.htm.

[9] Tore Refslund Hamming, "The Al Qaeda – Islamic State Rivalry: Competition Yes, but No Competitive Escalation" (2020) 32 *Terrorism and Political Violence* 1, 20–37.

[10] Olivier Roy, *Le Djihad et la Mort* (Seuil, 2016) 25, 137, 140–1:

> Contrairement à l'émirat islamique d'Afghanistan fondé par les talibans, il n'est pas question pour Daech d'accepter le concept d'État-nation, avec les frontières et le jeu diplomatique induits. En ce sens, le terme "État islamique" est trompeur: ce projet n'a rien à voir avec celui des Frères musulmans de toute nature. Le califat n'existe que dans l'expansion, et donc dans la guerre, car il ne peut accepter aucune négociation.

[11] Ibid., 97; William McCants, *The ISIS Apocalypse: The History, Strategy, and Doomsday Vision of the Islamic State*, Reprint edition (Picador, 2016); Fawaz A. Gerges, *ISIS: A History*, Reprint edition (Princeton University Press, 2017). In the last instance, even the prospect of creating a global Islamic society cannot be identified as the concrete agenda of these "new" non-state armed groups. Indeed, death and war are not the means toward the achievement of a political goal. Instead, war and death are ends in themselves:

fundamentally different from the state-centered and territorially delineated projects of traditional non-state armed groups, both deserve to be included in the scope of the present study.

Although I have decided to focus on ISIS and Al Qaeda and will highlight their divergences and common denominators, it should already be noted that the US, France, and to a certain extent the UK, as we shall see in the following chapters, do not distinguish between various jihadist groups when crafting their military strategy. Even more important, the US and France aggregate different non-state armed groups as part of a unique conflict (when they do not refer to them as interchangeable entities).[12] The consequence is that the characteristics of the groups identified in this section are inflated, thus intensifying the urge and strengthening the justification to adopt an extensive military strategy and permissive interpretations of the law to support it. Indeed, as has been shown, each transnational jihadist group on its own is characterized by a multiplicity of fronts. When, for instance, Al Qaeda is treated as part of the same enemy entity alongside ISIS, the Taliban, and other terrorist groups, the enemy appears to have an even greater number of fronts around the globe and a more significant degree of mobility.

ISIS members are convinced of the imminent end of the world and the state that precedes the apocalypse is a state of war. All in all, the ideology of ISIS is essentially nihilistic in that it revolves around death, which is the only key to heaven.

12 President Trump's Speech to the UN General Assembly, September 19, 2017, http://edition.cnn.com/2017/09/19/politics/president-trump-united-nations-speech/index.html:

> The United States and our allies are working together throughout the Middle East to crush the loser terrorists and stop the reemergence of safe havens they use to launch attacks on all of our people. Last month, I announced a new strategy for victory in the fight against this evil in Afghanistan. From now on, our security interests will dictate the length and scope of military operations, not arbitrary benchmarks and timetables set up by politicians. I have also totally changed the rules of engagement in our fight against the Taliban and other terrorist groups. In Syria and Iraq, we have made big gains toward the lasting defeat of ISIS. In fact, our country has achieved more against ISIS in the last eight months than it has in many, many years combined.

French Commission d'enquête parlementaire relative aux moyens mis en œuvre par l'Etat pour lutter contre le terrorisme depuis le 7 janvier 2015, Hearing Transcripts, www.assemblee-nationale.fr/14/cr-cemoyter/15-16/c1516032.asp: Military and state officials constantly identify the enemy broadly as "jihadist" groups and individuals. Unlike in the US and in France, it should be noted that in the UK the identification of the enemy group is precise.

Traditional non-state armed groups and jihadist terrorist groups can be distinguished as being respectively primarily and secondarily interested in, and defined by, state and territorial concerns. I make this distinction according to three main criteria: the center of gravity, the agenda, and the structure of these groups. Traditional non-state armed groups revolve around a unique and stable physical center of gravity, that is, a geographical focal point – either a country, or part of it, or a delineated territory that spills over several countries – from which the non-state armed group carries out its operations, recruits the majority of its members, and in which official authorities are the main target/object of conflict.[13] The well-established center of gravity of such groups does not exclude international cooperation, which is why I specified above that these groups *primarily* (and not solely) have state concerns and rootedness. Yet, despite international alliances around a common project or ideology, the actions of traditional non-state armed groups mainly consist of a series of national campaigns.[14] Indeed, no matter how extensive the international activities are, their aim, first and foremost, is to support the focal point of operations and to reinforce their core.[15]

By contrast, a multiplicity of fronts, a multiplicity of recruitment areas, and a multiplicity of enemies are typical of contemporary terrorist groups aspiring to global jihad. The diagnosis of an absence of a center of gravity is not merely based on the cross-border operations of those groups. The countries of action, the countries where the recruits come from, the countries where the families of the recruits originally come from, and the countries of residence and radicalization are all different.[16] Their theaters of operations are also geographically multiple: Spain, Indonesia, the UK, Tanzania, the US, France, Germany, Yemen, India, and so forth.[17] In fact, these groups can be expected to increasingly target a

[13] Peter Neumann, *Old and New Terrorism* (Polity, 2009) 18.

[14] David C. Rapoport, *Inside Terrorist Organizations* (2nd ed., Routledge, 2013), 34–8. For instance, the globalized nature of new non-state armed groups should be distinguished from the nineteenth-century anarchist movement that – if operating in and receiving support across Europe and North America – mainly consisted of a series of national campaigns with very little cross-border activity or exchange (common ideology but separate national-based campaigns).

[15] Neumann, *Old and New Terrorism*, 18.

[16] Olivier Roy, *Globalized Islam: The Search for a New Ummah* (Columbia University Press, 2006).

[17] Tim Lister, Ray Sanchez, Mark Bixler, Sean O'Key, Michael Hogenmiller, and Mohammed Tawfeeq, "ISIS Goes Global: 143 Attacks in 29 Countries Have Killed 2,043," CNN, last update February 12, 2018, http://edition.cnn.com/2015/12/17/world/

multiplicity of fronts as they turn to cyber-attacks and start using armed drones as a way to strike their opponents.[18]

With this multiplicity of fronts, a new virtual space supersedes the multiple physical locations of the group.[19] This virtual space is beyond the control or identity of any state, and crystallizes a new kind of social space – not only without a single, permanent geographical point of reference but also with a loose or no concern for geographical delineation.[20] Of course, the virtual community does not replace physical world relations, but it does play a role in loosening spatial constraints, and in changing the nature of the relationship between non-state armed groups and states. It is interesting to note that cross-border synergies and movements facilitated by social media do not threaten, and may even reinforce, the groups' strength and stability. This is, by the way, also true for the physical movements of the groups, and not only digital ones. Al Qaeda has moved headquarters at least three times and none of these moves has destroyed the organization altogether.[21]

Traditional non-state armed groups, in addition to being territorially based, have a state-centered narrative and agenda. If we compare Al Qaeda or ISIS and the guerilla movement of the Revolutionary Armed Forces of Colombia (hereafter, the FARC), both are non-state armed groups but the FARC has a state-centered and territorially delineated agenda. The FARC's enemy has always been the Colombian security forces and their claim has mainly concerned control over land.[22] To take

mapping-isis-attacks-around-the-world/index.html; "Timeline: Al-Qaeda," BBC News Special Reports, http://news.bbc.co.uk/2/hi/7546355.stm.

[18] Roy, *Globalized Islam*, 305; Thomas Gibbons-Neff, "ISIS Drones Are Attacking U.S. Troops and Disrupting Airstrikes in Raqqa, Officials Say," *The Washington Post*, June 14, 2017, Section Checkpoint, www.washingtonpost.com/news/checkpoint/wp/2017/06/14/isis-drones-are-attacking-u-s-troops-and-disrupting-airstrikes-in-raqqa-officials-say/; Cody Poplin, "Look Who Else Has Drones: ISIS and Al Nusra," *Lawfare*, October 24, 2014, www.lawfareblog.com/look-who-else-has-drones-isis-and-al-nusra.

[19] Thomas Hegghammer, "The Rise of Muslim Foreign Fighters: Islam and the Globalization of Jihad" (2010) 35 *International Security* 3, 53–94; Gabriel Weimann, "Terrorist Migration to the Dark Web" (2016) 10 *Perspectives on Terrorism* 3, 44; Leah Windsor, "The Language of Radicalization: Female Internet Recruitment to Participation in ISIS Activities" (2020) 23 *Terrorism and Political Violence* 3, 506–38.

[20] Neumann, *Old and New Terrorism*, 20; Roy, *Globalized Islam*.

[21] Peter L. Bergen, *Holy War, Inc.: Inside the Secret World of Osama Bin Laden* (Free Press, 2002).

[22] Andrea Fanta Castro, Alejandro Herrero-Olaizola, and Chloe Rutter-Jensen (eds.), *Territories of Conflict: Traversing Colombia through Cultural Studies* (University of Rochester Press, 2017); Marc Chernick, "FARC-EP: Las Fuerzas Armadas

another emblematic case of a non-state armed group in conflict with their government (before replacing it), the 1979 Islamic Revolution of Iran, although it was partly driven by the aim of exporting the ideology of political Islam and to influence the political landscape of the Muslim world, its primary goals were state-centered as Ayatollah Khomeini aimed at conquering state institutions and acquiring the power to change the regime.[23]

At the same time, interactions with state institutions and official local authorities, as well as rootedness in a given territory may represent a way to work toward a global Caliphate, but these interactions are never an end in themself for Al Qaeda and ISIS. Transnational jihadist groups distinguish themselves by a rejection of the state, the concept of sovereignty and the international society, where traditional non-state armed groups broadly accept it and might even aspire to be part of it once they have overthrown their own national government.[24] It is

Revolucionarias de Colombia-Ejército del Pueblo," in Marianne Heiberg, Brendan O'Leary, and John Tirman (eds.), *Terror, Insurgency, and the State: Ending Protracted Conflicts* (University of Pennsylvania Press, 2007), 51–82; Jonathan Watts, "Battle for the Mother Land: Indigenous People of Colombia Fighting for Their Lands," *The Guardian*, October 29, 2017, www.theguardian.com/environment/2017/oct/28/nasa-colombia-cauca-valley-battle-mother-land.

23 Gilles Kepel, *Jihad: The Trail of Political Islam* (trans. Anthony F. Roberts, Belknap Press: An Imprint of Harvard University Press, 2003), 120:

> The Iranian revolution's propaganda ... incited people to rise up against the impiety of their leaders, despite their claim to be following the dictates of the Koran and the sharia. The Saudi policy, on the other hand, was to finance the expansion of Islamism around the world, the better to control it ... and to prevent groups bent on changing the status quo from appropriating Islam to themselves.

24 Benedict Kingsbury, "Whose International Law? Sovereignty and Non-State Groups," *ASIL Proceedings* (1994) Theme Panel I, 11:

> An alternative approach for non-state groups is to deny the validity of the international law under which the sovereignty of the state is established, and under which colonization may have taken place. In so doing, however, they forgo whatever leverage the international legal system might provide. Such forbearance may be plausible for a group whose only interest is to be left alone, but complete isolation is a rare objective in the contemporary world. Similarly, it might be a strategy for a group that does not see the international legal system providing it any useful leverage: the relatively limited participation of Kurdish groups in international forums may manifest a view that these forums are unlikely to be of help. Otherwise, repudiation of existing international law must be accompanied by a massive effort to establish and legitimize a normative discourse to rival that of traditional international law: this was attempted most notably by the USSR after the

worth noting, however, that different jihadist groups reject the interstate community through diverse rationales and methods, and some play the Westphalian game more than others in order to achieve their objectives. This is true for some Taliban and Hayat Tahrir al-Cham or Al Qaeda – much more than it is for ISIS – particularly when such objectives are local and thus considered negotiable because they are geographically restrained. This practice recently appeared from the agreement reached between the US and the Taliban in Doha, which was based on the departure of US troops from Afghanistan within a year.[25] Concrete interactions with state institutions and leaders are also reflected in a statement by Jamaat Nusrat al-Islam wal Muslimeen[26] regarding similar calls for negotiations from the government of Mali featured in the organization's journal.[27] In the statement, the organization refuses to hold any sort of negotiations before the departure of

Bolshevik revolution, but the experience of revolutionary entities has been that after a transitional period the advantages of participating in the international legal system on negotiated terms outweigh the autochthonous alternatives. In general, non-state groups have opted to make their cases as participants in the international legal system, striving to adapt existing doctrines to their purposes, to delegitimize and eclipse unsatisfactory doctrines, and to create spaces in the architecture of international institutions. While this may appear as the general strategy of indigenous peoples, there is a sampling bias: voices heard in the United Nations are amplified through the international legal institutions and literature, whereas those remaining outside and preferring repudiation tend not to be heard. Even amongst the audible sample, there is a degree of tension in the discourse of indigenous peoples between the strategies of accepting and contesting particular principles of international law.

25 Agreement for Bringing Peace to Afghanistan between the Islamic Emirate of Afghanistan Which Is Not Recognized by the United States as a State and Is Known as the Taliban and the United States of America, February 29, 2020, www.state.gov/wp-content/uploads/2020/02/Agreement-For-Bringing-Peace-to-Afghanistan-02.29.20.pdf; Joint Statement on the Signing of the US-Taliban Agreement, by Special Envoys and Special Representatives of the European Union, France, Germany, Italy, Norway, the United Kingdom, the United Nations and the United States of America on the Occasion of the Signing of the US-Taliban Agreement on February 29 in Qatar, March 9, 2020, www.state.gov/joint-statement-on-the-signing-of-the-u-s-taliban-agreement-2/.

26 Jamaat Nusrat al-Islam wal Muslimeen is a Salafi-Jihadist militant organization operating in the African Sahel region. For more information about the organization, see https://cisac.fsi.stanford.edu/mappingmilitants/profiles/jamaat-nusrat-al-islam-wal-muslimeen.

27 Jamaat Nusrat al-Islam wal Muslimeen, *Az-Zallaqa Foundation Journal*, no. 152, March 8, 2020.

French troops and its foreign allies from Mali, after which it will consider discussing with the Bamako government if it proves "serious [enough] to serve the interest of the Malian people . . . in their legitimate pursuit of freedom from direct occupation."

These interactions with state institutions do not mean that the jihadist groups accept their existence. The goal of a universal Caliphate and the ambition to move beyond governments and the international legal order are shared by ISIS, Al Qaeda, and other jihadist groups with global aspirations, from those ones who play the Westphalian game, use its channels and vocabulary the most, to those that reject it the most, such as ISIS. In the late 1980s, the purpose of Al Qaeda was redefined as the pursuit of a transnational project and enlarged its priorities "from the near enemy to the far enemy" (*min al 'adou al qareeb ila al 'adou al ba'eed*).[28] The deterritorialization of the jihadist project did not mean that militant actions became unrooted; they all take place in concrete territories and situations. Instead, their becoming transnational in essence marked the intrinsic opposition of jihadist groups to the state and international legal order. In this sense, Ayse Zarakol explains that what is striking about Al Qaeda is that "it is not interested in replacing any *particular* regime in any one *particular* country, even if it supports its local affiliates in such quests."[29]

The trajectory of IS developed progressively, through concrete spaces and contexts, and in this sense it is deeply connected to territories even if the broader picture is transnational.[30] Yet, here too, this territorialized construction is not indicative of its embeddedness in the Westphalian order and its orderly following of national-territorial lines.[31] In fact, one could say that it reveals quite the opposite. First, its territorialized construct expresses a negation of the state located in the territories cited. Second, it reveals an understanding that a perennial

[28] Mohammad-Mahmoud Ould Mohamedou, *A Theory of ISIS: Political Violence and the Transformation of the Global Order* (Pluto Press, 2018), 40.

[29] Ayse Zarakol, "What Makes Terrorism Modern? Terrorism, Legitimacy and the International System" (2011) 37 *Review of International Studies* 5, 2311–36, 2334. *Emphasis added.*

[30] James Piscatori and Amin Saikal, *Islam Beyond Borders: The Umma in World Politics* (Cambridge University Press, 2019), 8: "The worldwide concern about ISIS was precisely centred on its capture of territory and ISIS itself acknowledged the imperative for control over Islamic lands (dar al-Islam) to which Muslims must migrate (*hijra*)."

[31] See Chapter 7 (this book), p. 200.

global expansion can only be achieved through concrete integration in space and time.[32]

These groups also ignore conflicts that Muslim communities may be confronted with around the world. The most meaningful illustration of this is Palestine: even if the names of Palestine or Gaza regularly come up in their campaigns, Al Qaeda and ISIS neither understand nor concretely support the Palestinian cause.[33] On the contrary, these groups have sometimes fought against Hamas in the Yarmuk camp, and against Hezbollah in the north of Damascus.[34] More generally, the photographs used for propaganda are rarely dated, are thus somehow interchangeable, and sometimes have nothing to do with the caption.[35] This, according to some, indicates that the Muslim community that the contemporary jihadist movements seek to "save" is neither historically nor spatially specified.[36] More cautiously, I would say that it reveals that the concrete theaters of operations are simply rites of passage that are part of a global struggle. Indeed, transnational jihadist movements, from Al Qaeda to ISIS, consider themselves involved in a protracted and transnational war against nonbelievers in order to realize a single and global pan-Islamic community or *umma*.[37]

> Islamic law enjoins Moslems to maintain a State of permanent belligerence with all non-believers, collectively encompassed in the *dar al-harb* the domain of war. . . . The Muslims are, therefore, under a legal obligation to reduce non-Muslim communities to Islamic rule in order to achieve Islam's ultimate objective, namely the enforcement of God's law (the Sharia) over the entire world.[38]

Finally, this global *umma* depends on the establishment of a Caliphate as a universal political and institutional project. It is interesting to note that

32 Mohamedou speaks of "a combination of an independently moving battle plan – now focused on Iraq, now centred on Syria – and an adaptation to domestic and regional contingencies." Mohamedou, *A Theory of ISIS*, 2204.

33 Roy, *Le Djihad et la Mort*, 81.

34 Ibid.

35 Ibid. Olivier Roy mentions the use of a photograph of a massacre of Harkis, Algerians who served in the French Army during the Algerian War of Independence, perpetrated by the FLN regime in Algeria, but attributed to the French.

36 Ibid., 80.

37 Piscatori and Saikal, *Islam Beyond Borders*.

38 Roda Mushkat, "Is War Ever Justifiable? A Comparative Survey" (1987) 9 *Loyola of Los Angeles International and Comparative Law Journal* 2, 227–317, 302.

before ISIS, few jihadist movements tried to define and conceptualize how such a Caliphate would be structured and legitimized. The purpose of declaring itself as *the* Islamic State is that the community will be unified spiritually not only through belief but also institutionally through a unique political authority.[39] This single command structure would cover the ever-expanding territory of the Muslim community until it replaced the current interstate community.

Finally, traditional non-state armed groups usually adopt formalized structures and have long imitated the structure of traditional armies by establishing "hierarchical systems with clear lines of command and control."[40] Alternatively, in order to be more stealthy, such groups adopted structures in cells that only allow the cell leader to have contact with the wider organization.[41] In this way, he points out, if individual members were caught, "they could only betray the other members of their cell rather than implicating the entire organization."[42] Still, this sort of cell structure implies the existence of both hierarchical control and central organization. On the other hand, transnational jihadist groups, even if they do have some hierarchical features, have a more diffuse structure, mainly characterized by loose networks based on multiple personal relationships.[43] For instance, personal relationships at the individual level (i.e., who an individual knows and what connections he or she can facilitate) may be more important than the formal rank held by the individual. This feature is in striking contrast to traditional state and non-state armies that leave very little room for lower-ranking soldiers to have any other role than that of obeying.

To conclude, transnational jihadist groups have a transnational character, or at least aspire to and narrate themselves as such, and this transnational character lies both in their modes of expansion and in the very purpose or essence of their actions. These features of transnational jihadist groups are the reason why states consider the recourse to armed drones necessary, and through them, the adoption of a military strategy that is individualized and based on

[39] Hussein Solomon, *Islamic State and the Coming Global Confrontation* (Palgrave Macmillan, 2016).
[40] Neumann, *Old and New Terrorism*, 17.
[41] Ibid.
[42] Ibid.
[43] Ibid., 46.

anticipation. The idea underlying such military strategy is that members of jihadist groups are dispersed, a feature that makes them difficult to identify. For this reason, states consider that they should be able to target individuals based on indications that they have allegiance to the group (and thus have a hostile intent vis-à-vis infidels).[44]

3.2 Drones: The *raison d'être* and the Stabilizing Force of a Bureaucratic Machinery

> We are never faced with objects or social relations; we are faced with chains which are associations of humans (H) and non-humans (NH).[45]

As a technological tool, drones appear to be an essential actor in the emergence of a stable and legitimate institution. Organizational theorists, such as Stephen Barley and Wanda Orlikowski, have demonstrated the role played by technologies in influencing organizational structures to some degree depending on the specific socio-historical context in which they emerge.[46] Their work has highlighted the importance to keep the contextual landscape in mind when studying the genealogy of a practice and/or institution. On the one hand, when examining the role played by technology, the point is certainly not to paint a picture of human agents as powerless and human activities as fully determined. At the same time, it is a mistake to neglect the influence that technology can have on practices and institutional

[44] Transcript: President Obama's Address to the Nation on the San Bernardino Terror Attack and the War on ISIS, December 6, 2015, CNN, http://edition.cnn.com/2015/12/06/politics/transcript-obama-san-bernardino-isis-address/index.html. Also American officials, and former President Obama himself in 2015, evoked the evolution of the terrorist threat into a new phase, one characterized by the multiplication of "less complicated acts of violence," the exploitation of the Internet in that it "erases the distance between countries," and poisons the minds of the people in different places.

[45] Bruno Latour, "Technology Is Society Made Durable," in John Law (ed.), *A Sociology of Monsters: Essays on Power, Technology and Domination*, Sociological Review Monograph, no. 38 (Routledge, 1991) 110.

[46] Stephen R. Barley, "Technology as an Occasion for Structuring: Evidence from Observation of CT Scanners and the Social Order of Radiology Departments" (1986) 31 *Administrative Science Quarterly* 78–108; Wanda Orlikowski, "The Duality of Technology: Rethinking the Concept of Technology in Organizations" (1992) 3 *Organization Science* 3, Focused Issue: Management of Technology, 398–427.

structures (as reinforcing and/or constraining them). Generally speaking, the objective is to strike a good balance between heavily deterministic or voluntarist perspectives of technology[47] both of which have dominated the literature on drones.

When contextualizing technological innovation in the military, it is important to look at the strategy implemented by these new tools. For drones, the military strategy that is facilitated could be broadly referred to as "find, fix, and finish" (hereafter referred to as the "FFF strategy") but this strategy predates the use of drones. The first time the idea that enemies had to be systematically, first found, then fixed in a location, and ultimately "finished," dates back to the Korean War and was used in that context by General Matthew Ridgway as an order to his troops.[48] During the Cold War, his orders became national security policy. Since then, the US military has been searching for the best way to "find, fix, and finish" its enemies.[49] In the Korean and Cold War contexts, but also later in Iraq, the FFF strategy was not difficult to implement in terms of finding and fixing targets, as the enemies were located in well-defined zones and easily identifiable. It was the "finishing" part that posed a challenge, not because destroying targets was materially difficult but because it was a tricky strategic choice, as neither side of those conflicts wanted (to risk) annihilation.[50] On the contrary, with the emergence of transnational jihadist networks, it initially appeared to be materially challenging to find, fix, and finish targets. Thus, FFF predates 9/11 but its salient features evolved with the emergence of transnational terrorist networks. In a way, before 9/11, the FFF equation simply reflected the routine tasks and goals of military operations and then appeared as a major military challenge with the emergence of the threat of transnational terrorism: all steps of the "find, fix, and finish" equation became materially difficult. First, ascertaining exactly who poses a threat and locating enemies became more problematic, considering that the groups are dispersed, and less visible. Second, fixing also became more difficult to achieve since the

47 Ibid., 402.

48 Matthew B. Ridgeway, *The Korean War* (Da Capo Press, 1967), 89; Aki Peritz and Erich Rosenbach, *Find, Fix, Finish: Inside the Counterterrorism Campaigns that Killed bin Laden and Devastated Al Qaeda* (PublicAffairs, 2013, Kindle Ed.), loc. 148.

49 William M. Arkin, *Unmanned: Drones, Data, and the Illusion of Perfect Warfare* (Little, Brown), 84.

50 Peritz and Rosenbach, *Find, Fix, Finish*, 160.

targets can be highly mobile individuals.[51] Third and last, it appeared difficult to finish targets, as we are often talking about difficult-to-access areas or territories of non-consenting states. Thus, finding a way to make the FFF steps feasible in that context became a top priority.

In order to achieve this goal and before recoursing to armed drones, several methods were adopted to navigate these challenges. To find and fix, a warrantless electronic surveillance program was adopted by the Bush administration. The goal was to identify individuals within the US who were in contact with terrorist networks abroad. This program, which had a heavy political cost and triggered strong legal objections, was not really adequate to identify threats abroad. If other surveillance programs followed, they cannot be considered as being at the core of extraterritorial counterterrorism policies in the US simply because they could not perform this function well enough. In extraterritorial counterterrorism policies, the goal was to coordinate intelligence and military operations as well as possible by combining different tools from human intelligence – which was significantly improved in Afghanistan,[52] – to on-the-ground technical analysis of cell phones and documents, to "debriefing" of captured militants on the ground and their interrogation/torture in Guantanamo. A number of different methods were also used to finish targets (to isolate, capture, or kill them) but the main role was still played by Special Forces on the ground. Cooperation with allies on the different steps of the process has also always been, and still is a solution. A 2017 Report shows that the UK for instance assisted the US in the targeted killings by providing intelligence and other support to facilitate the strike.[53] The UK would "find" and "fix" targets in Yemen for US strikes to take place.

Today, the combat drone appears to be the only available tool that combines the capability to conduct each step of the FFF process most precisely. Drones' technological capacities allow an acute focus on individuals, primarily through surveillance capacities that enable a precise

[51] Peritz and Rosenbach explain that "the US and other countries struggled for years to 'fix' Abu Musab al-Zarqawi, a Jordanian militant who arguably became the single most important instigator of sectarian carnage in Iraq from 2003. The fix did not occur until June 2006, three long, bloody years later," ibid., 200.

[52] Afghanistan. See Ibid., 135.

[53] Fiona Nelson, "Litigating Drone Attacks: ECCHR's Expert Workshop and Public Forum in Review," in Report "Litigating Drone Strikes," ECCHR, 2017, 22, www.ecchr.eu/fileadmin/Publikationen/Litigating_Drone_Strikes_PDF.pdf.

"finding" process. They have the capacity to gather several types of intelligence from the air such as signal intelligence (SIGINT) and image intelligence.[54] Utilizing satellite communication links, drones acquire real-time imagery beyond the line-of-sight, which means that their radio communications capabilities allow them to connect with systems that are normally too distant or too obscured by terrain specificities (weather situations, geological landform).[55] Following the surveillance step, drones' technological capacities facilitate the "fixing" and "finishing" parts of the process. To that end, Reaper drones carry the Multi-Spectral Targeting System, which comprises a set of powerful visual sensors for targeting: an infra-red sensor, a color/monochrome daylight TV camera, an image-intensified TV camera, a laser rangefinder/designator, and a laser illuminator.[56] In addition, MQ-9 Reaper drones are equipped with Air-to-Ground Missile-114 Hellfire missiles, which are the primary air-to-ground precision weapon.[57] It follows that drones offer the full material apparatus corresponding to the anticipatory and individualized warfare sought to target a highly mobile network of individual threats.

Because drones combine these specificities, the now Former French Chief of the Defense Staff General Lecointre forecasted that the future of aerial military operations abroad will include a replacement of piloted aircrafts by an army of drone pilots, or at least an assemblage of a large number of drones alongside some manned vehicles,[58] in a "strike package."[59] It is precisely because these technological capabilities are

[54] A source of The Intercept underscored the limitations of drones' SIGINT capabilities. See The Drone Papers, The Assassination Complex (The Intercept, October 15, 2015), https://theintercept.com/drone-papers/the-assassination-complex/.

[55] US Air Force, Fact Sheet, "MQ-9 Reaper," September 23, 2015; French Senate, "Drones d'observation et drones armés: un enjeu de souveraineté," Rapport d'information de MM. Cédric PERRIN, co-président, Gilbert ROGER, co-président, Jean-Marie BOCKEL et Raymond VALL, fait au nom de la commission des affaires étrangères, de la défense et des forces armées, no. 559 (2016–17), May 23, 2017, www.senat.fr/espace_presse/actualites/201705/les_drones_dans_les_forces_armees.html, 18.

[56] US Air Force, Fact Sheet, "MQ-9 Reaper."

[57] Ibid.

[58] Compte rendu, Commission de la défense nationale et des forces armées, Audition du général François Lecointre, chef d'état-major des armées, sur le projet de loi de finances pour 2019, October 18, 2018, Report no. 15, 13.

[59] Alice Pannier and Olivier Schmitt, "To Fight Another Day: France between the Fight against Terrorism and Future Warfare" (2019) 95 *International Affairs* 4, 913, part of a Special issue on "Re-visioning War and the State in the Twenty-First Century."

combined in one tool, with its promise of ubiquity, precision but also permanence,[60] that this tool emerges as the prior technique for conducting warfare against non-state actors who are difficult to identify and whose behavior is difficult to understand and predict with conventional tools.[61] Therefore, by its features and its emergence in a specific context, the combat drone became an indispensable tool, and will remain so until a better technological program capable of achieving the same aim is found. In the meantime, alternative techniques such as aircrafts or "boots on the ground," tend to disappear from the operational landscape.[62]

The convergence between context and tools explains the durability of drone programs. Because drone technologies correspond to a certain military strategy, which itself corresponds to a specific type of enemy, there is a convergence of tools, method, and end-goal. Of course, as mentioned above, it is also the story of what the enemy says about himself that corresponds to the story told by states about their enemy and how they should be targeted by using drones. This convergence is

60 Unlike traditional airplanes, which were not designed with such an objective in mind, drones promise permanence. First of all, they allow an economy of mean – especially of ground refueling. The Reaper drone can stay airborne for up to fourteen hours fully loaded and about twenty-four hours in total. General Atomic's updated drone, the Certifiable Predator B, is a turboprop-powered drone that can spend forty hours in the air. Eric Adams, "A Stronger, Faster Predator Drone Is Headed for European Airspace," *Wired*, December 12, 2016. The UK announced having ordered a fleet of the new Certifiable Predator B remotely piloted aircraft from the US in November 2016. Thomas Gibbons-Neff, "Britain Set to Purchase $1 Billion in Advanced U.S. Predator Drones," *Washington Post*, November 17, 2016, Section entitled Checkpoint, www.washingtonpost.com/news/checkpoint/wp/2016/11/17/britain-set-to-purchase-1-billion-in-advanced-u-s-predator-drones/. Besides, through a warden system, drones can ensure a 24/7 presence for each relevant area. The French Senate emphasized the potentially permanent (and discrete) presence of drones as facilitating an unprecedented control of time and space, as well as an essential understanding of the situation on the ground where the enemy is fleeting ("*fugace*") and hides among civilians. See French Senate, "Drones d'observation et drones armés," 14, 17, 77.

61 This is also what comes out from the annexed report to the law on military programming insisting that jihadist terrorism because of its "complexity and geographical spread," "recomposes and extends itself to new regions of the world," LOI no. 2018-607 du 13 juillet 2018 relative à la programmation militaire pour les années 2019 à 2025 et portant diverses dispositions intéressant la défense, Article 65, www.legifrance.gouv.fr/affichTexteArticle.do;jsessionid=094A3118E029E3E8DDAE747AEEA322D8.tplgfr33s_2?idArticle=JORFARTI000037192860&cidTexte=JORFTEXT000037192797&dateTexte=29990101&categorieLien=id.

62 Latour, "Technology Is Society Made Durable." This point echoes with his concept of anti-programs.

precisely what makes drone programs durable and why we can assume, since the context and rhetoric from both sides have not fundamentally changed, that drone programs will persist and even expand to other states.[63]

Because of the emergence of jihadist transnational networks and because of the convergence developed above, not exploiting technological improvements that took place between 2001 and 2009, and earlier, proved not only impossible but unthinkable for the Obama administration. In the light of the genealogy of the FFF strategy, the essential role of technology in facilitating a practice and making it durable, we must nuance the idea that drone programs resulted from the sole political choice made by state officials – the choice made by the Bush administration to use drones and that of the Obama administration to counter terrorism mainly at a distance through a further reliance on the use of combat drones.[64] First, the choice made by the Bush administration to make incarceration in Guantanamo its main counterterrorism policy does not mean that they made a choice of principle, in turn, not to use armed drones as their main counterterrorism tool. On the contrary, they were simultaneously testing and working to

[63] For Australia, see Minister for Defense, Rt. Hon. Christopher Pyne MP, Joint Media Release, "Australian-designed Unmanned 'Loyal Wingman' Aircraft to Be developed with Industry," February 27, 2019, www.minister.defence.gov.au/minister/steven-ciobo/media-releases/australian-designed-unmanned-loyal-wingman-aircraft-be. For Italy, see Andrea Shalal, "U.S. Government Approves Italy's Request to Arm Its Drones," *Reuters*, November 4, 2015, www.reuters.com/article/italy-usa-drones-idUSL1N12Z05620151104. It should be noted that Italy made an agreement with the US to deploy its armed drones exclusively for self-defense purposes. It is in line with the Italian agreement that the US uses a drone base in Sigonella, Sicily on the condition that US drones are used only for defensive missions and not offensive actions. See Italy country profile on European Forum on Armed Drones website, www.efadrones.org/countries/italy/. For the Netherlands see Ministerie van Defensie, "Defensie kiest Reaper als onbemand vliegtuig," November 21, 2013, www.defensie.nl/actueel/nieuws/2013/11/21/defensie-kiest-reaper-als-onbemand-vliegtuig. Although the government announced the acquisition of drones only for reconnaissance and surveillance purposes, their armament in the near future is not to be excluded, as a coalition of political parties was created to that end and no political party opposed armed drones per se. On March 1, 2017, a survey-based report written by the Dutch NGO PAX concluded that a majority of Dutch political parties remain concerned about the use of armed drones for extrajudicial killings, but no political party opposes armed drones *per se*. See also Defense Update, "Netherlands to Field Four MQ-9 Reaper Drones by 2017," February 8, 2015, http://defense-update.com/20150208_dutch_reapers.html; EFAD Country Profile on the Netherlands, 2017, www.efadrones.org/wp-content/uploads/2017/12/The-Netherlands.pdf.

[64] Arkin, *Unmanned: Drones, Data*, 134–5.

improve drones' capacities as we saw earlier. Second and reciprocally, the increased use of armed drones under Obama[65] does not reflect a sudden choice to over-rely on the technology but is part of a continuum and corresponds to the time where the system could finally become data-based, equipped with precise weapon systems, unmanned and thus capable of accessing hard-to-reach areas. The technological momentum did not only correspond to the strategy designed to fight jihadist groups, but also to the multiplication of jihadist transnational networks that were said to call for an intensification of the FFF strategy. In this context, drones also meant that this FFF strategy would be less challenging, as it assembled technical capabilities that facilitate each step of the process. Drones also meant that other tools that were more burdensome practically and politically were less needed.

Now that the convergence of factors was established as explaining the emergence of drone programs, it is worth zooming in on the technology to explain the persistence of drone programs. Borrowing from Wanda Orlikowski's analysis, "once developed and deployed, technology tends to become reified and institutionalized, losing its connection with the human agents *[and I would add, contextual factors]* that constructed it or gave it meaning, and it appears to be part of the objective, structural properties of the organization."[66] This phenomenon explains why, even when some of the converging elements that once gave rise to an institution evolve or disappear, this institution – here, drone programs – may still persist for two reasons. First, as we will further explore, technology is stabilized through bureaucratic interactions and infrastructures. Besides, it has been demonstrated that interactions of human actors with technology can influence the institutional properties of an organization by reinforcing structures and activities.[67] It is reasonable to imagine that

[65] Rosa Brooks, *How Everything Became War and the Military Became Everything: Tales from the Pentagon* (Simon & Schuster, 2016), 34. Bureau of Investigative Journalism. For instance, in Pakistan, in 2008, the last year of the Bush presidency, there were 36. In 2009, the first year of the Obama administration, there were 52 and in 2010, 122.

[66] Orlikowski, "The Duality of Technology," 406.

[67] "a" refers to technology as a product of human action as design, development, appropriation, and modification; "b" refers to technology as a medium of human action, facilitating and constraining it through the provision of interpretive schemes, facilities, and norms; "c" refers to institutional conditions of interaction with technology ("institutional properties influence humans in their interaction with technology, for example, intentions, professional norms, state of the art in materials and knowledge, design standards and available resources"); and "d" refers to institutional consequences of interaction with

the reinforced structures and activities established around the use of drones' technological capabilities, might not be immediately deconstructed when the importance of a contextual element decreases.

Second, when a technological tool is democratized in all spheres of society, and is not just bound to the military paradigm, its military use is highly likely to follow suit as it becomes woven into the social fabric. Drones are the dual-use type of tool. In other words they have both military and civilian applications and are used by the military in both weapons and non-weapons roles, for both surveillance and targeting.[68] In this regard, the use of the technological tool is entrenched in all societal spheres, but also serves different purposes in the military. Thereby, as Hughes and Latour suggest, the infrastructure that regulates the use of a technology that appears both at the micro (the military) and macro (all spheres of the society) levels is more likely to become almost seamless.[69] It is interesting to note that at the European level, military drones have been invoked for several years but mostly as part of the initiative seeking the common development and regulation of European civil and military MALE drones.[70] In France, official documents often refer to the dual-use of drones,[71] as if it made the military use of the tool less special, more ordinary and thus more acceptable.

technology, which "reinforces or transforms structures of signification, domination and legitimation."

68 Alex Roland, *War and Technology: A Very Short Introduction* (Oxford University Press, 2016), 90.

69 Thomas Hughes, "The Electrification of America: the System Builders" (1979) 20 *Technology and Culture* 1, 124–62; Thomas Hughes, *Networks of Power, Electric Supply Systems in the US, England and Germany, 1880–1930* (Johns Hopkins University Press, 1983); Latour, "Technology Is Society Made Durable," 103–1.

70 Discussed in detail by Chantal Lavallée and Océane Zubeldia, "Un Espace Européen des Drones," Note de Recherche IRSEM, no. 52, March 7, 2018.

71 Annexed Report to the French Law on Military Programming (it should be noted that it also has legislative value), Rapport annexé, (appears at the end of the legislation), www.legifrance.gouv.fr/affichTexte.do?cidTexte=JORFTEXT000037192797&dateTexte=20181122, 9: "D'autre part, l'innovation tiendra une place centrale dans la préservation de la supériorité opérationnelle des armées à long terme, au moyen d'équipements tirant pleinement avantage de la révolution numérique ou des technologies de rupture, désormais plus fréquemment issues des développements du secteur civil, dans des temps de plus en plus courts." French Ministry of Defense Strategic Review, 2017, §219: "La France jouit d'un statut de grande puissance technologique, qui contribue de manière décisive à son rang parmi les premiers exportateurs mondiaux de matériel militaire. Cette situation est le fruit d'un investissement continu et d'une politique qui garantit en permanence l'équilibre entre l'export, la dualité civilo-militaire et les acquisitions nationales."

Hughes and Latour also emphasize that the dual nature of a technological tool, in addition to making the innovation appear common and almost invisible, make the infrastructure that regulates its use more likely to last. Of course, durability does not mean permanence. Similarly, as with the power of bureaucracy, the results of this institutionalization process through technology itself can be deconstructed; but in the same way as for bureaucratic infrastructures and activities, a clear and robust decision would have to be made to stop the use of the technological tool. Looking at the technological tool, it is important to note that it interacts with human actors. The use of drones has involved, both in the US and UK, the interaction of a specific set of actors according to specifically designed procedures. Drones, in other words, became the *raison d'être* of a bureaucracy, particularly in the US.

Here the term "bureaucracy" is used descriptively, to refer to a complex organization with several features, including the interaction of a multitude of actors, forming a community, and a division of functions or responsibilities among those actors;[72] the reliance upon a hierarchy as the central device to coordinate the activities;[73] the use of a common terminology specific to the given institution;[74] and the interchangeability of the bureaucrats (which is more an outcome than a factor of institutionalization and will be further developed below).[75] This is not an exhaustive list. In addition to principles of office hierarchy, Weber identifies the reliance on written documents, the need for the full working capacity of the official (once the office is fully developed), and the existence of general rules "which are more or less stable, more or less exhaustive, and which can be learned."[76]

When observing the structures and practices related to drone strikes, constitutive elements of bureaucracy so defined emerge. Exploring the case of the US, the following developments identify

[72] These first elements derive from the typology established by Owen M. Fiss, "The Bureaucratization of the Judiciary" (1983) 92 *The Yale Law Journal* 8, 1442–68.

[73] Ibid.; Max Weber, *Economy and Society: An Outline of Interpretive Sociology* (Guenther Roth and Claus Wittich (eds.), University of California Press, 2013 [1978]), 957.

[74] The two last elements are inspired by the conceptualization of Mathilde Cohen, "Judges or Hostages? The Bureaucratization of the Court of Justice of the European Union and the European Court of Human Rights," in Bill Davies and Fernanda Nicola (eds.), *European Law Stories* (Cambridge University Press, 2017), 58–80.

[75] Ibid.

[76] Weber, *Economy and Society*, 957–8.

the features of the most advanced bureaucratic infrastructure for the use of drones that exists to this day. To understand how a social structure for the use of drones is assembled one should "follow the actors themselves," to borrow a slogan from Actors Network Theory (ANT),[77] which means to observe and catch up with their practices "in order to learn from them what the collective existence has become in their hands, which methods they have elaborated to make it fit together, which accounts could best define the new associations that they have been forced to establish."[78] In other words, the task is not to teach actors what they are, should be, or to reflect on their practice, but to make sense of what their coordinated activities have produced as an external observer.

A multiplicity of actors intervening in the use of drones in the US have been glued together by common procedures and hierarchical connectors, thus forming a full-blown community. In 2015, The Intercept obtained and published documents from a 2013 Pentagon study evaluating the intelligence and surveillance technology behind the military's Joint Special Operations Command (JSOC) killing campaign in Yemen and Somalia in 2011 and 2012.[79] These documents comprise a slide exhibiting the different steps and the chain of command leading to the approval of drone strikes.[80] In fact, two parallel procedures and two separate chains of commands exist depending on whether the strike is conducted as a targeted killing or as a signature strike, referred to on the slide as "actionable intelligence." The document shows that for a targeted killing to take place, an agent assesses that a suspected member of Al Qaeda or associated forces poses a threat to the US and raises that individual's name for consideration for lethal action. The proposal goes through different steps of review along which several task forces come into play: the Geographic Combatant Command, the Joint Staff, the Secretary of Defense, the Principals' Deputies Committee, up to the President of the United States for the final decision.[81] Signature strikes,

[77] Bruno Latour, *Reassembling the Social* (Oxford University Press, 2005), 12.
[78] Ibid.
[79] The Drone Papers, https://theintercept.com/drone-papers/the-kill-chain/.
[80] Ibid.
[81] John O. Brennan, Remarks of John O. Brennan, Assistant to the President for Homeland Security and Counterterrorism, "The Ethics and Efficacy of the President's Counterterrorism Strategy," Woodrow Wilson International Center for Scholars, Washington, DC, April 30, 2012, www.wilsoncenter.org/event/the-efficacy-and-ethics-uscounterterrorism-strategy; Department of Justice White Paper, "Lawfulness of a

or strikes conducted on the basis of "actionable intelligence," depend on a different review process. After having observed an individual and gathered intelligence on their behavior, a task force suggests striking them down. Then, it is for the Geographic Combatant Command, the Chief of Mission, and the Host Nation to give their approval for the strike to take place. It helps to understand that these institutions participate jointly in the drone program according to formally established procedures specifically designed for these activities. Generally speaking, this document puts the chain of command and the bureaucracy behind the drone campaign into stark relief.[82]

Although very little information is available on the decision-making process preceding the use of drones in the UK, it appears that, there too, the military has to take extra-procedural steps to conduct drone strikes compared to "conventional uses of lethal force in armed conflict."[83] The Parliamentary Joint Committee on Human Rights identified that Prime Ministerial, Attorney General, and National Security involvement are required at the stage of "in principle approval of target selection on the basis of intelligence."[84] Even if the chain of command and the decision-making process are not clearly presented, or even if it is still unclear whether a kill list is established,[85] whether government lawyers systematically provide legal advice throughout the decision-making process,[86] publicly available elements show that there is a heavy reliance upon hierarchy to coordinate drone activities. In its 2017 Joint Doctrine Publication on Unmanned Aircraft Systems, the Ministry of Defense speaks of normalization of drone operations:

> The last five years have seen much of the business of operating unmanned and remotely piloted aircraft normalized. . . . Early unmanned aircraft systems were bought under the urgent operational requirement process;

Lethal Operation Directed against a U.S. Citizen Who Is a Senior Operational Leader of Al-Qa'ida or an Associated Force," November 8, 2011, https://fas.org/irp/eprint/doj-lethal.pdf.

82 Jameel Jaffer, *The Drone Memos: Targeted Killing, Secrecy and the Law* (The New Press, 2010), 225.

83 Parliamentary Joint Committee on Human Rights, "The Government's Policy on the Use of Drones for Targeted Killing," Second Report of Session 2015–16, May 10, 2016, HL Paper 141, HC 574, §4.7, 62.

84 Ibid.

85 Ibid., §4.14.

86 Ibid., §4.18.

> the supporting processes needed to provide a complete capability were less comprehensive than normal, as the procurement process was accelerated. At the tactical level, tactics, techniques and procedures developed rapidly, but operational doctrine lagged behind systems' operational use. . . . The context for unmanned and remotely piloted aircraft operations has evolved over time, and this publication reflects that.[87]

What this passage shows is that technology was progressively accompanied not only by techniques and procedures, but also by operational doctrine that was specifically designed to consolidate best practices on drone operations. Just as in the US, such operational doctrines came along with the involvement of a tailor-made set of actors. The UK Ministry of Defence in fact explicitly mentioned that the use of drones has involved the existence and training of new actors such as of course drone pilots, but also sensor operators, image analysts and maintainers, and drone maintenance personnel.[88] These new actors also interact with the usual main body of operators, analysts, and commanders, and, with them, form a group that is more numerous and bound by more complex procedures than for manned systems.[89] There is no information, however, regarding the chain of command structuring the use of drones in the UK, thus leaving unanswered the question of whether the UK drone program involves a hierarchical structure that is specifically designed for the use of drones and separate from the usual military chain of command.

France has not disclosed information regarding the operational processes and associated chain of command that regulate the use of combat drones deployed in the Sahel region. While at the beginning of France's use of drones, expectations were that no special doctrine or rules of engagement would be implemented due to their small fleet of combat drones, recent practice has indicated the contrary. Data collection through drones and the decision to conduct a strike seem to go through a decision-making process involving a unique set of actors and chain of command, which involves military commanders specifically trained as drone operators, as well as – and in the last instance – the military

[87] UK Ministry of Defence, Joint Doctrine Publication 0-30.2, "Unmanned Aircraft Systems," August 2017, §1.9.

[88] Ibid., §3.16: "Logistics Considerations."

[89] Ibid.

command of the French Barkhane operation based in N'Djamena.[90] The specialized chains of command are not anecdotal when one considers that 58 percent of the strikes conducted in the Sahel-Saharan strip were conducted through combat drones in 2020. Besides, the strikes conducted through drones are emblematic of a military strategy revolving around the objective of anticipation where "behavioral analysis" as a mode of target selection is the usual modus operandi, thereby implying specific interpretations of the norms regulating the use of force.[91]

In the US, the procedures mentioned above are accompanied by specialized language created to name practices related to the use of drones.[92] The creation of new vocabulary testifies to the objectification of new practices by a community.[93] Following this creation, this vocabulary creates elements that "(1) can come before the mind and be grasped 'in a flash', in other words something isolable, but which (2) can serve as a guide for certain future actions, and also (3) can set a standard for the correctness of those actions."[94] The glossary of terms and acronyms established solely for the use of drones in the US reveals that there are a large number of specialized terms to identify specific procedures, events, individuals, or steps in the interagency process.[95] For instance,

90 "Drone Strike in the Malian Desert," transcription of the interview of Lieutenant-Colonel Romain, French Air Force officer and drone operator, conducted by Alexandre Jubelin (AJ), published on April 9, 2021, translated from French into English by M. Drevet, L. Mieusset, R. Mignot-Mahdavi, C. Pinel, and A. Yehiel, "Testimony of a French Drone Operator: Anticipatory Strikes in the Sahel," European Forum on Armed Drones (EFAD), February 16, 2022, www.irsem.fr/le-collimateur/dans-le-viseur-27-frappe-de-drone-dans-le-desert-malien09-04-2021.html; translation into English www.efadrones.org/wp-content/uploads/2022/02/Drone-strike-in-the-Malian-desert_interview-in-English-2.pdf.

91 "Testimony of a French Drone Operator."

92 Meredith Williams, "Rules, Community and the Individual," in M. Williams (ed.), *Wittgenstein, Mind and Meaning: Toward a Social Conception of Mind* (Routledge, 1999), 176–7, 177.

93 Barry Stroud, *Meaning, Understanding, and Practice: Philosophical Essays* (Oxford University Press, 2003), 80–94: chapter entitled "Wittgenstein on Meaning, Understanding, and Community."

94 Williams, "Rules, Community and the Individual," 159; Wittgenstein, *Philosophical Investigations*, §141, §198.

95 The Intercept, The Drone Papers (2015). The Intercept has obtained a cache of secret documents detailing the inner workings of the US military's assassination program in Afghanistan, Yemen, and Somalia. The documents, provided by a whistleblower, offer an unprecedented glimpse into Obama's drone wars.

"Military-Age Male" or MAM[96] refers to a person who is a male of fighting age, whose precise identity is not necessarily known and who is considered to be a potential enemy. In fact, based on their sex and age, some individuals who were not the primarily selected target are labeled Enemy Killed in Action (EKIA);[97] on the contrary, when drone operators kill the person intended, the strike is called a "jackpot."[98] Another acronym that populates the drone program language is FFF, which means "find, fix, and finish," another version of which is F3EA, "find, fix, finish, exploit/analyze." These terms refer to the different steps of tracking and ultimately killing a targeted person. The FFF doctrine has fueled the US post-9/11 counterterrorism policy and "is being refined and institutionalized" by drone programs.[99]

Even if there is no evidence that the UK uses such a detailed and sophisticated drone language, the Joint Doctrine Publication on Unmanned Aircraft Systems published in August 2017 by the British Ministry of Defence contains a chapter dedicated to relevant terminology and classification.[100] This chapter outlines terminology related to the use of drones and this terminology appears to be mostly standard military terminology, and thus differs from drone-specific terminology that appears in the leaked US official documents. It might mean that public documents on the UK use of drones do not contain the full range of linguistic tools associated to the use of drones, or that it does not have any.

The creation of specialized language in the US objectifies the practices conducted by the drone program community. Through the cognitive apparatus that it provides, language turns unnamed things into objects

[96] Jo Becker and Scott Shane, "Secret 'Kill List' Tests Obama's Principles," *The New York Times*, May 29, 2012.

[97] Tara McKelvey, "A Former Ambassador to Pakistan Speaks Out," November 20, 2012, www.thedailybeast.com/a-former-ambassador-to-pakistan-speaks-out. Interview of Cameron Munter, who had served as US ambassador to Pakistan between October 2010 and July 2012. Munter explained that "the definition [of a person who can be targeted] is a male between the ages of 20 and 40." He continues: "My feeling is one man's combatant is another man's – well, a chump who went to a meeting."

[98] Jeremy Scahill and The Intercept, *The Assassination Complex: Inside the Government's Secret Drone Warfare Program* (Simon & Schuster, 2016), 39.

[99] Ibid., 5.

[100] UK Ministry of Defence, Joint Doctrine Publication, "Unmanned Aircraft Systems," chapter 2.

to be apprehended as a reality by these individuals. On the contrary, without this linguistic creation, the experience of using drones and conducting strikes would only be inscribed in the consciousness of those individuals who live it. At the most, as this experience would still be shared by participants in the drone program, it would be intersubjective. However, once there is a linguistic designation of their activities, once their experiences are identifiable linguistically, they become accessible objects that can be observed, judged (including by those who do not directly share or participate in their activities), and serve as precedents to inform future practice.

Finally, language, like procedures and structures, is one of the factors that generate, or at least go hand in hand with the interchangeability of the bureaucrats, as exemplified at the end of this chapter. Even if certain practices are implemented by identifiable individuals and performed by others, these practices become detached from the individuals through their linguistic objectification; language, labels, acronyms anonymize the undertakings. In the last instance, language not only allows external actors to talk about a structure and its activities within it, but it also allows the whole range of activities to be easily transferred, like a system, to new agents. The transfer of language and procedures as "knowledge" to all new actors of institutionalized activities is a recognition that those activities are a "permanent solution to a permanent problem"[101] but also the insurance that both the vocabulary and the procedures outlive the individuals who, for a certain amount of time, compose and act within the bureaucracy.

What the US special and elaborate procedures for the use of drones, with the use of specialized vocabulary, practically lead to is normalizing practice and stabilizing it. Each actor in the interagency process coordinates their actions and judgments with those of the other agents, altogether creating a group of people that sustains certain habits and patterns of actions over time. Their actions are ultimately coordinated and embedded in a structure within which error or mistake can be easily discerned.[102]

[101] Berger and Luckmann, *The Social Construction of Reality*, 86–7.

[102] This echoes with the work of Wittgenstein on community and rule-following, and the analysis conducted by Williams on rule, community and the individual. See Ludwig Wittgenstein, *Philosophical Investigations*; Williams, "Rules, Community and the Individual," 176–7.

3.3 The Normalizing Power of Legal Rationales

The Obama administration adopted a hyper-legalistic approach to develop its drone policy. Legal reasoning and lawyers were integrated at every level of the described chain of command,[103] and legal rationales were meticulously crafted. This choice of the Obama administration automatically places the counterterrorism apparatus of the Obama era at the opposite end of the Bush administration's relationship to law.[104]

First, the integration of legal analysis at every stage of the process meant expanding the role of the interagency national security lawyers group, a bureaucratic institution set up in the 1990s that the Bush–Cheney administration had sidelined.[105] Reinforcing the legal team, as the 2013 Presidential Policy Guidance explains, ensured that all plans are subject to legal review within each structure and at each step of the processes cited above.[106] Internally, the legal team does not only

[103] Jack Goldsmith, *Power and Constraint: The Accountable Presidency After 9/11* (W. W. Norton, 2012), 136.

[104] See, for instance, Eric Holder's Speech before the American Constitution Society, June 13, 2008, www.youtube.com/watch?v=Mk3tKaEvFZ4 (4'50"), where he denounces the Bush–Cheney administration for violating the rule of law, standing in stark contrast with the constitutional history of the United States of America. See also Koh's hearing before a Senate Judiciary Subcommittee, entitled "Restoring the Rule of Law," September 2008: "To regain our global standing, the next president and Congress must unambiguously reassert our historic commitments to human rights and the rule of law as a major source of our moral authority."

[105] Savage, *Power Wars*, 64.

[106] Presidential Policy Guidance, 2013:

> All operational plans to undertake lethal operations against terrorist targets firstly undergo a legal review by the general counsel of the operating agency executing the plan and are submitted to the national security staff (NSS) for inter-agency review. Then, the NSS legal adviser and the general counsel of the proposing operating agency consult with other department and agency counsels. The NSS Legal Adviser submits the relevant legal conclusions to the Deputies Committee to inform its consideration of the proposed operational plan. All proposed operational plans to undertake direct action against terrorist target are reviewed by appropriate members of the Deputies and Principals Committees of the National Security Council (NSC) before weekly presentation to the President for decision.

Eric Holder, Remarks of Eric Holder, Attorney General of the United States, Northwestern University School of Law, Chicago, IL, March 5, 2012:

> If the Principal of the nominating operating agency, after review by Principals and Deputies, continues to support the operational plan the plan shall be presented to the President for decision, along with the views

deliberate within each Department but also across the Department of State, Defense, and Justice[107] on a wide range of topics from how to interpret international law, the limits of POTUS's power, how to define the notion of associated forces and which groups to consider as such, and so forth.[108] Externally, the legal task force drafted executive orders to be driven through the interagency process, and gave public speeches defending the Obama drone program.[109]

Second, as Chapters 2 to 4 unpack, the Obama administration crafted meticulous legal rationales to justify the drone program.[110] These

> expressed by departments and agencies during the NSC process. An appropriate NSS official will communicate, in writing, the President's decision, including any terms or conditions placed on any approval, to appropriate departments and agencies.

107 Savage, *Power Wars*, 628–9:

> In the months that followed, lawyers with the Departments of Defense, Justice, and State, along with the Joint Staff and the National Security Council – that is, Jeh Johnson, Virginia Seitz, Harold Koh, Rich Gross, Avril Haines, and their aides – gathered to analyze whether Obama had the authority to launch a punitive military strike if Assad crossed this red line. The lawyers group collectively produced a seventeen-page unsigned paper whose existence has never been reported. It assessed a legal case for the use of force in such a hypothetical situation . . . The Obama legal team decided Kosovo could nevertheless serve as a precedent. In their seventeen-page memo, they came up with a similar list of "factors" the United States could cite to justify an attack on Syria.

108 Savage, *Power Wars*, 149.

109 Harold Hongju Koh, made the following remarks before the American Society of International Law, Legal Adviser, US Department of State, Speech at the Annual Meeting of the American Society of International Law, "The Obama Administration and International Law," March 25, 2010: "It is the considered view of this administration – and it has certainly been my experience during my time as Legal Adviser – that U.S. targeting practices, including lethal operations conducted with the use of unmanned aerial vehicles, comply with all applicable law, including the laws of war," Koh declared. He added: "As a matter of international law, the United States is in an armed conflict with al-Qaeda . . . and may use force consistent with its inherent right to self-defense under international law. . . . A state that is engaged in an armed conflict or in legitimate self-defense is not required to provide targets with legal process before the state may use lethal force."

110 Clearly, the set of legal justifications proposed by the US and supported at least in some respects by the UK, Israel, France, Australia, and in specific contexts Russia and Turkey, is still highly debated in the literature and has been met by limited explicit approval from states. On Turkey, see the analysis of Tom Ruys, "Quo Vadit Jus ad Bellum?: A Legal Analysis of Turkey's Military Operations against the PKK in Northern Iraq" (2008) 9 *Melbourne Journal of International Law*, 334, 338, 342, 353. On Russia, see Permanent Representative of Georgia to the United Nations, Letter dated September 13, 2002 from the Permanent Representative of Georgia to the United Nations Addressed to the

sophisticated and combative legal theories were elaborated to deal with the legal problems that derived from being militarily involved against transnational terrorist networks. By exploiting uncertainties in the law that had not necessarily appeared as vectors for extensive practice until then, these legal rationales put pressure on accepted understanding of the norms regulating the use of force. These rationales have included arguments for (i) being in a non-international armed conflict against Al Qaeda and associated forces, (ii) targeting individuals under *jus in bello* and *jus ad bellum* when these individuals are neither currently participating in hostilities in the traditional sense of the term, nor planning an imminent attack that could be materially identifiable,[111] (iii) targeting

Secretary-General Transmitting a Statement by Russian Federation President V. V. Putin Dated September 12, 2002, UN Doc. A/57/409–S/2002/1035, Annex (September 16, 2002). On France, see Madame Florence Parly, Ministre des armées, Université d'été de la défense 2017, Discours de clôture, Toulon, September 5, 2017, www.defense.gouv.fr/salle-de-presse/discours/discours-de-florence-parly/discours-de-cloture-de-florence-parly-universite-d-ete-de-la-defense-2017; Loi de programmation militaire 2019–2025, July 2018, see also the Annexed report, Discours du président de la République devant le Parlement réuni en Congrès, November 16, 2015, www.elysee.fr/declarations/article/discours-du-president-de-la-republique-devant-le-parlement-reuni-en-congres-3/. These documents show that Elena Chachko and Ashley Deeks were, in my view, wrong to categorize France as an ambiguous case, see Elena Chachko and Ashley Deeks, "Which States Support the 'Unwilling and Unable' Test?," *Lawfare*, October 10, 2016; Rebecca Mignot-Mahdavi, "Will the War on Terror Ever End?," *La Revue des droits de l'homme*, Actualités Droits-Libertés, March 10, 2019, http://journals.openedition.org/revdh/6269.

111 Harold Hongju Koh, "The Obama Administration and International Law," March 15, 2010, www.state.gov/s/l/releases/remarks/139119.htm:

> [T]he United States is in an armed conflict with al-Qaeda, as well as the Taliban and associated forces, in response to the horrific 9/11 attacks, and may use force consistent with its inherent right to self-defense under international law. As a matter of domestic law, Congress authorized the use of all necessary and appropriate force through the 2001 Authorization for Use of Military Force (AUMF). These domestic and international legal authorities continue to this day.

Jeh Charles Johnson, General Counsel of the U.S., "The Conflict against al Qaeda and Its Affiliates: How Will It End?," Department of Defense at the Oxford Union, Oxford University, November 30, 2012, www.lawfareblog.com/jeh-johnson-speech-oxford-union; Barack Obama, "Statement by the President on Afghanistan," The White House, July 6, 2016; The White House, "Executive Order – United States Policy on Pre- and Post-Strike Measures to Address Civilian Casualties in U.S. Operations Involving the Use of Force," 2016, www.whitehouse.gov/the-press-office/2016/07/01/executive-order-united-states-policy-pre-and-post-strike-measures; Authorization for the Use of Military Force, Public Law 107–40, September 18, 2001, www.gpo.gov/fdsys/pkg/PLAW-107publ40/pdf/PLAW-107publ40.pdf; United States District Court

them on the basis of an accumulation of past events indicating a pattern of continuing armed activity or an intention to carry attacks in the near future,[112] (iv) using force against them on a third state's territory, without the latter's consent and without any direct support provided by that state to the non-state armed groups.[113] In other words, these legal rationales intend to reset the limits and reshape the content of key conceptual differentiations and oppositions (combatant/civilian, criminal/enemy, status/conduct, battlefield/non-battlefield).

Against this background, the role of the law in developing the US drone program can be understood in at least three ways. To start with the most common understanding of law's function in policymaking contexts, this race for legal justification can be understood as a race for legitimacy. Legal language and theories are powerful as they rub out the contingency and arbitrariness that generally characterize the creation of institutions.[114] Borrowing the words of Maurice Hauriou, "institutions are born, live and die legally."[115] Thereby, law does not only protect government officials who create those institutions, they also normalize the institutionalized practices, even if the legal theories that ground them are later doubted or even discredited.[116] President Obama himself explicitly embraced the idea that "when we cannot explain our efforts clearly and publicly, we face terrorist propaganda and international suspicion, we erode the legitimacy of our actions in the eyes of our partners and our

for the District of Columbia, Moath Hamza Ahmed Al-Alwi v. Barack Obama et al., No. 09-5125, July 22, 2011; United States Court of Appeals for the District of Columbia, Abdul Razak Ali v. Barack Obama, No. 11-5102, December 3, 2013; Presidential Policy Guidance, "Procedures for Approving Direct Action"; "Fact Sheet: U.S. Policy Standards and Procedures for the Use of Force in Counterterrorism Operations outside the United States and Areas of Active Hostilities," May 23, 2013.

[112] Daniel Bethlehem, "Self-Defense against an Imminent or Actual Armed Attack by Nonstate Actors" (2012) 106 *American Journal of International Law* 770, 773; ICJ, Military and Paramilitary Activities in and against Nicaragua v. US, Judgment, 1986 ICJ Reports 1986, 14 and Separate Opinions of Judge Ago and President Singh, 101, para. 191; ICJ, Oil Platforms (Islamic Republic of Iran v. United States of America), Judgment of November 6, 2003, ICJ Reports 2003, 161, and dissenting opinions of Judge Elaraby and Judge Simma, paras. 51 and 64.

[113] On the unwilling unable link of attribution, see Monica Hakimi, "Defensive Force against Non-State Actors: The State of Play" (2015) 91 *International Law Studies*, 31.

[114] Berger and Luckmann, *The Social Construction of Reality*, 82–8.

[115] Maurice Hauriou, "La Théorie de l'institution et de la fondation" (1925) 4 *Cahiers de la Nouvelle Journée* 89–128.

[116] Savage, *Power Wars*, 37.

people, and we undermine accountability in our own government."[117] As such, this first reading of the centrality of – if not obsession with – legal rationales in developing the US drone program is that it reflects a commitment to the long-standing US tradition of smart power as conceptualized by Joseph Nye:

> The important point is that the soft power that arises from qualities of benignity, competence, legitimacy, and trust can add leverage to the hard power of military force. Strategies that combine the two successfully represent smart military power.[118]

For Weber, the law brings rationality and legitimacy not because of the content of the rules but because the rules are enacted according to a clear procedural system. This idea is part of Weber's conceptualization of legal-rational authority that rests on "a belief in the legality of enacted rules and the right of those elevated to authority under such rules to issue commands."[119] The law is seen as constraining the power of the ruler and simultaneously depersonalizes power by practically triggering the elaboration of a complex chain of command in a bureaucracy.[120]

It is interesting to note that the design of legal rationales and their regular expression in the public sphere, although in line with the American tradition of smart power and the legal-rationality of liberal democracies, was nonetheless unusually frenetic. In a context where the state is challenged by transnational non-state security threats, it is plausible to say that legal justifications served to gain cohesion on policy orientations and to avoid political contestation domestically, but not just for legitimacy purposes. Going beyond the legitimacy quest

[117] Executive Order, July 2016, "Releasing Aggregate Data on Strikes Undertaken by the U.S. Government against Terrorist Targets outside Areas of Active Hostilities."

[118] Joseph Nye, *The Future of Power* (Broché, 2011), 48; Koh, "The Obama Administration and International Law," March 15, 2010:"'smart power' – a blend of principle and pragmatism" that makes "intelligent use of all means at our disposal," including promotion of democracy, development, technology, and human rights and international law to place diplomacy at the vanguard of our foreign policy." Jack L. Goldsmith and Eric A. Posner, *The Limits of International Law* (Oxford University Press, 2006); Bernard Harcourt, *The Counterrevolution: How Our Government Went to War against Its Own Citizens* (Basic Books, 2018): "Still today, the use and legal regulation of torture or drone strikes by American presidents work in a similar way: they stabilize and balance American interests in such a way as to secure and steady the political regime."

[119] Weber, *Economy and Society* (1978), 215.

[120] John R. Sutton, *Law/Society: Origins, Interactions, and Change*. Sociology for a New Century (Sage Publications, 2000), 99–111.

explanation, legal norms appear to have acted as a tool for stabilizing the community.[121] The community, here, can be defined both as the US institutions – executive, legislative, and judiciary – but also more broadly American citizens in general.[122] The design of an elaborate system of legal propositions based on previously established norms can be understood as a way of strengthening social groups. This is a strong hypothesis when one considers that the Obama administration proposed legal interpretations that radically departed from the most accepted understandings of certain norms, at times to such an extent that the norms in question lose their constraining function. As a result, and practically speaking, there might not be a great difference between drone operations that the Bush administration would have undertaken by openly rejecting any legal constraints and those undertaken by an administration committed to embracing international law. Against this background, the malleable use of the law to such an extent that practice is unconstrained and war potentially infinite in time and space, reveals that the law is used for a reason other than constraining practice. Instead, building a new practice on preestablished norms serves to integrate it into preexisting structures that are familiar to the social group (or at least to prevent the new practice from destabilizing the group). Durkheim explains that:

> *The first origins of all social processes of any importance should be sought in the internal constitution of the social group.* It is possible to be even more precise. The elements which make up this milieu are of two kinds: things and persons. Besides material objects incorporated into the society, there must also be included the products of previous social activity: law, established customs, literary and artistic works, etc.[123]

This idea is helpful to think of the laws regulating the use of force as a tool not only to stabilize a group but also, going further, as a way to

[121] Latour, *Reassembling the Social*, 7.

[122] Harcourt, *The Counterrevolution*: Harcourt analyzes counterterrorism policies through the lens of the counterinsurgency warfare paradigm. He considers that at the heart of these policies are the tactics aiming to win the hearts and minds of the population as a whole.

[123] Emile Durkheim, *The Rules of Sociological Method* (trans. Sarah A. Solovay and John H. Mueller, Free Press, 1966), 73; Latour, *Reassembling the Social*, 33: "There exist endless ways of rendering the group definition a finite and sure thing, so finite and sure that, in the end, it looks like the object of an unproblematic definition. You may appeal to tradition or to law."

"delineate" this group from "others" (enemy groups). By defining the circumstances in which the other can be fought, by organizing the conditions of delineation, these corpuses of norms hold the potential of stabilizing the group further.[124] If we pursue this chain of thought, we could even suggest that the attempt at delineating the group (and thus, at stabilizing it) is even more intense when these norms are interpreted in such a way that the other can be fought in a very vast amount of circumstances under very low legal thresholds.

Finally, the Obama administration's legal rationales were special in that they were always presented in a context and thus never embedded in totalizing discourses, or discourses of universality or neutrality about the content of the norms involved. Their legal rhetoric was one that clearly proposed norm interpretations in accordance with a specific context – the war against transnational jihadist groups – in accordance with a certain mode of warfare – data or surveillance warfare, and precise targeted killings, through drones – and, finally, adapted to a related military strategy – anticipation of threats and individualization of war. They were, in other words, perspectival discourses or historico-political discourses, defined as the idea that norms and their open-texture encapsulate possibilities for struggles and disagreements about their interpretation that are, and will always be, embedded in specific contexts and depend on contemporary goals and tactics. This marked a clear rejection of the idea that the content of norms is a science and can be determined in the same way at any point in time. This is how Foucault defines historico-political discourses:

[124] Andrew Linklater, *The Transformation of Political Community: Ethical Foundations of the Post-Westphalian Era* (Polity Press, 1998), 2.

> The survival of political community owes much to the fact, which Bodin (1967, p. 21) emphasized, that the social bond between citizens and the state does not extend to aliens. Political communities endure because they are exclusive, and most establish their peculiar identities by accentuating the differences between insiders and aliens. In the history of political community, distinctiveness has often been forged in war or in unifying struggles for national independence. But this phenomenon does not stand on its own: communities do not rely simply on contrasts with the outer world in order to purchase their identities. As Foucault argued, various distinctions between the allegedly competent members of the community and the marginal such as the criminal and the insane also play their part in the constitution of community . . . This book considers communities as systems of inclusion and exclusion.

> The subject who speaks in this discourse, who says "I" or "we", cannot, and is in fact not trying to, occupy the position of a universal, totalizing, or neutral subject. In the general struggle he is talking about, the person who is speaking, telling the truth, recounting the story, rediscovering memories and trying not to forget anything, well, that person is inevitably on one side or the other: he is involved in the battle, has adversaries, and is working toward a particular victory. Of course, he speaks the discourse of right, asserts a right and demands a right. But what he is demanding and asserting is "his" rights – he says: "We have a right". These are singular rights, strongly marked by a relationship of property, conquest, victory, or nature. It might be the right of a person's family or race, the right of superiority or seniority, the right of triumphal invasions, or the right of recent or ancient occupations. In all cases, it is a right that is both grounded in history and decentered from a juridical universality. And if this subject who speaks of right (or rather, rights) is speaking the truth, that truth is no longer the universal truth of the philosopher. It is true that this discourse about the general war, this discourse that tries to interpret the war beneath peace, is indeed an attempt to describe the battle as a whole and to reconstruct the general course of the war. But that does not make it a totalizing or neutral discourse; it is always a perspectival discourse. It is interested in the totality only to the extent that I can see it in one-sided terms, distort it and see it from its own point of view. The truth is, in other words, a truth that can be deployed only from its combat position, from the perspective of the sought for victory and ultimately, so to speak, of the survival of the speaking subject himself.[125]

At no point did the Obama administration pretend to produce a scientific discourse or a regime of truth about the content of the norms regulating the use of force. Instead, there is at the foundation of their legal rhetoric a commitment to the historicity of law. The refusal of totalizing discourse about the law (to the benefit of a historico-political discourse) appears as an anti-scienticist statement about legal norms. As such, it opposes, practically and theoretically speaking, the arguments developed in contemporary international legal scholarship in general,[126] and by legal scholars against the Obama administration's propositions about the law in particular, which, for the most part, were framed as absolute truth discourses about the content of the norm.[127]

[125] Michel Foucault, *Society Must Be Defended* (Editions de Seuil/Gallimard, 1997), 52.

[126] Jean d'Aspremont, "International Law and the Rage against the Scientistic Age" (2022) 33 *European Journal of International Law* 2, 679–94.

[127] See examples in Chapters 4 to 6.

This genealogical approach to legal interpretation not only explains why the legal rationales are tailor-made for the drone program and thus participated in institutionalizing the use of drones. It might also explain why the attempts of legal scholars to constrain it by following the opposite mode of legal argumentation (with pseudo-scientific pretense) were so unsuccessful. The present study of drone programs itself – that is, our demonstration of how the drone technology, the military strategy to tackle transnational terrorist threats and the law reshape one another in a specific context – illustrates that the only way to understand our present is to investigate present practices, including legal developments (both the evolution of concepts internally and, externally, of their role in the society), in all their successive mutations. Chapter 7 and the Epilogue further illustrate that committing to the historicity of the law, using and interpreting the law by making sense of the particularisms of its interpretation and developments spatially and temporally is a very powerful way, if not to win interpretative debates, at least not to lose them – and for states to stabilize new practices.

The drone program so institutionalized is imposed on newly elected presidents or governments as a seemingly objective construct crafted by the predecessor(s) and transmitted to future generations of presidents or governments. Unless one voluntarily engages in a deconstruction of the new institutional apparatus, the drone bureaucratic machinery assembled through technology, legal rationales, and discourses about a new type of enemy, survives the turnover of the bureaucrats. From one government to another, the US drone program – made stable and durable during the Obama administration – remains solid and largely unchanged, when it is not strengthened.

3.4 Testing the Institutionalization Hypothesis: The Interchangeability of Bureaucrats

When a drone program becomes a full-blown state apparatus with bureaucratic infrastructures, sophisticated rationale, and attractive/robust technology, bureaucrats – in this case, US Presidents – become almost interchangeable even when a number of personal features and political opinions apparently differentiate them. The smooth transition from President Obama to President Trump when it comes to the use of drones testifies to the institutionalization of the US drone program.

Analyzing the US drone program to test the hypothesis that an institution emerged is helpful in that four successive administrations have used drones at the time of finalizing this book. While it is common to read that the Trump administration dropped the crucial limits that Obama had imposed on drone strikes,[128] by allegedly increasing the pace of airstrikes,[129] the number of casualties, secrecy[130] and by expanding shadow wars,[131] this diagnosis is over-hasty and overstated. What can be observed, on the contrary, is a rather harmonious transition and overall continuity in the drone practices between the Obama and the Trump administration.

While it is true that Trump announced some changes related to the drone program, these were too inconsequential to constitute a policy or legal shift. Rather, they appear as logical developments in line with the framework set by the Obama administration in the first place. First, the Trump administration was said to have deemed parts of Yemen and Somalia as areas of active hostilities, when the Obama administration had characterized them as zones outside areas of active hostilities. The second and third change can be examined alongside this first development. The second explicit modification concerns the requirement that the Obama administration implemented in its Policy Guidance that outside areas of active hostilities, strikes should only be carried out if there is a "near certainty" that this will not cause civilian casualties. Third, on March 6, 2019, the Trump administration published an executive order revoking the requirement to disclose civilian casualties[132] that Obama had estab-

[128] Charlie Savage, "Trump Revokes Obama-Era Rule on Disclosing Civilian Casualties from US Airstrikes outside War Zones," *The New York Times*, March 6, 2019. In this article, Savage dramatically refers to the revocation of the disclosure requirement established in 2016 by the Obama administration as "the latest in a series of ways that Mr. Trump has dismantled the architecture that Mr. Obama built over time to constrain the use of drone strikes and commando raids targeting Islamist militants in places like tribal Pakistan and rural Yemen."

[129] The Editorial Board, "Preventing a Free-for-All with Drone Strikes," *The New York Times*, March 16, 2017; Alex Liautaud, "More Bombs, More Boots, More Casualties," *Vice News*, January 15, 2018.

[130] Liautaud, "More Bombs, More Boots, More Casualties."

[131] Declan Walsh and Eric Schmitt, "U.S. Strikes Qaeda Target in Southern Libya, Expanding Shadow War There," *The New York Times*, March 25, 2018.

[132] President Donald Trump, National Security and Defense, Executive Order on Revocation of Reporting Requirement, March 6, 2019, www.whitehouse.gov/presidential-actions/executive-order-revocation-reporting-requirement/.

lished in July 2016.[133] The executive order refers to two laws enacted by Congress after Obama's 2016 Executive Order, the first of which requires the Secretary of Defense to submit an annual report to Congress on civilian casualties resulting from US military operations,[134] and the second, expanding the scope of the civilian casualty report and requiring that it be made public.[135] Although the Trump administration considered that the Obama disclosure requirement became redundant with these two new laws,[136] it was correctly noted that Congress only required disclosure for civilian casualties caused by the Defense Department's operations and not those of the CIA. While the revocation of the disclosure obligation (established at the very end of Obama's mandate) is a step backwards in terms of transparency and accountability, it is important not to overestimate the step that was taken by Obama in that regard with his 2016 disclosure rule in order not to rush to hasty conclusions of a rupture between the two administrations.

Examining how meaningful these changes are requires analyzing how constraining the category of "area of active hostilities" and the near certainty requirement were in the first place. Similarly, the benefits of the disclosure requirement can be assessed by examining the quality of the information on civilian casualties shared by the Obama administration. When the Obama administration shared the official numbers of civilian casualties, the numbers delivered were explained in a vague way (if at all) and were systematically lower than the casualties estimated by reporters such as the independent *Bureau of Investigative Journalism*, the *Long War Journal* and *New America*.[137] This discrepancy between the number of civilian casualties disclosed by the Obama administration and those reported by outsiders can be explained by how these actors respectively identify individuals as legitimate targets.

133 The White House, Executive Order 13732, July 1, 2016 ("United States Policy on Pre- and Post-Strike Measures").

134 Section 1057 of the National Defense Authorization Act for Fiscal Year 2018 (Public Law 115–91).

135 Section 1062 of the National Defense Authorization Act for Fiscal Year 2019 (Public Law 115–232).

136 Charlie Savage reports in his March 2019 article in the *New York Times* the statement of the National Security Council that the Obama disclosure requirements were "superfluous reporting requirements, requirements that do not improve government transparency, but rather distract our intelligence professionals from their primary mission."

137 Savage, "Trump Revokes Obama-Era Rule."

As a preliminary step, it must be stressed that US counterterrorism efforts during both the Obama and the Trump era have been made also outside areas of active hostilities. No matter how Trump decides to characterize these zones, the US has *de facto* been targeting individuals when they are not participating in hostilities at the moment of the strike and in places where hostilities are not intense or ongoing. When they follow this practice, drone operators rely on evidence that is provided and collected by the drone and that suggests continuous engagement of a person in militant activity.[138] In fact, the distinction between areas of active hostilities and outside areas of active hostilities does not perform any restrictive function in practice, and was never meant to.[139] The most likely reason for the Obama administration to operate this rhetorical shift was that it eased their discussions with allies who did not agree on considering some places of US involvement as part of its armed conflict against Al Qaeda and associated forces. Exiting the *jus in bello* paradigm did not mean, however, that the US would not be able to target the individuals they considered as enemies and to provide a legal justification for it. It just meant that they would use the *jus ad bellum* paradigm instead and push for a permissive version of the right to self-defense to legitimize targeting individuals posing a continuing imminent threat.[140] In practical terms, the Obama administration pursued its policy in much the same way as it would have done under the *jus in bello* paradigm, without being burdened with tense discussions with allies on the scope of the US "war on terror."

Aside from these rhetorical and geopolitical choices, there is a continuity of the US drone program in the transition from the Obama to the Trump administration in practice. To empirically illustrate this continuity and the nuance the allegations of shift mentioned above, a comparison between drone strikes scenarios from each era is useful. The scenario from the Obama era should be a drone strike conducted after the near certainty requirement was adopted in order to accurately assess the

[138] Peter Bergen and Katherine Tiedemann, "The Year of the Drone: An Analysis of US Drone Strikes in Pakistan, 2004–2010," New America Foundation, 2010. This 2010 study by the New America Foundation concluded that many of the strikes in Pakistan were not aimed at specific known individuals at all: they were signature strikes. Scahill, *The Assassination Complex*, 56.

[139] Contrarily to what has been said on many occasions: Adam Rawnsley, "Family Says They're Innocent Victims of Trump's Drone War," *The Daily Beast*, May 7, 2018.

[140] Christian Tams and James Devaney, "Applying Necessity and Proportionality to Anti-Terrorist Self-Defence" (2012) 45 *Israel Law Review* 1, 91–106.

restraining function it operates; in other words, it should be a story post-May 2013 Presidential Policy Guidance, which established the requirement.[141]

The reported strike against the Razzo family took place on September 20, 2015 in ISIS-occupied Mosul, Iraq.[142] That day, Basim Razzo was with his wife, his brother, and brother's wife in the family house. That day, when he went to bed after his usual night hours of clicking through car reviews on YouTube, of the BMW Alpina B7, the Audi Q7, and other kinds of cars, a strike hit the house. Basim and his sister-in-law survived. Later that same day, the American-led coalition uploaded a video to its YouTube channel entitled "Coalition Airstrike Destroys Daesh VBIED Facility Near Mosul, Iraq 20 Sept 2015."[143] The target, the video explained, was a bomb-making factory, a hub in a network of "multiple facilities spread across Mosul used to produce VBIEDs for ISIL's terrorist activities" posing "a direct threat to both civilian and Iraqi security forces."[144] The building that appeared in the recording was the Razzo's family home. That day, the contextual and behavioral evidence and intelligence gathered on Basim Razzo led to his identification as a legitimate target. Presumably, his usual daily YouTube activity was a key element used to identify him as the head of a factory making car-bombs for ISIS. This story, among others, shows that the near certainty requirement does not prevent the US military from overestimating the information collected by drones and what can be deduced from it.[145] The Razzo family was considered a legitimate target. Some of his family members were hit by the strike, and yet were not counted as civilians either at the time of the strike or after, which shows both the limited restraining function of the near certainty test, and the limited value of the requirement to disclose civilian casualties.

[141] US Presidential Policy Guidance, "Procedures for Approving Direct Action."

[142] Azmat Khan and Anand Gopal, "The Uncounted," *The New York Times*, November 16, 2017, www.nytimes.com/interactive/2017/11/16/magazine/uncounted-civilian-casualties-iraq-airstrikes.html.

[143] Ibid. VBIED is the acronym for "Vehicle Borne Improvised Explosive Devices."

[144] Khan and Gopal, "The Uncounted."

[145] Corroborated, among other things, by declarations of senior military officials to Spencer Ackerman, "US to Continue 'Signature Strikes' on People Suspected of Terrorist Links," *The Guardian*, July 1, 2016: "We continue to reserve the right to take action not just against individual terrorist targets but when we believe we have, for instance, a force protection issue or information to suggest a continued imminent threat."

Similar events under the Trump administration occurred, showing continuity in the nature of the operations carried out, including the recourse to signature strikes. In March 2018 in Yemen, several drone strikes killed people considered as legitimate targets by US officials and as civilians by their local communities, NGOs, and other reporters. On the afternoon of March 5, a thirteen-year-old boy and his nineteen-year-old cousin were driving home along a desert highway after visiting relatives in the city of al-Hudhi, when they were hit by a US drone strike.[146] The cousin survived. He and his family have insisted that the thirteen-year-old boy had no link with Al Qaeda whatsoever. Two days later, a man stood on top of a hill in the same area, hoping to get cell service to make a telephone call and was killed by a drone strike. Following these two lethal episodes, members of the al-Mahashima tribe to which all the dead belonged decided to move away from the area and to relocate. Six of them, all male adult children and grandchildren of a local tribal leader were targeted and killed by a drone as they were driving out of the area. The NGO Reprieve and local communities reported that these people had nothing to do with Al Qaeda and were poor people from another Yemeni province who had been displaced because of fighting in the region. On March 29, a US drone strike hit a Toyota Land Cruiser heading toward the city of al-Sawma'ah and killed four of the five men traveling in the car.[147] Once again, family members, tribal leaders, and a human rights group claim that they were civilians and that the purpose of their trip was to pick up a local elder to witness a sale of land.[148]

These events indicate that civilian casualties are not caused by the lack of the "near certainty" requirement but by a decision to conduct warfare by anticipation of potential threats. This strategy and the practice of signature strikes had already taken place in the Obama era. When states consider as legitimate targets individuals who have not been witnessed as actually undertaking military operations when their behavior reveals either continuous combat function (*in bello*) or continuing imminent threat (*ad bellum*), the near certainty requirement is irrelevant. Indeed, in such a context of preemptive warfare, a near certainty requirement boils down to asking whether one is nearly certain that a target is potentially a

[146] Shuaib Almosawa and Maryam Saleh, "A 13-Year-Old Boy and Other Yemeni Civilians Were Killed in U.S. Drone Strikes This Month," The Intercept, March 26, 2018.

[147] Rawnsley, "Family Says They're Innocent Victims."

[148] Ibid.

threat. The number of accepted hypotheses is so high that the requirement does not perform any constraint on the targeting decision.

Generally speaking, in addition to the continuity between the two administrations, these elements indicate that characterizing a situation, or not, as being outside areas of active hostilities does not change anything in practice because in the relevant two bodies of norms, *ad bellum* and *in bello*, legal rationales were found to justify the same type of operations. With or without a near certainty requirement, the victims of drone strikes will not be reported as civilian casualties but as legitimate targets because of the anticipatory mode of warfare. The overinclusive definition of who is a legitimate target also casts doubt on the function of the disclosure requirement. The only relevant change it makes is that disclosure of official data helps to expose the discrepancy between official numbers and NGO or journalist's reports; a discrepancy that indicates, among other things, the persistence of such practices as signature strikes.

The other point raised to argue that there is discontinuity between the two administrations is the idea that Trump initiated the expansion of drone wars to Africa.[149] While until 2018 the US operation in Libya had consisted exclusively of attacks on ISIS, the first of a series of drone strikes against Al Qaeda militants was conducted in March 2018 in the south of the country.[150] Some considered that this step marked an abrupt expansion of the US counterterrorism efforts,[151] and others rightly emphasized that targeting Al Qaeda in Libya just appeared to be the continuation of an already expanding activity of the US Africa-Command, the organization for US military activities on the continent, known as AFRICOM, in Libya's ungoverned areas.[152] In fact, it comes as no surprise that US drone strikes move along with the objects of

[149] Joe Penney, Eric Schmitt, Rukmini Callimachi, and Christoph Koettl, "C.I.A. Drone Mission, Curtailed by Obama, Is Expanded in Africa under Trump," *New York Times*, September 9, 2018, www.nytimes.com/2018/09/09/world/africa/cia-drones-africa-military.html.

[150] US Report on the Legal and Policy Frameworks Guiding the United States' Use of Military Force and Related National Security Operations, 2018.

[151] Walsh and Schmitt, "U.S. Strikes Qaeda Target in Southern Libya." Luke Hartig, a former senior director for counterterrorism at the National Security Council during the Obama administration, quoted by Walsh and Schmitt, considers that "Beginning a concerted strike campaign against AQIM or other AQ elements in the Sahel, akin to what we are doing in Yemen and in Somalia, would mark a significant expansion of our counterterrorism efforts."

[152] Deborah K. Jones, former US ambassador to Libya from 2013 to 2015, quoted by Walsh and Schmitt.

America's counterterrorism preoccupations.[153] There is nothing to suggest that the Obama administration would not have conducted a similar operation had it identified Al Qaeda targets in Libya.

In the same vein, the move of US drones to the international airport of Dirkou, in north-eastern Niger, was cited as an expansion of the drone mission in Africa under Trump,[154] and somehow as marking a departure from Obama's efforts to curtail the mission there.[155] Here too, these conclusions are highly misguided. According to documents obtained by The Intercept, the secretive unit Task Force 48-4 carrying out covert actions in the region was operating from Yemen and Somalia and conducting missions in those countries, starting with headquarters in Djibouti, from where a secret Pentagon study shows that surveillance and armed drones operated in 2012.[156] The internal 2013 Pentagon study also mentions outposts in Nairobi, Kenya, Sanaa, and Yemen; Predator drones were already based in the city of Niamey in Niger[157] and in the city of N'Djamena in Chad,[158] and Reaper drones had been flown out of Seychelles International Airport.[159] Back in 2011, the US military had

[153] Echoes what Chris Woods of Airwars declared to Spencer Ackerman of *The Daily Beast*, in Spencer Ackerman, "Trump Ramped Up Drone Strikes in America's Shadow Wars," *The Daily Beast*, November 15, 2018.

[154] Walsh and Schmitt, "U.S. Strikes Qaeda Target in Southern Libya":

> [T]he strike came as the Trump administration has been reassessing the American military commitment in North and West Africa after the ambush in Niger last fall that killed four American soldiers. The Pentagon has been preparing to fly armed drone missions form Niger's capital, Niamey, a step that diplomats and analysts say could further widen the Pentagon's shadow war in this part of the continent.

[155] Penney et al., "CIA Drone Mission."

[156] Nick Turse, "Target Africa: America's Expanding Drone Network," in The Intercept, The Drone Papers, Article no. 8 of 8, October 15, 2015, see slide featuring the types of drones and surveillance and attack aircrafts operated from Camp Lemonnier, the based in Djibouti used by the US (a map in the Pentagon report indicates that in June 2012 there were four far-ranging MQ-9 Reaper and ten MQ-1 Predator; by August 2012, the report shows sixteen drones were taking off or landing in Camp Lemonnier each day). See also Craig Whitlock, "Remote US Base at Core of Secret Operations," *The Washington Post*, October 25, 2012.

[157] Craig Whitlock, "Pentagon Set to Open Second Drone Base in Niger as It Expands Operations in Africa," *The Washington Post*, September 1, 2014.

[158] "Dealing with Boko Haram," *The New York Times*, May 30, 2014, www.nytimes.com/2014/05/31/opinion/dealing-with-boko-haram.html.

[159] Julian E. Barnes, "U.S. Expands Drone Flights to Take Aim at East Africa," *Wall Street Journal*, September 21, 2011.

concluded twenty-nine agreements to use international airports in Africa as refueling centers. The Intercept was able to conclude that the Camp Lemonnier – the headquarters in Djibouti – "is so crucial to long-term military plans that last year the US inked a deal securing its lease until 2044, agreeing to hand over $70 million a year in rent – about double what it previously paid to the government of Djibouti," testifying to the already growing importance of US counterterrorism missions in Africa.

Even though the US presence in Africa developed under Trump – and operations were extended to new groups as was the case in Libya – what these developments revealed was continuity between the Trump and the Obama administrations and adaptation to the evolution of the threats and possibly to operational capacities. So, the US presence in Africa under Trump does not mark a break with the Obama administration policy in Africa. It shows that the efforts made by the Obama administration to build a legal rationale for the use of drones and normalize the geographical expansion of the drone program were conclusive.

Now that the changes have been thoroughly mapped out, they can be reassessed as less important than the patterns of continuity. From the identification of legitimate targets based on contextual and behavior elements other than the witnessed participation in hostilities, to the scope of the conflict established according to the concept of Al Qaeda and associated forces, which is elastic not only in terms of who it includes as the enemy but also in how it defines the temporal and geographical boundaries of the counterterrorism efforts, many elements show that too many commentators have underestimated the continuity of the drone program of the Obama and Trump eras. By falling into the trap of assuming that Trump would make more radical decisions and by downgrading the analyses and criticisms they had formulated against Obama's past choices, the stability of the US drone program with its legal paradigm, its actors, infrastructure, and procedures were neglected. This institutional machinery is just waiting for anyone taking over the seat dedicated to POTUS in the chain of command to continue its routine.

3.5 Concluding Remarks

This chapter has shown that *ad hoc* elements have been transformed into a stable infrastructure capable of sustaining a continuous military campaign against transnational terrorist networks and that the law played a key role in this process.[160] The law performed as a creative force in the institutionalization process and stabilized it by rationalizing practices that would otherwise appear as arbitrary.[161] Arriving before our granular genealogy of the legal norms on the use of force and their permissive interpretations in the drone techno-legal machinery, this chapter adopted an external point of view to unravel the socio-techno-legal processes through which the US drone program has been institutionalized. The institutionalization process took place in the US, not only through the technology itself, but also through strong legal narratives (crafted by credible and trusted policymakers) that all survive thanks to a stable bureaucratic infrastructure. What this implementation of drone programs in the normal functioning of the state entails in practice is that they become an attribute of the state. The new kind of deterritorialized and individualized warfare brought about by the use of drones against transnational jihadist groups is now consolidated.

The chapter argues that legal rhetoric has been instrumental in sustainably implementing drone practices in the normal functioning of the state through anti-scientific legal discourses. These discourses were tailor-made for a specific military strategy at a certain point in time and, as such, did not pretend to declare absolute truths about the content of the norms. In this, I offered another perspective in the current discussions of a forever war and demonstrated that drone programs are stabilized in a hyper-legalistic way, but also and perhaps even more importantly because it embraces the historicity of the law: a genealogical understanding of evolutions and discussions about the interpretation of legal norms. The three next chapters zoom in and unpack the legal narratives that have been established to align with a type of warfare that consists in targeting hostile individuals and is, as a result, infinite in time and space. Reflecting on infinite warfare and the blurring of peace/war, battlefield/non-battlefield because of stable drone programs, the last chapter inquires about the long-term effects once a machinery for individualized, dematerialized, and deterritorialized warfare is embedded in the normal functioning of the state. This inquiry starts from the premise that what became normal for the operating state also develops into a habitual situation for the host state and its population, which as we will see, automatically affects both the relationship between the operating

[160] Ibid., 10.
[161] Savage, *Power Wars*, 1.

state and populations living under its drones, and that of the operating state and the host state within the international legal order. The question of what governing paradigm drone programs allow and what impact they have on sovereignty once they are implemented in the normal functioning of the state is dealt with in the final chapter.

4

Targeting Hostile Individuals

The military strategy consisting in preemptively targeting hostile individuals finds its primary legal translation in the proposition of a very permissive interpretation of the right of self-defense. Drone strikes conducted by the US, the UK, and France against transnational terrorist groups take place on the territory of foreign states. As such, the extraterritorial use of drones *prima facie* violates the UN prohibition on the use of force.[1] However, some states active in the war on terror and some scholars argue that the *ad bellum* right of self-defense has evolved over the past decades to allow the use of force against individuals posing a

[1] Article 2(4) of the UN Charter, principle of the prohibition of the use of force. The principle of the prohibition of the use of force implies that every use of force by a state in its international relations is *prima facie* necessarily illegal. Prior to the UN Charter, the Kellogg–Briand Pact of 1928 marked the illegality of warfare but the true turning point in the international legal order came in 1945 with the UN Charter. When it was drafted in San Francisco in 1945, one of its aims was to redress the shortcomings of the Kellogg–Briand Pact. Not only did the Charter prohibit war to resolve "disputes or conflicts of whatever nature or of whatever origin they may be" that may arise among States, but it also prohibited any recourse to the use of force in international relations. Accordingly, Article 2(4) provides that "all members shall refrain in their international relations from the threat or use of force against the territorial integrity or political independence of any state, or in any other manner inconsistent with the Purposes of the United Nations." In 1986, the principle of the ban on force attained the status of customary international law through a decision of the International Court of Justice; see ICJ, Military and Paramilitary Activities in and against Nicaragua (Nicaragua v. United States of America), Judgment, [1986] ICJ Reports 1986, 14 and Separate Opinions of Judge Ago and President Singh (Nicaragua case). The principle of the ban on use of force is referred to as the cornerstone of the modern international system; see Nicaragua case at 153; Oil Platforms (Islamic Republic of Iran v. United States of America) (Oil Platforms case), Judgment of November 6, 2003, [2003] ICJ Reports, 161, dissenting opinions of Judge Elaraby and Judge Simma, at 291; ibid., separate opinion of Judge Simma, at para. 328; Armed Activities on the Territory of the Congo (DRC–Uganda case), [2005] ICJ Reports, 201, at para. 148 ("*The prohibition against the use of force is a cornerstone of the United Nations Charter*"); Christian J. Tams, "The Use of Force against Terrorists" (2009) 20 *EJIL* 2, 359–97; Nehal Bhuta and H. Y. Liu, "Targeted Killing, Unmanned Aerial Vehicles and EU Policy" (2013) 17 RSCAS Policy Papers.

continuous imminent threat.[2] First, I argue that the framework articulated by some states active in the transnational war on terror (US, UK, Australia, Israel, and France), while still highly contested on some points, offers a framework for the continuous anticipation of armed attacks against individuals who show signs of continuing armed activity. I show that under pressure from state practice and rhetoric, some limitations on using force that were initially interpreted restrictively are currently interpreted extensively. More importantly, I argue that even if some limitations remain in the narratives, the concessions to the extensive interpretation of other limitations appear to have a direct cascade effect on the remaining locks because these limitations are interconnected. In the last instance it is shown that this cascade effect is epitomized by the principle of proportionality, which is not only extended, but transformed to adapt to the individualization of war.

Against this backdrop, I describe how drone programs facilitate the individualization of war and, as a corollary, the dematerialization of the decision to use force: instead of using force in self-defense against an (imminent) act, the idea is to use force against individuals in the light of their personal or behavioral characteristics. In other words, drone programs are characterized by the objective of permanently addressing future threats before they materialize and this objective authorizes action against individuals who are not presently perpetrating, or even clearly preparing, threatening acts. The absence of material circumstances amounting to the level of an armed attack, in the *jus ad bellum* sense, means that the use of force is focused not on material circumstances but on personal or behavioral features other than the witnessed preparation of an armed attack. Therefore, drone programs strengthen the extensive version of self-defense both by making it materially possible (hence, the specific role played by drones' technological capacities) and by making it apparently more acceptable. In other words, because drones practically permit precise surveillance and targeting, they make the transformation of the right of self-defense into a justification to preemptively target hostile individuals appear more admissible.

[2] Harold H. Koh, "Twenty First Century International Law Making," October 17, 2012, Speech of the Legal Adviser of the Department of State at the Georgetown University Law Centre; Stephen Marks, "Branding the 'War On Terrorism': Is There a 'New Paradigm' of International Law?" (2006) 14 *Michigan State Journal of International Law* 1, 71–119; Anne-Marie Slaughter and William Burke-White, "An International Constitutional Moment" (2002) 43 *Harvard International Law Journal* 1, 2: "in this new paradigm, we need new rules."

4.1 The Extension of the Right of Self-Defense Conditions in a Cascade

Over the past two decades, we have witnessed some states articulate a chain of propositions on how to interpret the right of self-defense against terrorists. This chain of propositions about the conditions and limits of self-defense is reasonably viewed as having expanded that right relative to an earlier series of propositions.[3] What has not been directly shown is the interconnectedness of these limitations. Yet, what this codependent nature involves is that accepting only some of the proposed modifications to the different conditions or limitations of self-defense means triggering extensions to others. So, even if many only partially accept the proposed extensions of self-defense, the implications are potentially greater. The result of this cascade effect is that the proposed right of self-defense does not so much respond to threatening material circumstances as to threatening individuals in anticipation of their acts. In this cascade effect, the principle of proportionality is somewhat unique compared to the other conditions of self-defense because its very nature ends up being fully reshaped through the process rather than merely extended like the other conditions of self-defense. The purpose of this chapter is not to describe the law as it is, the *lex lata*, nor even to discuss on the normative level the law as it should be, but rather to understand how some states play with the boundaries and gray zones of the right of self-defense to justify their strategy for the use of force in the counterterrorism context. An examination of each limitation of self-defense will reveal their interconnected nature, starting with the armed *ratione personae* limitation, followed by the *ratione materiae* limitation and *ratione temporis* limitation. The *ratione conditions* limitation, the peak of the phenomenon will be dealt with in the end (Figure 4.1).

The long-standing discussion concerning the *ratione personae* limitation of the right of self-defense predates 9/11[4] and goes beyond the so-called link of attribution, that is the necessary level of involvement of the host state when the litigious armed attack is perpetrated by non-state actors. The aim here is not to go through all these conversations and evolutions in the course of the International Court of Justice (ICJ) case

[3] Christian J. Tams and James Devaney, "Applying Necessity and Proportionality to Anti-Terrorist Self-Defence" (2012) 45 *Israel Law Review* 1, 91–106.

[4] Claus Kreß, *Gewaltverbot und Selbstverteidigungsrecht nach der Satzung der Vereinten Nationen bei staatlicher Verwicklung in Gewaltakte Privater* (Duncker & Humblot, 1995); Yoram Dinstein, *War, Aggression and Self-Defense* (Cambridge University Press, 1988).

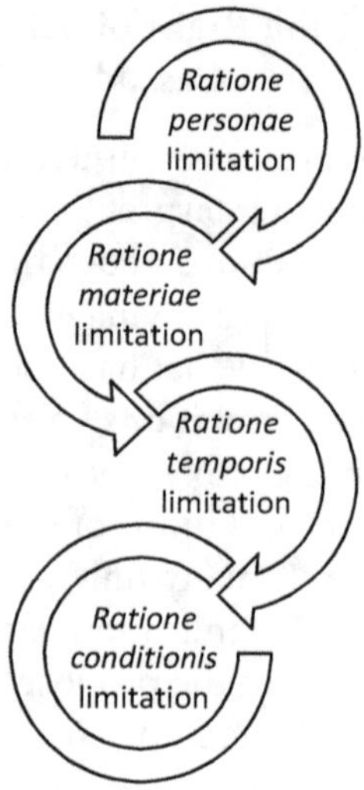

Figure 4.1 The interconnectedness of self-defense conditions

law on this *ratione personae* requirement – this has already been done with great care and scrupulousness elsewhere.[5] Instead, the goal is to focus on the reasoning used to include armed attacks perpetrated by terrorist non-state actors post-9/11.

Nonetheless, as a preliminary step, it should be noted that it is now widely accepted that non-state armed attacks can meet the *ratione personae* requirement, under certain conditions.[6] In the Nicaragua case, the ICJ established that for the conduct of irregular forces to be attributable to a state, that state has to exercise "effective control [over] the military or paramilitary operations" that are carried out against another

[5] Claus Kreß, "The International Court of Justice and the 'Principle of Non-Use of Force'," in Marc Weller (ed.), *The Oxford Handbook of the Use of Force in International Law* (Oxford University Press, 2015), 561–604.

[6] While the use of force against the territorial integrity or political independence of other states is expressly mentioned, Article 2(4) does not indicate that territorial integrity is considered to be threatened only when the menace comes from state actors. As such, Article 3 can be considered as banning "any use of inter-State force by Member States for whatever reason . . . unless explicitly allowed by the Charter." In support of this view, the UN General Assembly Resolution of the 2005 World Summit Outcome reiterated "the obligation of all Member States to refrain in their international relations from the threat or use of force in any manner inconsistent with the Charter" and reaffirmed that the purposes and principles guiding the United Nations are, *inter alia*, "to maintain international peace and security, to develop friendly relations among nations."

state.[7] In a series of further cases, the ICJ – referring to its Nicaragua decision – maintained a requirement for a link of attribution between the host state and the non-state armed attack.[8] A closer look at this case law allows to confirm that for a non-state armed attack to qualify as an armed attack in the sense of Article 51, the non-state armed attack has to be attributed to another state under rather demanding rules of attribution. Nonetheless, the link of attribution of "effective control" used in Nicaragua is sufficiently uncertain to discuss the possibility of a looser connection between the host state and the threatening non-state actors.[9]

[7] Nicaragua case, 14. s., at paras. 109 and 115; as well as para. 17 of Judge Ago's separate opinion. The effective control test has been subject to a lot of discussions and is therefore covered by a lot of literature. See, for instance, Christian Henderson, "Non-State Actors and the Use of Force," in Math Noortmann, August Reinisch, and Cedric Ryngaert (eds.), *Non-State Actors in International Law* (Hart Publishing, 2015), 88; ICJ, Case Concerning Application of the Convention on the Prevention and Punishment of the Crime of Genocide Bosnia and Herzegovina v. Serbia and Montenegro), Judgment, ICJ Reports 2007, 43. See Dissenting Opinion Judge Al-Khasawneh (dissenting opinion, [36]–[39]) and Judge ad hoc Mahiou (dissenting opinion, [113]–[117]). See also ICJ, *Independent International Fact-Finding Mission on the Conflict in Georgia*, Report, September 2009, vol. II, 260.

[8] ICJ, Legal Consequences of the Construction of a Wall in the Occupied Palestinian Territory, Advisory Opinion, July 9, 2004, ICJ Reports 2004, 136, para. 139: the Court reaffirmed that Article 51 applied only to "an armed attack by one State against another State" and because there was no state to whom the discussed non-state actions could be attributed (Israel being the occupying power), Article 51 was deemed inapplicable. See also, ICJ, Armed Activities on the Territory of the Congo (Democratic Republic of the Congo v. Uganda), Judgment of December 19, 2005, ICJ Reports 2005, 168, para. 146: the ICJ reaffirmed the necessity to attribute the acts perpetrated by non-state actors, which on another note could not be considered as constituting armed attacks in that case, to a State.

> The attacks did not emanate from armed bands or irregulars sent by the DRC or on behalf of the DRC, within the sense of Article 3 (g) of General Assembly resolution 3314 (XXIX) on the definition of aggression, adopted on 14 December 1974. The Court is of the view that, on the evidence before it, even if this series of deplorable attacks could be regarded as cumulative in character, they still remained non-attributable to the DRC.

See also ICJ, Application of the Convention on the Prevention and Punishment of the Crime of Genocide (Bosnia and Herzegovina v. Serbia and Montenegro), Judgment, ICJ Reports 2007, 43, para. 392: "Persons, groups of persons or entities may, for purposes of international responsibility, be equated with State organs even if that status does not follow from internal law, provided that in fact the persons, groups or entities act in 'complete dependence' on the State, of which they are ultimately merely the instrument."

[9] Kreß, "The International Court of Justice," 584:

> Those requirements are, in the alternative, the complete dependence of a group of violent non-state actors on the support of the state concerned or the latter's effective control over the specific forcible actions carried out

There are some convincing arguments in support of the departure from a more restrictive interpretation of Article 51, starting with the fact that this article does not require that the armed attack be perpetrated by a state actor.[10] Indeed, the terminology used by Article 2(4), which speaks of a use of force by one 'Member' against 'any state' is not reiterated in Article 51. Thus, the argument has been made that "there is nothing in Article 51 of the U.N. Charter that requires the exercise of self-defense to turn on whether an armed attack was committed directly by another state."[11] In addition to the letter of the norm, its purpose also arguably excludes such a requirement: given that Article 51 is intended to exceptionally allow states to use force when they face an attack that gravely endangers their security, and given that armed attacks perpetrated by non-state actors can actually reach this level of threat, it can actually comprise the armed attacks of non-state actors.[12]

If one is to remain within the scope of options made available by the semantic scope of Article 51, the remaining constraint is to establish some sort of link of attribution, but it can be a loose and indirect one.[13] This is the function that seems to be performed by the 'unwilling/unable'

from within such a group. The "harbouring" by a state of transnationally violent non-state actors on its territory, to take one specific and recently much discussed example, would seem to fall into that grey area.

10 On this posture, see Claus Kreß, "The Fine Line between Collective Self-Defense and Intervention by Invitation: Reflections on the Use of Force against IS in Syria," *Just Security*, February 17, 2015, www.justsecurity.org/20118/claus-kreb-force-isil-syria/; Sean Murphy, "Terrorism and the Concept of 'Armed Attack' in Article 51 of the UN Charter" (2002) 43 *Harvard International Law Journal* 1, 41, 50. For a seemingly more hesitant acceptance of non-state armed attacks entering the scope of Article 51, see Philip Alston, "Report of the Special Rapporteur on Extrajudicial, Summary or Arbitrary Executions," May 28, 2010, *United Nations Human Rights Council*, A/HRC/14/24/Add.6, §40: Philip Alston is not drawing any conclusion on whether Article 51's armed attacks criterion includes attacks perpetrated by non-State actors. However, he underlines that "it will only be in very rare circumstances that a non-state actor whose activities do not engage the responsibility of any State will be able to conduct the kind of armed attack that would give rise to the right to use extraterritorial force."

11 Murphy, "Terrorism and the Concept of 'Armed Attack'," 41, 50.

12 Ashley Deeks, "Unwilling or Unable, toward a Normative Framework for Extraterritorial Self-Defence" (2012) 52 *Virginia Journal of International Law* 483, 493.

13 On the contrary, some scholars consider that attacks committed by non-state actors without any link of attribution to the state constitute armed attacks under Article 51. Thomas M. Franck, "Terrorism and the Right of Self-Defense" (2001) 95 *American Journal of International Law* 839, 840; Christopher Greenwood, "International Law and the Preemptive Use of Force: Afghanistan, al-Qaida, and Iraq" (2003) 4 *San Diego International Law Journal* 7, 17; Raphaël Van Steenberghe, "Self-Defence in Response to Attacks by Non-State Actors in the Light of Recent State Practice: A Step Forward?"

doctrine that has gained increasing support.[14] This doctrine of the unwillingness or inability of the host state to counter the terrorist attacks that are perpetrated from its territory to recognize a right of self-defense against non-state armed attacks was set forth by states and by scholars but was never endorsed (neither was it rejected) by the ICJ.[15] It is also important to note that the doctrine predates 9/11 (and as such is not specific to the use of force in the context of counterterrorism) and was used as justification for action by numerous states as a trigger of the right to self-defense against non-state armed attacks.[16]

According to the unwilling/unable doctrine, a right to use force in self-defense against non-state actors exists if the foreign state is either unwilling to halt the activities of terrorists or unable to stop them.[17] This logic can be characterized as an attribution link, albeit lenient and indirect.

(2010) 23 *Leiden Journal of International Law* 183, 184; Dinstein, *War, Aggression and Self-Defense*, 214.

14 Some scholars still very strictly interpret the armed attack criterion of Article 51. Olivier Corten, "The 'Unwilling or Unable' Test: Has It Been, and Could It Be, Accepted?" (2016) 29 *Leiden Journal of International Law* 3, 777–99; Antonio Cassese, "The International Community's 'Legal' Response to Terrorism" (1989) 38 *International and Comparative Law Quarterly* 589, 597; Eric Myjer and Nigel White, "The Twin Towers Attack: An Unlimited Right to Self-Defense" (2002) 7 *Journal of Conflict and Security Law* 5, 7.

15 Strong normative arguments against the 'unwilling or unable' test are rare – see for an exception: Corten, "The 'Unwilling or Unable' Test," 777–99. Otherwise, see Elizabeth Wilmshurst, "The Chatham House Principles of International Law on the Use of Force by States in Self-Defence" (2006) 55 *International and Comparative Law Quarterly* 4, 963, 969. Or, more recently, Nico Schrijver and Larissa van den Herik, "Leiden Policy Recommendations on Counter-terrorism and International Law" (2010) 57 *Netherlands Yearbook of International Law* 531.

16 See for a detailed account and analysis of state practice and scholarly work in support and against this doctrine, Kreß, *Gewaltverbot und Selbstverteidigungsrecht nach.* See also, Deeks, "Unwilling or Unable, toward a Normative Framework," 483, 486–7. On Israel, see Tom Ruys, *"Armed Attack" and Article 51 of the UN Charter, Evolutions in Customary Law and Practice* (Cambridge University Press, 2010), 421–8. For the US, see Letter dated September 23, 2014 from the Permanent Representative of the United States of America to the United Nations addressed to the Secretary-General, UN Doc. S/2014/695, September 23, 2014:

> ISIL and other terrorist groups in Syria are a threat not only to Iraq, but also to many other countries, including the United States and our partners in the region and beyond. States must be able to defend themselves, in accordance with the inherent right of individual and collective self-defence, as reflected in Article 51 of the Charter of the United Nations, when, as is the case here, the government of the State where the threat is located is unwilling or unable to prevent the use of its territory for such attacks.

17 Deeks, "Unwilling or Unable, toward a Normative Framework," 486: "More than a century of state practice suggests that it is lawful for State X, which has suffered an

Indeed, in the first scenario, the unwilling state still bears the fault of willingly letting non-state actors threaten the victim state. In the second scenario, the unable state would arguably be willing to counter the threat if it were able to. In fact, if willing and unable, a state would either seek the support of a third state or at least consent to a third state intervention, if not explicitly and prior to the intervention in self-defense, then implicitly and/or without contestation afterward. We would thereby easily exit the self-defense paradigm as there would be no violation of sovereignty. If on the contrary, intervention in an unable state poses a diplomatic problem, this host state can easily be considered as unwilling to address the threat posed by non-state actors from its territory.[18] Understood as such, the unwilling test, as well as what we could call, instead of "unable," the "unable *and* unwilling" test, correspond in my view to an attribution link between the host state and non-state armed attack as it recognizes state fault. Following this analysis, the unwilling/unable test not only appears to be generally in line with the logic of the UN Charter, but it is also in line with the related ICJ case law requiring a link of attribution, even if it requires to adopt a much more flexible connection between the host state and the threat posed by non-state actors from its territory.[19]

armed attack by an insurgent or terrorist group, to use force in State Y against that group if State Y is unwilling or unable to suppress the threat."

[18] Eliav Lieblich, "On the Continuous and Concurrent Application of ad Bellum and in Bello Proportionality," in Claus Kreß and Robert Lawless (eds.), *Necessity and Proportionality in International Peace and Security Law* (Lieber Series, Vol. 4, Oxford University Press, 2020), 41–76. In this forthcoming paper, Lieblich expresses the idea that "In effect, this view constructs the problem of self-defense against non-state actors as a crude form of an 'innocent threat' dilemma: the state's territory is being used by the non-state actor – against its will – to stage attacks against other states; but a response against the non-state actor will inevitably violate the innocent state's territory." To use Lieblich's vocabulary, but in contrast to what he and others believe, I argue that a response against the non-state actor does not violate the innocent state's territory if that state is indeed innocent (only unable).

[19] This version of the link of attribution could even potentially reconcile judges within the ICJ. While on the one hand the ICJ as a whole maintains that Article 51 requires an attribution link, Judges Kooijmans and Simma, who argued in favor of an express acceptance of non-state armed attacks in separate individual opinions, could very well be satisfied with the indirect and loose attribution link that an unwilling unable test would require. ICJ, Legal Consequences of the Construction of a Wall, 194, para. 139: Article 51 recognizes the existence of an inherent right of self-defense in the case of an armed attack by one State against another. Since Israel did not claim that the attacks against it were imputable to a foreign State, however, Article 51 of the Charter had no relevance in the case of the wall. Separate opinion of Judge Kooijmans, 150, para. 30,

To summarize, this prospect of defining unwilling/unable as an attribution link is in theory compatible both with maintaining the cornerstone principles of the international legal order (even if the principle of sovereign equality can be considerably harmed by such a test if left undefined and open-textured),[20] and with the (reasonable) inclination to include non-state armed attacks within the scope of Article 51. This is how I explain that a broad range of actors have shown interest in, if not actually expressed approval of, the use of the unwilling/unable doctrine in the counterterrorism context. The unwilling/unable doctrine is more and more common and banal in justifications of the use of force, from states to scholars and UN special rapporteurs, such as Philip Alston who noted that the use of force by one state in the territory of another state does not violate the second state's sovereignty either if the second state consents, or if the first state acts under its right to self-defense because "the second State is unwilling or unable to stop armed attacks against the first State launched from its territory."[21]

The compromise that unwilling/unable can in principle achieve explains that it was central to states' narrative to justify post-9/11 extraterritorial use of force against non-state actors. The US interpretation of the *ratione personae* criterion of self-defense as only requiring "an assessment that the relevant governmental authorities in the country where action is contemplated cannot or will not effectively address the threat to U.S. persons"[22] took place in a context where it became common for states to identify non-state threats in other states' territories. The looser attribution link constituted by unwilling/unable was therefore welcomed with ease. As a result of the intense scholarly discussion under the

www.icj-cij.org/docket/files/116/10463.pdf. According to Judge Kooijmans, "if armed attacks are carried out by irregular bands from such territory against a neighbouring State, they are still armed attacks even if they cannot be attributed to the territorial State. It would be unreasonable to deny the attacked State the right to self-defence merely because there is no attacker State, and the Charter does not so require." Separate Opinion of Judge Simma, 173, para. 11, www.icj-cij.org/docket/files/116/10467.pdf. Judge Simma, in line with Judge Kooijmans' argument, declared that "in the light of more recent developments not only in State practice but also with regard to accompanying opinio juris, (reading of Article 51) ought urgently to be reconsidered, also by the Court."

20 The broader effects of the unwilling unable doctrine, if left undefined, on the international legal order are further explored in Chapter 7.

21 Alston, Report of the Special Rapporteur, UN Doc. A/HRC/14/42/Add. 6

22 "Fact Sheet: U.S. Policy Standards and Procedures for the Use of Force in Counterterrorism Operations Outside the United States and Areas of Active Hostilities," May 23, 2013, www.whitehouse.gov/the-press-office/2013/05/23/fact-sheet-us-policy-standards-and-procedures-use-force-counterterrorism.

Obama administration, when the UK and France now adopted a similar criterion to that of the US, it remained largely undiscussed. Indeed, the legal claim that strikes in Syria were justified by President Assad's unwillingness to deal with the attacks carried out by ISIS has been formulated by the US,[23] followed by the UK,[24] France,[25] and Australia.[26] In their May 10, 2016 Report, the House of Commons and House of Lords approved the British government's position that there is a right of self-defense against armed attacks by non-state actors "such as ISIL/Da'esh" if there is evidence that "the Assad regime is unwilling and/or unable to take action necessary to prevent ISIL's continuing attack on Iraq, or indeed attacks on [the UK]."[27] A few commentators have raised questions concerning the use of the unwilling/unable test in the Syrian case[28] and have discussed the actual fulfillment of the unwillingness or inability of the Syrian government to deal with the armed attacks perpetrated by Da'esh,[29] but without questioning the use of the doctrine itself.

[23] Letter from the President Barack Obama, War Powers Resolution Regarding Iraq, To the Speaker of the House of Representatives and the President Pro Tempore of the Senate, September 23, 2014, www.whitehouse.gov/the-press-office/2014/09/23/letter-president-war-powers-resolution-regarding-iraq.

[24] Prime Minister David Cameron, House of Commons Debate, November 25, 2015, column 1491.

[25] Discours du président de la République devant le Parlement réuni en Congrès, November 16, 2015, www.elysee.fr/declarations/article/discours-du-president-de-la-republique-devant-le-parlement-reuni-en-congres-3/. Interestingly completes the elements used for categorization by Elena Chachko and Ashley Deeks, "Which States Support the 'Unwilling and Unable' Test?," *Lawfare*, October 10, 2016, www.lawfareblog.com/which-states-support-unwilling-and-unable-test (leading them to, in my view, wrongly categorize France as an ambiguous case).

[26] Letter dated September 9, 2015 from the Permanent Representative of Australia to the United Nations addressed to the President of the Security Council, S/2015/693.

[27] House of Commons Debate, November 25, 2015, column 1491.

[28] Jennifer Daskal, Ashley Deeks, and Ryan Goodman, "Strikes in Syria: The International Law Framework," *Just Security*, September 24, 2014, www.justsecurity.org/15479/strikes-syria-international-law-framework-daskal-deeks-goodman; Nehal Bhuta, "On Preventive Killing," *EJILTalk!*, September 17, 2015, www.ejiltalk.org/on-preventive-killing/#more-13651.

[29] Kreß, "The Fine Line": According to Professor Kreß, it is impossible to say that Syria is unwilling to deal with ISIL's attacks considering President Assad's offer to fight the Islamic State in Syria in coordination with the US and its partners. He considers however Syria to be unable to deal with it on its own. Yet, he joins with Ryan Goodman's opinion that the inability is not sufficient to authorize self-defense measures. He says that

> If the goal to end a non-State armed attack can be effectively achieved through coordinated military action with the territorial State, then, in principle, this avenue must be pursued because it reconciles the needs to

Even if the unwilling/unable doctrine has not been adopted in positive law, states and scholars increasingly consider that the link of attribution is met when the unwilling or unable test is positive.[30] As will be explored below, the individualized conduct of warfare facilitated by the use of drones makes this extension of the *ratione personae* even more acceptable.

Once one accepts the inclusion of armed attacks perpetrated by non-state actors in the scope of self-defense through a link of attribution which is as loose and uncertain as unwilling/unable, in situations that concern terrorist transnational networks, the next step is to adapt self-defense to the modes of action of these actors. A new (extensive) version of the accumulation of events doctrine has been articulated over the past two decades precisely because states active in the counterterrorism context have adapted it to fit the use of force against threats posed by transnational terrorist networks.

This interpretative evolution should be examined step-by-step. The traditional interpretation of the *ratione materiae* limitation first entails that in order to give rise to a right of self-defense, the attack must be an armed attack.[31] Secondly, the armed attack must present a certain degree of gravity and one has "to distinguish the most grave forms of the use of force (those constituting an armed attack) from other less grave forms."[32] There is a view in the literature that the intensity requirement for

> protect the sovereignty both of the victim and the territorial State. It follows, that, again in principle, the right of collective self-defense in case of a non-State attack is subsidiary to "intervention by invitation."

See also, Ryan Goodman, "International Law on Airstrikes against ISIS in Syria," *Just Security*, August 28, 2014, www.justsecurity.org/14414/international-law-airstrikes-isis-syria/.

[30] This reasoning has been suggested in general by Michael Shaw, *International Law* (6th ed., Cambridge University Press, 2008) 89: "Generally, where states are seen to acquiesce in the behaviour of other states without protesting against them, the assumption must be that such behaviour is accepted as legitimate" (quoted by Monica Hakimi, "Defensive Force against Non-State Actors: The State of Play" (2015) 91 *International Law Studies* 31). On this specific doctrine by Daniel Bethlehem, "Self-Defense against an Imminent or Actual Armed Attack by Nonstate Actors" (2012) 106 *American Journal of International Law* 770, 773; Michael J. Glennon, "How International Rules Die" (2005) 93 *Georgetown Law Journal* 939, 960.

[31] Therefore, it does not comprise economic or ideological aggressions.

[32] Nicaragua case, 101, para. 191; Oil Platforms case, paras. 51 and 64. A minor use of force that violates Article 2(4), if it entails its author's responsibility, does not necessarily allow its victim to respond.

non-state armed attacks should be more demanding.[33] However, the opposite view that the qualitative threshold for an event to be qualified as an "armed attack" under Article 2(4) can be replaced by a quantitative one (accumulation of events doctrine) even for non-state armed attacks seems to have precedence. Therefore, while the introduction of a stricter intensity threshold would diminish the cascade effect, the expansion of the accumulation of events doctrine accelerates it.

Instead of having to identify one serious armed attack, the accumulation of events doctrine as discussed by the litigants in the DRC–Uganda[34] and Oil Platforms[35] cases means that the armed attack criterion is fulfilled by the existence of "*a series of minor incidents,* [which] *taken together, can be said to reach the threshold of an armed attack.*"[36] In other words, the doctrine admits a large-scale response both to a continuous series of attacks of a certain gravity and to less grave uses of force that amount to an armed attack when forming part of a chain of events.[37] In addition to the many occasions where states invoked the accumulation of events doctrine,[38] the ICJ did not expressly reject it, and can even be

[33] Wilmshurst, "The Chatham House Principles of International Law," principle 6; Schrijver and van den Herik, "Leiden Policy Recommendations on Counter-terrorism and International Law," paras. 38, 86; Claus Kreß, "Some Reflections on the International Legal Framework Governing Transnational Armed Conflicts" (2010) 15 *Journal of Conflict and Security Law* 2, 251; Report of the Special Rapporteur on Extrajudicial, Summary or Arbitrary Executions, Christof Heyns, Submitted in Accordance with Assembly Resolution 67/168, "Extrajudicial, Summary or Arbitrary Executions," September 13, 2013, A/68/382, §89.

[34] ICJ, Armed Activities on the Territory of the Congo (Democratic Republic of the Congo v. Uganda), Judgment of December 19, 2005, ICJ Reports 2005, 168.

[35] ICJ, Oil Platforms case, 161.

[36] Tams, "The Use of Force against Terrorists," 388. Oil Platforms case, para. 64:

> On the hypothesis that all the incidents complained of are to be attributed to Iran, and thus setting aside the question, examined above, of attribution to Iran of the specific attack on the Sea Isle City, the question is whether that attack, either in itself or in combination with the rest of the "series of . . . attacks" cited by the United States can be categorized as an "armed attack" on the United States justifying self-defence.

[37] Ruys, *Armed Attack and Article 51 of the UN Charter*, 168.

[38] See, for example, UN Doc. S/PV.749, October 30, 1956, §§33–9 (Israel); UN Doc. S/PV.749, October 30, 1956, §§154–73 (France); UN Doc. S/PV.749, October 30, 1956, §37 (Australia); UN Doc. S/PV.1106, April 2, 1964, §§39–48 (UK); UN Doc. S/PV.1111, April 9, 1964, §5 (US), §11 (Republic of China). For further example and deeper analysis, see Ruys, *Armed Attack and Article 51 of the UN Charter*.

considered as having implicitly followed the US argument that the attacks should be considered together.[39]

The UN Security Council, in its Resolution 2249 (2015), implicitly embraced what appears to be an extensive version of the accumulation of events doctrine. It condemns

> the horrifying terrorist attacks perpetrated by ISIL also known as Da'esh which took place on 26 June 2015 in Sousse, on 10 October 2015 in Ankara, on 31 October 2015 over Sinaï, on 12 November 2015 in Beirut and on 13 November 2015 in Paris, and all other attacks perpetrated by ISIL also known as Da'esh, including hostage-taking and killing, and *notes* it has the capability and intention to carry out further attacks and regards all such acts of terrorism as a threat to peace and security.[40]

The threat is assessed based on past events revealing a continuing threat, and the propensity of the members of terrorist groups to maintain this hostility. If this definition of 'threat' was endorsed as a way of framing the armed attack requirement and, more specifically, the accumulation doctrine, it would mark an additional step in the extension of the right of self-defense. Indeed, it goes even further than the initial idea that a series of minor incidents can be said to reach the threshold of an armed attack when taken together. This interpretation would entail that action in self-defense is taken on the basis of a series of *past* hostile activities and a diagnosis, on this basis, of the likelihood that individual groups maintain this hostile posture.

The reason why this excerpt of the UNSC Resolution is interesting is that the US, the UK, and France have adopted its reasoning when justifying the use of force, including through drones, in the counterterrorism context. Former British Prime Minister, David Cameron stated that it is clear "that ISIL's campaign against the UK and our allies has reached the level of an 'armed attack', such that force may lawfully be used in self-defense to prevent further atrocities being

[39] In the Oil Platforms case, even if the ICJ does not conclude that the incidents it analyzes constitute an armed attack, the Judges were ready to "take them cumulatively" to conduct the qualification, paras. 46–64. For concurring view and more detailed analysis, see Kreß, "The International Court of Justice," 582: "The question would lose some practical significance were the ICJ to finally endorse, as it seemed inclined to do in the *Oil Platforms* case as well as in the *Armed Activities* case, some form of accumulation of events doctrine for the purpose of measuring gravity in cases of a series of attacks." Tams, "The Use of Force against Terrorists," 388.

[40] UN Security Council Resolution 2249 (2015), Adopted by the Security Council at Its 7565th Meeting, on November 20, 2015, S/RES/2249(2015).

committed by ISIL."[41] In their Report on the government's policy on the use of drones for targeted killing of May 10, 2016, the British House of Lords and House of Commons' Joint Committee on Human Rights also endorsed this more lenient interpretation of the armed attack criterion.[42]

Former French President François Hollande, the then Prime Minister Manuel Valls, and Minister of Defense Jean-Yves le Drian also relied on a similar version of the right to self-defense for the strikes in Syria.[43] They argued that it was legitimate for France to conduct strikes in Syria under the right of self-defense because of the attacks that have been organized and perpetrated by ISIS members from Syria "against France and other countries."[44] On September 9, 2015, France addressed a letter to the UN Security Council, stating that:

> In accordance with Article 51 of the Charter of the United Nations, France has taken actions involving the participation of military aircraft in response to attacks carried out by ISIL from the territory of the Syrian Arab Republic.[45]

In an interview of April 2018, President Macron justified the expansion of France's war against jihadist terrorist groups overseas to Syria, by emphasizing that "in Syria, we wage war against IS, that is against the Islamist terrorist groups that had, I remind you, attacked our country,

41 House of Commons Debate, November 25, 2015, column 1491.

42 House of Lords and House of Commons' Joint Committee on Human Rights, The Government's Policy on the Use of Drones for Targeted Killing, Second Report of Session 2015–16, HL Paper 141, HC 574, May 10, 2016, 44.

43 Speech of Former French Prime Minister, Discours de Manuel Valls devant l'Assemblée Nationale, September 15, 2015, www.gouvernement.fr/syrie-la-france-est-en-guerre-contre-le-terrorisme-le-djihadisme-l-islamisme-radical-ce-sera-long-2873: "Il s'agit ainsi d'identifier et de localiser le dispositif de Daech pour être en mesure de le frapper sur le sol syrien et d'exercer ainsi notre droit à la légitime défense, comme le prévoit l'article 51 de la Charte des Nations unies." French National Assembly, Statement of French Former Minister of Defense, Déclaration de M. Jean-Yves Le Drian, Ministre de la Défense, en réponse à une question sur les frappes aériennes françaises en Syrie, à l'Assemblée nationale le 30 septembre 2015, Questions d'actualité à l'Assemblée nationale, September 30, 2015.

44 Public Lecture given by Former French President François Hollande, Sixième Conférence du Président de la République François Hollande [Sixth Conference of the French President on the Challenges and Priorities of the Executive Policy], September 7, 2015, Palais de l'Élysée, www.vie-publique.fr/discours/196108-conference-de-presse-de-m-francois-hollande-president-de-la-republique.

45 S/2015/745, Identical letters dated September 8, 2015 from the Permanent Representative of France to the United Nations addressed to the Secretary-General and the President of the Security Council, September 9, 2015.

considering that it is in Raqqa that the November 2015 attacks were planned."[46] In the Sahel region, the legal justification given by France since 2013 for the use of force is intervention by invitation.[47] In light of the explicit request for assistance by the government of Mali in 2013, this explanation first rested on solid grounds for the engagement in Mali. When engagement was extended to the region of the G5 Sahel – to Burkina Faso, Mauritania, Niger, and Chad – and the Serval Operation was replaced by the Barkhane Operation in 2014, France maintained that it was still acting by invitation of the territorial states.[48] This could be in itself a point for discussion in light of the numerous references to the right of self-defense hidden behind the veil of an 'intervention by invitation' justification.[49] What is most striking is France's continued military presence from the sky in Mali, after Mali withdrew its consent to the Barkhane and Takuba operations in 2022.[50] Following Mali's consent withdrawal, the French Ministry of the Armed Forces reported, in its

[46] Interview of President Macron, "Macron, un an après: le grand entretien en intégralité, Mediapart," YouTube, April 15, 2018, www.youtube.com/watch?v=mt0as7x-kfs&t=964s.

[47] French Ministry of Armed Forces, Presentation of the Serval Operation in Mali 2013–14, "Présentation de l'Opération," www.defense.gouv.fr/english/operations/missionsachevees/operation-serval-2013-2014/dossier/presentation-de-l-operation. See for an analysis, Karine Bannelier and Theodore Christakis, "Under the UN Security Council's Watchful Eyes: Military Intervention by Invitation in the Malian Conflict" (2013) 26 *Leiden Journal of International Law* 4, 855–74.

[48] News item on the announcement by French Minister of Defence Jean-Yves le Drian to extend the Serval Operation to the region and, hence, to rename it "Barkhane Operation"; see "Fin de Serval au Mali, lancement de l'opération 'Barkhane' au Sahel," France 24, July 13, 2014, www.france24.com/fr/20140713-operation-serval-mali-france-barkhane-le-drian-defensemilitaire-terroriste; Jean Guisnel, "Le Drian et Hollande installent l'opération Barkhane," *Le Point*, July 16, 2014, www.lepoint.fr/editos-du-point/jean-guisnel/le-drian-et-hollande-installent-l-operationbarkhane-16-07-2014-1846497_53.php.

[49] Rebecca Mignot-Mahdavi, "Le Silence des Agneaux: France's War Against 'Jihadist Groups' and Associated Legal Rationale" (2020) *ICCT Journal*, https://icct.nl/publication/le-silence-des-agneaux-frances-war-against-jihadist-groups-and-associated-legal-rationale/, 16–18.

[50] First, after diplomatic tensions escalated in February 2022, raising serious doubts on Mali's continued consent to French presence, France decided to withdraw its (on-the-ground) troops from Mali and announced it in a "Joint declaration on the fight against the terrorist threat and the support to peace and security in the Sahel and West Africa," February 17, 2022, www.elysee.fr/en/emmanuel-macron/2022/02/17/joint-declaration-on-the-fight-against-the-terrorist-threat. Then, on May 2, 2022, the Malian Foreign Minister Abdoulaye Diop formally announced the end of the 2014 defense cooperation agreement with France and the end of agreements signed in 2013 and 2020 on France's Barkhane and Europe's Takuba operations in Mali: see, for the video statement, "Mali: France Has Lost 'Legal Basis' for Military Operations," *Africanews*, www.africanews.com/2022/05/04/mali-france-has-lost-legal-basis-for-military-operations/.

weekly news release that they not only organized the relocation of the Barkhane operation from Mali to Niger, but also pursued the fight against "armed terrorist groups" in Mali.[51] Once consent of the host state is withdrawn and in the absence of a UN Security Council Resolution that approves a French intervention in the Sahel deprived of consent from host states, the only justification for the use of force is self-defense.[52] This is where the extensive self-defense logic of French officials to support military operations against terrorist groups in the Sahel on the basis of past attacks perpetrated by these (or other) groups in France and revealing continuing hostile intent takes all its importance.

Overall, this reasoning also recalls the US Department of Justice White Paper,[53] the subsequent Bethlehem Principles,[54] but also the British Attorney General's speech in January 2017,[55] and the Australian

[51] French Ministry of the Armed Forces, "Point de situation des opérations du vendredi 29 avril au jeudi 05 mai," News Release on the Operations Conducted from April 29 and May 5, 2022, www.defense.gouv.fr/point-situation-operations/point-situation-operations-du-vendredi-29-avril-au-jeudi-05-mai.

[52] To strengthen its legal basis for intervention in the Sahel, France had pursued a Security Council authorization. France proposed a resolution to obtain UN backing both for the G5 Sahel local task force and for French involvement in the region. In 2017, after two weeks of negotiation on the French draft text (and after France agreed to tone down the language to reassure its American allies who did not believe a resolution was necessary), the UN Security Council Resolution 2359 (2017) was adopted in June 2017. However, the resolution only serves to support and encourage the deployment of the task force and explicitly welcomes the efforts of the French forces to support joint military counter-terrorist operations in the region. The language used preconditions the involvement to the spirit of cooperation and thus to the consent of the states where France intervenes. See Security Council Resolution 2359 (2017), Adopted by the Security Council at Its 7979th Meeting, on June 21, 2017, http://unscr.com/en/resolutions/doc/2359. On the toning down of language, see analysis by Michelle Nichols, "France Softens Proposed U.N. Backing for Sahel Force to Appease U.S.," Reuters, June 20, 2017, www.reuters.com/article/us-africa-security-sahel-un/francesoftens-proposed-u-n-backing-for-sahel-force-to-appease-u-s-idUSKBN19B321.

[53] Department of Justice White Paper, "Lawfulness of a Lethal Operation Directed against a U.S. Citizen Who Is a Senior Operational Leader of Al-Qa'ida or an Associated Force," November 8, 2011, https://fas.org/irp/eprint/doj-lethal.pdf.

[54] Bethlehem, "Self-Defense against an Imminent," 770, 773.

[55] Rt. Hon. Jeremy Wright QC MP, UK Attorney General's Speech at the International Institute for Strategic Studies, Attorney General Discusses the Modern Law of Self-Defence at the International Institute for Strategic Studies, January 11, 2017, www.gov.uk/government/speeches/attorney-generals-speech-at-the-international-institute-for-strategic-studies.

Attorney General's Speech of June 2017.[56] These state representatives agree to assess the threat triggering the right to use force in self-defense on the basis of contextual and behavioral elements revealing the propensity of hostile individuals to act in the future. In practical terms, turning the armed attack requirement into an identification of hostile intent on the basis of past attacks marks the departure from the use of force to face material events: instead of using self-defense to repel a material threat, these states decide on certain occasions to use force to eliminate individuals who threaten them. This is an indication of the dematerialization of the decision to use force. Of course, strong objections against this proposition (and the dematerialization of the use of force that it entails) remain.[57] What is interesting here is not to say that the interpretative struggle ends here, but to show how the semantic scope of Article 51 has been exploited to formulate a very permissive proposition about the interpretation of self-defense.

This proposition about the *ratione materiae* condition of self-defense inevitably entails a temporal modification of the right. Three temporal propositions can be formulated to define the right of self-defense's *ratione temporis* limitation. First, responsive self-defense describes the use of force in response to an armed attack that may be completed or may still be ongoing, but which is in any case "an observable fact of reality."[58] Anticipatory self-defense includes two very different kinds of self-defense, that is, preemptive and preventive self-defense.[59] Preemptive self-defense refers to the use of force against an attack that has not yet taken place, but which is "imminent": the threat is "instant, overwhelming, leaving no choice of means and no moment for deliberation."[60] Preventive self-defense covers the use of force that seeks to

56 Senator the Hon. George Brandis QC, Attorney-General of Australia, "The Right of Self-Defence against Imminent Armed Attack in International Law," May 25, 2017, www.ejiltalk.org/author/gbrandis/.

57 While force in self-defense can generally be used against individuals without any formally required consideration of the group to which they belong, the accumulation of events doctrine could logically oblige statees to identify a link between these accumulated events. For instance, such a link could lie in a group affiliation. Practically speaking, it would not halt the evolution toward accepting the accumulation of events doctrine, but it would make it less extensive. See, in support of such a proposition, Kreß, "Some Reflections on the International Legal Framework," 249; Tams, "The Use of Force against Terrorists."

58 Ruys, *Armed Attack and Article 51 of the UN Charter*, 253.

59 Ibid.

60 For an explanation of the *Caroline* incident, see Matthew Allen Fitzgerald, "Note, Seizing Weapons of Mass Destruction from Foreign-Flagged Ships on the High Seas under Article 51 of the UN Charter" (2009) 49 *Virginia Journal of International Law* 473, 477–9, quoted by Deeks, "Unwilling or Unable, toward a Normative Framework," 502.

counter several potential future attacks, even without any concrete indication that those attacks will actually occur. It tries to prevent a prospective threat from becoming imminent.[61] Accepting the accumulation of events doctrine without carefully defining it, or even more strikingly, expressly endorsing the backward-looking version of the accumulation of events doctrine, carries the risk of a perpetuation of the timeframe during which the right of self-defense may be exercised.[62] This once more demonstrates the interconnectedness of the different conditions of that right.[63]

The official statements mentioned above, somehow validated by the Security Council in its Resolution 2249 (2015) also mentioned above,[64] mark not only a departure from the armed attack requirement, but also from the requirement that the threat of an armed attack be at least imminent to trigger a right of self-defense. In fact, affirming that an accumulation of past events can reveal a continuing threat from the part of non-state actors opens the door more to the idea of a "permanent imminence" of the threat of armed attack.[65] This idea that the right of self-defense is triggered because of the continuous imminence of the threat posed by certain individuals is not a specifically American notion. The UK drone strike against British national Reyaad Khan on August 24, 2014 initiated a discussion on the UK's interpretation of self-defense and showed that state practice and rhetoric beyond the US could further expand the condition of imminence of self-defense. Early in the discussion, David Cameron, in his first statement to the House of Commons, did not mention that the strike aimed to repel an imminent attack:[66]

[61] Ruys, *Armed Attack and Article 51 of the UN Charter*, 254.

[62] Marc Weller, "Permanent Imminence of Armed Attacks: Resolution 2249 (2015) and the Right to Self Defence against Designated Terrorist Groups," *EJIL: Talk!*, November 25, 2015, www.ejiltalk.org/permanent-imminence-of-armed-attacks-resolution-2249-2015-and-the-right-to-self-defence-against-designated-terrorist-groups/.

[63] Tams, "The Use of Force against Terrorists," 390.

[64] Weller, "Permanent Imminence of Armed Attacks."

[65] Ibid. See for similar (even more strongly claimed) analysis of the Resolution, Michael Scharf, Paul Williams, and Milena Sterio, *The Syrian Conflict's Impact on International Law* (Cambridge University Press, 2020), 174–5. The authors analyze the Resolution 2249 (2015) very straightforwardly as validating this flexible interpretation of self-defense: "After the United States and its allies conducted more than 5,500 air strikes on ISIS targets in Syria, the Security Council confirmed this new interpretation when it unanimously adopted Resolution 2249 on 20 November 2015, which stated that use of force against ISIS in Syria without Syria's authorization is permissible based on self-defense."

[66] David Cameron, Oral Statement to Parliament Syria: Refugees and Counter-terrorism – Prime Minister's Statement, September 7, 2015, House of Commons, www.gov.uk/government/speeches/syria-refugees-and-counter-terrorism-prime-ministers-statement.

> Both Junaid Hussain and Reyaad Khan were British nationals based in Syria who were involved in actively recruiting ISIL sympathizers and seeking to orchestrate specific and barbaric attacks against the West, including directing a number of planned terrorist attacks right here in Britain, such as plots to attack high profile public commemorations, including those taking place this summer.

The language used by David Cameron to identify the attacks planned by Reyaad Khan remained indeterminate and the justification focused on the role played by Junaid Hussain and Reyaad Khan within ISIS. Of course, the requirements of national security might explain the lack of clarity and precision of official pronouncements on such matters, but only partly. In fact, the UK government later explicitly made it clear that "it favours a more flexible approach to the meaning of 'imminence', to include an ongoing threat of a terrorist attack from an identified individual who has both the intent and the capability to carry out such an attack without notice."[67] Indeed, in his 2017 speech at the International Institute for Strategic Studies, Attorney General the Hon. Jeremy Wright QC MP referred directly to the Bethlehem Principles and insisted on Principle 8 as endorsed by the British government:

> Another observation by Sir Daniel, as part of Principle 8 addressing imminence, also warrants comment, namely:
> "[t]he absence of specific evidence of where an attack will take place or of the precise nature of an attack does not preclude a conclusion that an armed attack is imminent for purposes of the exercise of a right of self-defense, provided that there is a reasonable and objective basis for concluding that an armed attack is imminent."
> This statement reflects and draws upon what has been a settled position of successive British Governments. Sir Daniel's formulation must be right. In a world where a small number of committed plotters may be seeking to inspire, enable and direct attacks around the world, and indeed have a proven track record of doing so, we will not always know where and when an attack will take place, or the precise nature of the attack.[68]

This explicit reference to the Bethlehem Principles confirms that the UK has endorsed a position to respond proactively to a "continuous imminent threat" by looking backwards at an accumulation of events revealing the hostile intent of a terrorist network.

[67] House of Lords and House of Commons' Joint Committee on Human Rights, HL Paper 141, HC 574, May 10, 2016, 45, §3.33.

[68] Rt. Hon Jeremy Wright QC MP, Attorney General's Speech at the International Institute for Strategic Studies.

By accepting that the use of force against terrorists cannot depend on the identification of a precise armed attack, self-defense is not only dematerialized and focused on individuals as previously shown but also takes *de facto* an anticipatory turn. Even if preventive self-defense is still officially widely rejected, the acceptance of one of the previous propositions almost automatically affects the following propositions, through a cascade effect. The extension of the *ratione personae* condition affects the *ratione materiae* condition, which in turn impacts on the *ratione temporis* requirement in a way that no-one currently or fully admits. In the last instance, it is the *ratione conditionis* requirement, namely, the "necessity and proportionality criteria,"[69] that is reconfigured around the objective of targeting hostile individuals.

Even though the conditions of proportionality and necessity are not expressly mentioned in Article 51 of the UN Charter, their existence under customary law has constantly been reinstated by the ICJ.[70]

[69] Corten, "The 'Unwilling or Unable' Test," 421: "acceptance of preventive self-defence would consecrate the return to the 'law of necessity' that the Charter was devised to stamp out; the risk of abuse is greater when preventive self-defense makes the proportionality criterion inoperative." UN Doc. A/C.6/SR.413 (Czechoslovakia), November 3, 1954, para. 11.

[70] ICJ, Judgment of June 27, 1986, Nicaragua case, merits, para. 194. See also ICJ, Professor M. Brownlie, Audience Publique en l'affaire des activités armées sur le territoire du Congo, Translation, CR 2005/7, April 18, 2005, 31, para. 82. In this case, the US defended the forcible measures they had taken against Nicaragua. The main offensive that US measures were supposed to halt had occurred seven months before the US measures produced their first effects. Therefore, the Court decided that the measures were not necessary. ICJ, November 6, 2003, Oil Platforms case, paras. 73–7. In Oil Platforms, the Court concluded that the use of force did not lead to any military benefit for the US. The judges underlined the fact that the use of force was not even thought to be necessary by the US. Finally, see ICJ, Uganda v. DRC in which the Democratic Republic of Congo argued against Uganda on the basis that Uganda had not exhausted all peaceful means before actually using force. Therefore, according to the DRC, it was not necessary to use force. Uganda, for its part, argued that the criterion of exhaustion of peaceful means is not a proper definition of necessity, which only implies that "the conduct remains within the appropriate purpose." The ICJ first decided that according to the facts of the case no prior armed attack had been proven; therefore, the judges did not need to discuss the question of necessity. It should be emphasized that in this case, the ICJ was not faced with a threat of an armed attack, or in other words to the anticipatory use of force. If it had been the case, it is most likely that even in the absence of an armed attack that had actually occurred, the Court would have decided seeing whether the conditions of necessity and proportionality of the use of force to repel the threatening armed attack were actually met. Then, the Court addressed the series of transborder attacks, which according to Uganda amounted to an armed attack and gave rise to the right of self-defense. The Court analyzed the necessity of the use of force, even though it pointed out that the series of transborder attacks mentioned by Uganda did not reach the threshold

Traditionally, the principle of necessity requires that the state attacked – or threatened with imminent attack – must not have had any means of halting the attack other than recourse to armed force. The principle of proportionality entails that the attacked or threatened state must not have had any means to halt the attack other than recourse to *this scale* of armed force. If the attack could have been halted by using force on a lesser scale, the response is disproportionate. Under the ICJ case law, the use of force cannot be considered a self-defense measure when it is used by the state to pursue an aim that goes *beyond* the objective of halting and repelling an armed attack, for instance, to protect perceived security interests. In other words, the whole necessity and proportionality test revolves around the armed attack. To use our lexicon, it is based on the analysis of 'material circumstances'.

The temporal and material changes of self-defense automatically transform what is meant by necessity and proportionality. Indeed, if there is no identified armed attack in relation to which force should be necessary and proportional, these requirements cannot be based on such an attack. The tests are *de facto* impossible to conduct in relation to tangible or at least identified or expected material circumstances. Thus, the change from a material use of self-defense (i.e., to halt and repel an identified attack) to an individualized self-defense (i.e., to eliminate an individual posing a continuing imminent threat) means that the requirements of necessity and proportionality are not just affected in scope like the other limitations to self-defense but rather in nature.

The dematerialization of self-defense directly entails a proportionality test which differs from the evaluation of correspondence between the scope and intensity of the response to the (prospective assessment of the) harm caused by the armed attack. As Tams and Devaney rightly noted in 2012, accepting the idea of imminent threat already meant an evolution in the proportionality test toward a more prospective comparison of the scope and intensity of the response to the threat posed by the armed attack.[71] The more prospective the test, the more exacerbated the difference between the intensity of the response and that of the armed attack. But what is missing in the available analysis of how proportionality

expected for an armed attack to be characterized in accordance with Article 51 of the UN Charter. The ICJ concluded that the riposte, the use of force "many hundreds of kilometers from Uganda's border," was not necessary.

[71] Tams and Devaney, "Applying Necessity and Proportionality to Anti-Terrorist Self-Defence," 102.

adapts to a new reality is the detachment of the proportionality test from any precisely identified armed attack. When self-defense is used in the "absence of specific evidence of where an attack will take place or of the precise nature of an attack,"[72] to eliminate "plotters [who] may be seeking to inspire, enable and direct attacks around the world, and indeed have a proven track record of doing so,"[73] the test cannot consist of measuring (even in a prospective way) the harm caused by an abstract threat.

Instead, several states have shown readiness to accept that force be used in self-defense to weaken non-state armed groups.[74] And this is a direct consequence of the dematerialization and individualization of the use of force against terrorists. As a result, the restraining function of *ad bellum* proportionality is even more limited when the scope and intensity of the use of force are compared with the general threat posed by a transnational terrorist group or network. The proportionality test, thus defined, will solely involve the evaluation of circumstances such as (i) the intensity of the threat generally posed by the group to which the target is affiliated; and (ii) the role played by the specific individual in the group (eliminating an individual may prove excessive if this individual is a very low value member of the group).

4.2 Drones: Tailor-Made Machines for Individualized Warfare

Transnational terrorist groups have been described in Chapter 3 as calling, according to some states, for a systemic individualization of war.[75] Such an enemy, the narrative goes, cannot be successfully fought without accepting and responding to its dispersed nature and thus, without focusing on the members of the group individually. Simultaneously, because of the new modes of organization and action

72 Bethlehem, "Self-Defense against an Imminent."

73 Rt. Hon. Jeremy Wright QC MP, Attorney General's Speech at the International Institute for Strategic Studies.

74 On Turkey's Operation Sun, see Tom Ruys, "Quo Vadit Jus ad Bellum? A Legal Analysis of Turkey's Military Operations against the PKK in Northern Iraq" (2008) 12 *Melbourne Journal of International Law* 334–64, 334. On Israel's intervention in Lebanon, see UN Doc. A/60/937-S/2006/515, Letter sent to the Security Council dated July 12, 2006; Yaël Ronen, "The 2006 Conflict in Lebanon" (2008) 9 *Yearbook of International Humanitarian Law* 362–93.

75 See chapter 1, "Transnational Terrorist Networks, Calling for a Systemic Individualization of War."

used by the enemy, and also because new technological tools allow strategists to do otherwise, the idea is that states involved in the fight against jihadist terrorism should not have to wait to identify a specific armed attack in order to use force, but instead should be able to identify and eliminate individuals with a hostile intent.[76]

The technological capabilities of drones allow states to develop this strategy to the fullest; they can be used to facilitate a war conducted against a wide range of individuals and with the aim of anticipating threats. This objective of anticipation requires being in control of time, which in this context means to possess knowledge. Indeed, the characteristics of drone programs go beyond the capacity to target, as they also facilitate the aggregation of knowledge on individuals and, allegedly, the identification of the threat they may pose.

Drones are data machines: they involve a surveillance apparatus that allows a persistent collection of intelligence.[77] This surveillance apparatus is composed of premier satellite surveillance, capable of intercepting signal communications, collecting huge amounts of data, tracking enemies on various and distant territories for hours, and selecting and following targets. Today, unmanned aerial vehicles (UAVs) are able to collect several types of intelligence from the air such as signal intelligence (SIGINT) and image intelligence. Utilizing satellite communication links,

[76] Bethlehem, "Self-Defense against an Imminent," 770, 773. Bethlehem's considerations on "imminence," which according to him does not require "specific evidence of where an attack will take place or of the precise nature of an attack" and rather, on the importance of tracing a "concerted pattern of activity" clearly supports my observation that material circumstances revealing an actual or forthcoming armed attack are considered by some as too demanding. Instead, it implies that a hostile intent is sufficient to act in self-defense. Jeremy Wright, UK Attorney General's Speech at the International Institute for Strategic Studies:

> In a world where a small number of committed plotters may be seeking to inspire, enable and direct attacks around the world, and indeed have a proven track record of doing so, we will not always know where and when an attack will take place, or the precise nature of the attack. But where the evidence supports an assessment that an attack is imminent it cannot be right that a state is prevented from meeting its first duty of protecting its citizens without nailing down the specific target and timing of an attack. Apart from anything else, our enemies will not always have fixed plans. They are often opportunists.

Quoted by and supported by Senator the Hon. George Brandis QC, Attorney General of Australia, "The Right of Self-Defence."

[77] Jeremy Scahill and The Intercept, *The Assassination Complex: Inside the Government's Secret Drone Warfare Program* (Simon & Schuster, 2016), 44.

UAVs acquire real-time imagery beyond the line-of-sight, which means that their radio communications capabilities allow them to connect with systems that are normally too distant or too obscured by the terrain specificities (weather situations, geological landform). For this reason, UAVs "have replaced satellites and manned aircraft as the favored platform for intelligence collection."[78] In countries where drones have not yet been armed, UAVs are already the first source of intelligence in external operations.

Following the surveillance step, drones' technological capacities facilitate the "fixing" and "finishing" parts of the process. Thanks to the black boxes that are attached to them (known in the US as Gilgamesh), drones are equipped with metadata analysis and cell-phone tracking technologies.[79] Each drone is equipped with a geolocation device that locates the SIM cards of potential targets as the drone circles. These black boxes give drones minute geolocation capacities that greatly enhance their power to find and fix targets. In addition to the black box device attached to UAVs, US drones have devices on the ground that relay GPS data to the drone,[80] to other data collection tools such as the human intelligence collection (HUMINT),[81] and to mini and micro drones operating at lower altitudes.[82] To the end of "finishing" the target, drones carry a multi-spectral targeting system, which comprises a set of powerful visual sensors for targeting: an infrared sensor, a color/monochrome daylight TV camera, an image-intensified TV camera, a laser range-finder/designator, and a laser illuminator. In addition, US MQ-9 Reaper drones are equipped with Air-to-Ground Missile-114 Hellfire missiles, which is the primary air-to-ground precision weapon.

Unlike traditional airplanes, which were not designed with such an objective in mind, drones guarantee a permanent presence in several ways. First, they allow an economy of means – especially of ground

[78] Gabriel Margolis, "The Lack of HUMINT: A Recurring Intelligence Problem" (2013) 4 *Global Security Studies* 2, 43–60, 54.

[79] Jeremy Scahill and Glenn Greenwald, "Death by Metadata," in Jeremy Scahill and The Staff of The Intercept (eds.), *The Assassination Complex: Inside the Government's Secret Drone Warfare Program* (Simon & Schuster, 2016), 96–107.

[80] In the US, one of them is called ARTeMIS for Aerial Reconnaissance Tetraotor Mobile Intelligence System. See, William Arkin, *Unmanned: Drones, Data, and the Illusion of Perfect Warfare* (Little, Brown, 2015), 23; "Ground Unit," *ESD ARTeMIS*, April 30, 2014, https://esdartemis.wordpress.com/.

[81] Arkin, *Unmanned: Drones, Data*, 10. HUMINT has been devalued in the face of technical collection's capacity to infiltrate denied physical spaces.

[82] Arkin, *Unmanned: Drones, Data*, 14.

refueling. The Reaper drone, for instance, can stay airborne for up to fourteen hours fully loaded and about twenty-four hours in total. General Atomics' updated drone, the Certifiable Predator B, is a turboprop-powered drone that can spend forty hours airborne. Second, through a warden system, drones can ensure a 24/7 presence for each relevant area. The French Senate emphasized that this capacity offers the perspective of permanent (and discrete) presence of drones, as facilitating an unprecedented control of time and space, and an essential understanding of the situation on the ground where the presence of the enemy is transient and hidden among civilians.[83] Third, the fact that drone pilots operate their vehicles remotely makes permanence possible, as it overcomes physiological constraints. Retired US Air Force General Moseley insists on how the capacity to "launch a UAV from a remote field on the other side of the globe, then pilot that aircraft from a base in the United States [. . .] offer[s] unprecedented flexibility to combatant commanders worldwide."[84] Finally, UAVs have a low maximum cruising speed of around 230 mph (200 knots), and thereby ensure that each specific area is continuously covered.[85]

Some commentators have deduced from nongovernmental reports on civilian casualties resulting from drone strikes that drones' technological capabilities are not sufficiently precise to distinguish between civilians and combatants. However, this conclusion is incomplete. These casualties are not so much the result of a technical defect but rather of states defining legitimate targets in an over-inclusive manner. By all accounts, there is a broad gap between official assessments of such casualties and nongovernmental reports on civilian casualties resulting from drone airstrikes. For instance, in 2011, then senior counterterrorism advisor John Brennan argued that "for the [previous] year, there ha[d]n't been a single collateral death because of the exceptional proficiency, precision of

[83] French Senate, "Drones d'observation et drones armés: un enjeu de souveraineté," Rapport d'information de MM. Cédric Perrin, co-président, Gilbert Roger, co-président, Jean-Marie Bockel et Raymond Vall, fait au nom de la commission des affaires étrangères, de la défense et des forces armées, no. 559 (2016–17), May 23, 2017, www.senat.fr/espace_presse/actualites/201705/les_drones_dans_les_forces_armees.html.

[84] "'Reaper' Moniker Given to MQ-9 Unmanned Aerial Vehicle," *U.S. Air Force*, September 14, 2006, www.af.mil/News/Article-Display/Article/129780/reaper-moniker-given-to-mq-9-unmanned-aerial-vehicle/.

[85] "MQ-9 Reaper," September 23, 2015, www.af.mil/About-Us/Fact-Sheets/Display/Article/104470/mq-9-reaper/.

the capabilities that [they had] been able to develop."[86] On the other hand, for the year 2010 in Pakistan alone, 89 to 197 civilian deaths were reported as a result of US CIA-led drone strikes.[87] As is shown throughout the book, and particularly in Chapter 5, this difference in data, rather than revealing the limits of the technological tool, flows from a conceptual disagreement: The largest number of civilian casualties reflects a restrictive interpretation of who can be lawfully targeted, and the smallest number reflects an extensive interpretation thereof. In other words, drones do allow drone operators to target who they intend to kill, it is the framework they use to identify legitimate targets that is very inclusive.[88]

On the contrary, on the technical level, "from Desert Storm through Kosovo to Iraq 2006 and into [sic.] the current day, whether the task is synchronizing or searching deeper, the black box has grown smaller and smaller as the individual and minute target has also shrunk, all while operating on a larger and larger battlefield."[89] The capacity of geolocation devices that allows the machine to find individual cell phones even when they are not in use or when the caller does not answer,[90] the set of black boxes placed on aircrafts and on the ground, collecting intelligence and working together with the drones as a network, and all the capacities mentioned here not only facilitated the desired strategic change, but also intensified it, by prioritizing it as the way of using force. This does not mean that drones' technological capabilities caused the military strategy focused on individuals – considering that this strategic objective was at the heart of the scientific research on how to improve the technology for the past decades – but rather that drones made the implementation of such a strategy possible, including because the drone technology made the legal rationales associated to anticipatory use of force appear more acceptable. In Arkin's words, the military "has been transformed and become hyper precise, but it also has become able to do only one thing: drill down to the individual – a terrorist, a car, an armored vehicle, a

[86] Remarks of John O. Brennan, Assistant to the President for Homeland Security and Counterterrorism, on Ensuring al-Qa'ida's Demise – As Prepared for Delivery, *The White House*, June 29, 2010, https://obamawhitehouse.archives.gov/the-press-office/2011/06/29/remarks-john-o-brennan-assistant-president-homeland-security-and-counter.

[87] TBIJ, "Pakistan: Reported US Strikes 2010," www.thebureauinvestigates.com/drone-war/data/obama-2010-pakistan-strikes.

[88] Extensive enmity will be explored in more detail in Chapter 5.

[89] Arkin, *Unmanned: Drones, Data*, 183–4.

[90] Dana Priest and William M. Arkin, *Top Secret America: The Rise of the New American Security State* (New York: Back Bay Books, 2011), 242.

window in an office, the most hidden or fragile heart or brain of a machine or a network."[91]

In fact, the only two scenarios under which drone strikes are conducted are inherently centered on individuals. As was already mentioned in Chapter 1, drone strikes are either conducted as personality strikes against individuals appearing on a kill list because of their specific attributes,[92] or as signature strikes against individuals demonstrating an insurgent pattern of life, and suspicious behavior suggesting engagement in militant activity.[93] As reported by The Intercept, according to one of their sources, the target is always an individual person: "[E]very mission that is triggered begins as an objective to find one person for whatever reason."[94] Both drone strike scenarios align with the proposed interpretation of the material condition of self-defense. First, signature strikes are based on a suspicion of affiliation to a group identified as having a hostile intent and this suspicion is deduced by contextual or behavioral elements, such as an unusual feature in the pattern of life of the target. Second, drones are used as targeted killings against individuals who have not necessarily been witnessed as preparing imminent attacks, but rather as belonging to a group having perpetrated attacks in the past and/or showing signs that they might commit attacks in the future.[95]

Even in the UK, where the government says that it does not have a "targeted killing policy" focused on individuals, the UK Parliamentary Joint Committee on Human Rights concluded in its 2016 Report on the government policy on the use of drones for targeted killings that although they understand why the government does not want to call its policy a "targeted killing policy," its "policy on the use of lethal force outside of areas of armed conflict does contemplate the possibility of pre-identified individuals being killed by the State."[96] In the US, we know that the targeting process is facilitated by the existence of a "disposition matrix," a database that associates the names of suspected terrorists with

[91] Arkin, *Unmanned: Drones, Data*, 18.

[92] Alston, "Report of the Special Rapporteur," A/HRC/14/24/Add.6.

[93] Ibid.; Scahill and The Intercept, *The Assassination Complex*, 56; Grégoire Chamayou, *Théorie du drone* (La Fabrique éditions, 2013).

[94] Ryan Devereaux, "Manhunting in the Hindu Kush," in Jeremy Scahill and The Staff of The Intercept (eds.), *The Assassination Complex: Inside the Government's Secret Drone Warfare Program* (Simon & Schuster, 2016), 158.

[95] Alston, Report of the Special Rapporteur, §40.

[96] UK Joint Committee on Human Rights, Report on the Government's Policy on the Use of Drones for Targeted Killings, May 10, 2016, HC 574, HL Paper 141.

the resources being used to track them down.[97] This database collects real-time data on the specific individuals who interest the US. A nominating agency prepares a profile for each individual chosen for lethal action on the basis of all relevant disseminated information, "as well as any other information needed to present as comprehensive and thorough a profile of the individual as possible."[98]

France is an interesting example of how military strategy and technological tools interact, as it has shown signs of the individualization of decisions to use force in the Sahel. Former French President François Hollande admitted having personally authorized targeted killings in Syria and revealed the existence, beyond the Syrian situation, of a French hit list.[99] In this context, it was reported that the French military and the General Directorate for External Security have killed at least forty "High Value Targets" in Mali between 2012 and 2016.[100] This number corresponds to an average of one targeted killing per month. In 2015 and 2016, state officials confirmed France's targeted killing practice before the Parliamentary Commission.[101]

Beyond French state practice, the list of intelligence and communication systems that appears in the French law on military programming for 2019–2025 officially enacts French involvement in the era of data warfare.[102] The law insists that technological innovations have to be acquired and adapted to evolving threats, in particular combat aerial vehicles. French drones will be connected to data collection and

[97] Greg Miller, "Plan for Hunting Terrorists Signals U.S. Intends to Keep Adding Names to Kill Lists," *The Washington Post*, October 23, 2012, www.washingtonpost.com/world/national-security/plan-for-hunting-terrorists-signals-us-intends-to-keep-adding-names-to-kill-lists/2012/10/23/4789b2ae-18b3-11e2-a55c-39408fbe6a4b_story.html?hpid=z1&utm_term=.1143e2137871.

[98] Presidential Policy Guidance, "Procedures for Approving Direct Action against Terrorist Targets Located Outside the United States and Areas of Active Hostilities," May 22, 2013.

[99] Gérard Davet and Fabrice Lhomme (Interviews with President Hollande), *Un président ne devrait pas dire ça … les secrets d'un quinquennat* (Stock, French and European Publications Inc., 2016).

[100] Vincent Nouzille, *Erreurs fatales: Comment nos présidents ont failli face au terrorisme* (Fayard, Kindle Edition) location 426–7.

[101] See, for example, Audition, à huis clos, de M. Didier Le Bret, coordonnateur national du renseignement (CNR), May 18, 2016. One should note that like its American allies, France underlined that the capture option was preferred over the kill one.

[102] Statute, LOI no. 2018-607 du 13 juillet 2018 relative à la programmation militaire pour les années 2019 à 2025 et portant diverses dispositions intéressant la défense, (hereafter "Law on Military Programming"), Annexed Report, www.legifrance.gouv.fr/affichTexteArticle.do;jsessionid=3FA2F16A0C2BB9FE57FC2FBF9968154D.tplgfr33s_3?idArticle=LEGIARTI000037194585&cidTexte=JORFTEXT000037192797&dateTexte=20190413&categorieLien=id&oldAction=&nbResultRech=.

communication systems both of other drone machines and of robots on the ground,[103] and will be capable of lethal action.[104] From DESCARTES, to SYRACUSE IV, or Successeur MELCHIOR, to CONTACT, SCORPION, OMEGA, ASTRIDE, RIFAN, SIOC, SIA, GEODE, and ISSAN, the law marked the modernization of the means of communication of the military by the implementation of these new (and multiple) data collection networks to ensure "informational superiority."[105] Overall, the French example is interesting because it allows testing the above-mentioned hypothesis that, although drones do not initiate the individualization of warfare or cause a strategic change in that direction, their technological capacities intensify the individualization of war.

Not only do drones appear to correspond to the conduct of an individualized kind of warfare, but they also facilitate and intensify it, and they also somehow provide a strong incentive for embracing some of the legal changes initially proposed by the Obama administration and progressively adopted elsewhere. The proposed interpretation of the right of self-defense described above not only corresponds to the individualization of the use of force facilitated by drone programs but also makes it appear more acceptable. In a context where behavior could not be scrutinized from a distance, until the least accessible areas, in a context where no tool would allow the surveillance of the subject's lifestyle, habits, communication, and movements, the proposed extension of the right of self-defense would not appear as acceptable as it now is. If such

[103] LOI no. 2018-607 du 13 juillet 2018 relative à la programmation militaire pour les années 2019 à 2025 et portant diverses dispositions intéressant la défense, Article 65, §3.2.1:

> Les programmes d'armement qui seront lancés d'ici à 2025 permettront de faire face à l'évolution des menaces notamment celles que font à nouveau peser les États puissances. A cette fin, les programmes intégreront des technologies innovantes adaptées. En particulier, l'autonomisation des systèmes constitue un axe important de modernisation et d'innovation des capacités. Ainsi, les programmes de drones aériens (comme le drone MALE européen ou le système de drones aéromaritimes embarqués SDAM), le système de guerre des mines futur (SLAMF) ou encore les robots du domaine terrestre intégrés aux systèmes d'information et de communication infovalorisés du programme SCORPION apporteront des concepts entièrement nouveaux fondés sur la collaboration entre des plateformes et des systèmes de drones. Ces nouveaux systèmes seront intégrés aux capacités actuelles afin d'en améliorer la performance globale.

[104] Ibid., §3.2.1.4: "Les systèmes aéroportés de « drones aériens » poursuivront leur montée en puissance avec la mise en service des drones REAPER qui seront dotés de la capacité à délivrer des armements."

[105] "Law on Military Programming."

advanced technological capacities were not available, the idea that it could be lawful to target individuals not identified as preparing a forthcoming armed attack on the basis of the right of self-defense would not be as admissible to the same extent. Conversely, the extended version of the right of self-defense appears to be an acceptable framework for anticipating threats, even in the absence of an identified armed attack, in a world where drones' technological capacities combine the necessary elements to ensure persistent scrutiny of individuals and data collection. Besides, because drone strikes are preceded by a process of close-up surveillance of specific individuals, and have the capacity to precisely target, this gives the impression that the intrusion of state sovereignty is limited in comparison to more traditional uses of force. Indeed, individualized warfare and precise technological capacities may give the idea that contemporary warfare is less intrusive and, as such, does not need to establish a close link of attribution, or even attributability, between the members of transnational terrorist networks and their host state(s). In the light of these different factors – drones' technological capacities, the emergence of a new type of non-state actor, and the military strategy to fight transnational enemy groups – the initial strict necessity of linking the targets to the host state might appear practically and legally irrelevant to an increasing number of actors.

4.3 Concluding Remarks

This chapter highlights the interaction between technology, military strategy, and the law, and reveals how the evolution of the right of self-defense against transnational terrorist networks legitimizes and facilitates new military strategies, a use of force detached from material threats and focused on individual hostile intentions. It also demonstrates how this military strategy and the chain of legal propositions attached to it become more acceptable in light of drone technologies. The rationale, strategy, and technology of drone programs invite the operating state to observe the intimacy of people's daily lives, collect data on them including by tracking cell phones, and strike with precision[106] what operating

[106] The Intercept, The Drone Papers, September 2015, https://theintercept.com/drone-papers/; Arkin, *Unmanned: Drones, Data*; Rosa Brooks, *How Everything Became War and the Military Became Everything* (Simon & Schuster, 2016); Ian Shaw, *Predator Empire: Drone Warfare and Full Spectrum Dominance* (University of Minnesota Press,

states frame as a Hydra-headed dispersed enemy that calls for a change in military strategy.

As such, drone programs materialize the possibility of a full-fledged individualized warfare and pave the way for the dematerialization of the right of self-defense. Such a shift in the object of the use of force in self-defense, results in a metamorphosis of the principle of proportionality, from a material use of force in self-defense (i.e., to repel an identified attack) toward an individualized self-defense (i.e., to eliminate an individual posing a continuing imminent threat) against transnational terrorist networks. By providing the opportunity to collect individualized data, and behavioral scrutiny on an almost permanent basis and in areas that are virtually inaccessible, drone programs could almost make the legal opportunity to target individuals for their hostile intent acceptable, even if they are not preparing a threatening imminent attack. As a result, the *de facto* opportunity to individualize the conduct of warfare and the associated legal authorization to do so extensively through a revised *jus ad bellum* framework, at least partly explain the phenomenon of extension of enmity in today's war on terror.

Because the only question that seems to matter is, "Is this individual an enemy?," the next two chapters enter the *jus in bello* paradigm to demonstrate that the armed conflict is progressively extended to groups that have no or little link with the group initially fought. The extension of self-defense and the metamorphosis of proportionality caused by the extension of the other conditions of self-defense also reveals the overlap between *jus ad bellum* and *jus in bello* proportionality. Force is used outside so-called situations of active hostilities and is hence justified under an *ad bellum* rationale in a way that is systemic; first, because the same set of justifications can be articulated for each drone strike, and second, because this set of justifications rests on the general threat posed by members of a transnational terrorist network.

Although the lawfulness of a situation under *jus ad bellum* does not determine its lawfulness under *jus in bello*, the conditions under which a use of force is accepted in the first place have an impact on the kind of situation that results from this use. In the same vein, the purpose of the resulting situation of sustained violence is to target individuals who,

2016); Drone Warfare, *The Bureau of Investigative Journalism*, www.thebureauinvestigates.com/projects/drone-war.

based on all of the contextual and behavioral evidence, have a risk profile, rather than fighting an enemy who perpetrates actual hostile acts. As we will see, this kind of military operation is supported by a new version of direct participation in hostilities. Drone programs, for their part, go hand in hand with the contemporary objective of mastering time to such an extent that war is expected to consist in the prevention and deterrence of military action by the enemy.

5

Endless Wars

> The loss of the bounded battlefield makes time the essential element. Without any spatial constraints one cannot know where to expect war; one must, therefore, be aware of things as they happen everywhere. In addition, success is guaranteed by speed; acting too late is the same as defeat. The goal is to have knowledge of events and act upon that knowledge before they happen. The quest is to create, in the words of the former director of force transformation, an "inevitable military Leviathan." By already being everywhere, and by the "unblinking eye" being able to act at any time, a sort of pre-emptive deterrence is the goal. Future events will not happen because the opponent knows that the Leviathan will know and act before the opponent's deed can have effect. The event will never materialize. This is what "deterring forward" is about.[1]

For those states most active in the war on terror, action consists in detecting future events before they occur. This objective has three components. First, it means that action is taken wherever the enemy is. In order to pursue this objective, those states not only exploit the absence of geographical criteria to delineate armed conflicts in space as will be demonstrated in Chapter 6. From a strategic point of view, it means that whoever poses this threat must be targeted: if the threat is posed by a number of individuals that increases over time, enmity is extended to those individuals. This is true even if they act in the name of a terrorist group that did not exist when the conflict started. From a legal point of view, such a strategy is facilitated by the uncertainties related to the temporal delineation of conflicts. Second, the objective of addressing future threats means taking action against individuals who are not presently perpetrating hostile acts. This practice requires that the traditional interpretation of direct participation in hostilities (DPH) be

[1] Kristian Søby Kristensen, "Tourists or Vagabonds? Space and Time in the War on Terror" (2008) 33 *Alternatives* 249–66.

subject to a temporal change. Instead of suspending the protection of civilians only at the moment when – and for such time as – they engage in acts that reach a certain threshold of harm, targeting enemies on the basis of the threat they pose requires that DPH is extended not only to preparatory acts but also to signs indicating belonging to a group. This shift is supported by the notion of continuous combat function as currently defined.

This chapter explores how the law – its uncertainties and its new interpretations – can authorize the extension of enmity that takes place first of all factually to three types of targets. It will study the fact that the US and France consider that the group initially identified as the enemy group (let us call it the "nuclear group") can subsume members of the broader network, but also individuals located outside areas of active hostilities, and members of terrorist groups that spring up over time that states fight together with the nuclear group. These "extended enemies" might present very loose or no link with the nuclear group, and commentators or states might establish their affiliation to the nuclear group only posthumously.[2] Individuals located outside areas of active hostilities could be deemed to have a link with either the nuclear group, its broader network, or a new terrorist group. They are located and sometimes targeted at distance from areas of active hostilities, in Yemen, Pakistan, and Somalia, on the basis of their suspicious behavior. As already analyzed, suspicion can arise from different kinds of sources (telephone data, movements, location, change in pattern of life, etc.).

The case of individuals taking action in Western states is different because states' narrative for targeting them does not fully use the *jus in bello* language and, as such, it will be excluded from the scope of analysis. These individuals are generally targeted by the host state police forces *during* and *because of* their use of force; their (loose) connection with the terrorist group is only established posthumously. Instead, it is the threat to life posed by the individuals at the moment of action that makes them subject to the use of lethal force by the operating state. We cannot rule out, however, that if they appear during the search on national soil as being affiliated directly or indirectly to a terrorist group, the host state targets them as enemies under a *jus in bello* language.[3]

[2] Olivier Roy, *Le Djihad et la Mort* (Seuil, 2016).

[3] This hypothesis is substantiated by several political speeches, such as the speech delivered by President François Hollande on November 16, 2015, in front of Congress, after the second Paris attacks and which opened with the following statement (https://il.ambafrance

How does the extension of enmity to individuals beyond the nuclear group and beyond areas and actual moments of hostilities occur? When states strike targets where and when there are no active hostilities, how do they identify their enemies? Who are these individuals, and what did states identify in their behavior or in the context to trigger their characterization as enemies?

One could settle for the following remarks: states cannot just amalgamate different terrorist groups into a single non-international armed conflict when those groups show major differences and little cohesiveness.[4] Another point could be that states cannot aggregate to the enemy group any individual across the world who allegedly acts in their name of such groups, but who has little or no contact at all with this group and who are not targeted for their ongoing and apparent engagement in military operations.[5] However, while it may be valid, such reactions are

.org/Attentats-a-Paris-Discours-de-M-Francois-Hollande-president-de-la-Republique, our translation from the original version):

> France is at war. The acts perpetrated on Friday night in Paris and near the Stade de France are acts of war. They caused at least 129 deaths and a great many casualties. They consist of an act of aggression against our country, against its values, against its youth, against its way of life. They are the result of a jihadist army, the group Daesh that fights against us because France is a country of freedom, because we are the country of Human Rights.

Had the perpetrators been identified as individuals motivated or inspired by the ideology of Daesh at the time of the attack, it is likely that the French authorities would have used a *jus in bello* narrative to explain the killing of some of the perpetrators. If we read between the lines, this is actually the implicit message conveyed by Hollande when characterizing the events as acts of war a posteriori.

[4] Noam Lubell, "The War (?) against Al-Qaeda," in E. Wilmshurst (ed.), *International Law and the Classification of Conflicts* (Oxford University Press, 2012), 421–54, 436; Geoffrey Corn, "Making the Case for Conflict Bifurcation in Afghanistan: Transnational Armed Conflict, Al Qaeda, and the Limits of the Associated Militia Concept," Special issue in Michael N. Schmitt (ed.), *The War in Afghanistan: A Legal Analysis* (2009) 85 *International Law Studies* 182–218. For a deep analysis of the evolving narrative of modern co-belligerency theory and contestation of the assumption that co-belligerency is a well-established principle, see Rebecca Ingber, "Co-Belligerency" (2017) 42 *The Yale Journal of International Law* 1, 68–120.

[5] Marco Sassòli, "Transnational Armed Groups and International Humanitarian Law," *Program on Humanitarian Policy and Conflict Research* (Harvard, Occasional Paper Series, 2006, no. 6), 1–45, 10; Jens David Ohlin, "Targeting Co-belligerents," in Claire Finkelstein, Jens David Ohlin, and Andrew Altman (eds.), *Targeted Killings: Law and Morality in an Asymmetrical World* (Oxford University Press, 2012), 60–89. For an opposite view, see Peter Margulies and Matthew Sinnot, "Crossing Borders to Target Al-Qaeda and Its Affiliates: Defining Networks as Organized Armed Groups in Non-International Armed Conflicts," in T. D. Gill, R. Geiß, R. Heinsch, T. McCormack,

not sufficient or helpful to understand the socio-legal phenomenon at stake. This chapter argues that both norms regulating the conduct of hostilities and the technology and strategy of drone programs allow for the extension of enmity and, thereby, the extension of warfare in time.

There are several elements supporting these arguments. First, the law is ambiguous on the circumstances under which an armed conflict can be considered as having come to an end, or at least on the need to reevaluate the way armed conflict is characterized throughout the conflict in order to address the developments in exactly who states fight. Second, the notion of DPH understood as including temporal and material limitations – only and for such time as someone directly participates in hostilities – is no longer the only existing means of implementing the principle of distinction anymore. Two versions coexist in the legal landscape and they characterize different scenarios. Under the traditional version of DPH, non-state actors can only be targeted *during* the direct participation in harmful belligerent activities, whereas DPH as a continuous combat function opens the door to targeting suspicious behavior, other than the witnessed participation in hostilities. Finally, the technology and the zero-risk strategy of drone programs exploit this legal space for the extension of enmity.

5.1 Infinite Affiliation? The Uncertain Reevaluation of the Conflict Characterization and End of Conflicts

Norms regulating the conduct of hostilities do not set a clear obligation to reevaluate the existence of an armed conflict once it has been established. In the *jus in bello*, there is also an uncertainty on the end of conflicts. These gray areas, inherent to the law, only appear to facilitate extensive warfare under certain factual scenarios. It is the case of armed conflicts taking place in the counterterrorism context as they involve fighting against different groups, some that were initially fought and others who emerged later on. In this context, the extension of enmity does not only pertain to the multiplication of enemy groups over time but also, and maybe more importantly, to the discursive aggregation of these groups and their treatment as part of the same armed conflict. In the US these groups are called "affiliated forces," and in France they are

C. Paulussen, and J. Dorsey (eds.), *Yearbook of International Humanitarian Law* (T. M. C. Asser Press, 2013), 319–45.

named by the generic term "jihadist groups."[6] This aspect of the US and French wars on terror will also be dealt with in Chapter 6 but is useful to have in mind already when considering the temporal scope of these armed conflicts.

The umbrella terms "affiliated forces" in the US and "jihadist groups" in France drove the transformation of warfare from an armed conflict against a specific group, into a fight against a conglomerate of diverse enemy groups. The current French counterterrorism strategy made its first public appearance during parliamentary discussions under François Hollande's presidency and more recently in the law on military programming 2019–2025 under Emmanuel Macron's government. Already under President Hollande's administration – although the rationale was never clearly articulated – statements made by state and military officials suggested that the French military strategy and related (implicit) legal framework were much closer to the US narrative than anyone would like to admit.[7] Insisting on the Hydra-headed character of the threat, French officials affirmed the need for a holistic response irrespective of the enemy's location.[8] Rather than defining those multiple fronts as separate armed conflicts, jihadist groups from Al Qaeda, ISIS, Jabhat al-Nosra to Boko Haram were considered as forming part of the same conflict.[9]

Similarly, the 2018 French law on military programming defines a unique strategy and does not differentiate between conflict situations.[10]

[6] As far as the United Kingdom is concerned, Chapter 2, shows that the apparent dedication to analyzing each situation and non-state armed group separately might in fact reflect the strength of the legislative bodies across the Channel, more than the government's actual definition of the enemy. See Chapters 5 and 6. France's reference to "jihadist groups" framework and the US "Al Qaeda and associated forces" category.

[7] Parliamentary investigation, Commission d'enquête relative aux moyens mis en œuvre par l'État pour lutter contre le terrorisme depuis le 7 janvier 2015, *Comptes rendus*, www2.assemblee-nationale.fr/14/autres-commissions/commissions-d-enquete/moyens-pour-lutter-contre-le-terrorisme/(block)/ComptesRendusCommission/(instance_leg)/14/(init)/0-14.

[8] Parliamentary investigation, Général Pierre de Villiers, chef d'état-major des armées, Commission d'enquête relative aux moyens mis en œuvre par l'État pour lutter contre le terrorisme depuis le 7 janvier 2015, May 9, 2016, Séance de 14 heures, Compte rendu no. 20, Présidence de M. Georges Fenech, Président, www.assemblee-nationale.fr/14/cr-cemoyter/15-16/c1516020.asp#P324_120754.

[9] Ibid.

[10] Statute: Loi no. 2018-607 du 13 juillet 2018 relative à la programmation militaire pour les années 2019 à 2025 et portant diverses dispositions intéressant la défense, www.legifrance.gouv.fr/eli/loi/2018/7/13/ARMX1800503L/jo/texte; see together with Annexed Report to the French Law on Military Programming (it should be noted that it also has legislative value), Rapport annexé (appears at the end of the legislation), www.legifrance.gouv.fr/affichTexte.do?cidTexte=JORFTEXT000037192797&dateTexte=20181122.

The 2017 Strategic Review on Defense and National Security that preceded and influenced the adopted law established that the French military strategy consists in combating jihadist groups – ISIS, Al Qaeda, and the other current regional jihadist movements – which "share the same ideological matrix, Salafist jihadism, and the willingness to destroy the regimes of the Muslim world considered illegitimate, as well as the unholy societies."[11] In an interview given by Minister of Defense Florence Parly to *France 24* in November 2017,[12] when asked whether the French intelligence services were monitoring potential threats in the Sahel, in the Middle East and, more generally, French jihadists at home and abroad, Parly straightforwardly declared:

> You know, we don't really distinguish. This war is waged against terrorists and we don't ask these people for their identity cards, so we act, if I can put it that way, there and everywhere.[13]

This framework goes beyond the US "Al Qaeda and associated forces" framework established by Congress' 2001 Authorization for the Use of Military Force (AUMF).[14] In contrast to the all-inclusiveness of the "jihadist groups" category, the US notion of "associated forces" – albeit overinclusive – put some boundaries to the incorporation of new groups. In 2012, the Obama administration publicly articulated that in order for a group to be recognized and hit as an associated force of Al Qaeda it (1) had to be an organized armed group that (2) aligned itself with Al Qaeda and (3) had to have entered the fight against the United States and its coalition partners.[15]

[11] Strategic Defense Review, Revue stratégique de défense et de sécurité nationale, 2017, www.defense.gouv.fr/dgris/presentation/evenements/revue-strategique-de-defense-et-desecurite-nationale-2017.

[12] French Minister of the Armed Forces Florence Parly: "L'EI est d'ores et déjà en train de redéployer son action," *France 24*, November 15, 2017, www.france24.com/fr/20171511-entretien-florence-parly-etat-islamique-terrorisme-barkhane-g5-sahel.

[13] Translation from French: "Vous savez, nous ne faisons pas vraiment de tri. C'est une guerre qui se mène contre des terroristes et nous ne demandons pas leur carte d'identité à ces gens-là donc nous agissons, si je puis dire, tous azimuts."

[14] US Congress 2001 Authorization for the Use of Military Force (AUMF), www.gpo.gov/fdsys/pkg/PLAW-107publ40/pdf/PLAW-107publ40.pdf.

[15] Remarks by Jeh Charles Johnson, Dean's Lecture at Yale Law School, "National Security Law, Lawyers and Lawyering in the Obama Administration," February 22, 2012.

It should be emphasized that even if the US "associated forces test" performs a restraining function, this function is modest. The case of al-Shabaab is a good example of how it unfolds in practice. In the summer of 2011, the Obama legal team discussed whether al-Shabaab could be considered an associated force of Al Qaeda.[16] After an in-depth analysis of al-Shabaab, Harold Koh, Obama's legal advisor, came to the conclusion that it was not a sufficiently unified well-organized group but rather an association of several factions, led by different militants. As such, Koh considered, al-Shabaab as a whole could not be identified as an associated force of Al Qaeda. Jeh Johnson, a senior government official, entered into a heated debate with Koh, changing his mind several times but most of the time considering that the entire group qualified as an "associated force" of Al Qaeda.[17] In 2016, and contrary to Koh's idea, the decision was made to formally treat al-Shabaab as an associated force of Al Qaeda under the AUMF. This decision was made not because the group appeared to have gained in organization and cohesiveness, but because the context called for it: The US was carrying out an increasing number of strikes in Somalia to defend American personnel deployed there, as well as the African Union and Somali government partner forces.[18] The political pressure was so great and the strikes so numerous that it could not be justified by suspicious individual behavior alone. Al-Shabaab had to be declared an "associated force." For the purpose of our analysis, what can be deduced from this case is that signs of disorganization and lack of coordination between sporadic individual involvement in hostilities of its members do not exclude a group from being characterized as an affiliated force of Al Qaeda.

Al-Shabaab is only one example of the fragility of the link between Al Qaeda and groups deemed to be affiliated to it. Under the AUMF, ISIL is treated as an affiliated force of Al Qaeda, which implies that ISIL has aligned itself with Al Qaeda. Yet, the real story is much more complex and tormented. Jabhat al-Nusra, which was officially established by the

[16] Charlie Savage, *Power Wars: The Relentless Rise of Presidential Authority and Secrecy* (Little, Brown, 2015), 275.

[17] Ibid., 277. Before officially following Johnson's viewpoint in 2016, the administration's strategy was to target only individuals who had also links with Al Qaeda or who were identified to be part of specific plots against US interests. This element should be kept in mind for later discussion.

[18] Ibid.

leader of ISIL, Abu Bakr al-Baghdadi, as the Syrian branch of the Islamic State in Iraq on January 23, 2012, has a second-in-command called Abu Muhammad al-Jawlani.[19] When a disagreement broke out between the two men, al-Jawlani refused to pledge allegiance to Abu Bakr al-Baghdadi and subsequently pledged allegiance to Al Qaeda. Ayman al-Zawahiri, the leader of Al Qaeda, joined sides with al-Jawani and declared that al-Baghdadi's group, ISIL, deviated from Al Qaeda's methodology. Since then, Al Qaeda and ISIL exist side-by-side but certainly do not share aligned strategy and activity. More recently, an additional rupture took place when Jabhat al-Nusra broke with Al Qaeda.[20] In June 2016, Jabhat al-Nusra became Jabhat Fateh al-Sham (JFS). The latter was considered by some as a strawman, a sort of "al-Qaeda in new clothes, comprising the same people and pursuing the same ideological aspirations."[21] But the analysis proved wrong, as thoroughly explained by Tore Refslund Hamming and Pieter Van Ostaeyen. In fact, the rebranding in question reflected al-Jawlani's decision to break with Al Qaeda, to dissociate his group from the international terror campaign and to adopt a local focus. Tensions between jihadist groups are constant.

Given the differences in leadership, in ideology, in methods and goals, it is puzzling that the US considers that these groups have *aligned* with Al Qaeda and are thus affiliated forces.[22] It is equally revealing of the absence of a restraining function played by the associated forces criterion to read, for instance, Senator Richard Burr, chair of the powerful Senate Intelligence Committee, declaring in 2015 that:

> When you look around the world, whether it's Yemen, whether it's Syria, whether it's in Iraq, whether it's in Afghanistan or in North Africa with Boko Haram, we've got terrorist elements that are carrying out terrorist acts and if you put that collection together, what you've got is a war on Western civilization. It really doesn't matter which terrorist group we insert into the blank.

In this context of extensive enmity, international law provides very limited guidance when it comes to ascertaining the end of

[19] Tore Refslund Hamming and Pieter Van Ostaeyen, "The True Story of al-Qaeda's Demise and Resurgence in Syria," *Lawfare*, April 8, 2018, www.lawfareblog.com/true-story-al-qaedas-demise-and-resurgence-syria.

[20] Ibid.

[21] Ibid.

[22] Even more perplexing is the absence of a test similar to the US "affiliated forces test" in France, as far as the public knows, in order to consider these groups as part of the same conflict.

non-international armed conflicts[23] as per Common Article 3 and Additional Protocol II do not contain express provisions concerning the termination of non-international armed conflicts (NIACs). Legal uncertainty on the endpoint of the application of international humanitarian law (IHL) rests on four alternative theories on the end of armed conflicts, identified by Blum, Lewis, and Modirzadeh in their legal briefing "Indefinite War":

- The two-way-ratchet theory: as soon as at least one of the constituent elements of the NIAC – intensity of hostilities or organization of the non-state armed group – ceases to exist;
- The no-more-combat-measures theory: upon the general close of military operations as characterized by the cessation of actions of the armed forces with a view to combat;
- The no-reasonable-risk-of-resumption theory: where there is no reasonable risk of hostilities resuming; and
- The state-of-war-throwback theory: upon the achievement of a peaceful settlement between the formerly warring parties.[24]

Rather than seeing these alternative theories as a list, I suggest picturing them as a spectrum. At the extremes we find, on the one hand, the two-ratchet theory (the constitutive elements of a NIAC are not present anymore) and on the other hand, the no-reasonable-risk-of-resumption theory; in the middle, there is the achievement of a peaceful settlement theory and the no-more-combat-measures theory. The two-ratchet theory gives the assurance of marking the end of conflicts early. First because it includes a test based on factual elements: conflict can end without the subjective decision of the parties in order to resume hostilities through a peaceful settlement. Second, because logically, the conduct of hostilities should in principle reduce both the intensity of hostilities and the organization of a non-state armed group. Simultaneously, according to this theory, conflict can end before parties are in the extreme situation where they cannot conduct combat measures anymore. Overall, according to the two-ratchet theory, the end of hostilities can

[23] Dustin A. Lewis, Gabriella Blum, and Naz K. Modirzadeh, "Indefinite War: Unsettled International Law on the End of Armed Conflict," Harvard Law School Program on International Law and Armed Conflict, Legal Briefing, February 2017, https://pilac.law.harvard.edu/indefinite-war/.

[24] Ibid., 96.

potentially be identified sooner than according to the two other theories in the middle of the spectrum.

On the contrary, the no-reasonable-risk-of-resumption theory can lead to endless warfare, especially if the threshold to assess the absence of reasonable risk is high. First, it supports the continuation of hostilities and the application of IHL even after one or all constituent elements of the NIAC cease to exist, and even after combat has practically stopped. This is also the case for the peaceful settlement according to the ICTY, which in its 1995 Tadić Decision on Interlocutory appeal, declared that:

> On the basis of the foregoing, we find that an armed conflict exists whenever there is a resort to armed force between States or protracted armed violence between governmental authorities and organized armed groups or between such groups within a State. International humanitarian law applies from the initiation of such armed conflicts and extends beyond the cessation of hostilities until a general conclusion of peace is reached; or, in the case of internal conflicts, a peaceful settlement is achieved. Until that moment, international humanitarian law continues to apply in the whole territory of the warring States or, in the case of internal conflicts, the whole territory under the control of a party, whether or not actual combat takes place there.[25]

Second, and more importantly, it accepts the emerging idea among the most active states in the war on terror that conflict against terrorist networks only ends with their destruction is conducive to endless wars. Indeed, this idea could be read as a radical version of the "no-reasonable-risk-of-resumption theory," setting a very high threshold for the reasonableness assessment. When President Trump announced on December 19, 2018 that the US would withdraw its troops from Syria, he emphasized the "large defeat" of ISIS.[26] This declaration might simply mean that his administration considered ISIS incapable of mounting military operations in Syria from then on. In this, it could be seen as following either a moderate version of the "no-reasonable-risk-of-resumption theory" by locating the end of conflicts when the operational capacity of the enemy is degraded to such an extent that there is no reasonable risk that those organizations' forces will attack again; or the "no-more-

[25] ICTY, Prosecutor v. Dusko Tadić a/k/a "Dule," Decision on the Defence Motion for Interlocutory Appeal on Jurisdiction, ICTY Appeals Chamber, IT-94-1-I, October 2, 1995, §70 [hereinafter, "Tadić, Decision on Interlocutory Appeal"].

[26] Mark Landler, Helene Cooper, and Eric Schmitt, "Trump to Withdraw U.S. Forces from Syria, Declaring 'We Have Won Against ISIS'," *The New York Times*, December 19, 2018, www.nytimes.com/2018/12/19/us/politics/trump-syria-turkey-troop-withdrawal.html.

combat-measure theory" providing that war ends when actions of the armed forces with a view to combat have ended. On the contrary, some of the reactions that followed Trump's decision were quite alarmist and upheld that troops should remain in Syria because ISIS had not been eradicated and there was still a risk that hostilities might resume. In other words, the idea was that US troops should remain even if ISIS troops had been overpowered in order to avoid the resurgence of the latter.

In the wake of Trump's announcement, among the other state forces present in Syria, some state officials dissociated themselves from the President's decision. The British Defence Minister insisted that ISIS was "very much alive."[27] The French Minister of the Armed Forces Florence Parly acknowledged that the group had been significantly weakened, but that the battle was not over, because the "Islamic State has not been wiped from the map, nor have its roots. The last pockets of this terrorist organization must be defeated militarily once and for all."[28] What is apparent in their declarations is the commitment to the most extensive version of the no-reasonable-risk-of-resumption theory on the end of NIACs. In general, under this theory, the end of conflicts is submitted to the vague criterion of reasonableness of conflict resumption. In her declaration, French Minister of the Armed Forces Parly showed an understanding of the reasonableness assessment as requiring that a very high threshold for establishing the end of conflicts is met: It is only when ISIS is wiped off the face of earth that France will consider that there is no reasonable risk of a resumption of hostilities and the conflict will stop.

The strategy that this legal interpretation supports is of course that military presence and operations must be sustained, even when the enemy group has lost the capability of mounting military operations, even when the group is disorganized and consists in networks of dispersed individuals; instead, the goal becomes the annihilation of its

[27] "Isis Not Defeated in Syria Despite Trump Claim, Says UK," *The Guardian*, December 19, 2018, www.theguardian.com/politics/2018/dec/19/isis-not-defeated-in-syria-despite-trump-claim-says-uk.

[28] Official Twitter account of French Minister of the Armed Forces Florence Parly, December 20, 2018, https://twitter.com/florence_parly/status/1075667341546045441:

> 1- Daech est plus affaibli que jamais. Daech est passé à la clandestinité et en mode insurrectionnel dans sa manière de combattre. Daech a perdu plus de 90% de son territoire. Daech n'a plus de logistique comme il a pu en avoir. 2- Mais Daech n'est pas rayé de la carte, ni ses racines d'ailleurs, il faut vaincre militairement de manière définitive les dernières poches de cette organisation terroriste.

surviving members. Only then can they be almost certain that the group will not be able to rebuild up its strength.

For a close follower of the French counterterrorism strategy, this logic is not new. The 2017 French Strategic Review on Defense and National Security, in its section on "Rootedness and Dissemination of Jihadist Terrorism," insisted that "jihadist terrorism is going through a transformative phase that will not diminish its reach and the danger it represents for the forthcoming decade: the main jihadist organizations will decline in some areas, yet without disappearing, and their underpinning ideology will persist."[29] Indeed, thanks to their "operational and ideological matrix, where knowledge is transmitted from generation to generation," it further explains, "the current jihadist organizations, Daech, Al Qaida and their several affiliates managed to adapt and mutate despite the setbacks they have suffered."[30] Likewise, the annexed report to the law on military programming adopted on July 13, 2018 insists that jihadist terrorism "recomposes and extends itself to new regions of the world," being a "complex and geographically dispersed" phenomenon.[31] For this reason, France considers that troops should be deployed for as long as necessary, in any place where terrorist groups exist or emerge and until they are defeated.

This position reflects a rationale on the end of armed conflicts that might go beyond the US rationale. Under the Obama administration, the US considered that

> there will come a tipping point – a tipping point at which so many of the leaders and operatives of Al Qaeda and its affiliates have been killed or captured, and the group is no longer able to attempt or launch a strategic attack against the United States, such that Al Qaeda as we know it, the organization that our Congress authorized the military to pursue in 2001, has been effectively destroyed. At that point, we must be able to say to ourselves that our efforts should no longer be considered an "armed conflict" against Al Qaeda and its associated forces; rather, a counterterrorism effort against individuals who are the scattered remnants of Al Qaeda, or are parts of groups unaffiliated with Al Qaeda.[32]

29 French Strategic Defense Review, Revue stratégique de défense et de sécurité nationale.

30 Ibid.

31 Statute reference: Loi no. 2018-607 du 13 juillet 2018; Annexed Report to the French Law on Military Programming.

32 Jeh Charles Johnson, "The Conflict against Al Qaeda and Its Affiliates: How Will It End?," General Counsel of the US Department of Defense at the Oxford Union, Oxford University, November 30, 2012, www.lawfareblog.com/jeh-johnson-speech-oxford-union.

On the contrary, in January 2018, when the context suggested that American troops would remain in Syria, the US Secretary of State Rex Tillerson declared that the continued US "military presence in Syria" would be "focused on ensuring ISIS cannot re-emerge." It is worth noting that the US war on terror through drones, including in Afghanistan, continues,[33] – thus revealing that moderation may only be rhetorical. What this discussion shows is that the legal issue remains unresolved and that, in the meantime, the extension of enmity progresses.

This legal uncertainty on the end of conflicts partly explains the extension of enmity in the counterterrorism context. To grasp this fully, it has to be read with IHL norms and silence about the norms on the constituent elements of NIACs and their role throughout the conflict. While it is clear that in order for a NIAC to be identified, a non-state armed group must be identified as sufficiently organized, it is unclear whether the organized armed group requirement performs a restraining function throughout the conflict. For a NIAC to qualify as such, non-state armed forces must constitute an "organized armed group." According to Article 3 Common to the Geneva Conventions and Additional Protocol II to the Geneva Conventions, a non-international armed conflict takes place between the armed forces of a state and "dissident armed forces or other organized armed groups that, under responsible command, exercise such control over a part of its territory as to enable them to carry out sustained and concerted military operations."[34] The Appeal Chamber of the ICTY, in the Tadić case, defined NIACs as "protracted armed violence between governmental authorities and organized armed groups or between such groups within a State."[35] The idea behind this provision and case law is that an armed conflict can exist only between parties that are sufficiently organized to confront each other with military means. If state authorities have always been presumed to possess armed forces that satisfy this criterion, non-state armed forces do not presumably fulfill the organizational requirement. If the organizational test is inconclusive, non-state armed forces do not qualify as

[33] The Bureau of Investigative Journalism reported US drone strikes in 2020 and the last strike reported when finalizing this text in May 2020 dates back to March 24, 2020 and is thus quite recent. For more details on these strikes, see, www.thebureauinvestigates.com/drone-war/data/afghanistan-reported-us-covert-actions-2020#strike-47179.

[34] Additional Protocol II to the Geneva Conventions Relating to the Protection of Victims of Non-International Armed Conflicts (Protocol II), June 8, 1977, Art. 1.

[35] ICTY, Prosecutor v. Tadić (Judgment), Case No. IT-94-1-A. 38 ILM 1518 (1999), Appeals Chamber, July 15, 1999, para.70.

organized non-state armed groups under the Geneva Conventions and Additional Protocol II and the situation can only be characterized as internal disturbances as *jus in bello* is not applicable.[36]

Courts have established the set of factors that can be used to identify the level of group organization, that is (i) the close link between the group's members; and (ii) the close link between the group and the hostilities. In particular, the International Criminal Tribunal for the Former Yugoslavia (ICTY) has played a major role in mitigating the absence of a more detailed provision.[37] The sufficient level of organization of a group can for instance be deduced from the occupation of significant areas of the territory;[38] the existence of institutions dedicated to defense and a military structure;[39] the existence of an official joint command structure or established hierarchy;[40] the existence of headquarters;[41] designated zones of operation;[42] the ability to procure, transport and distribute arms;[43] the engagement in military tactics in order to achieve military objectives;[44] the ability to negotiate and conclude agreements such as ceasefire or peace accords;[45] and the existence of military training and camps.[46]

[36] Article 1, Protocol II to the Geneva Conventions; ICC Statute, Arts. 8(2)(d) and (8)(2)(f); ICTY, Prosecutor v. Tadić (Judgment), para. 70: NIACs exclude situations of internal disturbances and tensions, such as riots, isolated and sporadic acts of violence, or other acts of similar nature.

[37] ICRC, Commentary on the Geneva Convention for the Amelioration of the Wounded and Sick in Armed Forces in the Field 32 (Jean S. Pictet, ed., 1952), 49–50 (Common Article 3).

[38] ICTY Trial Chamber, Prosecutor v. Tadić, Trial Judgment, Case No. IT-94-1-T, May 7, 1997. ICTY, Prosecutor v. Mucić et al. (IT-96-21), Trial Judgment, November 16, 1998; ICTY, Trial Chamber, Prosecutor v. Halilović (IT-01-48), November 16, 2005.

[39] ICTY, Trial Chamber, Prosecutor v. Slobodan Milošević (IT-02-54), Rule 98 bis Decision, February 5, 2004; ICTY, Trial Chamber, Prosecutor v. Halilović (IT-01-48); ICTY, Trial Chamber, Prosecutor v. Limaj et al. (IT-03-66), November 30, 2005.

[40] ICTY, Trial Chamber, Prosecutor v. Limaj et al. (IT-03-66), November 30, 2005.

[41] ICTY, Trial Chamber, Prosecutor v. Slobodan Milošević (IT-02-54); ICTY, Trial Chamber, Prosecutor v. Mrkšić et al. (IT-95-13/1), Judgment, September 27, 2007; ICTY, Trial Chamber, Prosecutor v. Haradinaj et al. (IT-04-84), April 3, 2008, para. 60.

[42] ICTY, Trial Chamber, Prosecutor v. Slobodan Milošević (IT-02-54).

[43] Ibid.

[44] ICTY, Trial Chamber, Prosecutor v. Halilović (IT-01-48).

[45] Ibid.

[46] ICTY, Trial Chamber, Prosecutor v. Limaj et al. (IT-03-66); ICTY, Trial Judgment, Prosecutor v. Hadžihasanović & Kubura (IT-01-47), March 15, 2006; ICTY, Trial Chamber, Prosecutor v. Martić (IT-95-11), Judgment, June 12, 2007.

When Philip Alston, as the UN Special Rapporteur on extrajudicial executions, wrote his 2010 report he insisted that ignoring the organization requirement, for instance, "by using force against groups that are not the equivalent of an organized armed group capable of being a party to a conflict, whether because it lacks organization, or the ability to engage in armed attacks, or because it does not have a connection or belligerent nexus to actual hostilities," would contravene the object and purpose of international humanitarian law.[47] A non-state armed group must be identified as sufficiently organized for a NIAC to exist; and organization is defined, *inter alia*, as a group that has the capacity to engage in armed attacks, as having a sufficient level of connection and nexus among members and to hostilities.

However, while IHL provides that objective criteria should be met to establish that an armed conflict exists (and that IHL thus applies), it is not clear whether these objective criteria should be met *throughout* the hostilities for a situation to still be deemed an armed conflict under IHL. The alternative view, if we follow any of the three other theories on the end of armed conflict, is that this criterion only plays a role in the early stages of conflict, when we have to determine whether or not IHL applies. According to this alternative option, the organizational requirement is only a legal parameter relating to the scope of application of IHL, namely, an element of a concrete situation that has to appear for IHL to apply in the first place.

Regardless of the position taken from a normative viewpoint, it is safe to say that the norms are uncertain on this question and that lawyers are in a situation of reasonable disagreement where some plausible arguments can be, and in fact have been, formulated in support of each theory. Against the validity of the two-way-ratchet theory, one can argue that none of the norms and case law focusing on the organization and intensity requirements concerns the termination of armed conflicts but rather its onset: they concern the trigger of IHL application. In their 1987 ICRC Commentary on the Additional Protocols, Yves Sandoz, Christophe Swinarski, and Bruno Zimmerman understood Articles 1 and 2 AP II as expressing its field of application *ratione temporis* as follows:

47 UN General Assembly, Report of the Special Rapporteur on Extrajudicial, Summary or Arbitrary Executions, Philip Alston, May 28, 2010, www2.ohchr.org/english/bodies/hrcouncil/docs/14session/A.HRC.14.24.Add6.pdf, 18.

> The starting point of the application of the Protocol is determined by Article 1, (Material field of application), paragraph 1, and corresponds to the moment when the criteria laid down in that article are objectively fulfilled.
> The text does not contain any indication as regards the end of its applicability.[48] Logically this means that the rules relating to armed confrontation are no longer applicable after the end of hostilities, while the fundamental guarantees granted persons deprived of their liberty are dealt with in paragraph 2 commented on below.[49]

In an initial draft version of Additional Protocol II, Article 2 was entitled "beginning and end of application" but this terminology, along with the proposal to cease applying IHL upon "the general cessation of military operations" was abandoned. From these elements the authors of the commentary deduce that Article 1 APII and its criteria serve to establish the starting point of the application of IHL.

This is also the approach adopted by the ICTY in the Tadić decision, where the tribunal considers the intensity and organizational criteria only when trying to initially characterize the conflict. In the ICTY 2008 Haradinaj judgment, the Trial Chamber held that "since according to the Tadić test an internal armed conflict continues until a peaceful settlement is achieved, and since there is no evidence of such settlement during the indictment period, there is no need for the Trial Chamber to explore the oscillating intensity of the armed conflict in the remainder of the indictment period."[50] Such a formula could even be read as revealing an explicit rejection of the two-way-ratchet theory.

Another set of arguments against this theory can be found in the logic of *jus in bello* and its distinction with *jus ad bellum*. To understand this, one has to distinguish first between IHL rules relating to its scope of application and the rules relating to the conduct of hostilities. In contrast to *jus ad bellum* that requires us to examine the conditions for a lawful use of force each time an attack is carried out, the conditions for the application of *jus in bello* are not reviewed for each use of force once the

[48] An amendment that was not adopted proposed that the application of the Protocol should cease "upon the general cessation of military operations." See Official Records, Diplomatic Conference on the Reaffirmation and Development of International Humanitarian Law Applicable in Armed Conflicts, O.R. IV, 12, CDDHII/79.

[49] ICRC, Commentary on the Additional Protocols of June 8, 1977 to the Geneva Conventions of August 12, 1949 (Yves Sandoz, Christophe Swinarski, and Bruno Zimmerman, eds., 1987), www.legal-tools.org/doc/6d222c/pdf/, §§4491–2.

[50] ICTY, Prosecutor v. Ramush Haradinaj et al., Judgment, Trial Chamber I, IT-04-84-T, April 3, 2008, §100 [hereinafter, "Haradinaj, Trial Judgment"].

situation has been characterized as an armed conflict. If principles of proportionality, necessity, and distinction lead to casuistic tests, the characterization of armed conflict is generally discussed as an applicability issue of IHL which, once established, is set for the entire duration of the conflict.[51] Once the legal facts triggering the legal situation of armed conflict are identified, IHL is considered applicable "from the beginning to the end of the armed conflict."[52]

A final argument provides plausible grounds to dismiss the two-way-ratchet theory, and may explain the discomfort of the drafters to explicitly choose a restrictive theory to identify the end of non-international armed conflicts. Conflicts are supposed to weaken the opponent. Imagine a situation where a non-state armed group is deemed capable of mounting operations, controls some territory, and is organized according to an established hierarchy. The level of violence opposing this group to another party to the conflict is intense, so this state of affairs, defined as a NIAC, triggers the application of IHL. Weakening the enemy could be understood as making sure the enemy group loses the characteristics that allowed it to be initially characterized as an organized non-state armed group for the purposes of IHL applicability. Before the enemy is completely incapacitated, and in the meantime (during the process of reaching this end goal), the enemy can already be weakened and lose its initial characteristics; violence might become less intense to such an extent that such a situation would not have initially been characterized as a NIAC if presenting that amount of violence. Does it mean that IHL does not and should not apply? This can certainly be argued, but it will face competing theories on the end of armed conflict.

Why does it matter that the two-way-ratchet theory faces strong alternatives? Because it is the only theory that would place emphasis on the evolution of group characteristics, and constrain states in extending their conflict. The changing nature of terrorist groups has been identified as a challenge,[53] but it is challenging at least partly because there is no rule on conflict termination, and especially no rule stating that as soon as

[51] Robert Kolb, "Applicability Issues: Finding a Way Out of the Quagmire," in Robert Kolb (ed.), *Advanced Introduction to International Humanitarian Law* (Edward Elgar, 2014), 93.

[52] Ibid., 94.

[53] Emily Crawford, *International Humanitarian Law* (Cambridge University Press, 2018), 83.

the group evolves in such a way that it loses its initial organizational features, IHL ceases to apply.

Just as it is unclear whether IHL requires states to ensure that there is the same amount of initial organizational level and violence intensity each time force is used, there is no co-belligerency legal test to ensure that force is only used when there is a belligerent nexus between new non-state entities and the initial enemy group. It is interesting to note that, in order to address the criticisms on the extension of the enemy group to new affiliated forces, the Obama administration used a concept of co-belligerency. The concept was transposed from the law of neutrality's concept of co-belligerency, which was initially applicable to states that violated their obligation to remain impartial and refrain from participating in a conflict.[54] When transposed to NIACs, the ensuing principle entails that force may be used by a state against any new non-state entities that provide some kind of support to its enemy.[55] However, the option that these groups are co-belligerents in order to be considered as part of the same conflict does not appear in the law on NIACs.[56] Co-belligerency even appears rarely in treaty language concerning international armed conflicts and when it is mentioned, it is more of an informal term of identification than a well-established legal concept.[57] The law does not say that when multiple non-state armed groups do not just have affinities, but form a coherent group, then those groups can be considered as a party to the same conflict.

The uncertain legal options and requirements to address conflict evolutions partly explains why there is very little legal academic work on the personal scope of the conflict in the counterterrorism context (i.e., trying to address the question of who the enemy is and how to regulate the way states try to define it). If some scholars refer to the war on terror as consisting of a multiplicity of armed conflicts,[58] very few voices have been heard on this issue since the Obama administration departed from the "global war on terror" terminology and built his military strategy solely on the more nuanced statement that the US was at war with Al

[54] Lassa Oppenheim, *International Law: A Treatise* (5th ed., Longmans, 1935), 203–6.

[55] Ingber, "Co-Belligerency," 1, 87.

[56] UNGA, Report of the Special Rapporteur on Extrajudicial Summary or Arbitrary Executions, Christof Heyns, submitted in accordance with Assembly resolution 37/168, September 13, 2013, A/68/382, §§60–1.

[57] Ibid., 80.

[58] Philip Bobbitt, *Terror and Consent: The Wars for the Twenty-First Century* (First Anchor Books Edition, 2009).

Qaeda and its affiliated forces.[59] In the absence of a clear delineation of when conflicts end, how can the systematic identification of the existence of a new armed conflict, each time a new group or faction or network is targeted, be expected? One could argue that it is a matter of perspective, and that each group should be regarded as a potential party to separate armed conflicts. This instruction, although reasonable from a normative standpoint, appears to be disconnected from the specificity of a context where various groups may emerge at the same time, sometimes in similar state territories, or in neighboring states, or at least in the same region of the world. Such an option is also detached from the difficulty to unravel the many evolutions both within a group and between various groups. At least, both the US and France consider being in a unique conflict against several jihadist groups and little reaction is being voiced, including from the part of other states.[60]

All-in-all, the legal uncertainty on when and how to reevaluate the features of a conflict situation over time and on the endpoint of armed conflicts gives room for the extension of the enemy group to other individuals who either directly or indirectly support the group ideology from a distance or act for so-called affiliated groups. The practice of extending enmity to members of terrorist networks vaguely united by a common ideology accentuates the focus on individuals in the way war is conducted. This relationship between an obscure collective body, on the

[59] Before this, scholars gathered forces to make the legal case against the global war on terror, like Mary Ellen O'Connell, "The Legal Case against the Global War on Terror" (2004) 36 *Case Western Reserve Journal of International Law* 349–58, 349. Others noted that the break operated by the Obama administration was not that categorical, like Christine Gray, "President Obama's 2010 United States National Security Strategy and International Law on the Use of Force" (2011) 10 *Chinese Journal of International Law* 1, 35–53. But very few focused on the question, nonetheless. The exceptions, for their part, consider the importance of legal grey zones and do not make simplistic proposals. This is the case of Rebecca Ingber's work on co-belligerency: Ingber, "Co-Belligerency," 1, 68–119.

[60] Direct support for this holistic approach from Daniel Bethlehem, explicitly embraced by the US with the notion of "Al Qaeda and associated forced" and France, with the umbrella category "jihadist groups"; indirect support found in UN Security Council Resolutions, calling to "combat terrorism," in UN SC 6526th Meeting, May 2, 2011, UN Press Release SC/10239; to "take any measure to combat terrorism," in UN Security Council Resolution 2249 (2015), Adopted by the Security Council at Its 7565th Meeting, on November 20, 2015, S/RES/2249(2015). It cannot be excluded that this silence of states might be because the majority agrees that the operations against these multiple groups have to be considered holistically for, if not legal, at least contextual and strategic reasons.

one hand, and scrutinized individuals, on the other hand, is something to which we will return later on.[61]

5.2 Infinite Action? Direct Participants in Hostilities Outside Areas and Moments of Ongoing Hostilities

Beyond legal uncertainties on the endpoint of armed conflicts, the rules regulating the target selection process facilitate the conduct of individualized and anticipatory warfare where the group nexus is overstretched and obscure. The evolution from collective enmity in hot battlefields to individualized warfare outside moments and areas of ongoing hostilities can be described in light of the emergence and evolution of the law of NIACs. Before NIACs were included in *jus in bello*, armed conflicts under international law were characterized by interstate enmity in delineated battlefields.[62] Of course, civil wars had been witnessed – a great number of them had even marked history, and in particular the nineteenth century; but they had not been the object of an international legal framework.[63] When the framework for NIACs was designed, the factual NIAC scenarios corresponded to colonial wars or civil wars taking place within the confines of a given state.[64]

[61] Chapter 4.

[62] Fabian Klose, *Human Rights in the Shadow of Colonial Violence: The Wars of Independence in Kenya and Algeria* (University of Pennsylvania Press, 2013) (original edition published under the title *Menschenrechte im Schatten Kolonialer Gewalt*, by Oldenbourg Wissenschaftsverlag GmbH, Munich, 2009), 120:

> Traditionally, the colonial powers justified the unchecked use of force by arguing that colonial conflicts differed fundamentally from wars between "civilized states". "Small wars" in the overseas possessions, maintained the British military theoretician Charles Callwell, were "expeditions against savages and semi-civilized races by disciplined soldiers". In the opinion of U.S. president Theodore Roosevelt, such a conflict was a relentless race war that could not abide by the rules of international morality. From a Western military viewpoint, international treaties on warfare were not valid in such war scenarios.

[63] David Armitage, *Civil Wars: A History in Ideas* (Yale University Press, 2017), 161. There were some norms before 1949 but only very few provisions: see, Anthony Cullen, *The Concept of Non-International Armed Conflict in International Humanitarian Law* (Cambridge University Press, 2010), 25; Boyd Van Dijk, The Making of the Geneva Conventions: Decolonization, the Cold War, and the Birth of Humanitarian Law (PhD thesis, Florence: European University Institute, 2017), 30.

[64] For a thorough and scrupulous historical analysis of the Geneva Conventions, and for our purpose of the laws of non-international armed conflicts, see Van Dijk, The Making of

Common Article 3 thereby broke "the taboo against applying international norms to conflicts *within*[65] states and empires."[66] However, the combatant status was not attributed to members of non-state armed groups.[67] In 1949 when the discussion on the future of the laws of war was taking place among states, and what they had in mind was the experience of World War II where all individuals were engaged in serving the military in one way or another was what they had in mind. Most states were convinced that the notion of civilian as a legal category for persons who by definition never take part in hostilities was disappearing.[68] Accordingly, state delegates largely agreed that everybody had to be treated as a "potential soldier" under the laws of war.[69] Simultaneously, insurgency and resistance practices made states unwilling to confer combat status to non-state actors. This privilege would immediately give non-state actors very strong legitimacy when fighting states. DPH thus reflects the two ideas: (a) anybody is targetable the minute direct involvement in hostilities is identified; and (b) nobody is given a combatant status.[70]

Therefore, even if it was established that for a situation to be labeled as a NIAC, an organized non-state armed group should be identified,[71] there was no membership status. The *jus in bello* says what it takes for

the Geneva Conventions; see in particular, chapter 1 "Common Article 3: Internationalizing Civil and Colonial Wars."

65 Emphasis added.

66 Van Dijk, The Making of the Geneva Conventions, 28.

67 Helen M. Kinsella, *The Image before the Weapon: A Critical History of the Distinction between Combatant and Civilian* (Cornell University Press, 2011), 121. As Kinsella explains, the Geneva Conventions are premised on the logic of total war that dispenses with a definition of the *civilian*. It is only the Commentary on the IV Convention that institutes the category of individuals who by definition do not take part in the fighting. Thus, scholarship that considers DPH to be applicable to civilians and not to individuals who continuously take part in hostilities in support of a non-state armed group is wrong.

68 Ibid., 114.

69 Oscar M. Uhler and Henri Coursier, *Geneva Convention Relative to the Protection of Civilian Persons in Time of War: Commentary* (Geneva: International Committee of the Red Cross, 1958), 232.

70 Precisely because of the legitimacy derived from it, fighting insurgencies might have preferred to acquire the legal status of combatants. But on the other hand, it had the advantage of constraining the power of states to target them, which benefited the modus operandi of insurgent groups and gave them some valuable protection in between the acts of DPH.

71 Article 3 Common to the Four Geneva Conventions of 1949. Additional Protocol II to the Geneva Conventions.

a group to be considered a party to the conflict, but is silent on what it takes for an individual to be considered as a member of such a group. As a result, members of non-state armed groups were not targeted as such, contrary to members of state armed forces. Rather, the conduct of war was individualized through the notion of DPH and the target selection process was the object of a DPH case-by-case analysis. In the absence of a textual definition of who belongs to a non-state armed group, the identification of the enemy in NIACs derives from the application of the notion of DPH, and thus from the observation of the relevant individual behavior.[72] The notion of DPH, undefined in the text of Article 13 of Protocol II and Article 51 of Protocol I, provided the legal basis for developing the profile of the archetypical participant in hostilities in classic civil wars, that is, wars conducted on "hot" battlefields within the confines of a given state.[73] This archetypical participant conducts hostile acts, which are intended to cause actual harm to the personnel and equipment of the enemy.

The absence of a definition of the DPH category in the Geneva Conventions could have been a channel for extensive practice, but its temporal and material scope have been sufficiently limited for the status to apply to precise situations showing clear signs of hostile participation. The three cumulative constitutive elements of direct participation as crystallized by the International Committee of the Red Cross (ICRC) guidelines are that: (i) this person must engage in an act that reaches a certain threshold of harm; (ii) a direct causal link exists between the act and the harm; and (iii) the act is precisely designed to directly cause harm, in support of a party to the conflict and to the detriment of

[72] For the DPH category, see Protocol I, Article 51(3). The ICRC in its commentary (https://ihl-databases.icrc.org/applic/ihl/ihl.nsf/Comment.xsp?action=openDocument&documentId=5E5142B6BA102B45C12563CD00434741) expressly confirms that the DPH category applies both for civilians who participate alone or "as part of a group" to the conflict: "Thus a civilian who takes part in armed combat, either individually or as part of a group, thereby becomes a legitimate target, though only for as long as he takes part in hostilities."

[73] ICRC, Interpretive Guidance on the Notion of Direct Participation in Hostilities, 2009. HCJ 769/02 Public Committee against Torture in Israel v. Gov't. of Israel, PD 62(1) 507 [2006] (Isr.) [*Targeted Killings* case] (hereafter "Interpretive Guidance"); State of Israel, The 2014 Gaza Conflict: Factual and Legal Aspects (2015) [2014 Gaza Conflict Report], http://mfa.gov.il/ProtectiveEdge/Documents/2014GazaConflictFullReport.pdf. For a commentary of the Targeted Killing case, see Yahli Shereshevsky, "Targeting the *Targeted Killings* Case – International Lawmaking in Domestic Contexts" (2018) 39 *Michigan Journal of International Law* 2, 241–281.

another.[74] The direct causation requirement calls for a verification that the behavior of the individual goes beyond strengthening the capacity of a party to inflict harm.[75] The military has to check if the individual's participation goes beyond the mere "preparation of a general campaign of unspecified operations would not qualify as direct participation in hostilities,"[76] beyond the production, storage, purchase, or smuggling that are not considered as causing the necessary direct harm for a person to be labeled as DPH.[77]

Direct participation in hostilities only temporarily suspends civilian protection only for such time as the person directly participates in hostilities. Case law and scholarly works have established that in addition to a limited temporal scope, DPH has a limited material scope (i.e., only covers acts that are intended to cause and do cause actual harm to the opponent). If it were only for this version of DPH, the extension of targeting in warfare to individuals recognized as members of the enemy group when hostilities are not ongoing would thus be unlawful, as it permits targeting only and for such time as someone directly participates in hostilities. However, more recently, we have seen the concept of DPH defined as a continuous combat function emerge and be employed alongside the traditional DPH definition. With the arrival of CCF in today's NIACs, targeting moves away from the material circumstances of warfare and thus is intensely related to personal and behavioral characteristics of the target.

Limited to the ongoing perpetration of hostile acts, the traditional DPH "act-by-act" framework does not grant authorization to target individuals who are not conducting hostile acts. On the contrary, by creating a status-based mode of targeting derived from material elements, the continuous combat function offers a legal framework for targeting individuals outside areas or moments of ongoing hostilities. The targets are not actively involved in the conduct of hostile acts when they are targeted but, rather, they adopt a behavior that is found to suggest a

[74] ICRC, Interpretive Guidance, 16.

[75] Kenneth Watkin, "Opportunity Lost: Organized Armed Groups and the ICRC Direct Participation in Hostilities Interpretive Guidance" (2009) 42 *NYU Journal of International Law and Politics*, 658.

[76] ICRC, Interpretive Guidance, 66.

[77] The weaknesses of the ICRC's approach could be developed at length, but others have done it well before me. See for instance, Watkin, "Opportunity Lost: Organized Armed Groups," 680.

continuing militant activity.[78] As a result, the continuous combat function appears as an extensive version of the notion of DPH as it opens the scope of targeting possibilities if an individual appears to have a lasting integration into a non-state armed group. Lasting participation and integration into an organized armed group can for instance be deduced from "the preparation, execution, or command of acts or operations amounting to direct participation in hostilities," but do not need to include witnessed participation in hostilities.[79] Moreover, CCF does not have to be deduced from formal elements, such as official and public integration into permanent units, distinguishable by uniforms, insignia, and equipment. Instead, it is established on material or circumstantial elements related to the role played by an individual in the conflict, such as evidence of recruitment, training, or equipment related to the non-state armed group's activities.[80] If the CCF test is conclusive, that is, if the observation of material or circumstantial elements allows states to determine that a person maintains a "continuous function," then the individuals can be targeted at any moment, even when not involved in acts of combat "because they are treated as analogous to members of the armed forces, rather than as civilians who are directly participating in hostilities."[81] Contrary to the traditional version of DPH, the continuous combat function thus triggers a quasi-combatant status that suspends the protection continuously (the status is one of "quasi-"combatant only because this suspension of protection does not go hand-in-hand with the granting of the combatant privileges).[82]

[78] Peter Bergen and Katherine Tiedemann, "The Year of the Drone: An Analysis of US Drone Strikes in Pakistan, 2004–2010" (2010) New America Foundation, Counterterrorism Strategy Initiative Policy Paper, http://counterterrorism.newamerica.net/sites/newamerica.net/files/policydocs/bergentiedemann2.pdf. This 2010 study by the New America Foundation concluded that many of the strikes in Pakistan were not aimed at specific known individuals at all: they were signature strikes. Jeremy Scahill and The Intercept, *The Assassination Complex: Inside the US Government's Secret Drone Warfare Program* (Simon & Schuster, 2016), 56.

[79] ICRC, Interpretive Guidance, 34.

[80] Ibid., 33–4.

[81] Michael N. Schmitt and Eric Widmar, "'On Target': Precision and Balance in the Contemporary Law of Targeting" (2014) 7 *Journal of National Security and Policy* 379–409, 386.

[82] ICRC, Interpretive Guidance; Dapo Akande, "Clearing the Fog of War? The ICRC's Interpretive Guidance on Direct Participation in Hostilities" (2010) 59 *International and Comparative Law Quarterly* 1, 180–92, 190. Accordingly, the damages are enhanced in the case of CCF as compared to DPH if an error occurs when conducting the uncertain factual test.

This is how the CCF broke the initial compromise of DPH that restrained the states' targeting options substantially and temporally by offering a status-based targeting of non-state actors in NIACs. Interestingly, with the CCF concession in 2009, the ICRC responded to states' pre-9/11 frustration at the lack of possibility to target traditional types of non-state enemies whose activities were visible, geographically constrained, and their agenda state-centered. But it ended up giving a formulation to the interests of states at a time that gave it a completely different function from the way that the ICRC probably saw it.[83] Because the CCF test can rest on contextual and behavioral evidence other than the witnessed engagement in combat and because "lasting integration" is not defined, the CCF test as currently framed puts civilian populations at risk in a context of anticipatory warfare. The principle of distinction, when applied through the CCF framework, loses its protective strength. In fact, this risk had been highlighted by UN Special Rapporteur Philip Alston in his 2010 report. In line with our analysis and responding to the emergence of the notion of CCF and its increased use in practice, Alston sounded the alarm by insisting on the need to set a strong evidentiary standard for civilians who are targeted for their lasting integration into the military wing of a non-state armed group.[84]

The US drone program shows us that DPH defined as CCF has the practical function of validating signature strikes. The US Executive Order of July 2016 explains that

> The United States considers all available information about a potential target's current and historical activities to inform an assessment of whether the individual is a lawful target. For example, an individual may be targetable if the individual is formally or functionally a member of an armed group against which we are engaged in an armed conflict. As Administration officials have stated publicly, to determine if an individual is a member of an armed group, we may look to, among other things: the extent to which the individual performs functions for the benefit of the group that are analogous to those traditionally performed by members of a country's armed forces; whether that person is carrying out or giving orders to others within the group; or whether that person has undertaken certain acts that reliably connote meaningful integration into the group.[85]

83 ICRC, Interpretive Guidance; Akande, "Clearing the Fog of War?," 1, 180–92.

84 UN General Assembly, Alston, Report of the Special Rapporteur on Extrajudicial.

85 The White House, "Executive Order – United States Policy on Pre- and Post-Strike Measures to Address Civilian Casualties in U.S. Operations Involving the Use of Force,"

The Intercept Drone Papers – which documents detailing the inner workings of the US military's assassination program in Afghanistan, Yemen, and Somalia[86] – as well as Forensic Architecture's work and that of the Bureau of Investigative Journalism (TBIJ) and *The New York Times* in the report, "The Uncounted," but also the report "Living Under Drones" produced by the International Human Rights and Conflict Resolution Clinic, of Stanford Law School, and the Global Justice Clinic, of the NYU School of Law, and investigative work such as Charlie Savage's *Power Wars* all narrate some important stories of how some US drone strikes were approved.[87] They give a more precise idea of the material elements used to characterize a target as lawful outside moments and/or areas of active hostilities.

First, there have been successful signature strike stories, where persons who were actually and continuously involved in militant activities were targeted on the basis of the CCF test. In January 2015, Adam Gadahn and Ahmed Farouq were killed in US drone strikes in Pakistan. The government said neither of them had been approved for targeted killing, and it had not known that either of these men were present in the strike zones before missiles were fired. Instead, they had been approved under the signature strikes framework, on the basis of material elements demonstrating a continuous involvement in hostilities. The test was successfully conducted as both men *a posteriori* proved to be important Al Qaeda figures. Adam Gadahn was an Al Qaeda translator and key propagandist who frequently appeared in Al Qaeda videos, and Ahmed Farouq was Al Qaeda's deputy commander in Pakistan and one of the most senior members in the organization's central leadership.[88]

What elements were taken into consideration in the absence of profile identification? On January 19, 2015, CIA drones targeted a house in the Shawal area of North Waziristan killing between five and seven people, including US citizen Adam Gadahn. The Bureau of Investigative Journalism reported elements that seem to have led to the assumption

2016, www.whitehouse.gov/the-press-office/2016/07/01/executive-order-united-states-policy-pre-and-post-strike-measures.

86 The Intercept, The Drone Papers, September 2015, https://theintercept.com/drone-papers/.

87 Savage, *Power Wars*.

88 Ibid., 287–8; Robert Windrem, "Only One of Six Al-Qaeda-Linked Americans Killed by Drone on Purpose," *NBC News*, April 23, 2015, www.nbcnews.com/news/us-news/only-one-six-al-qaeda-linked-americans-killed-drone-purpose-n347046.

that the house was occupied by terrorist militants.[89] First, the Shawal is an area with steep valleys and thick woodland that makes it easily defensible, which is why it became a stronghold for armed groups in North Waziristan. Second, the area had become an even more convenient location for the armed groups since the Pakistan military operation in the area began in 2014. A senior Pakistani government official explained to *The News* that "all the militant groups, including members of Al Qaeda, had shifted to the mountainous Shawal Valley after the government launched a military operation against them in the plains of North Waziristan."[90] Ahmed Farouq, for his part, was killed in the January 14 drone attack that also killed the American hostage Warren Weinstein and Italian Giovanni Lo Porto, in the same region of Pakistan.[91] This drone attack was directed against a building suspected to be an Al Qaeda compound. Presumably, the drone operators in these two cases took into consideration the geographic location of the targeted buildings, the regular presence of male groups and gatherings. These elements most probably led them to suspect that the people in the compound had a continuous engagement in militant activity.

In 2015, in Yemen, Nasir al-Wuhayshi, the leader of Al Qaeda in the Arabian Peninsula – and at that time purportedly No. 2 of core Al Qaeda – was killed by a CIA strike, which seemed to be a signature strike and not a personality strike.[92] Although anonymous government officials told *Bloomberg View* that Wuhayshi had been the CIA's target, other anonymous government officials told the *Washington Post* that the CIA had been unaware of any high-value target in its sights before firing at a group of suspected militants, and only found out afterward that Wuhayshi was among the dead.[93] Yemeni officials reported that Wuhayshi was killed in a raid in Al Qaeda-held Mukalla, a seaport in Yemen's south-eastern Hadramawt province, against him and two other

[89] TBIJ, "Pakistan: Reported US Strikes 2015," www.thebureauinvestigates.com/drone-war/data/obama-2015-pakistan-drone-strikes.

[90] "Seven Killed in Shawal Drone Strike," *The News*, January 20, 2015, www.thenews.com.pk/print/10388-seven-killed-in-shawal-drone-strike.

[91] TBIJ, "Pakistan: Reported US Strikes 2015."

[92] Savage, *Power Wars*, 288–9.

[93] Eli Lake and Josh Rogin, "How the U.S. Tracked Down Al-Qaeda's Yemen Chief," *Bloomberg View*, June 16, 2015, http://goo.gl/kk526Q, 115; Greg Miller, "CIA Didn't Know Strike Would Hit al-Qaeda Leader," *Washington Post*, June 17, 2015, http://goo.gl/RCUSut.

men.[94] A US intelligence official attributed the killing of Wuhayshi and other Al Qaeda operatives to "the cumulative knowledge [they] have developed" of terrorist networks in the region.[95] In this particular instance, it seems that the strike was conducted on the basis of various sources: intelligence, contextual knowledge, geographical location of the targets within the country but also within the city, behavior demonstrating gatherings and group conversations, etc. The strike thus seems to have been a signature strike, and the way the US identified the targets can also be successful, as they were posthumously recognized as official terrorist militants. These instances, as probably many others, show that anticipatory warfare where targets are selected on elements other than their witnessed participation in hostilities do not necessarily lead to civilian casualties.

However, results are less fortunate in other cases, even though it aligns in principle with the CCF version of DPH. These instances reveal the danger of relying on contextual and behavioral evidence other than witnessed participation in hostilities in order to select targets. For instance, Azmat Khan and Anand Gopal, in the "The Uncounted," tell the story, already mentioned above, of the Razzo family, whose home was targeted on the evening of September 20, 2015 in ISIS-occupied Mosul, Iraq.[96] That evening, Basim Razzo, his wife, his brother, and brother's wife were preparing for bed in the family house. Basim usually spent his evening hours clicking through car reviews on YouTube, driven by his long-standing taste for fast cars and to alleviate the frustration generated by the prohibition on driving the family 1991 BMW car because of the ISIS occupation. The house was hit by a strike, which only Basim and his sister-in-law survived. Later the same day, the American-led coalition uploaded a video to its YouTube channel entitled "Coalition Airstrike Destroys Daesh VBIED Facility Near Mosul, Iraq 20 Sept 2015."[97] The target, the video explained, was a car-bomb factory, a hub in a network of multiple facilities spread across Mosul used to produce VBIEDs for ISIL's terrorist activities posing "a direct threat to both civilian and Iraqi

[94] "Yemen al-Qaeda Chief al-Wuhayshi Killed in US Strike," *BBC News*, June 16, 2015, www.bbc.com/news/world-middle-east-33143259.

[95] Miller, "CIA Didn't Know."

[96] Azmat Khan and Anand Gopal, "The Uncounted," *The New York Times*, November 16, 2017, www.nytimes.com/interactive/2017/11/16/magazine/uncounted-civilian-casualties-iraq-airstrikes.html?_r=0.

[97] Airwars, "Coalition Airstrike 20 Sept 15 in Mosul Iraq," May 12, 2017, www.youtube.com/watch?v=jn5cSZkfFSM.

security forces."[98] The buildings seen in the film footage were the homes of Basim and his brother. That day, the contextual and behavioral evidence and intelligence gathered on Basim Razzo, presumably, his YouTube and internet activity, led the US drone program chain of command to identify him as a participant in a car bomb-making for ISIL, and thus as a legitimate target.

The case of the Razzo family is not the only example of the lethal consequences of flawed or outdated intelligence and of misperceptions caused by other factors. On March 17, 2011, in the city of Datta Khel, North Waziristan, Pakistan, a US drone strike killed between forty to fifty people seated in two large circles.[99] US officials claimed that the men were all legitimate targets, stating that "these people weren't gathering for a bake sale. They were terrorists,"[100] and "not the local men's glee club."[101] Yet, it was then established by Forensic Architecture,[102] that the men who were targeted were in fact participating in a government-sanctioned meeting, and more specifically in a *jirga*, a traditional assembly of leaders that makes decisions by consensus and serves as a dispute-settlement system. The fact that a large group of men were seated in a circle, and appeared to be gathered together and discussing for two days, was sufficient to reach the conclusion that these men had a continuous militant activity. These men, other sources agree – from TBIJ, to the Stanford/NYU's Living Under Drones Report, to Forensic Architecture's report, which was used in turn by UN Special Rapporteur Ben Emerson,[103] – were mainly tribal leaders and local policemen discussing a local disagreement.[104] Despite the posthumous identity check of the

98 Khan and Gopal, "The Uncounted."

99 TBIJ, "Pakistan: Reported U.S. Strikes in 2011," www.thebureauinvestigates.com/drone-war/data/obama-2011-pakistan-strikes.

100 Salman Masood and Pir Zubair Shah, "C.I.A. Drones Kill Civilians in Pakistan," *New York Times*, March 17, 2011, www.nytimes.com/2011/03/18/world/asia/18pakistan.html.

101 Tom Wright and Rehmat Mehsud, "Pakistan Slams U.S. Drone Strike," *The Wall Street Journal*, March 18, 2011.

102 Forensic Architecture, "Case Study No. 1: Datta Khel, North Waziristan, March 16–17, 2011," www.forensic-architecture.org/case/drone-strikes/.

103 United Nations, U.N. SRCT Drone Inquiry, "Case 1 – Datta Khel," http://unsrct-drones.com/report/159.

104 International Human Rights and Conflict Resolution Clinic (Stanford Law School) and Global Justice Clinic (NYU School of Law), "Living Under Drones: Death, Injury, and Trauma to Civilians from US Drone Practices in Pakistan," September 2012, www-cdn.law.stanford.edu/wp-content/uploads/2015/07/Stanford-NYU-Living-Under-Drones.pdf.

deaths, US government officials reiterated that the strikes had not led to civilian casualties, but the deaths of a large group of heavily armed men, and had not violated international humanitarian law.[105]

In the evening of March 16, 2017, a US drone strike targeted Sayidina Omar Ibn Al-Khattab Mosque in Al-Jinah, in the province of Aleppo, Syria. Around forty dead were reported by the Syrian Observatory for Human Rights. The Forensic Architecture team reported that after the strike, the US Central Command claimed responsibility for the airstrike on the building, which it wrongly identified at first as located in the province of Idlib and as a "partially constructed community meeting hall" rather than a mosque.[106] The US officials further claimed that there were no civilian casualties. They then admitted that the building was in fact a mosque but maintained that they were "confident this was a meeting of Al Qaeda members and leaders; this was not a meeting of civilians."[107] However, on August 8, 2017, a United Nations Syria Commission report concluded that US forces "lacked an understanding of the actual target, including that it was part of a mosque where worshippers gathered to pray every Thursday," "failed to take all feasible precautions to avoid or minimize incidental loss of civilian life," and were "in violation of international humanitarian law."[108] Again in this case, a reunion of a group of people in a building apparently was the key element to characterize them as legitimate targets.

These are just some examples of the conundrum posed by the CCF as one way to apply the principle of distinction for those who conduct warfare. An increased risk of error is inherent in the process of selecting targets on the basis of contextual and behavioral evidence that do not include the witnessed participation in hostilities. The posthumous discussion on civilian casualties' assessment is confused: on the one hand,

[105] Scott Shane, "Contrasting Reports of Drone Strikes," *New York Times*, August 11, 2011, www.nytimes.com/2011/08/12/world/asia/12droneside.html?ref=asia&mtrref=undefined&gwh=AA5BB874ECB05EFD4B4F0EFBA50C0835&gwt=pay.

[106] Forensic Architecture, "Airstrikes on the Al-Jinah Mosque," https://forensic-architecture.org/investigation/airstrikes-on-the-al-jinah-mosque.

[107] Ibid. See also Thomas Gibbons-Neff, "U.S. Finds that March Airstrike that Struck Building Described as Mosque Was Legal," *The Washington Post*, June 7, 2017, www.washingtonpost.com/news/checkpoint/wp/2017/06/07/u-s-finds-that-march-airstrike-that-struck-building-described-as-mosque-was-legal-and-resulted-in-one-civilian-casualty/.

[108] UN General Assembly, Human Rights Council, "Report of the Independent International Commission of Inquiry on the Syrian Arab Republic," August 8, 2017, A/HRC/36/55, p. 13.

NGOs report civilian casualties after checking the identity of the targets and, on the other hand, the targeting state refuses to consider that the deceased are civilian, as they passed the CCF test. In fact, what happens is that the CCF makes the principle of distinction much more flexible and this leads to a high rate of false positives: the CCF test as currently defined may show that the person is a legitimate target, when in reality they do not hold a continuous combat function.

On January 3, 2021, the Barkhane forces conducted a strike on a group of individuals located in the village of Bounty, in Mali. In the aftermath of the strike, locals and journalists reported that the operation resulted in numerous civilian casualties. France, for its part, declared that its troops had targeted "members of a terrorist armed group" in full compliance with international humanitarian law. This event, and the divergent views on how to characterize what happened, led the MINUSMA to open an investigation that resulted in a report published on March 30, 2020. The report concludes that twenty-two casualties resulted from the strike, among which were nineteen civilian deaths and the death of three members of the terrorist group Katiba Serma, a semi-autonomous arm of the jihadist group Macina Liberation Front.

The casualties, including those identified as civilians by the MINUSMA, were the intended targets of the strike: France, both before and after the report, insists that only legitimate targets were hit. On January 7, 2021, the Ministry shared the following detailed information on what triggered the decision to strike (translated from French):

> On Sunday January 3, in the afternoon, after several days of intelligence gathering, the Barkhane force conducted an operation in the Douentza region, an area characterized by the presence and action of terrorist armed groups such as the Katiba Serma. . . .
> In this area, more than an hour before the strike, a REAPER drone had identified a motorcycle with two individuals at the north of RN16. The vehicle joined a group of about forty adult men in an isolated zone. All the intelligence gathered, including real time information, allowed us to identify this group as belonging to an armed terrorist group. The observation of the zone for more than an hour and a half also allowed to exclude the presence of women and children. Considering the behavior of the individuals, of the tools identified, and combining all collected intelligence, [the strike was ordered].

The MINUSMA report gets into interesting detail about the local tradition of having men and women spend part of the wedding celebrations in separate groups and concludes that only three of those men were presumably part of a violent non-state armed group.

Although the targets were not engaged in hostilities at the moment of the strike, it seems like their behavior, age, sex, and location were taken to reveal their role as part of the military arm of a terrorist group. Some elements of evidence might not have been released, and press releases from the French Ministry of the Armed Forces and the MINUSMA report might diverge on some elements, but one thing cannot be contested: The Barkhane forces gathered pieces of evidence other than witnessed participation in hostilities that taken together allowed them to identify the individuals as legitimate targets. These pieces of evidence seem to have included the facts that all individuals were men, apparently military-aged, unusually gathered, in a region known for terrorist groups' presence, and that some of them carried weapons.

In an era where data collection capacities are unprecedented and constantly growing, from current drone surveillance to the promise of their algorithmic capacities in the near future, the CCF test that is not conditioned upon witnessing someone engage in hostile acts exacerbates the risks of infinite warfare in time and space. Drone programs, by enhancing the phenomena of individualization and dematerialization of war, exacerbate the risk posed by the CCF test as currently defined in a way that further extends enmity.

5.3 Infinite Knowledge or Infinite Enmity?

As we have seen earlier and will further explore in Chapter 6, the technological capacities of drones facilitate a war conducted against a plethora of individuals and with the aim of preventing action. States, in order to prevent, must be in control of time, which in this context means to possess *knowledge*. When British Air Marshal Greg Bagwell was interviewed by Chris Cole from Drone Wars UK, the conversation turned at a certain point to the specificities of drone technologies:

> . . . GB: I have no problem with discussing the issues, but where I struggle is singling out drones. I think we have ended up pulling drones into a special place where they are singled out for commentary. When, actually, if it's the idea of having a "kill list" you want to talk about or the targeting of individuals, that's a legal argument. It's not about the tool you use, that's just the method. You could just as easily – well not just as easily – but you can possibly do that with a number of tools . . .

> CC: But that's the nub of the argument isn't it? When you say you can "just as easily do it with other tools," can you?
> GB: That's why I corrected myself. You're right, it's not just as easy.[109]

Drone programs are specific in that they combine all the technologies necessary to conduct an individualized and dematerialized kind of warfare. From satellite surveillance, interception of signal communications, geolocation devices, massive data collection, to capacities to conduct surgical strikes, drones are much more than killing machines.[110] Not only do drones facilitate and intensify the conduct of an individualized/dematerialized kind of warfare, but they also provide a strong incentive for embracing the emergence of the continuous combat function in support of such development. Indeed, similarly to what we observed for the right of self-defense extensive interpretation in Chapter 4, the technological capacities of drone programs seem to be the condition for accepting the continuous combat function as a means to implement the principle of distinction. In a context where behavior cannot be scrutinized from a distance, until the least accessible areas, in a context where no tool would allow the surveillance of people's private lives, habits, communication and movements, a legal category such as the continuous combat function does not seem to be adequate. Without advanced technological capacity, the idea that it could be lawful to target individuals who do not show any active participation in hostile acts, who are far from areas of active hostilities and who are not objectively identified as members of an enemy group, would not arise. Conversely, CCF appears to be a plausible and acceptable way of applying the principle of distinction in a world where drones' technological capacities combine the necessary elements to ensure persistent scrutiny of individuals and data collection, in other words elements that promise the minutiae of knowledge.[111]

[109] "Interview of Air Marshall Greg Bagwell by Chris Cole," Drone Wars UK, January 2018, https://dronewars.net/interview-of-air-marshall-greg-bagwell-drone-wars-uk/.

[110] Scahill and The Intercept, *The Assassination Complex*, 44.

[111] Against the acceptance of CCF, one could argue that in such a world, basing lethal decision-making on contextual and behavioral evidence is paradoxical, if not unacceptable. At least, a higher threshold than the one authorized by CCF could be demanded, such as the necessity to collect data allowing to objectively identify the target as a permanent and military active member of an organized armed group.

The dematerialized warfare that drones allow us to conduct derives from the availability of data collection tools[112] and the capacity to promptly eliminate a target once sufficient evidence has been collected to identify the individual as a threat. Although most of the attention has been focused on the elimination of the target, data collection capacities of drones seem to matter the most when it comes to how warfare has dematerialized; that is, I recall, has moved away from responding to material acts of hostilities. To understand the importance of data collection capacities, it suffices to imagine how this phenomenon of dematerialization of war will be exacerbated when knowledge superiority intensifies. For instance, we can argue that the knowledge provided by drones could in fact be exploited further if the analysis was done using algorithms. Indeed, for now, human drone operators spend most of their time trying to identify legitimate targets based on an enormous amount of data and metadata[113] but the speed and efficiency with which this data is processed and analyzed could potentially be greater. If the automation potential of the analytical process is ever exploited (the contrary would be surprising), knowledge and anticipation capabilities would multiply. Along with this technical acquisition, it would be surprising not to see the intensification of the phenomenon of dematerialization of warfare and its focus on individuals' personal characteristics and behavioral patterns.

In Kristensen's words,

> In addition, success is guaranteed by speed; acting too late is the same as defeat. The goal is to have knowledge of events and act upon that knowledge before they happen. The quest is to create, in the words of the former director of force transformation, an "inevitable military Leviathan." By already being everywhere, and by the "unblinking eye" being able to act at any time, a sort of pre-emptive deterrence is the goal. Future events will not happen because the opponent knows that the

[112] Such as the "disposition matrix" database in the US. Discussed here, Greg Miller, "Plan for Hunting Terrorists Signals U.S. Intends to Keep Adding Names to Kill Lists," *The Washington Post*, October 23, 2012, www.washingtonpost.com/world/national-security/plan-for-hunting-terrorists-signals-us-intends-to-keep-adding-names-to-kill-lists/2012/10/23/4789b2ae-18b3-11e2-a55c-39408fbe6a4b_story.html?hpid=z1&utm_term=.1143e2137871. Or, in France, the multiple data collection systems implemented by the new French Law on Military Programming, from DESCARTES, to SYRACUSE IV, or Successeur MELCHIOR, to CONTACT, SCORPION, OMEGA, ASTRIDE, RIFAN, SIOC, SIA, GEODE, and ISSAN.

[113] Jeremy Scahill and Glenn Greenwald, "Death by Metadata," in Jeremy Scahill and The Staff of The Intercept (eds.), *The Assassination Complex: Inside the Government's Secret Drone Warfare Program* (Simon & Schuster, 2016).

> Leviathan will know and act before the opponent's deed can have effect. The event will never materialize. This is what "deterring forward" is about.[114]

5.4 Concluding Remarks

This chapter highlighted another facet of the interaction between technology, military strategy, and the law. By offering the opportunity to collect individualized data and to scrutinize behavior on an almost permanent basis and to do this in areas that are difficult to access, drone programs make the legal opportunity to target individuals on the basis of contextual and behavioral evidence other than their witnessed participation in hostilities appear pragmatic. In a cascade effect, the material and technical opportunity to individualize the conduct of warfare and the associated legal authorization to do so extensively, at least partly explain the phenomenon of the extension of enmity: as warfare appears to be individualizable/ed, and as new legal interpretations support it, the conflict is progressively extended to individuals who belong to groups that have fragile links (if at all) with the nuclear group; and this partly because there is no clear obligation to reevaluate the organizational requirements in IHL.

The legal requirement to select a target throughout the conflict is whether a person is directly participating in hostilities or holds a CCF, while the group characteristics is a question that plays an explicit role solely at the onset of the conflict. It then plays an uncertain role throughout the conflict. DPH, on the contrary, is a constant condition when considering individual targets. Where DPH could limit targeting possibilities under its traditional interpretation, its CCF version extends them by allowing the operating state to ask, "Is this individual an enemy?" and not "is this individual currently conducting an act that directly supports the enemy group and harms us?" As such, the legal uncertainties related to the organizational requirement of the enemy group and the weight of this requirement throughout the conflict, combined with the CCF avenue paves the way for the extension of enmity to terrorist groups other than the nuclear group, members of the broader network and for the extension of enmity in time and space.

The extension of enmity through the continuous combat function reveals the dematerialization of war already explored in earlier chapters,

[114] Kristensen, "Tourists or Vagabonds?," 249–66.

understood as a shift away from acts of hostilities as a basis to target the enemy. The objective is to anticipate threats before they materialize, and it has been demonstrated that technology and data collection tools, as well as the continuous combat function doctrine itself, create space for, if not catalyze this phenomenon. Instead of conducting warfare to respond to ongoing hostilities, drones are used as a tool for profiling. These cases do not only bring to light the lethal consequences of flawed or outdated intelligence and of misperceptions caused by other factors, they also show that the data and evidence used to identify legitimate targets in armed conflicts against a party designated as a terrorist group include criteria such as, but not limited to: geographic location of individuals or buildings in an area of a city or region identified as concentrating terrorist activities; regular male gatherings; group gatherings; group conversations; cellphone communications or connections (the target does not need to have expressly communicated with an identified member of a terrorist group to trigger suspicion, as attempts of communication are also intercepted); internet activity (e.g., related to items associated with any terrorist group's activities); possession of weapons.

The dematerialization of warfare geared toward a focus on the personal and behavioral features of individual threats is related to the extension of the geographical scope of conflicts that will now be explored. Once it is accepted that people who are not currently perpetrating ongoing hostile acts can be considered as enemies under IHL, the parameters that trigger the enemy qualification, including those listed above, can be traced at a distance from active hostilities. At such a distance, the observable facts cannot consist of – but can only suggest – engagement in combat. Conversely, time and space management allowed by technical advances facilitate the loss of boundaries that delineate battlefields. Once again, the strategic logic is that because the enemy does not present any spatial constraints, states cannot know where to expect war and need to be aware of things before they happen, wherever this might be.[115]

[115] Ibid.

6

Anywhere Wars

In 2014, President Obama addressed the US population to announce the perspective of a geographical expansion of the US counterterrorism efforts against ISIS from Iraq to Syria, and potentially beyond:

> Our objective is clear: we will degrade, and ultimately destroy, ISIL through a comprehensive and sustained counter-terrorism strategy. First, we will conduct a systematic campaign of airstrikes against these terrorists. Working with the Iraqi government, we will expand our efforts beyond protecting our own people and humanitarian missions, so that we're hitting ISIL targets as Iraqi forces go on offense. Moreover, I have made it clear that we will hunt down terrorists who threaten our country, wherever they are. That means I will not hesitate to take action against ISIL in Syria, as well as Iraq. This is a core principle of my presidency: if you threaten America, you will find no safe haven.[1]

Drone programs, helped by the law, open the door to geographically unlimited war: an anywhere war. As must be clear by now, combat drones have been deployed against non-state actors extraterritorially, including in the territory of non-belligerent states where a member of a terrorist group is located. This is the context that the United States describes as "outside areas of active hostilities" or "outside hot conflict zones."[2] These non-legal concepts posit that *jus in bello* applies wherever there is a belligerent, including in the territory of a state where the hostilities are not taking place.[3] This practice, accompanied with

[1] Barack Obama, Statement by the President on ISIL, The White House, September 10, 2014, https://obamawhitehouse.archives.gov/the-press-office/2014/09/10/Statement-president-isil-1.

[2] The White House, "Executive Order – United States Policy on Pre- and Post-Strike Measures to Address Civilian Casualties in U.S. Operations Involving the Use of Force," 2016, www.whitehouse.gov/the-press-office/2016/07/01/executive-order-united-states-policy-pre-and-post-strike-measures.

[3] Conversely, they are not supporting a claim that *jus in bello* applies outside of armed conflicts as some have argued. See, for a similar understanding, Ryan Goodman, "Why the

supportive legal and political rationales, sparked a heated debate among scholars on the geographical scope of armed conflicts under *jus in bello*. This chapter demonstrates that there is no such thing as a legal geographical limitation of conflicts and that this absence is exploited by drone programs, thus materializing the prospect of a geographically unlimited war. This geographically unlimited war is what is referred to here as an "anywhere war," as it is inaccurate to characterize it as an "everywhere war" considering that it does not actually have a global spread.[4] Instead, its boundaries are potentially infinite as long as other conditions for an armed conflict to exist under international humanitarian law are met. In other words, it is these other conditions that will constrain the conduct of hostilities, not geography itself.

As *lex specialis*, and contrarily to *lex generalis* that covers a common situation (i.e., time of peace), *jus in bello* can be expected to cover a nonpermanent, geographically limited situation (i.e., time and space of war).[5] Yet, even if the *jus in bello* is *lex specialis*, it has only inchoate boundaries for where it applies[6] and does not explicitly rest on a bounded geography. This has given rise to a huge controversy on the geographical

Laws of War Apply to Drone Strikes Outside 'Areas of Active Hostilities' (A Memo to the Human Rights Community)," *Just Security*, 2017, www.justsecurity.org/45613/laws-war-apply-drone-strikes-areas-active-hostilities-a-memo-human-rights-community/.

4 Derek Gregory's work, that coined the term "everywhere war" is nonetheless extremely interesting and useful to think about the geographical scope of the wars on terror, to reflect on how drones and war by anticipation have accelerated the expansion of warfare and the blurring of boundaries between war and peace. See, Derek Gregory, "The Everywhere War" (2011) 177 *The Geographical Journal* 3, 238–50. See also, Derek Gregory, "From a View to a Kill: Drones and Late Modern War" (2011) 28 *Theory, Culture & Society* 7–8, 188–215.

5 Aaron X. Fellmeth and Maurice Horwitz, *Guide to Latin in International Law* (Oxford University Press, 2009).

6 ICJ, Legality of the Threat or Use of Nuclear Weapons, Advisory Opinion, July 8, 1996, ICJ Reports 1996, 226, §25:

> In principle, the right not arbitrarily to be deprived of one's life applies also in hostilities. The test of what is an arbitrary deprivation of life, however, then falls to be determined by the applicable lex specialis, namely, the law applicable in armed conflict which is designed to regulate the conduct of hostilities. Thus, whether a particular loss of life, through the use of a certain weapon in warfare, is to be considered an arbitrary deprivation of life contrary to Article 6 of the Covenant, can only be decided by reference to the law applicable in armed conflict and not deduced from the terms of the Covenant itself.

scope of conflicts especially since some states have been engaged in transborder NIACs against terrorist groups or networks.[7]

This debate takes its roots from the territorialized legal reasoning that originally framed *jus in bello*, despite the absence of an explicit geographical limitation of conflicts in the law. Prior to the Geneva Conventions of 1949, there was no substantive provision of *jus in bello* regarding situations of NIACs. When the extension of the *jus in bello*'s scope to situations not of an international character was raised at the time of the drafting of the Geneva Conventions, voices were raised against such an extension. The UK's Head of Delegation, Robert Craigie, spoke strongly against the adoption of draft Article 2, stating that it would "strike at the root of national sovereignty and endanger national security."[8] In other words, the opponents of the extension considered that armed conflicts could only take place between states (i.e., equal sovereign enemies), and that insurgents or rebels could not be recognized as belligerents. Thus, the exclusion of non-international armed conflicts from *jus in bello* prior to the Geneva Conventions reflected a state-centered vision of belligerency.

It is interesting to note that the shift undertaken by contemporary IHL – extending the application of *jus in bello* to non-international

[7] Marko Milanovic, "Accounting for Complexity of the Law Applicable to Modern Armed Conflicts," in Winston S. Williams and Christopher M. Ford (eds.), *Complex Battlespaces: The Law of Armed Conflict and the Dynamics of Modern Warfare*. The Lieber Studies Series (Oxford University Press, 2019) 33–59.

[8] Summary Records of the Joint Committee, *Final Record*, vol. II-B, 1st Meeting, April 26, 1949, 10. See also the similar position expressed by the US Head of Delegation, Leland Harrison, *Final Record*, ibid., 11: "The United States of America [does] not consider that it could bind itself to observe the provisions of the Convention except in the case of war as understood in international law"; the position of Australia, positing a set of very strict standards for the application of the Conventions to situations of non-international armed conflict, in *Final Record*, vol. III, Amendment proposed by Australia, May 4, 1949, Annex 11, 27; the criticism voiced by the Greek delegation regarding how it would affect the doctrine of belligerency in international law, and suggestion that the Conventions should be deemed applicable only if the belligerency of parties was recognized "individually by the majority of countries represented in the [United Nations Security] Council," in *Final Record*, vol. II-B, Summary Records of the Joint Committee, 3rd Meeting, 16; on the same matter, the firm state-centered suggestion of the Canadian delegation, in *Final Record*, vol. II-B, Summary Records, 2nd Meeting, 13: "[B]efore saying that a civil war [is] of the kind in which the Convention should be applied, the test should be: recognition of belligerency of the rebels by the lawful Government. Except in the instance of a civil war of that kind, the Canadian Delegation were not in favor of the provisions contained in paragraph 4, Article 2"; etc.

armed conflicts – perpetuates such territorialized legal reasoning.[9] The statist (and thus territorial) foundations of *jus in bello* are reflected in the provisions of the Geneva Conventions and Additional Protocols. On the one hand, Common Article 2 of the 1949 Geneva Conventions provides that the Conventions "apply to all cases of declared war or of any other armed conflict which may arise between two or more of the High Contracting Parties, even if the state of war is not recognized by one of them."[10] Only states may become parties to the Conventions. On the other hand, Common Article 3 of the Geneva Conventions defines NIACs as "those that are not of an international character occurring *in the territory of one of the High Contracting Parties.*"[11] Similarly, Additional Protocol II applies to conflicts that "take place in the territory of a High Contracting Party between its armed forces and dissident armed forces or other organized armed groups."[12] Again, the plain interpretation of Article 3 Common and Article 1 of Additional Protocol II leads to an apparent statist archetype for NIACs, according to which IHL governs the hostilities that take place within a state's borders.

Even when departing from this restrictive approach through case law, state borders remain the frame of reference. In the Tadić case, the International Criminal Tribunal for ex-Yugoslavia held that a NIAC consists in "protracted armed violence between governmental authorities and organized armed groups or between such groups *within a state*" (emphasis added).[13] As such, during a NIAC, IHL applies to the whole territory under the control of a party, whether or not actual combat takes place there. Even when extending the geographical scope of NIACs, the state's territory remained the point of reference. Furthermore, when observing spillover conflicts, the ICRC declared that when a NIAC extends into an adjacent territory, it does not absolve the parties of their

[9] Louise Arimatsu, "Territory, Boundaries and the Law of Armed Conflict" (2009) 12 *Yearbook of International Humanitarian Law*, 157–92, 168.

[10] Common Article 2 to the 1949 Geneva Conventions, https://ihl-databases.icrc.org/ihl/WebART/365-570005.

[11] Emphasis added.

[12] Additional Protocol II, Article 1(1).

[13] ICTY, Trial Chamber, Prosecutor v. Tadić, Trial Judgment, Case No. IT-94-1-T, May 7, 1997. ICTY, Prosecutor v. Mucić et al. (IT-96-21), Trial Judgment, November 16, 1998, Judgment, §70. Rome Statute, Article 8(2)(f): "It applies to armed conflicts that take place in the territory of a State when there is protracted armed conflict between governmental authorities and organized armed groups or between such groups."

IHL obligations simply because an international border has been crossed, explaining that the "ensuing legal vacuum would deprive of protection both civilians possibly affected by the fighting, as well as persons who fall into enemy hands."[14] Again, even when the interpretative logic favors the extension of the geographical scope of application of IHL, state borders remained the landmark.

However, despite the state-based logic that has characterized *jus in bello* and its developments, this chapter demonstrates that its norms were never designed to *confine* armed conflicts territorially but to *regulate* them. In this sense, the existence of a state-based logic when reflecting on the application of the law as well as the correspondence of the two types of armed conflict with two distinct geographical realities just existed as a matter of fact and not as a matter of law. Building on this legal reality, states involved in conflicts against non-state armed groups in the counterterrorism context cannot be said to adopt "expansive interpretations of IHL's geographical scope" as others have argued.[15] However, they do exploit the absence of geographical limitation in the law and the available options that the norms offer in that regard. This chapter illustrates how this absence is being particularly exploited by drone programs and thereby further demonstrates that the use of combat drones is not merely an example of broader phenomena related to the extraterritorial use of force in the war on terror.[16] On the contrary, a

14 International Committee of the Red Cross, International Humanitarian Law and the Challenges of Contemporary Conflicts, Report Prepared for the 31st International Conference of the Red Cross and Red Crescent, 31IC/11/5.1.2, October 2011, www.icrc.org/eng/assets/files/red-cross-crescent-movement/31st-international-conference/31-int-conference-ihl-challenges-report-11-5-1-2-en.pdf, 9–11.

15 For a similar understanding, see Michael N. Schmitt, "Charting the Legal Geography of Non-International Armed Conflict" (2013) 52 *Military Law and Law of War Review*, 109.

16 Noam Lubell and Nathan Derejko, "A Global Battlefield? Drones and the Geographical Scope of Armed Conflict" (2013) 11 *Journal of International Criminal Justice*, 1, 65–88, https://doi.org/10.1093/jicj/mqs096; Kenneth Anderson, *Targeted Killing and Drone Warfare: How We Came to Debate Whether There Is a "Legal Geography of War"* (Social Science Research Network, 2011); Gregory, "The Everywhere War," 238–50; Jennifer C. Daskal, "The Geography of the Battlefield: A Framework for Detention and Targeting Outside The 'Hot' Conflict Zone" (2013) 161 *University of Pennsylvania Law Review* 5, 1165–234; Noam Lubell and Nathan Derejko are the closest but fail in several ways to assess the specific role played by drones in the metamorphosis of armed conflicts. Their analysis considers this role to be specific only with regard to drone strikes frequently occurring outside areas of active hostilities. If this claim is correct, this chapter shows that this feature is not the only specificity of drone programs in challenging the scope of IHL.

number of elements help build the argument that drone programs intensify the prospect of a geographically infinite battlefield in the counterterrorism context. Against this background, the chapter takes a closer look at the arguments formulated by some legal scholars and actors trying to establish the existence of a legal limit to the geographical scope of conflicts and finds that their attempts to impede the realization of a geographically unconstrained war are unconvincing. They are an expression of the positivist idea that because we can give content to a norm, therefore we can know the "truth" about what the law exactly requires of us. These scholarly propositions thus omit that the opportunity to give the norm content means that the structure of concepts *limits* (and this only to a certain extent) the set of reasons that are available to justify action, and not that it gives only *one* meaning on the basis of which conduct can be criticized as clearly falling inside or outside the concept.

This chapter explores yet another interaction between military strategy, technology, and the law. On its own, the technological instrument is not sufficient to deterritorialize war (loss of geographical marker to conduct hostilities).[17] On its own, *jus in bello* does not lead to the emergence of anywhere wars. On its own, the strategic change does not entrench the reality of anywhere wars. Together, though, law, political/strategic change, and technological change, bring about anywhere wars. Making an argument both about the law and about war, one being a function of the other, the chapter shows what specific role is played by drone programs in the equation.

6.1 The Absence of a Geographical Limitation of Conflicts in the Law

There is no unitary concept of armed conflict: the Geneva Conventions recognize two types of armed conflict that are distinguished according to

[17] Lee Feinstein and Anne-Marie Slaughter, "A Duty to Prevent" (2004) *Foreign Affairs*, www.foreignaffairs.com/articles/2004-01-01/duty-prevent, 136–50, 136.

> Because danger and insecurity are imported into the system via the bad nature of particular regimes, the existence of, for instance, weapons of mass destruction do not in itself constitute a problem. They do turn noxious, however, as soon as they are in the hands of "rulers without internal checks on their power", "rulers who menace their own citizens as much as they do their neighbours and potential adversaries" or "individuals who seek absolute power at home or sponsor terrorism abroad."

the status of the parties.[18] As such, an interstate conflict qualifies as an international armed conflict (IAC), while a conflict between a state and a non-state actor qualifies as a non-international armed conflict (NIAC). Traditionally, the distinction between the two types of armed conflict informally corresponded to a territorial reality. On the one hand, an IAC was considered as involving border crossing, whereas a NIAC was presumed to be confined to the territory of one state. Therefore, IHL would apply to the whole territory of the warring parties or, in the case of NIACs, the whole territory under the control of a party to the conflict.[19]

Notwithstanding these factual scenarios and the legal assumptions that they created, *jus in bello* was never designed to confine armed conflicts territorially and it applies irrespective of the parties' geographical location. Indeed, in the absence of an express territorial limitation in the law, *jus in bello* applies "wherever belligerent confrontations occur, including international air space, the high seas, cyberspace, and, indeed, the territory of third States, whether hostile, co-belligerent, occupied, or neutral. What is decisive is not where hostile acts occur but whether, by their nexus to an armed conflict, they actually do represent 'acts of war'."[20] Hence, the coincidence of the two legal categories with a geographical distinction simply existed as a matter of fact. Although a territorialized legal reasoning originally framed *jus in bello* and although the two types of armed conflicts established by contemporary IHL used to implicitly correspond to two distinct geographical realities, it is hard to deny that there are no geographical criteria in *jus in bello* that delimit armed conflicts. As such, the possibility of geographical extension is present in the scope of available conditions for action that the norm provides for, but this possibility never appeared because the context was different.

Because no legal provision limits the scope of applicability of IHL rules to the battlefield, and if one accepts the Tadić logic as valid, the idea that

[18] Common Article 2, Geneva Conventions.

[19] ICTY, The Prosecutor v. Dragoljub Kunarac, Radomir Kovač and Zoran Vuković, Case No. IT-96-23 and IT-96-23/1-A, Judgment, June 12, 2002, para. 57, www.icty.org/x/cases/kunarac/acjug/en/kun-aj020612e.pdf; Jelena Pejic, "Extraterritorial Targeting by Means of Armed Drones: Some Legal Implications" (2014) 96 *International Review of the Red Cross* 67–106, 1–40.

[20] Nils Melzer, "Human Rights Implications of the Usage of Drones and Unmanned Robots in Warfare, Study," European Parliament, Directorate-General for External Policies, Policy Department, May 2013. Nils Melzer refers here to Art. 15(2) of the European Convention on Human Rights on derogation in time of emergency: "No derogation from Article 2, except in respect of deaths resulting from lawful acts of war, or from Articles 3, 4 (para. 1) and 7 shall be made under this provision."

NIACs do not suddenly stop because a border is crossed is applicable irrespective of how many borders are crossed. As Ryan Goodman rightly points out, "once it is understood that the laws of war extend transnationally to other States not involved in the conflict, it seems practically, if not also conceptually, unsustainable to draw the line around only immediately adjacent or neighboring States."[21] Why would the purpose of IHL suddenly evolve into preventing armed conflicts or confining them territorially (rather than regulating them wherever they occur)? Those who claim otherwise should be clear about the fact that they are speaking in normative terms and consider that it is not *desirable* for the scope of application of IHL in NIACs to remain unlimited in principle.[22]

As far as the application of the law is concerned in a NIAC, IHL provisions first consist in imposing IHL obligations on the parties and in regulating their conduct. Hence, as the ICRC has stated, the "spillover of a NIAC into adjacent territory cannot have the effect of absolving the parties of their IHL obligations."[23] Second, contemporary IHL also aims to protect civilian populations and prisoners of war. The decision not to apply IHL merely on the grounds of border crossing "would deprive of protection both civilians possibly affected by the fighting, as well as persons who fall into enemy hands."[24] This would go against Additional Protocol II, which provides for its applicability to "all persons affected by an armed conflict,"[25] but also against the Commentary to the Protocols that stresses the

[21] Goodman, "Why the Laws of War Apply to Drone Strikes." Interestingly, in support of our view, Ryan Goodman adds: "What's more, how can limiting the scope of the laws of war to immediately adjacent and neighboring States remain viable in the age of drone warfare or especially cyber conflict in which belligerents may attack from a continent away?"

[22] Some scholars are sharper in their analysis and admit the absence of geographical limitation in the law and then explaining why it is problematic. See Emily Crawford, "The Temporal and Geographic Reach of International Humanitarian Law," 2016, https://papers.ssrn.com/sol3/papers.cfm?abstract_id=2785420. The different approaches supporting the existence (or the introduction) of a territorial limitation in *jus in bello* will be further explored below.

[23] ICRC, International Humanitarian Law and the Challenges of Contemporary Armed Conflicts, Report of the 31st Conference, 9–10. See also Dapo Akande, "Classification of Armed Conflicts: Relevant Legal Concepts," in Elizabeth Wilmshurst (ed.), *International Law and the Classification of Armed Conflicts* (Oxford University Press, 2012), 70–2 and Nils Melzer, *Targeted Killing in International Law* (Oxford University Press, 2008), 259–60.

[24] ICRC, International Humanitarian Law and the Challenges of Contemporary Armed Conflicts, Report of the 31st Conference, 9–10.

[25] Article 2(1), Additional Protocol II..

applicability of Protocol II under criteria related to "persons, and not places,"[26] and finally against the intent of the 1972 Government of Experts that "persons affected by the armed conflict should be entitled to the protection of the Protocol, wherever they might be."[27]

It is not surprising, therefore, that in the Hamdan case involving a Yemeni national captured during hostilities between the US and Taliban fighters in Afghanistan, the US Supreme Court supported the application of Common Article 3 to the conflict with Al Qaeda without explicitly limiting the armed conflict's geographical scope to Afghanistan.[28] In much the same way, in cases concerning suspects captured in Pakistan and even in Bosnia-Herzegovina, the US courts considered that IHL applies to people taking part in hostilities wherever they are, regardless of whether they have crossed borders and whether or not they are located on a battlefield.[29]

Jus in bello does not include any explicit geographical criteria (and does not aim to) delimiting the scope of armed conflicts. This legal leeway was unimportant while there is an implicit link between the geographical scope of conflicts and their classification; and still is in conflict situations where it is easy to identify the places in which hostilities are underway. The emergence of drones in the counterterrorism context altered the implicit geographical delineation of conflicts, because of their technological features, because of the military strategy that they help materialize and because of the accompanying discourse insisting on the mobility and diffuse presence of transnational non-state enemy groups. In order to respond with as much (spatial) leeway as possible to emerging transnational non-state armed groups, the absence of geographical criteria in the law is being intensively exploited by drone programs.

6.2 Drone Programs' Targeted and Anywhere Wars: First Encounter with the Perils of Precision

Previous chapters have examined the rationale for drone programs based on the emergence of transnational jihadist groups. Building on this

[26] Additional Protocol Commentary, at 1360.

[27] ICRC, Commentary on the Draft Additional Protocols to the Geneva Conventions of August 12, 1949 (1973), 134.

[28] US Supreme Court, Salim A. Hamdan v. Donald H Rumsfeld et al., No. 05-184, June 29, 2006.

[29] US Court of Appeals DC, Mohammed Al-Adahi v. Barack Obama et al., No. 09-5333, July 13, 2010; US Court of Appeals DC, Belkacem Bensayah v. Barack Obama et al., No. 08-5537, June 28, 2010.

analysis and following the description of the resulting state rationale, which asserts that because the enemy is multiple, mobile and dispersed, the military response should be individualized, this chapter focuses on the impact it has on the geography of conflict: the idea is that a state should be able to act in (m)any place(s) at the same time to fight such an enemy. In order to implement this additional step in the strategy, combat drones again appear to have the required precision and ubiquity to face the described threat.

In France's fight against "jihadist groups," or the US fight against "Al Qaeda and associated forces," the rationale is that conflicts can and should take place anywhere as long as the right individuals are targeted. Chapters 4 and 5 have already demonstrated that drone programs exacerbate the individualization of war, understood as the conduct of war (and more generally the use of force) based on the personal and behavioral features of individuals rather than on (visible) material acts that they conduct in order to harm the enemy. If the individualization of war were not so materialized by drones, the absence of a geographical limitation of conflicts would not be so significant. While the precision offered by drones' technological capacities is often mentioned to praise their marked capacity to distinguish between combatants and civilians in principle, the present developments reveal another facet of precision. Because drones have capacities for high precision and ubiquity in observation, surveillance, and targeting, they simultaneously facilitate the implementation of military strategies that focus on the individual rather than on the armed group and make all geographical concerns and boundaries in conducting war virtually irrelevant.

In a context where operations focus on individuals belonging to transnational jihadist groups, targets that are all potentially itinerant, and where the operator does not wait for these actors to undertake hostile actions in order to strike, drone operations are deployed in multiple locations. Two elements are said to call for the absence of geographical constraint in order to conduct hostilities against such an enemy. First, several enemy groups are commingled and considered part of the same conflict by the US to a certain extent, even more so by France, and implicitly by the UK. Because these groups are present in different territories, the amalgam of enemy groups as part of a single conflict considerably extends the geographical scope of hostilities. Second, the focus is on individual targets, who are considered to "carry the hostilities" wherever they go.

The US position is that it is engaged in an armed conflict with Al Qaeda and associated forces. The first drone strike was conducted more than fourteen years ago by the US[30] and since then, drone strikes have been conducted in Afghanistan, Pakistan, Yemen, Somalia, Iraq, and Syria. For the time being, the 2001 AUMF is being relied upon for authority to use military force against "Al Qaeda and associated forces," a category that determines the scope of application of this Congress authorization but with uncertainty. Despite its ambiguity, the category "Al Qaeda and associated forces" has been used by all three branches of the US government to name the enemy in the non-international armed conflict that the US considers it has been part of since the 9/11 attacks.[31] As Rebecca Ingber explains with clarity in her article on co-belligerency, the Executive successfully established the principle in both the courts and Congress that it should read the Executive's statutory authority in a broad manner, to cover groups that did not exist at the time of the

[30] CIA Director George Tenet, "Written Statement for the Record of the Director of Central Intelligence before the National Commission on Terrorist Attacks upon the United States," March 24, 2004, 16, http://govinfo.library.unt.edu/911/hearings/hearing8/tenet_statement.pdf: "Subsequent to 9/11, approval was quickly granted to ship the missiles, and the Predator aircraft and missiles reached their overseas location on September 16, 2001. The first mission was flown over Kabul and Qandahar on September 18 without carrying weapons. Subsequent host nation approval was granted on October 7 and the first armed mission was flown the same day."

[31] Harold Hongju Koh, Legal Adviser, US Department of State, Speech at the Annual Meeting of the American Society of International Law, Washington, DC, "The Obama Administration and International Law," March 25, 2010, https://2009-2017.state.gov/s/l/releases/remarks/139119.htm:

> [T]he United States is in an armed conflict with al-Qaeda, as well as the Taliban and associated forces, in response to the horrific 9/11 attacks, and may use force consistent with its inherent right to self-defense under international law. As a matter of domestic law, Congress authorized the use of all necessary and appropriate force through the 2001 Authorization for Use of Military Force (AUMF). These domestic and international legal authorities continue to this day.

Jeh Charles Johnson, General Counsel of the US, "The Conflict against al Qaeda and Its Affiliates: How Will It End?," Department of Defense at the Oxford Union, Oxford University, November 30, 2012, www.lawfareblog.com/jeh-johnson-speech-oxford-union; Barack Obama, "Statement by the President on Afghanistan," The White House, July 6, 2016; The White House, "Executive Order – United States Policy"; US Congress 2001, Authorization for the Use of Military Force, September 18, 2001, www.gpo.gov/fdsys/pkg/PLAW-107publ40/pdf/PLAW-107publ40.pdf, 107–40; US District Court for the District of Columbia, Moath Hamza Ahmed Al-Alwi v. Barack Obama et al., No. 09-5125, July 22, 2011; US Court of Appeals for the District of Columbia, Abdul Razak Ali v. Barack Obama, No. 11-5102, December 3, 2013.

AUMF's enactment.[32] The application of the AUMF to all areas where drone strikes have been conducted gives us some indication as to which non-state armed groups are considered as "associated forces" of Al Qaeda. In fact, the concept has allowed the use of force against the Taliban, al-Shabaab, Al Qaeda in Iraq (AQI), Al Qaeda in the Arabian Peninsula (AQAP), and even ISIS. Until now, the government's official position has relied upon the 2001 AUMF and the associated concept of co-belligerency.

As mentioned before, halfway into the Obama administration, the executive started to define criteria for a group to be considered as an associated force: "(1) an organized armed group that has entered the fight alongside Al Qaeda, and (2) a co-belligerent with Al Qaeda in hostilities against the United States or its coalition partners."[33] At first glance, some of the vocabulary employed in this definition seems to suggest that direct participation in hostilities is needed for individuals to deserve to be targeted such as "entered the fight" or "hostilities against the United States." But the insistence that "ISIS grew out of Al Qaeda in Iraq"[34] as a justification of the use of force against ISIS shows that the US government puts the threshold of support for Al Qaeda quite low in order to consider that another group falls into the scope of the AUMF; and apparently lower than "direct participation in hostilities."[35] While some Congress members consider that Obama should have called on Congress for a new authorization to use force to complement or replace AUMF, at least when its government started fighting ISIS,[36] the

[32] Rebecca Ingber, "Co-Belligerency" (2017) 42 *Yale Journal of International Law* 68–120, 67.

[33] Jeh Johnson, General Counsel, Department of Defense, Dean's Lecture at Yale Law School: "National Security Law, Lawyers and Lawyering in the Obama Administration," February 22, 2012.

[34] House Foreign Affairs Committee Chairman Ed Royce (R-Fullerton) opposing Barbara Lee's amendment, quoted in, Sarah D. Wire, "Essential Politics May Archives: U.S. House Rejects Rep. Barbara Lee's Push to End War Authorization," *Los Angeles Times*, May 2016, www.latimes.com/politics/essential/la-pol-sac-essential-politics-20160501-htmlstory.html#u-s-house-rejects-rep-barbara-lees-push-to-end-war-authorization.

[35] Ingber, "Co-Belligerency," 82.

[36] In May 2016, the House voted 285 to 138 to reject an amendment Rep. Barbara Lee introduced to end Obama's authority to use the military against ISIS. However, on June 29, 2017, Congresswoman Barbara Lee's amendment to repeal the 2001 AUMF passed the Appropriations Committee in a bipartisan vote. This amendment would repeal the 2001 AUMF 240 days after enactment of the DOD Appropriations bill. See, https://lee.house.gov/news/press-releases/congresswoman-lee-statement-on-passage-of-aumf-amendment.

2001 AUMF has neither been repealed nor amended. The Trump administration made clear in August 2017 that the US has "sufficient legal authority to prosecute the campaign against al-Qa'ida [sic.] and associated forces, including against the Islamic State of Iraq and Syria (ISIS)," including on the basis of the 2001 AUMF.[37]

The US has never tried to identify a series of separate NIACs with the Taliban in Afghanistan, al-Shabaab in Somalia, al-Shabaab in Yemen, AQI in Iraq, Al Qaeda in Afghanistan, or AQAP in Yemen. Instead, they are considered as part of the same conflict. The Bush administration expressly claimed that 9/11 led to their declaration of a global war on terror.[38] If the Obama administration did not invoke the existence of a "global war," its legal narrative supported the existence of a single conflict against Al Qaeda and associated forces as a whole, expandable over the emergence of new groups and irrespective of any geographical delineation.[39] Finally, the Trump administration considered ISIS to be part of the same unique armed conflict against Al Qaeda and associated forces.[40] All groups are considered as enemies in the same conflict, wherever they are.

As mentioned earlier, and in much the same way, the emerging French rationale is that France is not only at war against ISIS,[41] but against

[37] Charles Faulkner, "Letter from the US Department of State Bureau of Legislative Affairs, to Foreign Relations Chairman Bob Corker on the Legal Basis for the Use of Force," August 2, 2017, https://assets.documentcloud.org/documents/3911844/8-2-17-Corker-Response.pdf.

[38] George Bush, "Address to a Joint Session of Congress and the American People," The White House, September 20, 2001, https://georgewbush-whitehouse.archives.gov/news/releases/2001/09/20010920-8.html.

[39] Barack Obama, "Remarks by the President at the National Defense University," National Defense University, Fort McNair, Washington, DC, The White House, May 23, 2013, www.whitehouse.gov/the-press-office/2013/05/23/remarks-president-national-defense-university: "Beyond Afghanistan, we must define our effort not as a boundless global war on terror – but rather as a series of persistent, targeted efforts to dismantle specific networks of violent extremists that threaten America. This will involve partnerships with other states: Pakistan, Yemen, Somalia, and Mali. Beyond Afghanistan we only target al Qaeda and its associated forces."

[40] Faulkner, "Letter from the US Department": "the United States is using force in Syria against al-Qa'ida and associated forces, *including ISIS*" (emphasis added).

[41] President François Hollande, Conférence Internationale Sur la Paix et la Sécurité en Irak , September 15, 2014 www.youtube.com/watch?v=Lwf2tpzcl4U; Laurent Fabius, Ministère des Affaires étrangères et du Développement international, "Le groupe terroriste Daech n'est pas un Etat; nous devons les neutraliser" (QAG,10/09/2014), 2014 www.youtube.com/watch?v=NmolpluNdpY.

"jihadist groups" in general.[42] French state officials insist on the multiplicity of groups that have to be fought and thus, on the necessity to respond globally.[43] The former Chief of Staff, Général Pierre de Villiers, emphasized that the threat is in constant mutation and has several faces: "Yesterday al Qaïda, today Daech, Jabhat al-Nosra or Boko Haram." He insisted that France is at war against numerous, mobile, and scattered jihadist groups. Because of these features, it is argued that the response should be "global."[44] In the same vein, in October 2017, the French Minister of Defense Florence Parly insisted that France does not "sort through enemies" but fights them "globally."[45] Conforming to this strategy, the French military is engaged in multiple countries[46] and conducts cross-border operations in partnership with G5 Sahel (i.e., with Burkina Faso, Mali, Mauritania, Niger, and Chad) against Al Qaeda in the Islamic Maghreb (AQIM) but also against ramifications of Al Qaeda and ISIS (Ansar Dinee, Katitba Macinaa, Islamic Stat in the Greater Sahara, Ansaroul Islam, etc.),[47] in Afghanistan against the Taliban and the Haqqani network, and against ISIS in Iraq, Libya, and Syria.

[42] Parliamentary investigation, Commission d'enquête parlementaire relative aux moyens mis en œuvre par l'Etat pour lutter contre le terrorisme, Audition, à Huis Clos du Général Pierre de Villiers, Chef D'état-Major Des Armées Compte Rendu de L'audition, May 9, 2016. (Hearing of Chief of Staff Général Pierre de Villiers.)

[43] Ibid.

[44] Minister of Defense Jean-Yves Le Drian, "Qui est l'ennemi ?" [Who Is the Enemy], Opening Speech of the 2015 National Conference on Strategic Research," December 1, 2015, www.asafrance.fr/item/officiel-discours-d-ouverture-des-assises-nationales-2015-de-la-recherche-strategique-de-m-jean-yves-le-drian-ministre-de-la-defense-a-paris-le-1er-decembre-2015-extrait.html. By "global," Jean-Yves Le Drian pinpoints the necessity to cooperate with allies, to provide responses other than the military response to terrorism, but also on the necessity to intervene militarily in multiple areas.

[45] French Minister of Defense Florence Parly, Radio France Inter, October 6, 2017, 8:25 a.m., www.franceinter.fr/emissions/l-invite-de-8h20/l-invite-de-8h20-06-octobre-2017.

[46] It should also be noted that French military troops (between 7,000 and 10,000) were deployed on the national soil, in the framework the *Opération Sentinelle*, in January 2015 after the first Paris attacks. The contribution of the militaries is described as going beyond a dissuasive dimension. Their mission is described as a mission of intervention and crisis management. The nature of the mission is obscure. When describing the Opération Sentinelle, many state officials locate this operation in the war against ISIS; and more precisely as being its tool for the domestic level (as opposed to the extraterritorial level). See, Rapport D'enquête Relative Aux Moyens Mis En œuvre Par l'Etat Pour Lutter Contre Le Terrorisme Depuis Le 7 Janvier 2015. Hearing of Général Bruno Le Ray, gouverneur militaire de Paris, and of Colonel Marc Boileau, chef de cabinet, March 21, 2016; Hearing of M. Marc Trévidic, premier vice-président du TGI de Lille, April 6, 2016.

[47] Héni Nsaibia and Caleb Weiss, "The End of the Sahelian Anomaly: How the Global Conflict between the Islamic State and Al Qaida Finally Came to West Africa," CTC, July

Rather than defining these situations as separate armed conflicts, France seems to define them as part of a unique war against "jihadist groups." France's fight against terrorism acquired a new dimension after the attacks made on French soil.[48] Numerous French state officials were heard by a Parliamentary Investigation Committee from January 7, 2015 onward to examine France's tools to fight against terrorism.[49] The hearings of government and military officials conducted by the deputies, as well as other declarations, reveal that both the Executive and the Parliament consider that France is at war and refer to "jihadist groups" as being the enemy.[50] When such a category delimits the scope of the armed conflict that France conducts, its geographical scope goes beyond the already extensive war of the US against "Al Qaeda and associated forces."

The UK has been using drones for targeted killings in Afghanistan since 2007, in Iraq since 2014, and in Syria since at least 2015.[51]

2020, https://ctc.usma.edu/the-end-of-the-sahelian-anomaly-how-the-global-conflict-between-the-islamic-state-and-al-qaida-finally-came-to-west-africa/.

48 From January 7, 2015 to January 9, 2015, terrorist attacks occurred across the Île-de-France region, particularly in Paris. Three attackers killed a total of seventeen people in four shooting attacks, and police then killed the three assailants. "Charlie Hebdo Attack: Three Days of Terror," *BBC News*, January 14, 2015, section Europe, www.bbc.com/news/world-europe-30708237. On Friday November 13, 2015, a few months later, a series of coordinated terrorist attacks occurred in Paris, France and the city's northern suburb, Saint-Denis. The attackers killed 130 people. Another 368 people were injured. Eleanor Steafel, "Paris Terror Attack: Everything We Know on Saturday Afternoon," *Telegraph*, November 21, 2015, www.telegraph.co.uk/news/worldnews/europe/france/11995246/Paris-shooting-What-we-know-so-far.html.

49 Parliamentary report, Rapport d'enquête relative aux moyens mis en œuvre par l'Etat pour lutter contre le terrorisme depuis le 7 Janvier 2015, Assemblée Nationale, July 2016, www.assemblee-nationale.fr/14/rap-enq/r3922-t1.asp.

50 Gérard Davet and Fabrice Lhomme (Interviews with President Hollande), *Un président ne devrait pas dire ça … les secrets d'un quinquennat* (Stock, French and European Publications, 2016); Minister of Defense Jean-Yves Le Drian, *Qui est l'ennemi ?* (Editions du Cerf, 2016); Prime Minister Manuel Valls, *L'Exigence* (Grasset, 2016); Commission d'enquête parlementaire relative aux moyens mis en œuvre par l'Etat pour lutter contre le terrorisme (Hearing of Chief of Staff Général Pierre de Villiers).

51 It should be noted for the future that an information tribunal upheld the MoD's refusal to release the number of British armed drones deployed against ISIS and their location: First-Tier Tribunal, General Regulatory Chamber, Chris Cole vs. The Information Commissioner and the Ministry of Defence, July 11, 2017, No. EA/2016/0290, https://dronewarsuk.files.wordpress.com/2017/08/023-150817-open-decision.pdf. Besides, it should be noted that the tribunal upheld the MoD's decision that the public will only know how many *manned* British aircrafts are deployed but not unmanned aircraft, while the MoD has been insisting "that there is in effect no difference between its armed drones and its manned aircraft" (see, on this point: Chris Cole, "Information Tribunal Dismisses Drone Wars Appeal over British Drone Secrecy," Drone Wars UK, August 17, 2017,

In general, the UK's fight against terrorism has been taking place in Afghanistan against Al Qaeda and the Taliban, in Iraq and in Syria against ISIS, in Nigeria against Boko Haram, and in Somalia against al-Shabaab.[52] In a similar manner to the US and French governments, the UK confronts multiple non-state armed groups in the context of counterterrorism. However, the UK implicitly merges the different terrorist groups into a single enemy in a slightly different way from the US and France. The UK's enemy is often referred to as "terrorism" rather than "the Taliban," "ISIS," "Boko Haram," or "al-Shabaab."[53] This disembodiment is counterbalanced by the *prima facie* distinction made by the UK between different conflicts, which can be explained by the Executive's need to obtain parliamentary authorization for each new area of engagement.

The distinction of conflicts as well as their apparent geographical delineation seems more formalistic than deeply representative of the UK drone war strategy. The need to obtain the authorization of the House of Commons prior to using force precludes the government from officially undertaking strategies that go beyond the scope of these authorizations, which are geographically delineated. Two British nationals were killed by drone strikes in August 2015 in Syria.[54] At the time, the House of Commons had only granted authorization to the government to use force in Iraq.[55] In August 2015, the UK ignored this restriction and

https://dronewars.net/2017/08/17/information-tribunal-dismisses-drone-wars-appeal-over-british-drone-secrecy/.

52 UK Ministry of Defence, Joint Doctrine Note 2/11, "The UK Approach to Unmanned Aircraft Systems," March 30, 2011; UK Ministry of Defence, Joint Doctrine Publication 0-30.2, "Unmanned Aircraft Systems," August 2017.

53 Rt. Hon. Amber Rudd MP, "Home Secretary Statement on Recent Terrorist Attacks to the Parliament," June 22, 2017, www.gov.uk/government/speeches/home-secretary-statement-on-recent-terrorist-attacks. Statement on Counterterrorism by Ambassador Jonathan Allen, UK Deputy Permanent Representative to the United Nations, "Multilateral Cooperation Must Continue to Effectively Counter Terrorism and Violent Extremism," September 29, 2017, www.gov.uk/government/speeches/multilateral-cooperation-must-continue-to-effectively-counter-terrorism-and-violent-extremism; Theresa May's Speech to the UN General Assembly 2017, September 29, 2017, www.gov.uk/government/speeches/multilateral-cooperation-must-continue-to-effectively-counter-terrorism-and-violent-extremism.

54 Ewen MacAskill and Richard Norton-Taylor, "How UK Government Decided to Kill Reyaad Khan," *The Guardian*, September 8, 2015, www.theguardian.com/world/2015/sep/08/how-did-britain-decide-to-assassinate-uk-isis-fighter-reyaad-khan-drone-strike.

55 Andrew Sparrow and Claire Philipps, "UK Parliament Approves Air Strikes against Isis in Iraq – As It Happened," *The Guardian*, September 26, 2014, www.theguardian.com/

crossed the border into Syria, first to undertake intelligence gathering missions and then to carry out air strikes. The UK could by no means publicly claim to be at war with ISIS in Syria. However, when discussing the UK strikes in Syria of August 2015, neither Michael Fallon in his hearing,[56] nor David Cameron in his oral statement,[57] nor any other UK official clearly identified these strikes as exclusively conducted in the exercise of self-defense. On the contrary, *jus in bello* was used to justify the strikes and it was clearly stressed out that the strikes in Syria were not only in self-defense of the UK but were also a result of the extension of the already existing armed conflict in Iraq.[58]

Later on, the Intelligence and Security Committee of Parliament issued a report confirming that the UK government used a mixed *jus ad bellum and jus in bello* justification for the strike on Khan.[59] The Committee confirmed that the government's policy involves conducting extraterritorial strikes against individuals in areas that Parliament has not primarily recognized as zones of armed conflict, both under *jus ad bellum* and

politics/blog/live/2014/sep/26/mps-debate-and-vote-on-air-strikes-against-islamic-state-politics-live-blog.

[56] Rt. Hon. Michael Fallon, "Oral Evidence: The UK Government's Policy on the Use of Drones for Targeted Killing," 2015, http://data.parliament.uk/writtenevidence/committeeevidence.svc/evidencedocument/human-rights-committee/the-uk-governments-policy-on-the-use-of-drones-for-targeted-killing/oral/27633.html.

[57] David Cameron, "Oral Statement to Parliament, Syria: Refugees and Counter-Terrorism – Prime Minister's Statement," House of Commons, 2015, www.gov.uk/government/speeches/syria-refugees-and-counter-terrorism-prime-ministers-statement.

[58] Government Legal Department, Leigh Day, "Proposed Application for Judicial Review by Caroline Lucas MP and Baroness Jones of Moulescoomb," October 23, 2015:

> It was also lawful as an act in the collective self-defence of Iraq in that it was directed at persons who were members of a group engaged in planning and perpetrating attacks against Iraq. The attack was lawful on both (and each independently) of these bases. It was also consistent with principles of the law of armed conflict in that the airstrike was directed at Reyaad Khan in the ongoing armed conflict within and against Iraq who was actively engaged in attack planning and perpetration, and the strike was fully in accordance with principles of military necessity, proportionality and related law of armed conflict principles.

Fallon, "Oral Evidence": When asked to define the incidental killing of the Belgium national in August 2015, Fallon explained that the death could not be identified as a "civilian casualty" providing that the Belgium national was "not a civilian."

[59] UK Intelligence and Security Committee of Parliament, Report on UK Lethal Drone Strikes in Syria, April 26, 2017, HC 1152, 5: individual and collective self-defense are set as a basis for extraterritorial drone strikes against non-state actors, as well as the laws of armed conflict.

jus in bello justifications.[60] Such a policy amounts to allowing an extraterritorial use of force against non-state actors wherever they go, including when they travel outside "hot conflict zones," to use the US expression. Such a policy amounts to considering that the armed conflict simply moves along with the participants in the conflict.

These elements strongly suggest that the British government had already considered itself to be in an NIAC against ISIS, also in Syria, in August 2015 before getting the Parliamentary authorization. It is worth noting that the authorizations granted by Parliament – while they are supposed to be a valuable check and push for accountability and transparency – do not actually shape the military strategy of the UK government. In this sense, the state-by-state determination of the scope of the conflict requested by the parliamentary authorization mechanism may well be a mere formality hiding the fact that the UK places a similar emphasis on the targets and their transnational trajectory as do France and the US.

The military strategy of drone programs, to conduct war wherever its participants go in anticipation of their participation in hostilities, would neither materialize nor hold without the technological capacities of drones and their promise of precision and ubiquity introduced at the beginning of this book. Overall, drones' technological capacities allow a precise focus on individuals, primarily through surveillance capacities that enable a precise selection process. Combat drones gather both signal intelligence and image intelligence, which is acquired in real time, thanks to the use of satellite communication links and to their powerful visual sensors.[61] This air-to-ground precision weapon it is equipped with closes the precision loop by ensuring that the person selected by the drone operator is accurately targeted.[62] Combat drones, through their capacity to stay airborne for hours on end and their effective AirWarden detection system, promise permanent surveillance.

[60] For a striking example of the intertwined *jus in bello/jus ad bellum* rationale, and even of the confusion between both legal frameworks, see UK Intelligence and Security Committee of Parliament, Report on UK Lethal Drone Strikes in Syria, 17–19. It is unclear whether and when the principles of necessity and proportionality are examined in terms of *jus in bello, jus ad bellum*, or both.

[61] A source of the Intercept underscored the limitations of drones' SIGINT capabilities. See The Intercept, The Drone Papers, The Assassination Complex, 2015, https://theintercept.com/drone-papers/the-assassination-complex/.

[62] Ibid.

The precision and ubiquity of drones allow the materialization of a war conducted anywhere a conflict participant may be. Thus, all three states have built their argument and military strategy on drones' technological capacities. The US argument has centered on the distance allowed by drones and issuing protection of their military troops, on the one hand, and the precision of the strikes, on the other hand. For instance, President Obama's speech on drone policy of May 2013 emphasized the fact that "fewer of our troops [were] in harm's way" since his administration considerably increased the use of combat drones, and the proof is that he had "already brought nearly 150,000 troops home."[63]

Drone technologies are indispensable to materialize France's aspiration to conduct war from a distance:[64] the technology is already at the core of the French rationale in favor of drone programs. Government and military officials expressed their disapproval of ground intervention and urged its limitation mainly to protect its troops.[65] In the same vein, Former Minister of Defense Jean-Yves le Drian advertised air intervention as allowing: (i) countries to decide for themselves how they want to handle the conflict on the ground for their region; and (ii) to "act preventively by destroying the enemy's epicenter."[66] The Minister of the Armed Forces (the new

[63] Obama, "Remarks by the President at the National Defense University."

[64] Le Drian, "Qui est l'ennemi ?," mentions the acquisition of drones by 2025. Institut de Recherche Stratégique de l'École Militaire, "Quels Drones Pour Quels Usages à L"horizon 2020 ?," May 18, 2016, www.defense.gouv.fr/irsem/page-d-accueil/nos-evenements/quels-drones-pour-quels-usages-a-l-horizon-2020-le-mercredi-18-mai-2016; "Discours de clôture de Florence Parly – Ministre des armées, Université d'été de la Défense 2017, Toulon, September 5, 2017, www.defense.gouv.fr/salle-de-presse/tout-discours/discours-de-cloture-de-florence-parly-universite-d-ete-de-la-defense-2017.

[65] Hearing of Chief of Staff Général Pierre de Villiers, May 9, 2016: He believes that the enemy wants to attract European military forces on the ground to "take hostages, cut off heads and sway public opinion," by denouncing for instance a return to the crusades and blaming the Western countries for allegedly conquering the two historical seats of the Caliphate, Baghdad and Damascus. Rapport D'enquête Relative Aux Moyens Mis En œuvre Par l'Etat Pour Lutter Contre Le Terrorisme Depuis Le 7 Janvier 2015, Hearing of Pierre Razoux, former director of the Ministry of Defense Research Center, May 19, 2016: Razoux considers ground intervention to be a "huge strategical mistake."

[66] Jean-Yves Le Drian, Minister of Defense, Commission d'enquête relative aux moyens mis en œuvre par l'État pour lutter contre le terrorisme depuis le 7 janvier 2015, June 1, 2016, Report no. 32, www.assemblee-nationale.fr/14/cr-cemoyter/15-16/c1516032.asp:

> Il ne faut pas envoyer de soldats au sol, ni en Libye ni au Levant. Notre rôle est de faire en sorte que les territoires concernés disposent de forces que nous formons, que nous aidons à manœuvrer, auxquelles nous livrons éventuellement du matériel; de faire en sorte que ces territoires se libèrent par eux-mêmes. Le précédent en Irak n'a en effet pas donné de

terminology for Ministry of Defense) Florence Parly praised drone technologies as allowing France "to permanently combine surveillance, endurance in the confidentiality and precision of the strike," as increasing the efficiency of military operations while "limiting the risk of collateral damages."[67] Parly also emphasized that this "new usage will also allow us to optimize the use of aircrafts and subsequent air refueling."[68]

Finally, the UK rationale in favor of drone programs is also very much focused on drones' technological capacities in particular to perform operations to conduct "dull, dirty, dangerous and deep tasks" better than any other engine and by protecting the lives of British soldiers.[69] Dull tasks are "low workload, low intensity tasks" that do not necessarily need direct and constant control of a human being and thus should be mostly automated.[70] Dirty tasks are operations "in environments that would be hostile to a manned aircraft or its crew."[71] Dangerous tasks are operations conducted in such high-risk areas that they may well lead to a sacrifice (for instance, when penetrating the enemy engagement zone for the sake of gathering information).[72] Finally, deep operations target "deep" or "strategic" targets who are not located in what is referred to as "close operations" (and in fact corresponds to the US notion of "areas of active hostilities").[73] Because combat drones allow for distant, permanent, and precision surveillance and strikes, they simultaneously ensure successful and protective operations that are "dull, dirty, dangerous and deep."

It has now been shown that drone programs have materialized the opportunity for a geographically unlimited war, and that this opportunity is encouraged by the absence of a geographical criterion in *jus in bello* to delineate hostilities. Despite the legal, strategic, and technological world

> bons résultats et, si nous nous substituions aux forces locales, ce serait ingérable. Aussi nous revient-il de former les forces locales et, par des frappes, non seulement d'accompagner leurs opérations, mais aussi d'agir préventivement en détruisant des centres de commandement, des centres d'entraînement, des lieux de ressource.

[67] Speech of French Minister of the Armed Forces, Discours de clôture de Florence Parly.
[68] Ibid.
[69] UK Ministry of Defence, Joint Doctrine Note 2/11; UK Ministry of Defence, Joint Doctrine Publication 0-30.2; UK House of Commons, Louisa Brooke-Holland, "Overview of Military Drones Used by the UK Armed Forces," Briefing paper, no. 06493, October 8, 2015, 8.
[70] UK Ministry of Defence, Joint Doctrine Note 2/11§308.
[71] Ibid., §309.
[72] Ibid., §310.
[73] Ibid., §311.

validating a geographically unlimited war – an anywhere war – some legal scholars still try to argue that there is a geographical criterion in the law that makes such an expansion of warfare illegal.

6.3 The Failed Attempts to Establish a Legal Constraint to the Geography of Drone Wars

Today, the idea that a NIAC can extend to the territory of neighboring states into which a conflict has spilled over is generally accepted. However, the idea that the territory of a NIAC can in principle be the world, as long as the other requirements for a NIAC to exist are met is still rejected by some scholars. Unfortunately, the idea that this rejection is not motivated by legal justifications but by normative or policy goals is not always acknowledged. It has been argued that "there has to be a territory in which 'protracted armed violence' is taking place [and t]hat territory cannot be the world," before inviting those "professing a novel theory" to prove that this theory has become legally accepted.[74] Yet, given the absence in *jus in bello* of any apparent geographical delineation requirement, the burden of proof seems to rest on those who believe that such a criterion exists. Some scholars do undertake this task, and the purpose of the current section is to examine their case for recognizing a territorial condition in IHL that would constrain conflicts geographically.

The first approach consists of choosing a state-by-state analysis of conflict situations. The ICRC for example explained that "it does not share the view that a conflict of global dimensions is or has been taking place. . . . the ICRC has taken a case-by-case approach to legally analyzing and classifying the various situations of violence that have occurred in the fight against terrorism."[75] The other approach is to rest on the territorial thinking that originally framed *jus in bello*. Some scholars, for instance, while they accept the Tadić logic and ensuing extension of *jus in bello* to neighboring non-belligerent states, consider that the "legal

[74] In response to a comment to his blog post, Marko Milanovic, "On Whether IHL Applies to Drone Strikes Outside 'Areas of Active Hostilities': A Response to Ryan Goodman," *EJIL: Talk!*, October 5, 2017, www.ejiltalk.org/on-whether-ihl-applies-to-drone-strikes-outside-areas-of-active-hostilities-a-response-to-ryan-goodman/.

[75] International Committee of the Red Cross, International Humanitarian Law and the Challenges of Contemporary Armed Conflicts, Report of the 31st International Conference of the International Red Cross and Red Crescent, 10, www.icrc.org/eng/assets/files/red-cross-crescent-movement/31st-international-conference/31-int-conference-ihl-challenges-report-11-5-1-2-en.pdf.

concept of a 'global battlefield' . . . does not appear to be supported by the essentially territorial focus of IHL, which appears to limit IHL applicability to the territory of states involved in an armed conflict."[76] However, some proponents of this idea do simultaneously admit its legal shortcoming and that it is policy or normative reasons that lead them to reject the idea that a member of an armed group moving around the world carries the NIAC with them wherever they go.[77] Indeed, as noted earlier, the original territorial thinking is insufficient to conclude that there is a legal criterion that limits the geographical scope of conflicts. This insufficiency becomes clear when authors deduce the existence of a legal criterion calling for a geographical limitation of conflicts from the mere presence of a lexical field of territory in the Geneva Conventions.[78] Pejic, for instance, explains that she refuses to understand IHL as automatically applicable to "the use of lethal force against a person located outside the territory of the parties involved in an ongoing NIAC," since it would "imply that a member of an armed group or an individual civilian directly participating in hostilities moving around the world would be deemed to automatically 'carry' the 'original' NIAC with them wherever they go, and based on IHL, would remain targetable within a potentially geographically unlimited space."[79] While expressing a policy concern, the author does not establish that her conclusion is the only possible interpretation of the norm. Instead of seriously articulating a normative argument in support of her preferred interpretation, Pejic prefers to simplistically try to convince us that the only "true" interpretation of the norm is hers.

[76] See, for instance, Pejic, "Extraterritorial Targeting," 36.

[77] Ibid.

[78] See, for example, Daskal, "The Geography of the Battlefield," 1203:

> While not explicitly articulated, the notion of a distinct zone of active hostilities where fighting is underway is implicit in treaty law. The Geneva Conventions, for example, specify that prisoners of war and internees must be moved away from the "combat zone" in order to keep them out of danger, and that belligerent parties must conduct searches for the dead and wounded left on the "battlefield." While there are no explicit definitions provided, the context suggests that these terms refer to those areas where fighting is currently taking place or very likely to occur. The related term "zones of military operations", which is spelled out in a bit more detail in the Commentaries to the Geneva Conventions, is described as covering those areas where there is actual or planned troop movement, even if no active fighting.

[79] Pejic, "Extraterritorial Targeting," 36–7.

In the same vein, although arguably in a more interesting and creative manner, some commentators attribute a territorial objective to provisions that help to identify armed conflicts. For example, Emily Crawford identifies a "third approach" according to which the law pushes for a geographical delineation of conflicts by requiring a sufficient nexus between the situation of violence and the target.[80] Crawford explains that:

> rather than hewing to a strict geographical limit on the applicability of the law, or espousing a broad, potentially vast, scope of applicability, this approach suggests that it is the "persons, objects, and the like that are affected by the armed conflict and the conduct at issue rather than any geographic location [that] would provide a more appropriate solution to the question of the geographic scope of application of the law."[81]

Yet, the condition that the target belongs to an organized armed group is already a condition of the law of non-international armed conflicts, which indeed applies to situations of violence between a state and non-state organized armed groups. As it stands, this requirement does not aim at geographically delineating conflicts. It is one thing to say it has logical repercussions on the location of hostilities (as it defines what can be considered as part of the armed conflict), and another to claim that this requirement constitutes a limitation to the geographical scope of armed conflicts.[82]

[80] Emily Crawford, "The Temporal and Geographic Reach of International Humanitarian Law," in Ben Saul and Dapo Akande (eds.), *The Oxford Guide to International Humanitarian Law* (Oxford University Press, 2020), 57–75.

[81] Ibid., 74. Crawford quotes here: Sandesh Sivakumaran, *The Law of Non-International Armed Conflict* (Oxford University Press, 2012), 252.

[82] Jennifer Daskal makes the same move when she claims to initiate a new approach to define the geographical scope of armed conflicts (the "zone" approach), while in fact using existing criteria of a non-geographical nature or concern in order to distinguish armed conflicts from the absence of armed conflict. See Daskal, "The Geography of the Battlefield," 1233: Daskal claims that

> the zone approach proposed by this Article fills the international law gap, effectively mediating the multifaceted liberty and security interests at stake. It recognizes the broad sweep of the conflict, but distinguishes between zones of active hostilities and other areas in determining which rules apply. Specifically, it offers a set of standards that would both limit and legitimize the use of out-of-battlefield targeted killings and law of war–based detentions, subjecting their use to an individualized threat assessment, a least-harmful-means test, and significant procedural safeguards.

Finally, a proposition recently endorsed by the ICRC interprets the law of IACs as applicable to the force used by a state on the territory of a non-consenting state against non-state actors.[83] This proposition can be interpreted as bringing back a state-based dimension to the classification of the conflicts, which subsequently partly depends on the territory where hostilities are conducted rather than only on the status of the parties. Yet, Common Article 2(1) to the Geneva Conventions defines IACs as any difference arising between two or more states and leading to the intervention of armed forces, regardless of the intensity, duration, and scale of violence.[84] On this basis, in the 1950s the ICRC declared that an IAC required the intervention of members of the armed forces of two or more opposing states.[85] This interpretation of the law led legal scholars to widely reject the Bush administration's claim that the use of force against Al Qaeda in the war on terror on a global scale qualified as an international armed conflict.[86] Although the US position was declared unacceptable at the time, now, two decades after the Bush administration formulated this argument, different ways of extending IACs to conflicts between state and non-state groups have been proposed. The new Commentary issued by the ICRC in 2016 concludes that the

In reality, Daskal does not exactly fill the "geographical scope" gap but rather refers to other existing criteria – unrelated to the geography of war – such as the existence of protracted armed violence or the minimum level of intensity that violence has to reach in order to qualify as an NIAC.

83 Akande, "Classification of Armed Conflicts," 32; Dapo Akande, "When Does the Use of Force against a Non-State Armed Group Trigger an International Armed Conflict and Why Does This Matter?," *EJIL: Talk!*, October 18, 2016, www.ejiltalk.org/when-does-the-use-of-force-against-a-non-state-armed-group-trigger-an-international-armed-conflict-and-why-does-this-matter/; Adil Ahmad Haque, "The United States Is at War with Syria (according to the ICRC's New Geneva Convention Commentary)," *EJIL: Talk!*, April 8, 2016, www.ejiltalk.org/the-united-states-is-at-war-with-syria-according-to-the-icrcs-new-geneva-convention-commentary/; Geneva Conventions, ICRC Commentary of 2016, para. 223, https://ihl-databases.icrc.org/applic/ihl/ihl.nsf/Comment.xsp?action=openDocument&documentId=BE2D518CF5DE54EAC1257F7D0036B518#51_B.

84 Geneva Conventions I to IV, Common Art. 2(1); ICRC, Commentary on the Geneva Convention for the Amelioration of the Wounded and Sick in Armed Forces in the Field, 3 (Jean S. Pictet, ed., 1952).

85 Frederic Siordet and Jean S. Pictet, Geneva Conventions, Commentary (Four Volume Set): For the Amelioration of the Condition of the Wounded and Sick in Armed Forces in the Field – The Geneva Conventions of August 12, 1949 (International Committee of the Red Cross, 1995).

86 Communication of the US regarding the Killing of Harithi al-Yemeni, May 4, 2006, A/HRC/4/20/Add.1, 344.

status-based interpretation of IACs is "too narrow."[87] To reach this conclusion, the ICRC delivers an extensive interpretation of Article 2 by insisting on the territorial component of the state:

> International armed conflicts are fought between states. The government is only one of the constitutive elements of the State, while the territory and the population are the other constitutive elements. Therefore, any attack directed against the territory, population, or the military or civilian infrastructure constitutes a resort to armed force against the State to which this territory, population or infrastructure belongs.[88]

For a while, the proposals to extend IACs to conflicts involving non-state actors did not depart from the actor-based logic of the classification. It was argued that conflicts should be regarded as IACs when: (i) non-state actors can be defined as the official government, thus resting on the mutation of a non-state actor into a state-like entity;[89] (ii) when the non-state armed group acts on behalf of a third state; or (iii) a non-state armed group is supported by third states in its fight against another state. All three of these scenarios build upon the legal status of the parties to the conflict. In contrast, the application of IAC law to conflicts between states and non-state armed groups in the absence of the territorial state's consent pays attention to the location of hostilities and to state borders. When read together with the ICRC's state-by-state approach to identify and delineate NIACs, the position in favor of the extension of IAC law to the use of force in a non-consenting third state appears as an act of resistance against a non-geographically focused and non-state-based *jus in bello* paradigm.

Overall, the four approaches pushing for the recognition or the introduction of a geographical criterion to confine armed conflicts territorially are not convincing because they are framed, not as normative propositions of what the law should be, but as attempts to convince the reader

[87] International Committee of the Red Cross, Commentary on the First Geneva Convention: Convention (Cambridge University Press, 2017). On this point, see §222 of the online version of the 2016 Commentary, https://ihl-databases.icrc.org/applic/ihl/ihl.nsf/Comment.xsp?action=openDocument&documentId=BE2D518CF5DE54EAC1257F7D0036B518.

[88] Geneva Conventions, ICRC Commentary of 2016, para. 224, https://ihl-databases.icrc.org/applic/ihl/ihl.nsf/Comment.xsp?action=openDocument&documentId=BE2D518CF5DE54EAC1257F7D0036B518#51_B.

[89] Marko Milanovic, "What Exactly Internationalizes an Internal Armed Conflict?," *EJIL: Talk!*, May 7, 2010, www.ejiltalk.org/what-exactly-internationalizes-an-internal-armed-conflict/.

that they reveal the true meaning of these norms. The search for leverage to limit the scope of armed conflicts, on the one hand, and to internationalize NIACs, on the other hand, both aim at offering the widest protection possible to people who do not take part in hostilities through different means. First, restraining the scope of NIACs aims at increasing the number of situations where IHRL instead of IHL would apply to the attacks. Second, increasing the number of situations that can qualify as IACs rather than NIACs leads to the application of a more complete and more protective regime. Contrary to what their authors often seem to claim, these propositions do not discuss what the law *is* but what the law, in their view, *ought* to be.

6.4 Concluding Remarks

This chapter showed that, although affiliated with a territorial thinking and long identified as corresponding to a geographical reality, *jus in bello* never categorically limited armed conflicts in space. Instead, the objective of the laws regulating the use of force has always been to regulate hostilities wherever they constitute armed conflicts. Building on the definition presented in the previous chapters of the distinctive features of transnational jihadist groups (a multiplicity of fronts; a global, abstract and non-state-centered agenda; a loose network organization), this chapter has shown how states extend the geographical scope of armed conflicts and how this extension is exacerbated when states aggregate all jihadist groups together in the same armed conflict.

The recourse to armed drones, because of their technology and the military strategy they implement, is presented as the most suitable tool to face a dispersed enemy. The chapter has illustrated the interdependence between drones' technological capacities, norms of IHL, and the emergence of a military strategy consisting of dispensing the conduct of hostilities with territorial concerns or constraints. By building on the detailed assessment of combat drones' technological capacities in previous chapters, Chapter 6 has argued that drones enable states to go potentially anywhere and to be precise enough to target individuals labeled as enemies individually and accurately. In conclusion, combat drones not only allow and validate the military strategy of anticipatory warfare but also arguably catalyze its development, in the absence of geographical criteria in *jus in bello*: the interaction between military strategy, technology, and the law has concretized the prospect of anywhere wars.

The lack of consideration for borders when conducting hostilities or regulating them both legally in *jus in bello* and practically in drone programs recalls the project of "spaceless universalism" which is unwilling to draw lines and spatial distinctions.[90] The geographically delineated system of relations among sovereign states does not function as a framework for "bracketing" the war on terror.[91] On the contrary, the departure from state-centricity relies on discursive practices and technological tools that emphasize and pursue a constructed universal imperative to fight against global terrorism everywhere. Yet, Chapters 4 to 6 have shown that waging war in the name of humanity in order to annihilate terrorist groups and to purportedly obtain the ideal of perpetual peace produces exactly the opposite: perpetual and anywhere wars.[92] The indefiniteness of wars waged through drone programs, in time and space calls for a study of its long-term effects. When institutionalized, drone programs and their endless and anywhere wars have deep effects on people living under drones, as well as on the international legal order and its power dynamics.

[90] Carl Schmitt, *Theory of the Partisan: A Commentary/Remark on the Concept of the Political* (Duncker & Humblot, 1963) 22–3, http://users.clas.ufl.edu/burt/spaceshotsairheads/carlschmitttheoryofthepartisan.pdf:

> Their basis [the Geneva Conventions'] remains the statist foundation of warfare and the achieved containment of war, with their clear distinctions of war and peace, military and civil, enemy and criminal, state war and civil war. While they, thus, relax these essential distinctions and even question them, they open the door for a kind of war that would knowingly destroy such clear divisions. At that point many carefully formulated compromise-rules will look like the fragile bridges over an abyss concealing portentous metamorphoses in the concepts of war, peace, and the partisan.

Louiza Odysseos, "Crossing the Line? Carl Schmitt on the 'Spaceless Universalism' of Cosmopolitanism and the War on Terror," in Louiza Odysseos and Fabio Petito (eds.), *The International Political Thought of Carl Schmitt: Terror, Liberal War and the Crisis of Global Order* (Routledge, 2007), 124–44.

[91] Carl Schmitt, *The* Nomos *of the Earth in the International Law of the* Jus Publicum Europaeum (Telos Press Publishing, 2006).

[92] Ibid. For the temporal aspect of the matter, see Mark Danner, *Spiral: Trapped in the Forever War* (Simon & Schuster, 2016); Samuel Moyn, "Why the War on Terror May Never End," *The New York Times*, June 24, 2016, www.nytimes.com/2016/06/26/books/review/spiral-by-mark-danner.html; Michelle Bentley and Jack Holland, *Obama's Foreign Policy: Ending the War on Terror* (Routledge, 2013); Obama, "Remarks by the President at the National Defense University."

7

Rituals of Sovereignty

The fact that state practices involve the rational activities of a bureaucracy does not prevent power from expressing itself in a symbolic and experiential way.[1] The stabilization of drone programs and their implementation as part of the normal functioning of the state deserve much more attention than it has received, since the power it conveys goes far beyond occasional and finite lethal strikes in foreign territories. The institutionalization of a drone program not only means that the extensive warfare that drones bring about is stable, but also, and perhaps even more importantly, because a drone program consists of the constant surveillance of populations who live, quite literally, under drones. Behavioral changes (in addition to the evident psychological ramifications) of populations living under drones have been proven, at both the individual and community level.[2] This chapter explores how populations living under drones are concretely affected by the permanent scrutiny of their behavior, recording and analysis of their personal data, and how the identification and killing of individuals deemed to be a threat impacts on them. It is argued that states operating through an institutionalized drone program end up governing the daily life of these populations and disciplining their behavior along with, or sometimes in lieu of the local power. The presence of drones is experienced and felt and targeting patterns are recognized and incorporate in how behaviors and routines are shaped. Even if this does not present the features of an exercise of sovereignty

[1] David I. Kretzer, *Ritual, Politics and Power* (Yale University Press, 1988), 4–5.

[2] International Human Rights and Conflict Resolution Clinic at Stanford Law School and Global Justice Clinic at NYU School of Law, "Living Under Drones: Death, Injury, and Trauma to Civilians from US Drone Practices in Pakistan," September 2012, www-cdn.law.stanford.edu/wp-content/uploads/2015/07/Stanford-NYU-Living-Under-Drones.pdf. It is important to note that psychological effects, which will not be at the core of our developments, are considered to be potentially irreversible. Drones have been found to cause mental disorders such as anticipatory anxiety, depression, insomnia, Post Traumatic Stress Disorder (PTSD), and Disorder of Extreme Stress (DESNOS).

over the populations living under drones, and could not be characterized as full-fledged occupation, the US drone program goes beyond the one-off use of force to tackle threats. The way in which drone programs disrupt the principle of sovereign equality is indeed different – as being much less explicit, but not necessarily less intense in the long run – from that posed by the American project of "transformative occupation" of Iraq, for instance.[3] However, this chapter makes clear that a transborder drone program cannot be viewed as occasional interventions in self-defense. Instead, through an institutionalized drone program, a state performs rituals of governance and sovereignty over the populations it monitors.

The chapter conceptualizes the extension of state power over the populations of third states and explores what it means for the international legal order that the law is essential to such an extension. Based on analyses of the war on terror and associated legal framework, several scholars have already concluded that "new imperialism" is underway,[4] or that some doctrines and practices replicate the "standard of civilization" that characterized the international legal order in the nineteenth century.[5] Despite the usefulness of these studies, the prism of sovereignty on its own does not account for the concrete mechanisms of power exercised over and through bodies. This is because describing the effects of power negatively (such as excluding, repressing, concealing), prevents us from describing what reality power actually produces.[6] Therefore, dissecting the concrete circumstances and tangible processes through which drone programs disrupt principles of equal sovereignty and territorial integrity, distinctions between battlefield and non-battlefield, enemy and criminal prove useful.[7] Such an analysis also reveals that states put different

[3] On this issue and the US project to transform the material and formal constitution of Iraq from 2004, see Nehal Bhuta, "The Antinomies of Transformative Occupation" (2005) 16 *The European Journal of International Law* 4, 721–40.

[4] Antony Anghie, *Imperialism, Sovereignty and the Making of International Law* (Cambridge University Press, 2007).

[5] Ntina Tzouvala, "TWAIL and the 'Unwilling or Unable' Doctrine: Continuities and Ruptures" (2015) 109 *AJIL Unbound*, 266–70.

[6] Put slightly differently, describing the effects of power negatively (such as excluding, repressing, concealing) prevents us from describing what reality power actually *produces*. Michel Foucault, *Discipline and Punish: The Birth of the Prison*, trans. Alan Sheridan, New ed. (Penguin, 1991), 194: "We must cease once and for all to describe the effects of power in negative terms: it 'excludes', it 'represses', it 'censors', it 'abstracts', it 'masks', it 'conceals'. In fact, power produces; it produces reality; it produces domains of objects and rituals of truth."

[7] Nehal Bhuta, "States of Exception: Regulating Targeted Killing in a 'Global Civil War'," in Philip Alston and Euan Macdonald (eds.), *Human Rights, Intervention, and the Use of Force* (Oxford University Press, 2008), 243–74.

degrees of pressure on the norms and the international legal order according to the degree of "otherness" that separates them from the concerned actor. To deal with otherness within the international legal order, states use law to tame other, often weaker, states; to face otherness outside the international legal order – transnational jihadist groups – law is used to allow annihilation.

7.1 Infiltrating the Bodies of Populations Living under Drones: Extension of the Operating State's Power

"Power" is an "essentially contested concept," meaning that its use and definition involve disputes that are endless and unresolvable.[8] As such, the point here is not to vindicate a particular use of the term "power." Instead, power is used as an analytical category that is helpful to understand an actuality or operation,[9] deriving from the newly acquired capacity of agents or entities to act. The point is not to ask normative questions either such as "How can this practice be constrained?," "What is the appropriate way to use this tool?," "How can we ensure accountability?," and so on. The acquisition of technological capability that drones are equipped with, enables the operating state to perform a range of actions. This section analyzes the concrete bearing that this technological acquisition has in the counterterrorism context through the prism of power and rituals.

"Ritual" is also a helpful analytical category to capture the symbolic but also organic ways in which an institutionalized drone program infiltrates the bodies of individuals living under drones. Until the 1950s, sociologists and anthropologists defined rituals as the standardized, repetitive, and symbolic activity influencing human affairs and involving a supernatural dimension.[10] Yet even then, Kretzer explains that the link with the supernatural was not an essential feature in the articulated definitions of rituals: if Durkheim, for instance, asserts that rituals are the "rules of conduct which prescribe how a man should comport himself in the presence of these sacred objects," a closer look

[8] W. B. Gallie, "Essentially Contested Concepts" (1955–6) 56 *Proceeding of the Aristotelian Society, 1955–1956*, 167–98.

[9] Mitchell M. Dean, *The Signature of Power: Sovereignty, Governmentality and Biopolitics* (Sage, 2013).

[10] For instance, see Raymond Firth, *Elements of Social Organization* (Watts, 1951), 222. For more references, see Kretzer, *Ritual, Politics and Power*, 9.

shows that in his work the sacred refers more to people's social dependence and societal arrangements than to a supernatural entity.[11] What prevails in contemporary literature about rituals – a conceptualization that will be adopted here – is the symbolic and repetitive dimension of an action that shapes or affects human behavior and activity.[12] The symbolic nature of action, which is a key characteristic of rituals, entails that the given action channels emotion, guides cognition, and organizes social groups.[13] A ritual, therefore, is established not through the state of mind of its creator but through the psychological matrix of those who experience it. On the contrary, a repetitive standardized action that does not have this symbolic dimension is a custom or habit.[14]

Drone programs are deployed through micro-procedures, processes, modalities, or techniques usually used by states over their own citizens to discipline them or to "conduct their conduct."[15] Conceptual keys are to be found in Foucault's work to discern what is taking place for populations living under drones. Of course, the goal is not to propose a Foucauldian theory of drones but his categorizations of techniques and mechanisms of government in many ways echo the kind of power that drone programs convey, not only in what they do but also in what they do not perform. Drawing parallels and identifying divergences allow us to respond better to the question posed here.

If we think of power relations through the concept of discipline, multiple commonalities and one major divergence allow us to define the type of power conveyed by drone programs. The first common feature lies in that discipline is achieved through a multiplicity of processes investing human bodies individually and precisely. This is what Foucault explores in the chapter entitled "Docile Bodies" in *Discipline*

11 Kretzer, *Ritual, Politics and Power*; Emile Durkheim, *The Elementary Forms of the Religious Life* (trans. Joseph Swain, Free Press, 1974 [1915]), 37, 41.

12 Kretzer, *Ritual, Politics and Power*; Edmund Leach, *Political Systems of Highland Burma* (Beacon, 1954), 12–13; Roberto Da Matta, "Constraint and License: A Preliminary Study of Two Brazilian National Rituals," in Sally F. Moore and Barbara G. Myerhoff (eds.), *Secular Ritual* (Van Gorcum, 1977), 256–7.

13 Edmund Leach, "Ritualization in Man in Relation to Conceptual and Social Development" (1966) 251 *Philosophical Transactions of the Royal Society* 772, 404; Roy Rappaport, *Ecology, Meaning and Religion* (North Atlantic Books, 1979), 175–6.

14 Kretzer, *Ritual, Politics and Power*, 9; Barbara Myerhoff, "We Don't Wrap Herring in a Printed Page: Fusion, Fictions and Continuity in Secular Ritual," in Sally F. Moore and Barbara G. Myerhoff (eds.), *Secular Ritual* (Van Gorcum, 1977), 200.

15 Foucault, *Discipline and Punish*.

and Punish.[16] Discipline is presented as "a political anatomy of detail."[17] The meticulousness of how bodies are invested and inspected is emphasized by Foucault, through a well-known study of different sites of governmentality, from schools and hospitals to army barracks, where, he says a "supervision of the smallest fragment of life and of the body" takes place.[18] The investment of human bodies he describes practically proceeds from the "distribution of individuals in space," which can be achieved in different ways, including by enclosing and confining individuals in spaces where they can be distinguished and observed individually. Ideally, the spatial architecture allows states to observe and ultimately distinguish between infected bodies from healthy ones, and bad pupils from good ones.[19] Acting upon the body also involves manipulating behavior. This is what Foucault identifies as the control of activity, be it through establishing rhythms, imposing occupations, or regulating habits;[20] it can also involve articulating the relationship that the body entertains with certain objects.[21]

The means through which bodies are invested – individualized and constant observation – on the one hand, and the result of the scrutiny of bodies in the form of modified habits and behavior, on the other hand, are almost mechanically linked. However, this link does not need to rest on explicit rules. The previous chapters have explained in detail what makes drones adequate tools for individualized and continuous

[16] Ibid., 135–69.
[17] Ibid., 139.
[18] Ibid., 140.
[19] I use the medical terminology in relation to the example of the hospital used by Foucault to develop the art of spatial distributions but also because it will appear to be relevant, in a metaphorical sense, to the present case study. He also uses the school context to explain his idea. See Foucault, *Discipline and Punish*, 147, where he quotes J.-B. de la Salle, *Conduite des écoles chrétiennes*, B.N. Ms. 11759, 248–9: "Things must be so arranged that 'those whose parents are neglectful and verminous must be separated from those who are careful and clean; than an unruly and frivolous pupil should be placed between two who are well behaved and serious, a libertine either alone or between two pious pupil'."
[20] Foucault, *Discipline and Punish*, 149.
[21] Even if we explore this major difference in another paragraph, I must stress that even if these elements may echo the power conveyed through drones, someone familiar with Foucault's concept of discipline will have in mind that the power exercised through human bodies in the cases he explores and our case are driven by a completely different purpose. This key difference is what makes the analogy so helpful, but at this stage the reader may be puzzled by the comparison. Just to clarify things, Foucault talks about how disciplinary control teaches gestures as well as the best relation between the body and a gesture (of the pupil, the worker, etc.), to manage the population's behavior with the idea that the fruits of such disciplinary control will optimize life within the state.

observation. The minutiae of knowledge that has to be acquired in order to act on human bodies can certainly be achieved through the use of drones, thanks to their enhanced capacity to collect many different types of intelligence, the fact that they are connected to engines placed at lower altitudes that also collect evidence, their capacity to not only observe in a precise manner thanks to their powerful visual sensors, but also to record this data.[22]

Drone observation – when they are also equipped with the option to kill – also demonstrably leads the operating state to invest human bodies living under drones. This is a crucial element to take into consideration as it appears from discussions with drone operators that over 90 percent of their work consists of observation, data collection, and analysis, and only around 10 percent in carrying out strikes.[23] Reported information shows that the presence of drones affects the habits of populations living under drones, from their daily routines to more fundamental cultural traditions.[24] The lethal threat posed by combat drones and the kind of material circumstances that are known to trigger a strike (gatherings, especially gatherings of men, carrying weapons, circulating close to a zone where a strike just took place), leads people to avoid risk by modifying their routines. Some will simply lock themselves up alone in a room,[25] farmers will stop irrigating their land at night as it involves the use of flashlights which, an Afghani farmer believes, the US military thinks are used exclusively by the opposition.[26] Some families take their

[22] See, Chapter 4, Section 4.2.

[23] Interview 1 with a former US drone operator, *Anonymized*. Interview 2 with French drone operator, *Anonymized*.

[24] For Pakistan, see International Human Rights and Conflict Resolution Clinic, "Living Under Drones." On Afghanistan, see Alex Edney-Browne, "The Psychosocial Effects of Drone Violence: Social Isolation, Self-Objectification, and Depoliticization" (2019) 40 *Political Psychology* 6, 1–15.

[25] International Human Rights and Conflict Resolution Clinic, "Living Under Drones."

[26] Edney-Browne, "The Psychosocial Effects of Drone Violence," 10–11:

> Mohammed (40 years old) and Amidullah live in a Wardak village where the economy is primarily based on agriculture. Most of the families own farms, and all share a water-irrigation pipe; the families take turns throughout the day and night to ensure everyone's farms are irrigated and that the water is not wasted, and this is organized through a randomized "ballot system". Since the United States began flying drones over their village, Mohammed and Amidullah (along with friends in their community) feel frustrated and afraid when they draw a night shift from the ballot. Mohammed said that if he hears a drone while irrigating his land at night he will "switch off the flashlight and leave the irrigation to go home". He

children out of school or, as teachers, stop going to school to teach to avoid traveling backwards and forwards, but also more generally to avoid the risk of being identified as part of a "suspicious gathering."[27]

Changes in cultural traditions have also taken place, as was reported in the case of Pakistan but also of Afghanistan as a result of drone strikes targeting mosques,[28] burials, weddings, or Eid celebrations,[29] all of which involve meetings and collective ceremonies. The traditions of washing and covering the body and burying it as soon as possible after death, preferably within the first twenty-four hours is no longer followed, not only because of the suspicion triggered by lengthy and large collective gatherings but also in light of double tap practices.[30] When rituals such as funerals or weddings are the object of drone strikes, people start to behave in ways that depart from tradition and culture.[31] More generally,

> described to me that this takes its toll on his family's income: "If I miss the water on my turn to leave and go home, then my wheat dries out because I then have to wait till my next turn. The water comes out without control because I am not there to control it, and I lose that water. It is wasted." Amidullah similarly stated that if he irrigates his farm at night, he is "afraid [he] will be attacked": "The military think that flashlights are used only by the opposition, but they should understand that normal people use them also – for their irrigation or if they are going somewhere."

27 Ibid., 89. Their fear and decision derive from actual events; the most well-known school strike was on October 6, 2006 strike on a religious school in Bajaur that killed over eighty people, including sixty-nine children. See, "Most Bajaur Victims Were Under 20," *The News*, November 4, 2006, www.thenews.com.pk/archive/print/646502-'most-bajaur-victims-were-under-20'.

28 International Human Rights and Conflict Resolution Clinic, "Living Under Drones," 98.

29 Edney-Browne, "The Psychosocial Effects of Drone Violence," 7:

> Interviewees reported that fear of indiscriminate bombing had also led to the avoidance and sometimes discontinuation of communal activities and traditions. Festivities (such as Eid festival and wedding parties), funerals, and local political meetings have been affected. As Gul Mohammed, a 35-year-old driver from Maidan Shar (Wardak province), explained: "Before the drones, for 3–4 days in the evening over Eid, 4–5 families would cook one evening and they would feed the rest of the community and then the next night 4–5 different families would feed the community. So, it was like a culture or relationship between the families in the community, and now that culture has almost completely gone."

30 International Human Rights and Conflict Resolution Clinic, "Living Under Drones," 92–3.

31 "10 Killed in Two South Waziristan Drone Attacks," *The News*, June 3, 2012, www.thenews.com.pk/archive/print/622794-10-killed-in-two-south-waziristan-drone-attacks; Chris Woods and Christina Lamb, "CIA Tactics in Pakistan Include Targeting Rescuers and Funerals," *The Bureau of Investigative Journalism*, February 4, 2012, www.thebureauinvestigates.com/stories/2012-02-04/cia-tactics-in-pakistan-include-targeting-rescuers-and-funerals; "A Wedding That Became a Funeral | US Drone Attack on

group gatherings even at home when inviting friends or family are reported as being significantly reduced by the effect of drones.[32] A major change also took place with the erosion of the *jirga* system, a community-based conflict resolution process in Pashtun society.[33] In Edney-Browne's words, "people are made to see themselves through the eyes of American drone operators and change their behaviors [sic.] accordingly."

The second main feature of discipline after the "investment of bodies" to make them docile lies in "the means of correct training."[34] These means include observation, normalizing judgment, and examination. When these features are unpacked, it turns out that disciplinary power is exercised through techniques and tools of observation – "*observatoires*": eyes that must see without being seen, but whose presence must simultaneously be known or at least always be suspected. This surveillance takes place continuously and everywhere, leaving no zone of shade. The idea of normalizing judgement refers to the specific mode of punishment implemented by discipline:

> [T]he whole indefinite domain of the non-conforming is punishable. . . . The order that the disciplinary punishments must enforce is of a mixed nature: it is an "artificial" order, explicitly laid down by a law, a program, a set of regulations. But it is also an order defined by natural and observable processes. . . . In a disciplinary régime punishment involves a double juridico-natural reference.[35]

Thanks to this, the norm is mainly integrated through the observation of phenomena rather than by the application of a body of laws.[36] In other words, it is through a special system of command that this influence over bodies and behavior takes place: the order does not need to be explained or formulated; a simple signal triggering off the behavior suffices to conduct conducts.

Marriage Procession in Yemen," *Human Rights Watch*, February 19, 2014, www.hrw.org/report/2014/02/19/wedding-became-funeral/us-drone-attack-marriage-procession-yemen.

32 International Human Rights and Conflict Resolution Clinic, "Living Under Drones," 96–7: "Sadaullah Wazir, a teenager, told us that drone[s] have 'made life quite difficult [in that] more than two can't sit together outside because they are scared they might be struck by drones . . . We often discuss that too many people shouldn't sit together outside because they are vulnerable then'."

33 Forensic Architecture, "Case Study No. 1: Datta Khel, North Waziristan, March 16–17, 2011," www.forensic-architecture.org/case/drone-strikes/.

34 Foucault, *Discipline and Punish*, 170–94.

35 Ibid., 179.

36 Ibid., 183.

As argued in earlier chapters of the book, drones offer the opportunity of a permanent and discrete presence thanks to their unprecedented capability to stay airborne for around forty hours, at low maximum cruising speed to cover each area precisely and because it overcomes the physiological constraints associated with piloted aircrafts. As such, they present the opportunity "for a single gaze to see everything constantly [or a] central point [that is] both the source of light illuminating everything, and a locus of convergence for everything that must be known: a perfect eye that nothing would escape and a center towards which all gazes would be turned."[37] The constant thought of being potentially flown over by a combat drone, without paralyzing populations, arguably infiltrates minds and bodies.

Through repeated practice, patterns of drone activities are identified and recognized by the population, which is able to recreate mentally the profile of drone targets and contextual elements that are common to drone strikes. Once this profile is painted, the time comes for the population to adapt its way of life, both by remodeling individual daily routines and by abandoning the rituals of major community events as shown earlier. Without an explicit or advertised target selection process, drone operators give signals. Each time that the buzz sound of drones is heard, the same behavioral rearrangements take place. This reminds us of what Foucault describes as "a policy of coercions that act upon the body, a calculated manipulation of its elements, its gestures, its behavior," before concluding that under these conditions, "the human body [enters] a machinery of power that explores it, breaks it down and rearranges it."[38] It is interesting to note that Foucault's description of discipline and our findings on drone programs converge insofar as individuals adapt their conduct to what is signaled as the best behavior in order to respect the norm. For drone programs, remaining alone with a minimum of mobility and interactions would be the norm and, as the individuals involved know that anything less than the total respect of the norm can be characterized as misconduct, they will usually choose to never sit in a circle with a group of people.[39]

[37] Ibid., 173.

[38] Ibid., 138.

[39] International Human Rights and Conflict Resolution Clinic, "Living Under Drones," 96:

> The fears the interviewees described were not limited to ceremonial gatherings or other large group activities. Many said that they were afraid even to congregate in groups or receive guests in their home. Umar Ashraf, who

Another key characteristic of discipline concerns the functions of disciplinary surveillance that allows state forces to "qualify, to classify and to punish." Foucault himself actually talks about rituals when describing this mechanism, explaining that examination is highly ritualized as it combines "the ceremony of power and the form of the experiment, the deployment of force and the establishment of truth."[40] This examination is accompanied by documentary techniques that make each individual a "case."[41] This case consists of a detailed description of the individual concerned, information obtained through day-to-day observation, allowing states to define, measure, and compare him to others, and identify whether he has to be corrected or excluded. This leads us to Chapter 3 on panopticism that concludes the reflections on discipline. Foucault distinguishes between exceptional surveillance and generalized surveillance; the latter being represented by Foucault's conceptualization of Bentham's Panopticon. In contrast to the leper colony, where the physically marked lepers are excluded and confined in a separate space, the disciplinary society individualizes and scrutinizes the masses by capturing every detail of everyday life through constant examination and recording of events ("permanent registration").[42]

Generalized surveillance capacities to simultaneously record data about all observed individuals and to individualize surveillance through case-by-case analyses, the formulation of individual profiles that will ultimately allow them to define the dangerousness of an individual and, if established as a legitimate target, to kill them, is precisely the set of capabilities that drones offer. Drones videotape anything that goes on below, even in high definition thanks to sensors that work day and night, stormy weather conditions, and narrow or wide views.[43] They can

has noticed the changes in community dynamics over the past few years, observed that "[W]e do not like to sit like this, like friends [gesturing in front of him at the small circle of interviewer, interviewee, and translator], because we have fear, since [they] usually attack people when they sit in gatherings." Sameer Rahman, whose family's house was hit in a strike, confessed that "there are barely any guests who come anymore, because everyone's scared." He also stated that he does not allow his children to visit other people's homes when they have guests over, because he believes having guests makes it more likely that the house will be attacked.

40 Foucault, *Discipline and Punish*, 184.

41 Ibid., 191.

42 Ibid., 196.

43 Michel Foucault, *Security, Territory, Population: Lectures at the College De France, 1977–1978* (Picador, 2009).

include equipment that can listen and record radio and cell phone communications and identify where the communications come from. The amount of data collected and recorded is literally gigantic. Although surveillance is massive, it is also so precise that it allows profiling and observation of a single individual while the machine keeps on gathering data on other individuals. The intimacy between drone operators and the subject of their surveillance has been reported as transcending the kind of information you could obtain on the ground or with a traditional airplane with limited autonomy and less sophisticated sensors and imagery. As is now apparent, the final decision to kill with drones is highly individualized, be it with targeted killings or signature strikes, precisely because of these enhanced surveillance capacities that allowed what the panopticism seeks: scrutiny, control, measurement, and examination of individuals before deciding whether they must be "excluded."

In an institutionalized drone program, the operating state generally conveys power in the same ways as a state over its population, but also in ways that the host state (the actual sovereign) does not necessarily do at that point in time, namely, they operate by managing individual bodies and retaining the final power of life and death over the population.

However, and this is the crucial difference with Foucault's notion of discipline, a specific project motivates the disciplinary power: manufacturing useful individuals, shaping and correcting their behavior, in order, in the last instance, to improve the society that they compose. Discipline is not "simply an art of distributing bodies, of extracting time from them and accumulating it, but of composing forces in order to obtain an efficient machine."[44] It is unlikely that the US, French, or UK governments intend to manage the daily life of people living under drones or to make their society more efficient. They conduct certain rituals that convey power, but this power is not necessarily intended to make the population perform efficiently in order to achieve a well-managed society.[45]

The behavioral reactions of people living under drones are not even expected and exploited to achieve a certain goal. The operating state does not expect these individuals to stop organizing weddings and funerals.

[44] Foucault, *Discipline and Punish*, 164.

[45] As such, drone programs do not echo certain features of the disciplinary state such as the double system of gratification-punishment described by Foucault (*Discipline and Punish*, 180) as operating in the process of training and correction, to achieve an ever-greater performance.

Although it could be argued that these reactions may make pursuit easier – as the legitimate targets, which will logically remain mobile and continue to interact with each other, will become more apparent compared to the invisible civilians – it would be erroneous to attribute this objective to the operating states. For instance, it would even be grotesque to claim that the negative impacts of drones in Pakistan on economic and social activities, or even on education, were part of the Obama administration's plan.[46] Thus, it begs the questions: are human bodies living under drones only the instruments of power and not its objects, contrary to Foucault's disciplinary mechanisms? If human minds and bodies living under drones are vehicles of power, what are the actual objects of drone programs?

It appears insufficient to use the sole prism of power or discipline and that the described rituals of power in fact deserve to be renamed as "rituals of sovereignty." The resulting mechanisms of power are concrete and multiple: They do apply primarily to bodies, but they also implicate not only mechanisms of domestic discipline and the art of governing individuals, but also relations of sovereignty. A combination of the two conceptual frameworks, therefore, accounts for this concrete, complex, and multilayered exercise of power. Whereas Foucault's examination of discipline mechanisms corresponds to a governmental shift from "sovereignty and territory" to "security and population," the context at the heart of this study prompts us to reconcile discipline and sovereignty in the same paradigm. Building on the epistemological work of Mitchell Dean on Foucault's *Signatures of Power*,[47] power is understood here as a "triangle: sovereignty, discipline, governmental management which has population as its main target *[we could add, at home and abroad]* and apparatuses of security as its essential mechanisms."[48]

While there is no project on the part of the disciplining state to optimize the society of people living under drones, the operating state arguably disciplines the host state through the bodies of its "own" population, and indirectly other states that suspect such operations could be imposed on them under the unwilling or unable doctrine. The society thus "optimized," from the point of view of the operating state, is not the domestic sphere but the international legal order. The unique effects that

[46] On the impact on economic activities, see International Human Rights and Conflict Resolution Clinic, "Living Under Drones," 97.

[47] Dean, *The Signature of Power*, 36 f.

[48] Foucault, *Security, Territory, Population*, 108.

drone programs have on sovereignty have been neglected and underestimated. This neglect can be explained by the fact that the technicalities of drone programs make the expansion of state power that it allows almost invisible. If surveillance is the main activity of drone operators, it is also the most discrete. Yet, as was explained above, surveillance is precisely what leads the operating state to monitor the populations living under drones; it is in fact the main means through which the operating state perpetrates rituals of sovereignty.

The sovereign nature of these power rituals is substantiated when contemplating how this sort of situation would be defined by the courts, by analogy of how human rights courts define the situations where member states' jurisdiction (and thus, that of the court) applies extraterritorially. Two models of extraterritorial jurisdiction emerge from the ECHR case law: the spatial model of jurisdiction, according to which jurisdiction is triggered when inhabitants of a territory are under the effective territorial control of an ECHR contracting state,[49] and the personal model of jurisdiction, which refers to the situation where a state agent exercises (physical) authority and control over individuals.[50] In Al Skeini, the Court has shown that these versions were not mutually exclusive. For this, it relied on its own case law on the personal model of jurisdiction and on the exercise of "elements of governmental authority" and "public powers" that are normally exercised by a sovereign government.[51] The requirement of elements of governmental authority was analyzed as one version of the "effective control doctrine," and above all as a looser territorial model of jurisdiction. Indeed, elements of governmental authority includes various modes of exercise of public powers over a given territory that are not limited to occupation or control over diplomatic premises.[52] At the same time, some exercises of authority by state agents may not consist of elements of governmental authority.

[49] Bankovic and Others v. Belgium and Others, Appl. No. 52207/99 (ECtHR, December 12, 2001), para. 80.

[50] Al Skeini and Others v. United Kingdom, Appl. No. 55721/07 (ECtHR, July 7, 2011), paras. 136–7.

[51] Ibid., para 149. See also for a complete analysis, Cedric Ryngaert, "Clarifying the Extraterritorial Application of the European Convention on Human Rights" (2012) 28 *Utrecht Journal of International and European Law* 74, 59.

[52] For a case of occupation, see Cyprus v. Turkey [GC], Appl. No. 25781/94, ECHR 2001-IN. For situations of control over diplomatic premises, see Al-Saadoon and Mufdhi v. the United Kingdom (Dec.) Appl. No. 61498108 (ECtHR, June 30, 2009).

At this stage, one must return to the claim made earlier on drone strikes as the main object of scholarship on drones, if one only observes the conduct of extraterritorial drone strikes, jurisdiction will most certainly be considered as not characterized under spatial models of extraterritorial jurisdiction (i.e., models that require more than exercise of authority by a state agent). In fact, under either a strict spatial model or a loose one, the ECHR would consider that drone strikes are neither a mark of effective territorial control nor elements of governmental authority usually conducted by a sovereign government. On the contrary, if one expands the analysis to drone programs as a whole, taking into consideration the main activity that this involves – that is, permanent presence and surveillance – with the deep effects described above, my hypothesis is that the Court would not only recognize the exercise of authority by a state agent, but also the exercise of "elements of governmental authority" and "public powers" that are normally exercised by a sovereign government. Therefore, even with a threshold that is higher than the open-ended personal model,[53] drone programs could be recognized as triggering jurisdiction if all their features are taken into consideration. To conclude, the institutionalized drone programs convey and extend state power by facilitating rituals of sovereignty.

This extension of state power through rituals of sovereignty is directed toward two groups of actors – (weaker) states and transnational non-state jihadist groups – both of which lead to the articulation of different legal justifications. These rituals of sovereignty and the legal rhetoric that accompany them have been explored throughout this book without being distinguished according to the actors they concern. It is now argued that depending on the level of otherness of the actor concerned, law is used in a more or less malleable way. Malleability is preferred to the term flexibility because if both refer to the action of putting something under pressure, a flexible object resumes in its original shape, its "normal state," after having yielded under pressure. A malleable object remains deformed after the pressure is gone.

[53] For a more thorough discussion of the open-ended nature of this model, see Martin Scheinin, "Extraterritorial Effect of the International Covenant on Civil and Political Rights," in F. Coomans and M. Kamminga (eds.), *Extraterritorial Application of Human Rights Treaties* (Intersentia, 2004), 76: "Authority and control over individuals as a basis for state jurisdiction simply boils down to the proposition that a state has obligations under human rights treaties towards all individuals whose human rights it is able to violate." Ryngaert, "Clarifying the Extraterritorial Application," 60.

7.2 The Law as an Instrument to Tame the "Other Inside": States

The focus on drone *strikes* to the detriment of the entire drone *machinery* has allowed operating states to escape criticisms of violations of sovereignty that go beyond the occasional use of force. This focus is not fortuitous, and the Obama administration arguably achieved it by being very vocal on its drone program and legal justifications from the outset: they framed the debate. The main legal tool used to justify the use of force in third states without their consent is the unwilling/unable doctrine, which has served to establish a loose link of attribution between the threat posed by a non-state armed group and the territorial state. As explained in Chapter 4, this link of attribution constitutes the *ratione persone* criterion of the right of self-defense when force is used against non-state actors. As such, the unwilling/unable doctrine is used to justify the use of *force* in self-defense.

If discussions had revolved around the rituals of sovereignty deployed through the drone program's surveillance apparatus and bureaucratic machinery, states would have had to justify violations of territorial integrity that go beyond the use of force and are continuous. In other words, the law would have had to be used in such a malleable way that the norms used would no longer be recognizable. Instead of this, the right of self-defense has been extended, including through the unwilling/unable doctrine, and lost most of its constraining function because of the chain of interconnected propositions that the unwilling/unable doctrine is part of and the context in which it is mobilized. Yet, it still recognizably serves to justify the use of force, in violation of a third state's sovereignty, to protect the attacking state against a threat posed from the territory of that third state.

Certainly, states' use of the doctrine to justify force in self-defense, as it remains an undefined and unconstrained tool, exacerbates the sovereignty of the operating state to the detriment of the host state. As sharply described by Sara Kendall,

> As an articulation of contingent sovereignty, the "unwilling or unable" theory divides the international order into states that can adequately handle threats of force and those who cannot, either due to a lack of will or capacity. The hinge on which this division turns is effective territorial control, itself a product of many historical, geopolitical, and economic factors. As a political claim masquerading as a legal standard, "unwilling or unable" reorients the international legal imaginary. It shifts its starting premise from a field of uniformly sovereign states toward a relative orientation, where states appear in relation to one another according to

> their capacity to project territorial control and uphold shared security priorities. In many ways this logic marks a political realist appropriation of international legal forms.[54]

The unwilling/unable doctrine is a legal tool that serves to arbitrarily and authoritatively resolve tensions between weaker and stronger states, to the detriment of the weaker ones. The masquerade is clear when unpacking the different scenarios the doctrine claims to support. First, there is the case where the host state is *unable* to tackle the threat posed by the group acting from its territory. As explained in Chapter 4, an unable (and *willing*) state would either seek the support of a third state or at least consent to a third state's intervention when faced with a threatening armed attack; if not explicitly and prior to the intervention in self-defense, at least implicitly and/or without contestation afterwards. As such, the self-defense paradigm can easily be exited as there would be no violation of sovereignty. Now, despite this logic, when a state nonetheless justifies its use of force on the basis of the unable state scenario, Article 51 is invoked not only to avoid entering diplomatic discussions but also because entering such discussions and seeking the expression of consent from weak states is considered burdensome or useless. The logic is clear when considering that the same actors who use the unwilling or unable doctrine are also those who argue in favor of a relaxed temporal limitation for the right of self-defense. When a state is suspected of being unable to tackle threatening non-state actors on its territory and when the imminence of the threat is identified on the basis of continuous imminent hostile intentions rather than identified material circumstance (what we have called the individualization and dematerialization of the right to self-defense), it would not be unreasonable to expect the operating state to enter such diplomatic discussions.[55]

[54] Sara Kendall, "Cartographies of the Present: 'Contingent Sovereignty' and Territorial Integrity," in Martin Kuijer and Wouter Werner (eds.), *Netherlands Yearbook of International Law: The Changing Nature of Territoriality in International Law* (Asser Press and Springer, 2016), 83–106, 100.

[55] For similar views on the prospect of requiring from the operating state to undertake cooperative measures before taking action, see Michael N. Schmitt, "'Change Direction' 2006: Israeli Operations in Lebanon and the International Law of Self-Defense" (2008) 29 *Michigan Journal of International Law* 2, 161: "before a state may act defensively in another [state's] territory, it must first demand that the state from which the attacks have been launched act to put an end to any future misuse of its territory." Noam Lubell, *Extraterritorial Use of Force against Non-State Actors* (Oxford University Press, 2010), 42.

The second scenario, under the *unwilling* state scenario, is when the unwilling state is responsible for willingly allowing non-state actors to threaten the victim state and thereby reveals the possibility, as argued in Chapter 4, of identifying a link of attribution between non-state actors and the host state. In this situation, the principle of sovereign equality can be considerably harmed by such a doctrine if left undefined as it is today, and if there is no control of the operating state's evaluation of the host state's willingness. Besides, the operating state may have genuine (long term) security concerns, leading it to refuse foreign intervention to tackle threats that do not meet an urgent threshold of imminence (but instead, consist in targeting individuals with hostile intentions). Such unwillingness, in other words, is not necessarily the reflection of a link between the state and the non-state armed group. It is one thing to accept the proposition that a threatened state should have the possibility to use force when the host state is ineffective in preventing its territory from being used to launch attacks against another state, or is unwilling to do so, especially if the state threatened with hostile action has attempted to cooperate without a satisfactory outcome. It is quite another thing to support the view that where a host state has decided not to use force against non-state actors operating from its territory, identified by another state as having a hostile intent, the other state should be able to intervene. Yet, the unwilling/unable doctrine is precisely used in such circumstances to make the security choice of the operating state prevail.

However, the link of attribution under the unwilling/unable doctrine does not in itself and in abstract terms deprive of most of its constraining function the version of the right of self-defense proposed by states active in the war on terror. It is the use of the doctrine in this specific context and together with the propositions pertaining to other limitations of self-defense that does. Here, we should recall the broader framework in which the doctrine applies: It is part of a set of propositions explored in Chapter 4 that stretches the other limitations of the right of self-defense, and that is used to sustain the targeting of individuals with continuous hostile intent. This is the reason why the unwilling/unable doctrine practically serves to exacerbate the power of the operating states extraterritorially.

The use of the unwilling/unable doctrine certainly is a signal sent to sovereign states that the security strategies of stronger states can systematically trump those of weaker states. States using drones have used the unwilling/unable doctrine to subjugate other states on the territories where they want to intervene to track and target members of transnational jihadist groups. This has required to intensely exploit the uncertainties and grey zones of Article 51 of the UN Charter and related case law. The proposed version of the right of self-defense is, as a result, quite extensive, but it was never suggested that a link of attribution was quite unnecessary, neither was it explicitly claimed that drones could be permanently deployed in states which are unwilling/unable to tackle the terrorist threats with a full-fledged surveillance apparatus. After all, the link of attribution thus defined still concerns the regulation of a use of force that violates *a priori* the prohibition to use force on another state's territory; where in fact the drone program, if observed as a whole, is much more intrusive in states where drones are deployed. The choice was made to stick to the justification of one-off drone strikes under a recognizable self-defense paradigm, with a recognizable exception to the cornerstone principle of equal sovereignty of states.

By developing the unwilling/unable doctrine as loosely defined and used as it might be, states preserve the structural equilibrium of the interstate system and its set of arrangements. This shows that legal categories are stretched only insofar as the system of justification upholds the formal and structural equal sovereignty of its unequal members.[56] In other words, to justify the oppression of the "other" who is "inside" and a part of the system, the malleability of the law is only exploited to a limited extent. On the contrary, Chapters 4 to 6 have shown how legal uncertainties are exploited to breaking point when legal rhetoric concerns actions not involving territorial states directly, but transnational jihadist groups.

7.3 The Law as an Instrument to Annihilate the "Other Outside": Jihadist Groups

Chapters 4 to 6 explored states' legal rationales mostly in conditions where members of transnational jihadist groups can be targeted. In fact, only the unwilling/unable doctrine directly addresses the violation of state sovereignty. Above all, the exploitation of *jus ad bellum* and *jus in bello* norms aims at justifying the expansion of warfare against members of (any) jihadist group in time and space. Targeting individuals based on their personal characteristics and signs of continuous hostile intent rests

[56] Anne-Marie Slaughter, "International Law and International Relations Theory: A Dual Agenda" (1993) 87 *AJIL* 2, 226; Stanley Hoffmann, "International Systems and International Law" (1961) 14 *World Politics* 1, Special issue on "The International System: Theoretical Essays," 230.

on a permissive chain of propositions about the right of self-defense, on the exploitation of the open texture of the law on the endpoint of armed conflicts, on the uncertainties pertaining to the geographical scope of war, and on the emergence of a new form of direct participation in hostilities with the concept of continuous combat function. All legal propositions formulated on these issues converge toward the objective of continuously anticipating threats posed by individuals, wherever they are, and until the groups that they belong to are annihilated. All these propositions – and their backing up by precision and ubiquitous surveillance tools and weapons – also make it difficult to comfortably assess what constitutes an eligible and non-eligible use of the legal concepts and norms that they use. As a result of such doubts on the permissible reasons for action, one is left wondering what constraint norms still exert in these situations.

Infinite warfare to the point of annihilation is at the core of this legal rhetoric and motivates states to exploit law's open texture to a greater extent than in the unwilling/unable case. Indeed, with DPH as continuous combat function, or proportionality of the use of force (in self-defense) to the threat posed by a group (and not by armed attacks) radical extensions, if not shifts, of concepts are proposed. As already stated, while rules do not explicitly stipulate what follows from them, they are usually formulated in such a way that only a finite number of justifications for actions can be articulated within their semantic framework. In a given context at a certain point in time, in the light of dominant interpretations and practices, the contents and meanings of a norm can be sufficiently clear to have a good idea about which sort of behavior is correct or incorrect.[57] When circumstances change, either we see the justification for action evolve within the semantic scope of the concept or, as seems to be the case here, we witness proposals to shift its content and transform norms' boundaries.[58] Such a shift suddenly reveals

[57] Robert Brandom, "A Hegelian Model of Legal Concept Determination," in Graham Hubbs and Douglas Lind (eds.), *Pragmatism, Law, and Language* (Routledge, 2014), 22–3.

[58] Nehal Bhuta and Rebecca Mignot-Mahdavi, "Dangerous Proportions: Means and Ends in Non-Finite War," in Nehal Bhuta, Florian Hoffmann, Sarah Knuckey, Frédéric Mégret, and Margaret Satterthwaite (eds.), *The Struggle for Human Rights*. Essays in Honour of Philip Alston (Cambridge University Press, 2021), 301–27. See also, Nehal Bhuta and Rebecca Mignot-Mahdavi, "From Brownlie to Brandom: Recollective Stories of the Right of Self-Defense and a Theory of the Pragmatic Semantics of Legal Conceptual Change," *Opinio Juris*, April 20, 2021, https://opiniojuris.org/2021/04/20/from-brownlie-to-brandom-recollective-stories-of-the-right-of-self-defense-and-a-theory-of-the-pragmatic-semantics-of-legal-conceptual-change/.

what had crystallized, at least for a while, as the concept's boundaries that were not apparent before.

An explanation for this is that the shifting concepts are used in a scenario that uncouples them from the concrete conditions that they previously presupposed: a certain level of mutual acceptance between the parties to a conflict. Transnational jihadist groups are the "others outside." Depending, more or less radically, on the group, they are themselves firmly opposed to sovereignty and the international community. Not only do these groups show no intention of undergoing a process of recognition and have no intention whatsoever to become part of the interstate system, they also negate the latter and are willing to fight until they see the dawn of a universal caliphate to replace it.[59] The goal of a universal caliphate and the ambition to move beyond governments and the international legal order are shared by all jihadist groups, even those that play the Westphalian game, use its channels and vocabulary the most, to the ones that reject it most, like ISIS. In the late 1980s, the purpose of Al Qaeda was redefined as pursuing a transnational project and enlarged its priorities "from the enemy nearby to the enemy afar" (*min al 'adou al qareeb ila al 'adou al ba'eed*).[60] The deterritorialization of the jihadist project did not mean that militant actions became unrooted; they all take place in concrete territories and situations. Instead, their transnational turn basically marked the intrinsic opposition of jihadist groups to the state and the international legal order. In this regard, Ayse Zarakol explains that what is noteworthy about Al Qaeda is that "it is not interested in replacing any *particular* regime in any *particular* country, even if it supports its local affiliates in such quests."[61] She goes on to explain:

[59] Taking jihadist group's political project seriously in order to understand better what is at stake in the war on terror is inspired by the work of Darryl Li. See among other things, Darryl Li, "A Jihadism Anti-Primer" (2015) 276 *Middle East Report*, 12–17:

> The statist discourse and its liberal opposition present a choice between demonizing the enemy and banalizing him. But there is a third option: taking radicalism seriously as a political orientation, whether its idiom is Islamic, communist or anarchist. . . . Jihadi groups may have very different ideas of the good and may operate in forms unfamiliar to those who can only think of politics in terms of the state and its categories. But that does not render any less concrete the ideas and interests at stake in their antagonisms, nor does it make thinking clearly about them any less urgent.

[60] M.-M. O. Mohamedou, *A Theory of ISIS:* Political Violence and the Transformation of the Global Order (Kindle, ed., Pluto Press, 2018), 40.

[61] Ayse Zarakol, "What Makes Terrorism Modern? Terrorism, Legitimacy and the International System" (2011) 37 *Review of International Studies* 5, 2334. Emphasis added.

> Increasingly, the international system as a whole becomes the subject of revolutionary ire. This is why, with each subsequent wave of terrorism since the nineteenth century (and with each expansion of the international society), system-threatening variants of terrorism have made a stronger comeback, each time less willing to compromise with principles of Westphalian legitimacy. Therefore, when Al-Qaeda is eventually defeated (and/or coopted into the Westphalian model), it is likely to be replaced by an organisation with an even broader reach and an ideology with a legitimacy claim to a more universalising authority.[62]

When she wrote this article, what was then called the Islamic State in Iraq had engineered a refocusing on the local level, thus apparently departing from Al Qaeda's transnational dynamic. This is probably why IS does not appear in support of the author's prediction that a more universalizing jihadist project would soon emerge. The IS rapidly seized the opportunity afforded by the Syrian civil war that began in March 2011 to establish itself beyond the Iraqi borders and to start its "Levantine expansion."[63] This move, officialized by the adoption of the name, Islamic State in Iraq and the Levant (ISIL, al Dawla al Islamiya fil Iraq wal Shaam, or ISIS for Islamic State in Iraq and Syria) in April 2013 was not just the sign of an Iraqi story that evolved into a Syrian or regional one. The IS was first driven by a provincial ambition, built up momentum with the Syrian civil war, to then "pursue and deepen Al Qaeda's transnational mode of force projection while focusing on the territorial centre of gravity it controlled between Mosul and Raqqa."[64] In other words, the IS trajectory developed in a progressive manner, through concrete spaces and contexts, and in this sense it is deeply connected to local territories while simultaneously becoming more and more transnational.[65]

This territorialized construct, however, should not be misinterpreted: it is not indicative of its embeddedness in the Westphalian frame with its orderly following of national-territorial lines. In fact, one could say that it reveals quite the opposite. First, the fact that it is built-up locally expresses a negation of the state authorities located in the said territories.

[62] Ibid., 2336.
[63] Mohamedou, *A Theory of ISIS*, 89.
[64] Ibid., 101.
[65] James Piscatori and Amin Saikal, *Islam Beyond Borders: The Umma in World Politics* (Cambridge University Press, 2019), 8: "The worldwide concern about ISIS was precisely centred on its capture of territory and ISIS itself acknowledged the imperative for control over Islamic lands (*dar al-Islam*) to which Muslims must migrate (*hijra*)."

Second, it reveals an understanding that a perennial global expansion can only be achieved through concrete integration in space and time.[66]

On June 29, 2014, ISIS announced its goal as the global caliphate and articulated a narrative on how to bring about a virtuous future for the *umma*, a concept that refers to a pan-Islamic community as explored in more detail below. Al Adnani, official spokesman and senior leader of ISIS proceeded in certain quite illuminating statements:

> Therefore, the shūrā (consultation) council of the Islamic State studied this matter after the Islamic State – by Allah's grace – gained the essentials necessary for khilāfah (caliphate), which the Muslims are sinful for if they do not try to establish it. In light of the fact that the Islamic State has no shar'ī (legal) constraint or excuse that can justify delaying or neglecting the establishment of the khilāfah such that it would not be sinful, the Islamic State – represented by ahlul-halli-wal-'aqd (its people of authority), consisting of its senior figures, leaders, and the shūrā council – resolved to announce the establishment of the Islamic khilāfah, the appointment of a khalīfah for the Muslims, and the pledge of allegiance to the shaykh (sheikh), the mujāhid, the scholar who practices what he preaches, the worshipper, the leader, the warrior, the reviver, descendent from the family of the Prophet, the slave of Allah, Ibrāhīm Ibn 'Awwād Ibn Ibrāhīm Ibn 'Alī Ibn Muhammad al-Badrī al-Hāshimī al-Husaynī al-Qurashī by lineage, as-Sāmurrā'ī by birth and upbringing, al-Baghdādī by residence and scholarship. And he has accepted the bay'ah (pledge of allegiance). Thus, he is the imam and khalīfah for the Muslims everywhere. Accordingly, the "Iraq and Shām" in the name of the Islamic State is henceforth removed from all official deliberations and communications, and the official name is the Islamic State from the date of this declaration.[67]

From then on, ISIS would officially start its successful growth across the global chess board, through centrifugal dynamics working along different layers from the Middle East to the Sahel and sub-Saharan Africa and attracting an expansive lineup of fighters from around the world.

Understanding the group's conception of the Caliphate and *umma* helps clarify their political project and tells us about the alternative structure of the world order they envisage to replace the current inter-state system with. The concept of *umma*, which has qur'anic roots, is interpreted in different ways not only by the Sunni and the Shia, but also

[66] Mohamedou speaks of "a combination of an independently moving battle plan – now focused on Iraq, now centred on Syria – and an adaptation to domestic and regional contingencies." Mohamedou, *A Theory of ISIS*, 105.

[67] Speech by Al Adnani, June 29, 2014, "This Is the Promise of Allah."

by the Saudi State and by jihadist groups such as Al Qaeda and ISIS.[68] All of them use this concept to endorse the ultimate goal of one community of the faith (*umma wahida*); but some believe in the *umma* as a statement of fact, others as an aspiration; some perceive it in non-territorial terms; and others explicitly frame it as a model that competes with the nation-state or other parochial forms of community.[69] ISIS, which espouses a highly literalist interpretative reading of the Qur'an, deduces from the text that *umma* imposes on it a legal duty to establish the caliphate. This would, according to the qur'anic prophecy, imply the fall of Rome and the conquest of global authority, thus ensuring prosperity, safety, and well-being for the *umma*. This claim of ISIS stems from their interpretation of Surat al-nur (Chapter of Light) in the Qur'an (24:55), which reads as follows:

> Allah has promised those who have believed among you and done righteous deeds that He will surely grant them succession [to authority] upon the earth just as He granted it to those before them and that He will surely establish for them [therein] their religion which He has preferred for them and that He will surely substitute for them, after their fear, security, [for] they worship Me, not associating anything with Me. But whoever disbelieves after that – then those are the defiantly disobedient.

Abu Bakr al-Baghdadi builds on this promise of authority to guarantee the *umma* that "If you hold to it, you will conquer Rome and own the world, if Allah wills."[70] The conceptualization of ISIS of the *umma* has its roots in the Salafist movement that itself emerged in the mid-nineteenth century as a reaction to European colonization and domination of the Muslim world. The consequent diffusion of foreign ideas and practices "caused deep concerns amongst those who wanted their countries to develop as sovereign and independent societies, according to a pristine Islam."[71] The Wahhabi tradition of Salafism followed by ISIS is primarily about adopting a literalist approach to Islamist texts and espousing a vision of the world that is strictly divided between Muslim believers in the land of Islam (*dar al-Islam*) on the one hand, and infidels and the

[68] For a complete study of these differences, see Piscatori and Saikal, *Islam Beyond Borders*.
[69] Ibid., 1.
[70] Abu Bakr al-Baghdadi, Mosul speech, quoted in Amaryllis Maria Georges, "ISIS Rhetoric for the Creation of the Ummah," in Daniel Ochieng Orwenjo, Omondi Oketch, and Asiru Hameed Tunde (eds.), *Political Discourse in Emergent, Fragile, and Failed Democracies* (IGI Global, 2016), 196.
[71] Piscatori and Saikal, *Islam Beyond Borders*, 135.

land of disbelief (*dar al-kufr*), on the other hand. As a result of this starting point, conflict must expand over time and space as long as *dar al-kufr* exists. A sermon delivered by al-Baghdadi on July 4, 2014 after his forces captured Mosul, encapsulates this vision of the world order that is at the heart of the ISIS political project:

> O *umma* of Islam, indeed the world today has been divided into two camps and two trenches, with no third camp present: The camp of Islam and faith, and the camp of kufr [disbelief] and hypocrisy – the camp of the Muslims and the mujahidin everywhere, and the camp of the Jews, the crusaders, their allies, and with them the rest of the nations and religions of kufr, all being led by America and Russia, and being mobilized by the Jews.[72]

Certainly, any solution other than this binary approach to structure the world order, with the caliphate in sight, is entirely rejected. The interstate community in particular, as being the prominent structure of the contemporary world order, is simply dismissed and members of the community are instructed to reject it: They are, among other things, prohibited from "being divided among states";[73] they are required to reject their nationality and national borders;[74] finally, the *umma* is expected to contest the established order. As Piscatori and Saikal explain, jihadi Islamism

> sits at the extreme end of this ideological spectrum, rejecting participation within the existing political system and legitimising the use of violence to achieve its overthrow and the installation of a new order. Jihad, which is mentioned in the Qur'an primarily in the sense of a "sustained struggle," has evolved to assume two dimensions: jihad al-kabir (greater jihad), which refers to an internal, personal struggle for self-improvement ("to be a selfless, decent and virtuous human being"), and jihad al-saqhir (lesser jihad), which refers to physical combat in defence of Islam.[75]

[72] Quoted by Remy Low, "Making up the Ummah: The Rhetoric of ISIS as Public Pedagogy" (2016) 38 *Review of Education, Pedagogy, and Cultural Studies* 4, 306.

[73] Hassan al-Banna, quoted in Cole Bunzel, "From Paper State to Khilafat" (2015) Analysis Paper 19, Brookings Project on US Relations with the Islamic World, www.brookings.edu/wp-content/uploads/2016/06/The-ideology-of-the-Islamic-State.pdf, 8.

[74] *Dabiq*, official online journal of ISIS, full citation: "Amongst the greatest deeds the muwahhid performs is his rejection of nationalism. Rather, his Islam is not correct until he disbelieves in nationalism, as nationalism declares people equal regardless of their religion, it does not discriminate between them accordingly, it limits the religion to a nationalist border, and it prohibits its expansion beyond."

[75] David Cook, *Understanding Jihad* (University of California Press, 2005); Piscatori and Saikal, *Islam Beyond Borders*, 140.

Contemporary jihadist movements, from Al Qaeda to ISIS, consider themselves involved in a protracted and transnational war against non-believers that will only end when a single and global *umma* replaces the current interstate order, a global non-state body of believers, a community of faith that negates any division. In this sense, the *umma* constitutes a universal and holistic ideal:

> Islamic law enjoins Moslems to maintain a state of permanent belligerence with all non-believers, collectively encompassed in dar al-harb the domain of war. . . . The Muslims are, therefore, under a legal obligation to reduce non-Muslim communities to Islamic rule in order to achieve Islam's ultimate objective, namely the enforcement of God's law (the Sharia) over the entire world.[76]

This global *umma* for contemporary jihadist movements depends on the establishment of a caliphate as a universal political and institutional order. Before ISIS, few jihadist movements made any effort to define and conceptualize how such caliphate would be structured and legitimized. The purpose of declaring itself as *the* Islamic State, Hussein Solomon explains, is that the community will be unified spiritually through belief, but also institutionally under a unique political authority. The single command structure will cover the ever-expanding territory of the Muslim community until it replaces the current interstate community altogether. Piscatori and Saikal explain that the caliphate takes its authority from its recognition of the sovereignty of God (intrinsic source) and the consensus of the *umma* on its right to enforce that authority (extrinsic source).[77] This political project calls for every community member to act to the best of their abilities to establish it; if not through physical combat, at least by acting to bring down the nation-states they are located in.[78]

[76] Roda Mushkat, "Is War Ever Justifiable? A Comparative Survey" (1987) 9 *Loyola of Los Angeles International and Comparative Law Journal* 2, 227–317, 302.

[77] Piscatori and Saikal, *Islam Beyond Borders*, 151.

[78] Ibid., 150. They refer to a passage of the *Dabiq* that declares:

> This is the order of the Khalifa. . . . Either one performs hijrah to the Wilayat of the Khilafa or, if he is unable to do so, he must attack the crusaders, their allies, the Rafidah, the tawaghit, and their apostate forces, wherever he might be with any means available to him. . . . He should attack after declaring his bay'ah to the Khilafa, so as not to die a death in Jahiliyyah.
>
> ("And Allah Is the Best of Plotters," *Dabiq*, Issue 9, 54)

The commitment to mutually exclusive ideas of how to structure the world order triggers a project of mutual annihilation. Very differently, groups that try to overthrow and replace their government, those that seek secession and establishment of their own states or those whose objective is to profit from trade in illegal goods, all have one thing in common: they accept (and even want to become part of) the interstate system.[79] In the absence of this acceptance, states and transnational jihadist groups recognize each other as infinite enemies, which entails infinite conflict in time and space. This project of infinite enmity breaks with the basis of international legal norms, namely, with regulation of conflicts between, if not equals in the Schmittian sense,[80] then at least between entities that mutually accept each other's existence, reflected in the desire on the part of non-state actors to acquire the attributes of a state. In the absence of such mutual acceptance, the parties are prepared to exclude or destroy entities that are not only dissimilar but also reject the other's existence/attributes and, to that end, states are ready to radically and vigorously exploit any uncertainty in the norms even if it means proposing their metamorphosis.

7.4 Concluding Remarks

Drone programs establish rituals of sovereignty: from the investment of human bodies through individualized and constant observation, thereby modifying habits and behavior; to the collection and recording of knowledge, and ultimately the examination and identification of those individuals who have to be "corrected" or excluded. After examining these rituals, this chapter offered an understanding of who the objects of these rituals were and reflected on how this extension of power through law could be explained. It distinguished between levels of malleable uses of the law depending on the degree of otherness of the actor directly concerned by the intensification of power: states, on the one hand, and transnational jihadist groups, on the other hand. The potential of the law

[79] Tanisha M. Fazal, "Rebellion, War Aims & the Laws of War" (2017) 146 *Dædalus, the Journal of the American Academy of Arts & Sciences* 1, 75.

[80] Carl Schmitt, *Verfassungslehre* (Duncker & Humblot, 2017 [1928]), 375–6. Schmitt defines substantial similarity as the "concrete and real correspondence between the member states that prevents the occurrence of the extreme conflict within the association."

as a tool for taming states emerged through the development of the unwilling/unable doctrine. The discourse articulated with this doctrine has concealed the invasiveness of drone programs by focusing on air strikes and individual threats. Therefore, although the doctrine is far from being accepted, it establishes and cultivates a belief of the international legal community in the compatibility of the doctrine with the international legal order. On the one hand, in practical terms the unwilling/unable doctrine acts as a basis for the stronger state that in turn exercises authority and normalizes the power asymmetry of the international legal order.[81] On the other hand, however, the link of attribution remains recognizable through the unwilling/unable doctrine. On the contrary, states exploit legal norms concerning the targeting of members of transnational terrorist groups to such an extent that these norms undergo a metamorphosis: this is the case for instance of the principle of proportionality in self-defense, or direct participation in hostilities defined as continuous combat function. The uncertainties of the temporal and geographical limits of war, for their part, are exploited to such an extent that boundaries between war and peace, criminal and combatant now seem more fluid than ever.

Distinguishing between actors affected by the legal rationales, and thus between levels of otherness allowed us to formulate the hypothesis that states make radical techno-legal efforts of self-preservation only insofar as the other rejects the interstate system. The malleable use of the unwilling/unable doctrine reveals that the international legal system is established and preserved to arrange and secure, through structures and constitutive principles, an interest that is shared by all these entities: their

[81] Nehal Bhuta, "On Preventive Killing," *EJIL: Talk!*, September 17, 2015, www.ejiltalk.org/on-preventive-killing:

> This juridical asymmetry has consequences for what we understand to be the purpose of the strict limits placed on the use of force by the Charter framework. The framework protects states' right to defend themselves, but balances this with the aim of restraining as much as possible uses of force which could escalate into larger conflicts. As such, the Charter framework presumes and indeed requires that temporary defensive uses of force between states can be quickly subjected to peaceful forms of dispute resolution, where the underlying clash of interests leading to the outbreak of conflict can be mediated or even adjudicated. All of this presupposes the legal symmetry of states, and that each state's interests have in principle the possibility of being recognized and negotiated, as means of containing the use of force.

preservation and survival.[82] Dedicated to state preservation, the interstate system revolves – only as much as necessary for its entities to survive – around the principle of sovereign equality and the other rules of the game resulting from this cornerstone principle. Far from prohibiting exceptions to this principle, the interstate system allows tensions to unfold internally; but only to such an extent that entities endure these inevitable interstate power struggles. Going a step further, the project of universalization of the interstate system is also driven by the practical interest derived from mutual acceptance and recognition – self-survival and mutual preservation – which is itself multiplied when it concerns an expanded community: the bigger the community, the safer its members are from remaining external competing powers. It is generally accepted that non-state armed groups should be treated with restraint as long as they accept or aspire to being part of the interstate system themselves. It is also true that states are aware that what they can do on their own is limited in a global world order.[83] Alderson and Hurrell's account of Bull on international society is interesting in that regard:[84]

> Similarly, the main thrust of the argument of *The Anarchical Society* is that the international society of states represents the best, albeit very fragile and imperfect, answer to the dangers of international anarchy by providing the basis for the promotion of certain basic goals: such as the survival of the state system itself, the maintenance of the independence of individual states, the setting of limits to use and severity of military force.

[82] See also, Bardo Fassbender, "The United Nations Charter as Constitution of the International Community" (1998) 36 *Columbia Journal of Transnational Law* 3, 614; Bhuta, "On Preventive Killing," 15:

> Nations, and claim sovereign immunity in other states' courts for certain governmental acts are deeply embedded as constitutive rules of the game in the international law system. This set of arrangements, established partly on the basis of mutual interest and reciprocity, has become a structural equilibrium. Each actor has incentives to be part of this membership system, both for reasons of efficacy in the conduct of international affairs and because of benefits conferred on leaders in internal politics by international recognition. No significant powerful actors have an incentive to defect from the system. It is self-enforcing, self-perpetuating, and reinforced to some degree by cognitive entrenchment. It is likely to change only incrementally unless it becomes grossly inefficient to its purposes, or suffers a crisis of legitimacy.

[83] Fassbender, "The United Nations Charter," 557: "Today, there is an increasing awareness of the limits of the nation-state in the face of the tasks it is meant to fulfill."

[84] Kai Alderson and Andrew Hurrell, *Hedley Bull on International Society* (Macmillan, 2000), 10; Bhuta, "On Preventive Killing," 11.

This common objective of self-preservation means that the interstate community is basically a system of inclusion and exclusion. Its *raison d'être* is not only the preservation (and accentuation?) of demarcations between inside and outside,[85] but also the protection of "Us" from the "Other," if necessary, until its annihilation if the "Other" continues to reject the interstate community.

[85] R. B. J. Walker, "Genealogy, Geopolitics and Political Community: Richard K. Ashley and the Critical Social Theory of International Politics" (1988) 13 *Alternatives*, 85; Andrew Linklater, *The Transformation of Political Community: Ethical Foundations of the Post-Westphalian Era* (Polity Press, 1998), 2.

Epilogue

In the distant horizon of fake cockpits in Nevada, the ghost (or fantasy?) of the all-powerful sovereign haunting the weakened state, is masked behind the objective of ensuring the security of its population. Drone programs appear as a techno-legal machinery discreetly intensifying or undermining state power. My interest in drone programs was not motivated by a desire to study the state; the state imposed itself when scrutinizing drone programs in their concrete details. In fact, the study started out on drone strikes but very soon became a study of drone *programs*, as I was immediately struck by their implementation in bureaucratic infrastructures, their use according to formalistic procedures and sophisticated legal rationales. In other words, it was never a question of asking "What is the state?" and using drones as a symbol of contemporary state power. Instead, I looked at the new legal rationales created by state representatives to justify the extraterritorial use of drones against non-state actors and was intrigued by the following questions: is there anything specific to drones that explains the intensification of the pressure put on the international norms regulating the use of force? What is it about drone strikes that calls for the formulation of hyper-legalistic discourses? Hence, I looked at all "acting agents"[1] of drone programs – drones' technological capacities, bureaucratic procedures, warfare and its contemporary features, the law – and decided to make sense of their interaction.

In addressing these questions, this book has shown how this interaction works, what it produces and how, and has explored the long-term and theoretical implications of how drone programs work and what they produce. The book demonstrates that the main role played by the law has not been to constrain drone programs – although one cannot rule out that norms and debate about their interpretation has performed some

[1] Pierre Bourdieu, *Sur L'État*. Cours au Collège de France 1989–1992 (Éditions du Seuil, 2012), Cours du 18 janvier 1990, 25.

kind of regulatory function considering the hyper-legalistic rhetoric that accompanied the development of drone programs in the US and to some extent in the UK. Rather, the law has performed a normalizing and even an institutionalizing function. Through the additional demonstration that the legal disagreement is not only reasonable but sometimes tilts toward the interpretation proposed by states (consider, for example, the geography of conflicts), this book offers a plausible explanation for why the legal fight undertaken by some scholars to constrain state practice since 9/11 has failed.

Throughout the book, I have tried to understand what drone programs produce, to which the answer is an extension of warfare and state power. I have also asked how they do this, and the answer is through technology and the law. Hypotheses have also been formulated regarding *why* this exacerbation of state power resting on enhanced technological capacities and de-/reconstructed legal frameworks, is taking place. This question, however, needs to be explored further.

A key claim made in the book is that warfare is extended because the enhanced technological capacities of drones permit it. Drones have been shown to practically trigger the extension of the geography and temporality of the battlefield. Their technological capacities made the military strategy shift toward individualized and dematerialized warfare possible. It also made the associated legal rationales and conceptual shifts somehow more acceptable. This is true for instance of the shifts in *jus ad bellum* self-defense criteria or *jus in bello* direct participation in hostilities that presuppose the ability to identify continuous hostile intent in an individual. Drones' technological capacities also make possible the exercise rituals of sovereignty over foreign populations with ease and stealthily.

Furthermore, the surveillance and data collection capacities of drones chronologically correspond to the infancy of the era of massive data collection systems. Drones' capacity to store large amounts of information built a bridge between techniques of governmentality used domestically and extraterritorially. Concretely, the drone as a data machine is at the core of the emergence of a program. This program conveys rituals of sovereignty (police powers and daily disciplinary techniques) and undermines the sovereignty of other states. As a data machine deployed at distance, it facilitates a tangible expansion of the geographical reach of the state. Enhanced data collection and analysis capacities offer the promise of mastering space and time, which are both key components of a successful find, fix, and finish process for targets belonging to evolving and dispersed transnational networks.

Although drones can collect massive amounts of data, they are not a big data platform. Indeed, "big data" is the practice of accumulating huge amounts of information from a variety of sources (Phase 1: storage) and processing of that information using algorithms and statistical analysis (Phase 2: analysis).[2] On the contrary, drone operations have not yet been reliant on algorithmic decision-making since the analytical part has only been managed by human operators. The future will probably be the automation of target selection processes, or at least of decision support systems, as big data increasingly appears to be essential when the goal is to detect dangerous individuals within an enormous number of interactions, information, and networks. The amount and variety of data that can already be collected by drones is such that without acute algorithms, we would struggle to make sense of the data and locate the relevant pieces of information. It is very likely that the difficulty to analyze such an enormous amount of data can explain the lack of precision of the criteria used to identify dangerousness – legitimate targets – as well as of their application in practice and the errors committed by drone operators such as the drone strike on the Razzo family's home.[3] In order to grasp the technological phenomenon better, let us imagine that the data net is a labyrinth in the form of a rhizome, described by Deleuze and Guattari as a structure that cannot be described globally, since it is a "potential sum of local descriptions":

> In a structure without outside, the describers can look at it only by the inside; as Rosenstiehl suggests, a labyrinth of this kind is a *myopic algorithm*; at every node of it no one can have the global vision of all its possibilities but only the local vision of the closest ones: every local

[2] Jonathan Stuart Ward and Adam Baker, "The Big Data Conundrum: How to Define It?," *MIT Technology Review*, 2013, www.technologyreview.com/2013/10/03/82990/the-big-data-conundrum-how-to-define-it/; Andrew Guthrie Ferguson, "Big Data and Predictive Reasonable Suspicion" (2015) 163 *University of Pennsylvania Law Review* 2, 352–3.

[3] Azmat Khan and Anand Gopal, "The Uncounted," *The New York Times*, November 16, 2016, www.nytimes.com/interactive/2017/11/16/magazine/uncounted-civilian-casualties-iraq-airstrikes.html?_r=0.

> description of the net is a *hypothesis*, subject to falsification, about its further course.[4]

The capacities acquired through algorithms and statistical analysis perform as an enhanced Ariadne's thread to navigate within the labyrinth and observe the net globally from the outside. In the not-so-distant future, this technological reality may lead to the full automation of drones, which will multiply the numbers of individuals identified as legitimate targets and arguably further radicalize the individualization, dematerialization, and deterritorialization of warfare.

Another finding of the book, and one that deserves to be further developed, is the object of preliminary reflections in Chapter 7; that a conflict where participants have a mutual intention to wipe each other from the face of the earth, means proposing legal justifications for action that shift the shape and content of norms as they had previously (and temporarily) crystallized, in a way that opens the door to infinite warfare.[5]

Until recently, the legal gray zones explored in the book did not appear to be problematic because conflicts were not motivated, or at least not so intensely, by the desire and project of mutual annihilation. I suggest that rules of IHL and the UN Charter were created to regulate conflicts and the use of force either between *equal public powers* or between states and *aspiring* states willing to challenge the sovereign exercising its power over them, in order to replace it. None of these scenarios features a desire for or a project of mutual annihilation, and all of them take place in an interstate paradigm thereby preserving the latter. The hypothesis is that once we depart from this premise to reach a new scenario, namely, the use of force against anti-statist transnational terrorist networks, the attacking public forces seek to annihilate the enemy (and vice versa). This dynamic conceals significant consequences: such conflicts are potentially infinite. The legal uncertainties relating to the end of conflicts did not emerge as a factor of unlimited warfare before the emergence of

[4] Umberto Eco, *Semiotics and the Philosophy of Language* (Indiana University Press, 1986), 80.

[5] This proposition was first formulated and then further developed jointly with Nehal Bhuta in "Dangerous Proportions: Means and Ends in Non-Finite War," in N. Bhuta, F. Hoffmann, S. Knuckey, F. Mégret, and M. Satterthwaite (eds.), *The Struggle for Human Rights: Essays in Honour of Philip Alston*. Collected Volume in Honor of Philip Alston (Cambridge University Press, 2021), 301–27. See also, Rebecca Mignot-Mahdavi, "Will the War on Terror Ever End?," *La Revue des droits de l'Homme*, Actualités Droits-Libertés, March 10, 2019, http://journals.openedition.org/revdh/6269.

war aims to annihilate members of transnational terrorist networks. In much the same way, this book shows that the absence of geographical criteria in the law to delineate armed conflicts never appeared as a factor of extensive warfare before war became a question of conducting hostilities against individuals belonging to transnational terrorist networks. Finally, the notion of direct participation in hostilities defined as a continuous combat function does not appear to give free rein for targeting individuals anywhere if it were not for the existence of transnational terrorist networks spread at a distance from hostile activities.

"Traditional" is a term that I have often used for interpretations of the norms that had crystallized as mainstream and differ from the interpretative propositions of states in the war on terror. This book demonstrates that it is not only a working concept helpful to clarify evolutions in how the law is interpreted, but also stresses the historical rootedness of the determination and deconstruction of the contents and meanings of legal norms. At this point in time, with drones in their possession, and a specific enemy to fight, states active in the war on terror push ambiguities and uncertainties in the law to their limits to allow for infinite warfare and enhanced state power. If attempts to curtail this war remain unrooted and if corresponding arguments remain a-historical, these attempts will inevitably fail.

BIBLIOGRAPHY

Scholarly Literature

Agamben, G, *State of Exception* (University of Chicago Press, 2005).

Akande, D, "Classification of Armed Conflicts: Relevant Legal Concepts," in Wilmshurst, Elizabeth (ed.), *International Law and the Classification of Conflicts* (Oxford University Press, 2012), 32–79.

"Clearing the Fog of War? The ICRC's Interpretive Guidance on Direct Participation in Hostilities" (2010) 59 *International and Comparative Law Quarterly* 1, 180–92.

"When Does the Use of Force against a Non-State Armed Group Trigger an International Armed Conflict and Why Does This Matter?," *EJIL: Talk!*, October 18, 2016, www.ejiltalk.org/when-does-the-use-of-force-against-a-non-state-armed-group-trigger-an-international-armed-conflict-and-why-does-this-matter/

Alderson, K, and Hurrell, A, *Hedley Bull on International Society* (Macmillan, 2000).

Anderson, K, "Targeted Killing in U.S. Counterterrorism Strategy and Law: A Working Paper of the Series on Counterterrorism and American Statutory Law" (2009) Digital Commons of the American University Washington College of Law, Working Papers, https://digitalcommons.wcl.american.edu/cgi/viewcontent.cgi?referer=&httpsredir=1&article=1007&context=fac_works_papers

Targeted Killing and Drone Warfare: How We Came to Debate Whether There Is a "Legal Geography of War" (Social Science Research Network, 2011).

Anghie, A, *Imperialism, Sovereignty and the Making of International Law* (Cambridge University Press, 2007).

Arimatsu, L, "Territory, Boundaries and the Law of Armed Conflict" (2009) 12 *Yearbook of International Humanitarian Law* 157–92.

Arkin, W, *Unmanned: Drones, Data, and the Illusion of Perfect Warfare* (Little, Brown, 2015).

Armitage, D, *Civil Wars: A History in Ideas* (Yale University Press, 2017).

d'Aspremont, J, *Formalism and the Sources of International Law* (Oxford University Press, 2011).

"International Law and the Rage against the Scientistic Age" (2022) 33 *European Journal of International Law* 2, 679–94.

Austin, J, *The Province of Jurisprudence Defined* (Cambridge University Press, 1995 [1832]).

Bannelier, K, and Christakis, T, "Under the UN Security Council's Watchful Eyes: Military Intervention by Invitation in the Malian Conflict" (2013) 26 *Leiden Journal of International Law* 4, 855–74.

Barley, SR, "Technology as an Occasion for Structuring: Evidence from Observation of CT Scanners and the Social Order of Radiology Departments" (1986) 31 *Administrative Science Quarterly* 78–108.

Bassou, A, and Guennoun, I, "Le Sahel Face aux Tendances Al Qaeda et Daech: Quel Dénouement Possible ? / Al Qaeda vs. Daech in the Sahel: What to Expect?," *AfricaPortal*, January 2017, www.africaportal.org/publications/le-sahel-face-aux-tendances-al-qaeda-et-daech-quel-d%C3%A9nouement-possible-al-qaeda-vs-daech-in-the-sahel-what-to-expect/

Bentley, M, and Holland, J, *Obama's Foreign Policy: Ending the War on Terror* (Routledge, 2013).

Benvenisti, E, "The Legal Battle to Define the Law on Transnational Asymmetric Warfare" (2010) 20 *Duke Journal of Comparative & International Law* 339–59.

Bergen, P, and Tiedemann, K, "The Year of the Drone: An Analysis of US Drone Strikes in Pakistan, 2004–2010" (2010) New America Foundation, Counterterrorism Strategy Initiative policy paper, http://counterterrorism.newamerica.net/sites/newamerica.net/files/policydocs/bergentiedemann2.pdf.

Bergen, PL, *Holy War, Inc.: Inside the Secret World of Osama Bin Laden*, 1st Touchstone ed. (Free Press, 2002).

Berger, PL, and Luckmann, T, *The Social Construction of Reality: A Treatise in the Sociology of Knowledge* (Penguin, 1991).

Bethlehem, D, "Self-Defense against an Imminent or Actual Armed Attack by Nonstate Actors" (2012) 106 *American Journal of International Law* 4, 770–7.

Bhuta, N, "The Antinomies of Transformative Occupation" (2005) 16 *The European Journal of International Law* 4, 721–74.

"On Preventive Killing," *EJILTalk!*, September 17, 2015, www.ejiltalk.org/on-preventive-killing/#more-13651

"States of Exception: Regulating Targeted Killing in a 'Global Civil War'," in Alston, Philip, and Macdonald, Euan (eds.), *Human Rights, Intervention, and the Use of Force* (Oxford University Press, 2008), 243–74.

Bhuta, N, and Liu, H-Y, "Targeted Killing, Unmanned Aerial Vehicles and EU Policy" (2013) 17 RSCAS Policy Papers.

Bhuta, N, and Mignot-Mahdavi, R, "From Brownlie to Brandom: Recollective Stories of the Right of Self-Defense and a Theory of the Pragmatic

Semantics of Legal Conceptual Change," *Opinio Juris*, April 20, 2021, https://opiniojuris.org/2021/04/20/from-brownlie-to-brandom-recollective-stories-of-the-right-of-self-defense-and-a-theory-of-the-pragmatic-semantics-of-legal-conceptual-change/

"Dangerous Proportions: Means and Ends in Non-Finite War," in Bhuta, N, Hoffmann, F, Knuckey, S, Mégret, F, and Satterthwaite, M (eds.), *The Struggle for Human Rights: Essays in Honour of Philip Alston* (Cambridge University Press, 2021), 301–27.

Blank, LR, "After Top Gun: How Drone Strikes Impact the Law of War" (2012) 33 *University of Pennsylvania Journal of International Law* 3, 675.

Blum, G, "The Individualization of War: From War to Policing in the Regulation of Armed Conflict," in Sarat, A, Douglas, L, and Umphrey, MM (eds.), *Law and War* (Stanford University Press, 2014), 48–83.

Bobbio, N, *The Future of Democracy: A Defense of the Rules of the Game* (Polity Press, 1987).

Bobbitt, P, *Terror and Consent: The Wars for the Twenty-First Century* (First Anchor Books Edition, April 2009).

Bourdieu, P, *Sur L'État.* Cours au Collège de France 1989–92 (Éditions du Seuil, 2012).

Brandom, R, "A Hegelian Model of Legal Concept Determination," in Hubbs, G, and Lind, D (eds.), *Pragmatism, Law, and Language* (Routledge, 2014), 19–39.

Brooks, R, "Drones and the International Rule of Law" (2014) 28 *Ethics & International Affairs* 1, 83–103.

How Everything Became War and the Military Became Everything (Simon & Schuster, 2016).

Bunzel, C, "From Paper State to Khilafat" (2015) Analysis Paper 19, Brookings Project on US Relations with the Islamic World, www.brookings.edu/wp-content/uploads/2016/06/The-ideology-of-the-Islamic-State.pdf

Byman, D, "Understanding the Islamic State – A Review Essay" (2016) 40 *International Security* 4, 127–65, 147.

Casey-Malsen, S, "Pandora's Box? Drone Strikes under *jus ad bellum, jus in bello* and International Human Rights Law" (2012) 94 *International Review of the Red Cross* 886, 597–625.

Cassese, A, "The International Community's 'Legal' Response to Terrorism" (1989) 38 *International and Comparative Law Quarterly* 589–608.

Castro, AF, Herrero-Olaizola, A, and Rutter-Jensen, C (eds.), *Territories of Conflict: Traversing Colombia through Cultural Studies* (University of Rochester Press, 2017).

Chachko, E, and Deeks, A, "Which States Support the 'Unwilling and Unable' Test?," *Lawfare*, October 10, 2016, www.lawfareblog.com/which-states-support-unwilling-and-unable-test.

Chafer, T, Cumming, G, and van der Velde, R, "France's Interventions in Mali and the Sahel: A Historical Institutionalist Perspective" (2020) 43 *Journal of Strategic Studies* 4, 482–507.

Chamayou, G, *Drone Theory* (Broché, 2015).

Théorie du drone (La Fabrique, 2013).

Chernick, M, "FARC-EP: Las Fuerzas Armadas Revolucionarias de Colombia-Ejército del Pueblo," in Heiberg, M, O'Leary, B, and Tirman, J (eds.), *Terror, Insurgency, and the State: Ending Protracted Conflicts* (University of Pennsylvania Press, 2007), 51–82.

Chesney, R, "Airstrikes Outside Areas of Active Hostilities: Attacks in Somalia and Questions about the Current Shape of the Policy," *Lawfare*, March 7, 2016, www.lawfareblog.com/airstrikes-outside-areas-active-hostilities-attacks-somalia-and-questions-about-current-shape-policy

de Cock, C, "Counter-Insurgency Operations in Afghanistan. What about the 'Jus ad Bellum' and the 'Jus in Bello': Is the Law Still Accurate?," in Schmitt, MN, Arimatsu, L, and McCormack, T (eds.), *Yearbook of International Humanitarian Law* (Stichting, T.M.C. Asser Instituut, Vol. 13, 2010), 97–132.

Cohen, M, "Judges or Hostages? The Bureaucratization of the Court of Justice of the European Union and the European Court of Human Rights," in Davies, B, and Nicola, F (eds.), *European Law Stories* (Cambridge University Press, 2017), 58–80.

Coleman, J, "Negative and Positive Positivism" (1982) 11 *Journal of Legal Studies* 139–64.

Coll, S, *Ghost Wars: The Secret History of the CIA, Afghanistan, and bin Laden, from the Soviet Invasion to September 10, 2001* (Penguin Books, 2004).

Cook, D, *Understanding Jihad* (University of California Press, 2005).

Corn, G, "Making the Case for Conflict Bifurcation in Afghanistan: Transnational Armed Conflict, Al Qaeda, and the Limits of the Associated Militia Concept," in Special Issue, Schmitt, MN (ed.), *The War in Afghanistan: A Legal Analysis* (2009) 85 *International Law Studies* 182–218.

Corten, O, "The 'Unwilling or Unable' Test: Has It Been, and Could It Be, Accepted?" (2016) 29 *Leiden Journal of International Law* 3, 777–99.

Crawford, E, *International Humanitarian Law* (Cambridge University Press, 2018).

"The Temporal and Geographic Reach of International Humanitarian Law," in Saul, B, and Akande, D (eds.), *The Oxford Guide to International Humanitarian Law* (Oxford University Press, 2020), 57–75.

Cullen, A, *The Concept of Non-International Armed Conflict in International Humanitarian Law* (Cambridge University Press, 2010).

Danner, M, *Spiral: Trapped in the Forever War* (Simon & Schuster, 2016).

Daskal, JC, "The Geography of the Battlefield: A Framework for Detention and Targeting outside the 'Hot' Conflict Zone" (2013) 160 *University of Pennsylvania Law Review* 5, 1165–234.

Daskal, JC, Deeks, A, and Goodman, R, "Strikes in Syria: The International Law Framework," *Just Security*, September 24, 2014, www.justsecurity.org/15479/strikes-syria-international-law-framework-daskal-deeks-goodman

Davet, G, and Lhomme, F (Interviews with President Hollande), *Un président ne devrait pas dire ça … les secrets d'un quinquennat* (Stock, French and European Publications, 2016).

Dean, MM, *The Signature of Power: Sovereignty, Governmentality and Biopolitics* (Sage, 2013).

Deeks, A, "'Unwilling or Unable': Toward a Normative Framework for Extraterritorial Self-Defence" (2012) 52 *Virginia Journal of International Law* 483–551.

Demuynch, M, and Coleman, J, "The Shifting Sands of the Sahel's Terrorism Landscape," *ICCT Journal*, March 12, 2020, https://icct.nl/publication/the-shifting-sands-of-the-sahels-terrorism-landscape/

Desgrais, N, "La Force conjointe du G5 Sahel ou l'émergence d'une architecture de défense collective propre au Sahel" (2018) 1 *Les Champs de Mars* 30, 211–20.

Devereaux, R, "Manhunting in the Hindu Kush," in Scahill, J, and The Intercept (eds.), *The Assassination Complex: Inside the Government's Secret Drone Warfare Program* (Simon & Schuster, 2016), 154–78.

van Dijk, B, The Making of the Geneva Conventions. Decolonization, the Cold War, and the Birth of Humanitarian Law (PhD thesis, Florence: European University Institute, 2017).

Dinstein, Y, *War, Aggression and Self-Defense* (Cambridge University Press, 1988).

War, Aggression and Self-Defence (5th ed., Cambridge University Press, 2011).

Durkheim, E, *The Elementary Forms of the Religious Life* (trans. by Joseph Swain, Free Press [1915] 1974).

The Rules of Sociological Method (trans. by Sarah A. Solovay and John H. Mueller, Free Press, 1966).

Eco, U, *Semiotics and the Philosophy of Language* (Indiana University Press, 1986).

Edney-Browne, A, "The Psychosocial Effects of Drone Violence: Social Isolation, Self-Objectification, and Depoliticization" (2019) 40 *Political Psychology* 6, 1–15.

Elden, S, *The Birth of Territory* (Broché, 2013).

Fassbender, B, "The United Nations Charter as Constitution of the International Community" (1998) 36 *Columbia Journal of Transnational Law* 3, 529–619.

Fauchille, P, *Traité de droit international public* (8th ed., Rousseau, 1925).

Fazal, TM, "Rebellion, War Aims & the Laws of War" (2017) 146 *Dædalus, the Journal of the American Academy of Arts & Sciences* 1, 71–82.

Feinstein, L, and Slaughter, A-M, "A Duty to Prevent" (2004) *Foreign Affairs*, www.foreignaffairs.com/articles/2004-01-01/duty-prevent, 136–50.

Fellmeth, AX, and Horwitz, M, *Guide to Latin in International Law* (Oxford University Press, 2009).

Ferguson, AG, "Big Data and Predictive Reasonable Suspicion" (2015) 163 *University of Pennsylvania Law Review* 2, 327–410.

Firth, R, *Elements of Social Organization* (Watts, 1951).

Fiss, OM, "The Bureaucratization of the Judiciary" (1983) 92 *The Yale Law Journal* 8, 1442–68.

Fitzgerald, MA, "Note, Seizing Weapons of Mass Destruction from Foreign-Flagged Ships on the High Seas under Article 51 of the UN Charter" (2009) 49 *Virginia Journal of International Law* 473–505.

Foucault, M, *Surveiller et Punir: Naissance de la prison* (Gallimard, 1993) [*Discipline and Punish: The Birth of the Prison*, trans. by Alan Sheridan, New ed. (Penguin, 1991)].

Society Must Be Defended (Editions de Seuil/Gallimard, 1997).

Les Anormaux. Cours au Collège de France. 1974–1975 (Gallimard, 1999).

Sécurité, Territoire, Population (Gallimard and Seuil, 2004).

Security, Territory, Population: Lectures at the College De France, 1977–1978 (Picador, 2009).

Franck, TM, "Terrorism and the Right of Self-Defense" (2001) 95 *American Journal of International Law* 4, 839–43.

de Galbert, S, "After the Paris Attacks, a European Anti-ISIS Coalition Comes Together," Center for Strategic and International Studies, December 3, 2015.

Gallie, WB, "Essentially Contested Concepts" (1955–6) 56 *Proceedings of the Aristotelian Society* 167–98.

Georges, AM, "ISIS Rhetoric for the Creation of the Ummah," in Orwenjo, DO, Oketch, O, and Tunde, AH (eds.), *Political Discourse in Emergent, Fragile, and Failed Democracies* (IGI Global, 2016), 178–198, 196.

Gerges, FA, *ISIS: A History* (reprint ed., Princeton University Press, 2017).

Glennon, MJ, "How International Rules Die" (2005) 93 *Georgetown Law Journal* 939.

Goldsmith, JL, *Power and Constraint: The Accountable Presidency after 9/11* (W. W. Norton, 2012).

Goldsmith, JL, and Posner, EA, *The Limits of International Law* (Oxford University Press, 2006).

Goodman, PS, *Change in Organizations* (Jossey-Bass, 1982).

Goodman, R, "International Law on Airstrikes against ISIS in Syria," *Just Security*, August 28, 2014, www.justsecurity.org/14414/international-law-airstrikes-isis-syria/

"Why the Laws of War Apply to Drone Strikes outside 'Areas of Active Hostilities' (A Memo to the Human Rights Community)," *Just Security*, October 4, 2017, www.justsecurity.org/45613/laws-war-apply-drone-strikes-areas-active-hostilities-a-memo-human-rights-community/

Gordon, Y, *Soviet/Russian Unmanned Aerial Vehicles* (Midland Publishing, 2005).

Gray, C, *International Law and the Use of Force* (3rd ed., Oxford University Press, 2008).

"President Obama's 2010 United States National Security Strategy and International Law on the Use of Force" (2011) 10 *Chinese Journal of International Law* 1, 35–53.

Greenwood, C, "International Law and the Preemptive Use of Force: Afghanistan, al-Qaida, and Iraq" (2003) 4 *San Diego International Law Journal* 7–38.

Gregory, D, "The Everywhere War" (2011) 177 *The Geographical Journal* 3, 238–50.

"From a View to a Kill: Drones and Late Modern War" (2011) 28 *Theory, Culture & Society* 7–8, 188–215.

Griffin, C, "Operation Barkhane and Boko Haram: French Counterterrorism and Military Cooperation in the Sahel" (2016) 27 *Small Wars & Insurgencies: Jihadist Insurgent Movements* 896–913.

Gross, M, *Moral Dilemmas of Modern War: Torture, Assassination, and Blackmail in an Age of Asymmetric Conflict* (Cambridge University Press, 2009).

Gusterson, H, *Drone: Remote Control Warfare* (The MIT Press, 2016).

Hakimi, M, "Defensive Force against Non-State Actors: The State of Play" (2015) 91 *International Law Studies* 31.

"The Jus Ad Bellum's Regulatory Form" (2018) 2 *The American Journal of International Law* 112, 151–90.

Hamming, TR, "The Al Qaeda–Islamic State Rivalry: Competition Yes, but No Competitive Escalation" (2020) 32 *Terrorism and Political Violence* 1, 20–37.

Hamming, TR, and Van Ostaeyen, P, "The True Story of al-Qaeda's Demise and Resurgence in Syria," *Lawfare*, April 8, 2018, www.lawfareblog.com/true-story-al-qaedas-demise-and-resurgence-syria

Haque, AA, "The United States Is at War with Syria (according to the ICRC's New Geneva Convention Commentary)," *EJIL: Talk!*, April 8, 2016, www.ejiltalk.org/the-united-states-is-at-war-with-syria-according-to-the-icrcs-new-geneva-convention-commentary/

Harcourt, B, *The Counterrevolution: How Our Government Went to War against Its Own Citizens* (Basic Books, 2018).

Hart, HLA, *The Concept of Law* (2nd ed., Clarendon Press, 1997 [1961]).

Hauriou, M, "La Théorie de l'institution et de la fondation" (1925) 4 *Cahiers de la Nouvelle Journée* 89–128.

Hegghammer, T, "The Rise of Muslim Foreign Fighters: Islam and the Globalization of Jihad" (2010) 35 *International Security* 3, 53–94.

Henderson, C, "Non-State Actors and the Use of Force," in Noortmann, M, Reinisch, A, and Ryngaert, C (eds.), *Non-State Actors in International Law* (Hart Publishing, 2015), 77–96.

Hoffmann, S, "International Systems and International Law" (1961) 14 *World Politics* 1, Special issue on "The International System: Theoretical Essays," 205–37.

Hughes, T, "The Electrification of America: the System Builders" (1979) 20 *Technology and Culture* 1, 124–62.

Networks of Power, Electric Supply Systems in the US, England and Germany, 1880–1930 (John Hopkins University Press, 1983).

Ingber, R, "Co-Belligerency" (2017) 42 *The Yale Journal of International Law* 1, 68–120.

Jaffer, J, *The Drone Memos: Targeted Killing, Secrecy and the Law* (The New Press, 2010).

Jeangène Vilmer, J-B, "Légalité et légitimé des drones armés" (2013) *Politique étrangère* 3, 199–32.

Jinks, D, "September 11 and the Laws of War" (2003) 28 *The Yale Journal of International Law* 1, 1–45.

Kelsen, H, *The General Theory of Law and State* (trans. by A. Wedberg, Russell & Russell, 1961).

Kendall, S, "Cartographies of the Present: 'Contingent Sovereignty' and Territorial Integrity," in Kuijer, M, and Werner, W (eds.), *Netherlands Yearbook of International Law: The Changing Nature of Territoriality in International Law* (T.M.C. Asser Press and Springer, 2016), 83–106.

Kepel, G, *Jihad: The Trail of Political Islam*, Edition Unstated (trans. by Anthony F. Roberts, Belknap Press: An Imprint of Harvard University Press, 2003).

Kfir, I, "Organized Criminal-Terrorist Groups in the Sahel: How Counterterrorism and Counterinsurgency Approaches Ignore the Roots of the Problem" (2018) 19 *International Studies Perspectives* 4, 344–59.

Kingsbury, B, "Whose International Law? Sovereignty and Non-State Groups" *ASIL Proceedings* (1994) Theme Panel I.

Kinsella, HM, *The Image before the Weapon: A Critical History of the Distinction between Combatant and Civilian* (Cornell University Press, 2011).

Klose, F, *Human Rights in the Shadow of Colonial Violence: The Wars of Independence in Kenya and Algeria* (University of Pennsylvania Press, 2013).

Koh, H, *The Trump Administration and International Law* (Global Oxford University Press, 2018).

Kolb, R, *Advanced Introduction to International Humanitarian Law* (Edward Elgar, 2014).

"Applicability Issues: Finding a Way Out of the Quagmire," in Robert Kolb (ed.), *Advanced Introduction to International Humanitarian Law* (Edward Elgar, 2014), 93–123.

Kreß, C, "Extraterritorial Targeted Killings of Non-State Actors by States in Response to Transnational non-State Violence," in Robert Schuman Centre for Advanced Studies Policy Papers, 2013/17, Global Governance Programme, Targeted Killing, Unmanned Aerial Vehicles and EU Policy, (contributions by Nehal Bhuta, Claus Kreß, Ian Seiderman, Christof Heyns, Nils Melzer, Martin Scheinin, Eyal Benvenisti, and Anthony Dworkin).

Gewaltverbot und Selbstverteidigungsrecht nach der Satzung der Vereinten Nationen bei staatlicher Verwicklung in Gewaltakte Privater (Duncker & Humblot, 1995).

"The Fine Line between Collective Self-Defense and Intervention by Invitation: Reflections on the Use of Force against IS in Syria," *Just Security*, February 17, 2015, www.justsecurity.org/20118/claus-kreb-force-isil-syria/

"The International Court of Justice and the 'Principle of Non-Use of Force'," in Weller, M (ed.), *The Oxford Handbook of the Use of Force in International Law* (Oxford University Press, 2015) 561–604.

"Some Reflections on the International Legal Framework Governing Transnational Armed Conflicts" (2010) 15 *Journal of Conflict and Security Law* 2, 245–74, 251.

Kreps, S, and Kaag, J, *Drone Warfare* (Polity Press, 2014).

Kretzer, DI, *Ritual, Politics and Power* (Yale University Press, 1988).

Kretzmer, D, "Targeted Killing of Suspected Terrorists: Extrajudicial Killing or Legitimate Means of Self-Defence?" (2005) 16 *The European Journal of International Law* 2, 171–212.

Kristensen, KS, "Tourists or Vagabonds? Space and Time in the War on Terror" (2008) 33 *Alternatives* 249–66.

Latour, B, *Reassembling the Social* (Oxford University Press, 2005).

"Technology Is Society Made Durable," in Law, J (ed.), *A Sociology of Monsters: Essays on Power, Technology and Domination*. Sociological Review Monograph, no. 38 (Routledge, 1991), 104–31.

Lavallée, C, and Zubeldia, O, "Un Espace Européen des Drones," Note de Recherche *IRSEM*, no. 52, March 7, 2018.

Law, J, *Aircraft Stories: Decentering the Object in Technoscience* (Duke University Press, 2002).

After Method: Mess in Social Science Research (Routledge, 2004).

Leach, E, *Political Systems of Highland Burma* (Beacon, 1954).

"Ritualization in Man in Relation to Conceptual and Social Development" (1966) 251 *Philosophical Transactions of the Royal Society* 772, 403–8.

Lewis, DA, Blum, G, and Modirzadeh, NK, "Indefinite War: Unsettled International Law on the End of Armed Conflict," Harvard Law School Program on International Law and Armed Conflict, Legal Briefing, February 2017, Harvard Public Law Working Paper.

Li, D, "A Jihadism Anti-Primer" (2015) 276 *Middle East Report*.

Lieblich, E, "On the Continuous and Concurrent Application of ad Bellum and in Bello Proportionality," in Kreß, C, and Lawless, R (eds.), *Necessity and Proportionality in International Peace and Security Law*. Lieber Series, Vol. 4 (Oxford University Press, 2020), 41–78.

Linklater, A, *The Transformation of Political Community: Ethical Foundations of the Post-Westphalian Era* (Polity Press, 1998).

Llewellyn, KN, *Jurisprudence: Realism in Theory and Practice* (Transaction Publishers, 2008 [1962]).

Low, R, "Making up the Ummah: The Rhetoric of ISIS as Public Pedagogy" (2016) 38 *Review of Education, Pedagogy, and Cultural Studies* 4, 297–316.

Lubell, N, *Extraterritorial Use of Force against Non-State Actors* (Oxford University Press, 2010).

"The War (?) against Al-Qaeda," in Wilmshurst, E (ed.), *International Law and the Classification of Conflicts* (Oxford University Press, 2012), 42–54.

Luban, D, "Risk Taking and Force Protection" (2011) Georgetown Public Law and Legal Theory Research Paper No. 11–72.

"War as Punishment" (2012) 39 *Philosophy & Public Affairs* 4, 299–330.

Lubell, N, and Derejko, N, "A Global Battlefield? Drones and the Geographical Scope of Armed Conflict" (2013) 11 *Journal of International Criminal Justice* 1, 65–88, https://doi.org/10.1093/jicj/mqs096

MacGibbon, IC, "The Scope of Acquiescence in International Law" (1954) 31 *British Yearbook of International Law* 143–86.

Margolis, G, "The Lack of HUMINT: A Recurring Intelligence Problem" (2013) 4 *Global Security Studies* 2, 43–60.

Margulies, P, and Sinnot, M, "Crossing Borders to Target Al-Qaeda and Its Affiliates: Defining Networks as Organized Armed Groups in Non-International Armed Conflicts," in Gill, TD, Geiß, R, Heinsch, R, McCormack, T, Paulussen, C, and Dorsey, J (eds.), *Yearbook of International Humanitarian Law* (T.M.C. Asser Press, 2013), 319–45.

Marks, S, "Branding the 'War On Terrorism': Is There a 'New Paradigm' of International Law?" (2006) 14 *Michigan State Journal of International Law* 1, 71–119.

Martin, MJ, and Sasser, CW, *Predator: The Remote Control Air War over Iraq and Afghanistan: A Pilot's Story* (Zenith Press, 2010).

da Matta, R, "Constraint and License: A Preliminary Study of Two Brazilian National Rituals," in Moore, SF, and Myerhoff, BG (eds.), *Secular Ritual* (Van Gorcum, 1977), 244–64.

Mazzetti, M, *The Way of the Knife: The CIA, a Secret Army, and a War at the Ends of the Earth* (Penguin Books, 2014).

McCants, W, *The ISIS Apocalypse: The History, Strategy, and Doomsday Vision of the Islamic State* (Picador, 2016).

Melzer, N, "Human Rights Implications of the Usage of Drones and Unmanned Robots in Warfare, Study," European Parliament, Directorate-General for External Policies, Policy Department, May 2013.

Targeted Killing in International Law (Oxford University Press, 2008).

Michel, AH, *Eyes in the Sky: The Secret Rise of Gorgon Stare and How It Will Watch Us All* (Mariner Books, 2019).

Mignot-Mahdavi, R, "Drone Programs, the Individualization of War and the Ad Bellum Principle of Proportionality," in Kress, Claus, and Lawless, Robert (eds.), *Necessity and Proportionality in International Peace and Security Law*. Lieber Series, Vol. 4 (Oxford University Press, 2020).

"Le Silence des Agneaux: France's War against 'Jihadist Groups' and Associated Legal Rationale" (2020) *ICCT Journal*, https://icct.nl/publication/le-silence-des-agneaux-frances-war-against-jihadist-groups-and-associated-legal-rationale/

"Will the War on Terror Ever End?," *Revue des Droits de l'Homme, Actualités Droits-Libertés*, March 10, 2019, http:// journals.openedition.org/revdh/6269

Milanovic, M, "What Exactly Internationalizes an Internal Armed Conflict?," *EJIL: Talk!*, May 7, 2010, www.ejiltalk.org/what-exactly-internationalizes-an-internal-armed-conflict/

"On Whether IHL Applies to Drone Strikes Outside 'Areas of Active Hostilities': A Response to Ryan Goodman," *EJIL: Talk!*, October 5, 2017, www.ejiltalk.org/on-whether-ihl-applies-to-drone-strikes-outside-areas-of-active-hostilities-a-response-to-ryan-goodman/

Mohamedou, M-MO, *A Theory of ISIS. Political Violence and the Transformation of the Global Order* (Kindle ed., Pluto Press, 2018).

Moyn, S, "Why the War on Terror May Never End," *The New York Times*, June 24, 2016, www.nytimes.com/2016/06/26/books/review/spiral-by-mark-danner.html

Murphy, S, "Terrorism and the Concept of 'Armed Attack' in Article 51 of the UN Charter" (2002) 43 *Harvard International Law Journal* 1, 41–52.

Mushkat, R, "Is War Ever Justifiable? A Comparative Survey" (1987) 9 *Loyola of Los Angeles International and Comparative Law Journal* 2, 227–317.

Myerhoff, B, "We Don't Wrap Herring in a Printed Page: Fusion, Fictions and Continuity in Secular Ritual," in Moore, SF, and Myerhoff, BG (eds.), *Secular Ritual* (Van Gorcum, 1977), 199–226.

Myjer, E, and White, N, "The Twin Towers Attack: An Unlimited Right to Self-Defense" (2002) 7 *Journal of Conflict and Security Law* 5.

Neumann, P, *Old and New Terrorism* (Polity, 2009).

Nouzille, V, *Erreurs fatales: Comment nos présidents ont failli face au terrorisme* (Kindle ed., Fayard, 2017).

Noorman, M, and Johnson, DG, "Negotiating Autonomy and Responsibility in Military Robots" (2014) 16 *Ethics and Information Technology* 51–62.

Nye, J, *The Future of Power* (Broché, 2011).

O'Connell, ME, "The Legal Case against the Global War on Terror" (2004) 36 *Case Western Reserve Journal of International Law* 349–58.

"Seductive Drones: Learning from a Decade of Lethal Operations" (2011) 21 *Journal of Law, Information & Science* 2, 116–39, Notre Dame Legal Studies Paper No. 11–35.

Odysseos, L, "Crossing the Line? Carl Schmitt on the 'Spaceless Universalism' of Cosmopolitanism and the War on Terror," in Odysseos, L, and Petito, F (eds.), *The International Political Thought of Carl Schmitt: Terror, Liberal War and the Crisis of Global Order* (Routledge, 2007), 124–44.

Ohlin, JD, "Targeting Co-belligerents," in Finkelstein, C, Ohlin, JD, and Altman, A (eds.), *Targeted Killings: Law and Morality in an Asymmetrical World* (Oxford University Press, 2012), 60–89.

Oppenheim, L, *International Law: A Treatise* (5th ed., Longmans, 1935).

Orlikowski, W, "The Duality of Technology: Rethinking the Concept of Technology in Organizations" (1992) 3 *Organization Science*, Focused Issue: Management of Technology, 398–427.

Pannier, A, and Schmitt, O, "To Fight Another Day: France between the Fight against Terrorism and Future Warfare" (2019) 94 *International Affairs* 4, 897–916.

Paulus, A, and Vashakmadze, M, "Asymmetrical War and the Notion of Armed Conflict – A Tentative Conceptualization" (2009) 91 *International Review of the Red Cross* 873, 95–125.

Pejic, J, "Extraterritorial Targeting by Means of Armed Drones: Some Legal Implications" (2014) 96 *International Review of the Red Cross* 893, 67–106.

Peritz, A, and Rosenbach, E, *Find, Fix, Finish: Inside the Counterterrorism Campaigns that Killed bin Laden and Devastated Al Qaeda* (Kindle ed., PublicAffairs, 2013).

Piscatori, J, and Saikal, A, *Islam Beyond Borders: The Umma in World Politics* (Cambridge University Press, 2019).

Poplin, C, "Look Who Else Has Drones: ISIS and Al Nusra," *Lawfare*, 2014 www.lawfareblog.com/look-who-else-has-drones-isis-and-al-nusra

Priest, D, and Arkin, WM, *Top Secret America: The Rise of the New American Security State* (reprint ed., Back Bay Books, 2011).

Rapoport, DC, *Inside Terrorist Organizations* (2nd ed., Routledge, 2013).

Rappaport, R, *Ecology, Meaning and Religion* (North Atlantic Books, 1979).

Raz, J, *The Authority of Law* (Oxford University Press, 1979).

Ridgeway, MB, *The Korean War* (Da Capo Press, 1967).

Roberts, A, "The Equal Application of the Laws of War: A Principle under Pressure" (2008) 90 *International Review of the Red Cross* 872, 931–62.

Roland, A, *War and Technology: A Very Short Introduction* (Oxford University Press, 2016).

Ronen, Y, "The 2006 Conflict in Lebanon" (2008) 9 *Yearbook of International Humanitarian Law* 362–93.

Rossiter, A, "Drone Usage by Militant Groups: Exploring Variation in Adoption" (2018) 34 *Defense and Security Analysis* 2, 113–26.

Roy, O, *Globalized Islam: The Search for a New Ummah* (Columbia University Press, 2006).

Le Djihad et la Mort (Seuil, 2016).

Ruys, T, *Armed Attack and Article 51 of the UN Charter, Evolutions in Customary Law and Practice* (Cambridge University Press, 2010).

"Quo Vadit Jus ad Bellum?: A Legal Analysis of Turkey's Military Operations against the PKK in Northern Iraq" (2008) 9 *Melbourne Journal of International Law* 334–64.

Ryngaert, C, "Clarifying the Extraterritorial Application of the European Convention on Human Rights" (2012) 28 *Utrecht Journal of International and European Law* 74, 57–60.

Sassòli, M, "Transnational Armed Groups and International Humanitarian Law" (2006) Program on Humanitarian Policy and Conflict Research, Harvard, Occasional Paper Series 6, 1–45.

Savage, C, *Power Wars: The Relentless Rise of Presidential Authority and Secrecy* (Little, Brown, 2017).

Scahill, J, and Greenwald, G, "Death by Metadata," in Scahill, J, and The Intercept (eds.), *The Assassination Complex: Inside the Government's Secret Drone Warfare Program* (Simon & Schuster, 2016), 96–109.

Scahill, J, and The Intercept, *The Assassination Complex: Inside the Government's Secret Drone Warfare Program* (Simon & Schuster, 2016).

Schachter, O, "New Custom: Power, Opinion Juris, and Contrary Practice," in Makarczyk, J (ed.), *Theory of International Law at the Threshold of the 21st Century.* Essays in Honour of Krzysztof Skubiszewski (Kluwer Law International, 1996), 531–40.

Scharf, M, Williams, P, and Sterio, M, *The Syrian Conflict's Impact on International Law* (Cambridge University Press, 2020).

Scheinin, M, "Extraterritorial Effect of the International Covenant on Civil and Political Rights," in Coomans, F, and Kamminga, M (eds.), *Extraterritorial Application of Human Rights Treaties* (Intersentia, 2004), 73–82.

Schmitt, C, *Verfassungslehre* (Duncker & Humblot, 2017 [1928]).

The Nomos *of the Earth in the International Law of the* Jus Publicum Europaeum (Telos Press Publishing, 2006).

Theory of the Partisan: A Commentary/Remark on the Concept of the Political (Duncker & Humblot, 1963).

Schmitt, MN, "'Change Direction' 2006: Israeli Operations in Lebanon and the International Law of Self-Defense" (2008) 29 *Michigan Journal of International Law* 2, 127–64.

"Charting the Legal Geography of Non-International Armed Conflict" (2013) 52 *Military Law and Law of War Review* 93–112.

"Drone Attacks under the Jus ad Bellum and Jus in Bello: Clearing the 'Fog of Law'," in Schmitt, MN, Arimatsu, L, and McCormack, T (eds.), *Yearbook of International Humanitarian Law*, Vol. 12 (T.M.C. Asser Press, 2010), 313.

Schmitt, MN, and Widmar, E, "'On Target': Precision and Balance in the Contemporary Law of Targeting" (2014) 7 *Journal of National Security and Policy* 379–409.

Schnell, F, "Pour une approche longitudinale de la lutte antiterroriste au Sahel" (2018) 1 *Les Champs de Mars* 39, 221–9.

Schrijver, N, and van den Herik, L, "Leiden Policy Recommendations on Counter-terrorism and International Law" (2010) 57 *Netherlands Yearbook of International Law* 531.

Shaw, IGR, *Predator Empire: Drone Warfare and Full Spectrum Dominance* (University of Minnesota Press, 2016).

Shaw, M, *International Law* (6th ed., Cambridge University Press, 2008).

Shereshevsky, Y, "Targeting the *Targeted Killings* Case – International Lawmaking in Domestic Contexts" (2018) 39 *Michigan Journal of International Law* 2, 241–81.

Sivakumaran, S, *The Law of Non-International Armed Conflict* (Oxford University Press, 2012).

"Re-envisaging the International Law of Internal Armed Conflict" (2011) 22 *The European Journal of International Law* 1, 219–64.

Slaughter, A-M, "International Law and International Relations Theory: A Dual Agenda" (1993) 87 *AJIL* 2, 205–39.

Slaughter, A-M, and Burke-White, W, "An International Constitutional Moment" (2002) 43 *Harvard International Law Journal* 1, 2–21.

Solomon, H, *Islamic State and the Coming Global Confrontation* (Palgrave Macmillan, 2016).

Stroud, B, *Meaning, Understanding, and Practice: Philosophical Essays* (Oxford University Press, 2003).

Sutton, JR, *Law/Society: Origins, Interactions, and Change*. Sociology for a New Century (Sage, 2000).

Tams, CJ, "The Use of Force against Terrorists" (2009) 20 *The European Journal of International Law* 2, 359–97.

Tams, CJ, and Devaney, J, "Applying Necessity and Proportionality to Anti-Terrorist Self-Defence" (2012) 45 *Israel Law Review* 1, 91–106.

Tams, CJ, and Devaney, JG, "Jus ad Bellum: Crossing Borders to Wage War against Individuals," in Barela, SJ (ed.), *Legitimacy and Drones* (Taylor & Francis, 2016), 25–47.

Tzouvala, N, "TWAIL and the 'Unwilling or Unable' Doctrine: Continuities and Ruptures" (2015) 109 *AJIL Unbound* 266–70.

Uhler, OM, and Coursier, H, *Geneva Convention Relative to the Protection of Civilian Persons in Time of War: Commentary* (International Committee of the Red Cross, 1958).

Van Steenberghe, R, "Self-Defence in Response to Attacks by Non-State Actors in the Light of Recent State Practice: A Step Forward?" (2010) 23 *Leiden Journal of International Law* 1, 83–208.

Walker, RBJ, "Genealogy, Geopolitics and Political Community: Richard K. Ashley and the Critical Social Theory of International Politics" (1988) 13 *Alternatives* 85.

Ward, JS and Baker, A, "The Big Data Conundrum: How to Define It?" (2013) *MIT Technology Review*, www.technologyreview.com/2013/10/03/82990/the-big-data-conundrum-how-to-define-it/#:~:text=%E2%80%9CBig%20data%20is%20a%20term,can%20agree%20is%20certainly%20overdue.

Watkin, K, "Opportunity Lost: Organized Armed Groups and the ICRC Direct Participation in Hostilities Interpretive Guidance" (2009) 42 *NYU Journal of International Law and Politics* 658.

Waxman, M, "The Structure of Terrorism Threats and the Laws of War" (2010) 30 *Duke Journal of Comparative and International Law* 429; Columbia Public Law Research Paper No. 10–240.

Weber, M, *Economy and Society: An Outline of Interpretive Sociology* (ed. Roth, Guenther, and Wittich, Claus, University of California Press, 2013 [1978]).

Weimann, G, "Terrorist Migration to the Dark Web" (2016) 10 *Perspectives on Terrorism* 3, 44.

Weller, M, "Permanent Imminence of Armed Attacks: Resolution 2249 (2015) and the Right to Self Defence against Designated Terrorist Groups," November 25, 2015, *EJIL: Talk!*, www.ejiltalk.org/permanent-imminence-of-armed-attacks-resolution-2249-2015-and-the-right-to-self-defence-against-designated-terrorist-groups/

Williams, MJ, *The Good War: NATO and the Liberal Conscience in Afghanistan* (Palgrave Macmillan, 2011).

Williams, M, "Rules, Community and the Individual," in Williams, M (ed.), *Wittgenstein, Mind and Meaning: Toward a Social Conception of Mind* (Routledge, 1999), 176.

Williams, WS, and Ford, CM (eds.), *Complex Battlespaces: The Law of Armed Conflict and the Dynamics of Modern Warfare*. The Lieber Studies Series (Oxford University Press, 2019), 33–59.

Wilmshurst, E, "The Chatham House Principles of International Law on the Use of Force by States in Self-Defence" (2006) 55 *International and Comparative Law Quarterly* 4, 963.

Windsor, L, "The Language of Radicalization: Female Internet Recruitment to Participation in ISIS Activities" (2020) 23 *Terrorism and Political Violence* 3, 506–38.

Winter, Y, "The Asymmetric War Discourse and Its Moral Economies: A Critique" (2011) 3 *International Theory* 3, 488–514.

Wittgenstein, L, *Philosophical Investigations* (4th ed., Wiley-Blackwell, 2009, trans. and ed. by PMS Hacker and Joachim Schulte).

Woods, C, *Sudden Justice: America's Secret Drone Wars* (Oxford University Press, 2015).

Zarakol, A, "What Makes Terrorism Modern? Terrorism, Legitimacy and the International System" (2011) 37 *Review of International Studies* 5, 2311–36.

Zoller, E, "The War Powers in French Constitutional Law" (1996) 90 *Proceedings of the Annual Meeting (American Society of International Law)* 46–51.
Zubeldia, O, *Histoire des drones* (Perrin Editions, 2012).

Official Statements and Discourses

United States

Summary Records of the Joint Committee, *Final Record*, vol. II-B, 1st Meeting, April 26, 1949, p. 10.
President G. W. Bush Addresses the Nation, September 20, 2001, Transcript available in *The Washington Post*, www.washingtonpost.com/wp-srv/nation/specials/attacked/transcripts/bushaddress_092001.html
George W. Bush, "Address to a Joint Session of Congress and the American People," The White House, September 20, 2001, https://georgewbush-whitehouse.archives.gov/news/releases/2001/09/20010920-8.html
Presidential Address to the Nation, October 7, 2001, https://georgewbush-whitehouse.archives.gov/news/releases/2001/10/20011007-8.html
Remarks of Harold Hongju Koh, Legal Adviser, US Department of State Annual Meeting of the American Society of International Law, Washington, DC, March 25, 2010, "The Obama Administration and International Law," https://2009-2017.state.gov/s/l/releases/remarks/139119.htm
Remarks of John O. Brennan, Assistant to the President for Homeland Security and Counterterrorism, on Ensuring al-Qa'ida's Demise – As Prepared for Delivery, The White House, June 29, 2010, https://obamawhitehouse.archives.gov/the-press-office/2011/06/29/remarks-john-o-brennan-assistant-president-homeland-security-and-counter
Justice Department White Paper, "Legality of a Lethal Operation by the CIA against a US Citizen," May 25, 2011 (available in Jameel Jaffer, *The Drone Memos: Targeted Killing, Secrecy and the Law* (The New Press, 2010, document 4).
John Brennan, White House Homeland Security & Counterterrorism Adviser, Obama Administration Counterterrorism Strategy (C-Span television broadcast), June 29, 2011, www.c-spanvideo.org/program/AdministrationCo
Remarks of John O. Brennan, Assistant to the President for Homeland Security and Counterterrorism, Harvard Law School, Cambridge, Massachusetts September 16, 2011, "Strengthening Our Security by Adhering to Our Values and Laws."
Department of Justice White Paper, "Lawfulness of a Lethal Operation Directed against a U.S. Citizen Who Is a Senior Operational Leader of Al-Qa'ida or

an Associated Force," November 8, 2011, https://fas.org/irp/eprint/doj-lethal.pdf.

President Obama's Google + Hangout, WHITEHOUSE.GOV, January 30, 2012, www.whitehouse.gov/photos-andvideo/video/2012/01/30/president-obama-s-googlehangout

Jeh Charles Johnson, Dean's Lecture at Yale Law School, "National Security Law, Lawyers and Lawyering in the Obama Administration," Yale Law School, February 22, 2012, www.cfr.org/national-security-and-defense/jeh-johnsons-speech-national-security-law-lawyers-lawyering-obama-administration/p27448

Remarks of Eric Holder, Attorney General of the United States Northwestern University School of Law, Chicago, March 5, 2012, www.justice.gov/iso/opa/ag/speeches/2012/ag-speech-1203051.html

Remarks of John O. Brennan, Assistant to the President for Homeland Security and Counterterrorism, "The Efficacy and Ethics of US Counterterrorism Strategy," Woodrow Wilson International Center for Scholars, Washington, DC, April 30, 2012, www.wilsoncenter.org/event/the-efficacy-and-ethics-uscounterterrorism-strategy

Letter from Amnesty International et al. to Barack Obama, President of the United States, May 31, 2012, www.justforeignpolicy.org/node/1242

Speech by John Brennan to the Council on Foreign Relations, Washington, DC, August 9, 2012, www.lawfareblog.com/2012/08/transcript-of-john-bren nans-speech-at-the-council-on-foreign-relations

Harold H. Koh, "Twenty First Century International Law Making," October 17, 2012, Speech of the Legal Adviser of the Department of State at the Georgetown University Law Centre.

Jeh Charles Johnson, "The Conflict against Al Qaeda and Its Affiliates: How Will It End?," General Counsel of the US Department of Defense at the Oxford Union, Oxford University, November 30, 2012, www.lawfareblog.com/jeh-johnson-speech-oxford-union

Remarks by the President at the National Defense University, National Defense University, Fort McNair, Washington, DC, The White House, May 23, 2013, www.whitehouse.gov/the-press-office/2013/05/23/remarks-president-national-defense-university

Barack Obama, "Statement by the President on ISIL," The White House, September 10, 2014, https://obamawhitehouse.archives.gov/the-press-office/2014/09/10/Statement-president-isil-1

Transcript: President Obama's Address to the Nation on the San Bernardino Terror Attack and the War on ISIS, December 6, 2015, CNN, http://edition.cnn.com/2015/12/06/politics/transcript-obama-san-bernardino-isis-address/index.html

US Department of Defense, "Statement from Pentagon Press Secretary Peter Cook on Airstrike in Somalia," Press Operations, Release No. NR-076-16,

March 7, 2016, www.defense.gov/News/News-Releases/News-Release-View/Article/687305/statement-from-pentagon-press-secretary-peter-cook-on-air strike-in-somalia?source=GovDelivery

Remarks of Brian J. Egan, Legal Adviser, US Department of State Annual Meeting of the American Society of International Law, Washington, DC, April 1, 2016, "International Law, Legal Diplomacy, and the Counter-ISIL Campaign."

President Barack Obama, "Statement by the President on Afghanistan," The White House, July 6, 2016.

Charles Faulkner, "Letter from the US Department of State Bureau of Legislative Affairs, to Foreign Relations Chairman Bob Corker on the Legal Basis for the Use of Force," August 2, 2017, https://assets.documentcloud.org/documents/3911844/8-2-17-Corker-Response.pdf

President Trump's Speech to the UN General Assembly, September 19, 2017, http://edition.cnn.com/2017/09/19/politics/president-trump-united-nations-speech/index.html

United Kingdom

UK Defence Secretary Michael Fallon, "UK to Provide Further Support to Forces Fighting ISIL," November 5, 2014, www.gov.uk/government/news/uk-to-provide-further-support-to-forces-fighting-isil

David Cameron's Oral Statement to Parliament, "Syria: Refugees and Counter-terrorism – Prime Minister's Statement," September 7, 2015, www.gov.uk/government/speeches/syria-refugees-and-counter-terrorism-prime-ministers-statement

Letter of the UK Permanent Representative, United Kingdom Mission to the UN, to the President of the Security Council, September 7, 2015.

UK Mission to the United Nations, September 7, 2015, "Letter on Drone Strike," www.justsecurity.org/wp-content/uploads/2015/09/UK_UNSC_Letter_on_Drone_Strike_7Sept2015.pdf

House of Commons, "Oral Evidence: The Work of the Attorney General," Rt. Hon. Jeremy Wright QC MP, Attorney General, HC 409, Tuesday, September 15, 2015.

Joint Committee on Human Rights, Rt. Hon. Michael Fallon, "Oral Evidence: The UK Government's Policy on the Use of Drones for Targeted Killing," 2015, http://data.parliament.uk/writtenevidence/committeeevidence.svc/evidencedocument/human-rights-committee/the-uk-governments-policy-on-the-use-of-drones-for-targeted-killing/oral/27633.html

House of Lords and House of Commons, Joint Committee on Human Rights, "The Government's Policy on the Use of Drones for Targeted Killing," Second Report of Session 2015–16, April 27, 2016.

Rt. Hon. Jeremy Wright QC MP, Attorney General's Speech at the International Institute for Strategic Studies, Attorney General Discusses the Modern Law of Self-defence at the International Institute for Strategic Studies, January 11, 2017, www.gov.uk/government/speeches/attorney-generals-speech-at-the-international-institute-for-strategic-studies

Prime Minister Theresa May, Full Speech on London Bridge Attack, June 4, 2017, http://time.com/4804640/london-attack-theresa-may-speech-transcript-full/

Rt. Hon. Amber Rudd MP, "Home Secretary Statement on Recent Terrorist Attacks to the Parliament," June 22, 2017, www.gov.uk/government/speeches/home-secretary-statement-on-recent-terrorist-attacks

Theresa May's Speech to the UN General Assembly 2017, September 29, 2017, www.gov.uk/government/speeches/multilateral-cooperation-must-continue-to-effectively-counter-terrorism-and-violent-extremism

Statement on Counterterrorism by Ambassador Jonathan Allen, UK Deputy Permanent Representative to the United Nations, "Multilateral Cooperation Must Continue to Effectively Counter Terrorism and Violent Extremism," September 29, 2017, www.gov.uk/government/speeches/multilateral-cooperation-must-continue-to-effectively-counter-terrorism-and-violent-extremism

Theresa May, Full Speech at the Munich Security Conference, February 17, 2018, www.gov.uk/government/speeches/pm-speech-at-munich-security-conference-17-february-2018

Australia

Letter Dated September 9, 2015 from the Permanent Representative of Australia to the United Nations Addressed to the President of the Security Council, S/2015/693.

Public Lecture on "The Right of Self-Defence against Imminent Armed Attack in International Law," Delivered in April 2017 by Australian Attorney-General, Senator the Hon. George Brandis Q, www.ejiltalk.org/author/gbrandis/

Minister for Defense, the Hon. Christopher Pyne MP, Joint Media Release, "Australian-Designed Unmanned 'Loyal Wingman' Aircraft to Be Developed with Industry," February 27, 2019, www.minister.defence.gov.au/minister/steven-ciobo/media-releases/australian-designed-unmanned-loyal-wingman-aircraft-be

Russia

Permanent Representative of Georgia to the United Nations, Letter Dated September 13, 2002 from the Permanent Representative of Georgia to the United Nations Addressed to the Secretary-General Transmitting a Statement by Russian Federation President V. V. Putin dated September 12, 2002, UN Doc. A/57/409–S/2002/1035, Annex (September 16, 2002).

France

President François Hollande, "France Supporting Mali against Terrorists," Statement Following the Select Defense Council, Paris, January 12, 2013, https://uk.ambafrance.org/France-supporting-Mali-against

Laurent Fabius, Ministère des Affaires étrangères et du Développement international, "Le groupe terroriste Daech n'est pas un Etat; nous devons les neutraliser" (QAG,10/09/2014), 2014, www.youtube.com/watch?v=Nmolp1uNdpY

President François Hollande, Conférence Internationale Sur la Paix et la Sécurité en Irak, September 15, 2014, www.youtube.com/watch?v=Lwf2tpzcl4U

Sixth Conference of the French President on the Challenges and Priorities of the Executive Policy, Sixième Conférence du Président de la République François Hollande, September 7, 2015, Palais de l'Élysée, www.vie-publique.fr/discours/196108-conference-de-presse-de-m-francois-hollande-president-de-la-republique

Letters Dated September 8, 2015 from the Permanent Representative of France to the United Nations Addressed to the Secretary-General and the President of the Security Council, September 9, 2015.

Speech of Former French Prime Minister, Discours de Manuel Valls devant l'Assemblée Nationale, September 15, 2015, www.gouvernement.fr/syrie-la-france-est-en-guerre-contre-le-terrorisme-le-djihadisme-l-islamisme-radical-ce-sera-long-2873

President François Hollande, Speech in Front of Parliament, November 16, 2015, www.youtube.com/watch?v=d6Hdlq3DLAM

Loi de programmation militaire 2019–2025, July 2018, see also the Annexed report, Discours du président de la République devant le Parlement réuni en Congrès, November 16, 2015, www.elysee.fr/declarations/article/discours-du-president-de-la-republique-devant-le-parlement-reuni-en-congres-3/

Discours de Manuel VALLS, Premier ministre à l'Assemblée nationale – Engagement des forces en Syrie [Prime Minister Manuel Valls, Speech at the National Assembly, "French Involvement in Syria"], November 25, 2015, www.gouvernement.fr/sites/default/files/document/document/2016/01/20151125_discours_de_manuel_valls_premier_ministre_-_engagement_forces_en_syrie_relu.pdf

French Minister of Defense Jean-Yves Le Drian, "Qui est l'ennemi ?" [Who Is the Enemy], Opening Speech of the 2015 National Conference on Strategic Research, Paris, December 1, 2015, www.asafrance.fr/item/officiel-discours-d-ouverture-des-assises-nationales-2015-de-la-recherche-strategique-de-m-jean-yves-le-drian-ministre-de-la-defense-a-paris-le-1er-decembre-2015-extrait.html

Institut de Recherche Stratégique de l'École Militaire, "Quels Drones Pour Quels Usages à L'horizon 2020 ?," May 18, 2016, www.defense.gouv.fr/irsem/page-d-accueil/nos-evenements/quels-drones-pour-quels-usages-a-l-horizon-2020-le-mercredi-18-mai-2016

Joint Statement of Intent by Mr Jean-Yves Le Drian (then) Minister of Defense of the French Republic (Currently Minister of Foreign Affairs), and the Honorable Ashton Carter, Secretary of Defense of the United States of America, Signed in Washington, DC, November 28, 2016.

Le Drian, J-Y, *Qui est l'ennemi ?* (Editions du Cerf, 2016).

Former French Prime Minister, Manuel Valls, M, *L'Exigence* (Grasset, 2016).

Airwars, "Coalition Airstrike 20 Sept 15 in Mosul Iraq," May 12, 2017, www.youtube.com/watch?v=iglfe4h4crQ

French Minister of the Armed Forces, Madame Florence Parly, "Discours de clôture de Florence Parly – Ministre des armées, Université d'été de la Défense 2017," September 5, 2017, www.defense.gouv.fr/salle-de-presse/discours/discours-de-florence-parly/discours-de-cloture-de-florence-parly-universite-d-ete-de-la-defense-2017

French Minister of the Armed Forces, Florence Parly, Radio France Inter, October 6, 2017, 8:25 a.m., www.franceinter.fr/emissions/l-invite-de-8h20/l-invite-de-8h20-06-octobre-2017

Minister of the Armed Forces Florence Parly, Speech at Global Leaders Forum, CSIS, Washington DC, October 20, 2017, www.csis.org/events/global-leaders-forum-he-florence-parly-minister-armed-forces-france

Florence Parly, "L'EI est d'ores et déjà en train de redéployer son action," France 24, November 15, 2017, www.france24.com/fr/20171511-entretien-florence-parly-etat-islamique-terrorisme-barkhane-g5-sahel

Florence Parly, Assemblée nationale, XVe législature, Session ordinaire de 2017–2018, Compte rendu intégral, Première séance du mardi 20 mars 2018, www.assemblee-nationale.fr/15/cri/2017-2018/20180160.asp#P1204140

Interview of President Macron, "Macron, un an après : le grand entretien en intégralité," Mediapart, YouTube, April 15, 2018, www.youtube.com/watch?v=mt0as7x-kfs&t=964s

Compte rendu, Commission de la défense nationale et des forces armées, Audition du général François Lecointre, chef d'état-major des armées, sur le projet de loi de finances pour 2019, October 18, 2018, Report No. 15.

Official Twitter Account of French Minister of the Armed Forces Florence Parly, December 20, 2018, https://twitter.com/florence_parly/status/1075667341546045441

Minister of the Armed Forces, Press release, Barkhane Operation, "Frappe contre un rassemblement de membres d'un groupe armé terroriste dans la région de Douentza," January 7, 2021, https://archives.defense.gouv.fr/salle-de-presse/communiques/communique-de-presse_operation-barkhane_frappe-contre-un-rassemblement-de-membres-d-un-groupe-arme-terroriste-dans-la-region-de-douentza

Minister of the Armed Forces, Press release, Barkhane Operation, "Réaction au rapport de la Minusma sur les frappes de janvier au Mali," March 30, 2021, www.asafrance.fr/item/communique-de-presse-du-ministere-des-armees-reaction-au-rapport-de-la-minusma-sur-les-frappes-de-janvier-au-mali.html

French Minister of the Armed Forces, Florence Parly, Déclaration de Mme Florence Parly, ministre des armées, "Speech on the Ethics of Air Power and Controlling the Air Space," October 19, 2021, www.vie-publique.fr/discours/282081-florence-parly-19102021-ethique-de-la-puissance-aerienne

French Ministry of the Armed Forces, "Point de situation des opérations du vendredi 29 avril au jeudi 05 mai," News Release on the Operations Conducted from April 29 and May 5, 2022, www.defense.gouv.fr/point-situation-operations/point-situation-operations-du-vendredi-29-avril-au-jeudi-05-mai

Netherlands

Ministerie van Defensie, "Defensie kiest Reaper als onbemand vliegtuig," November 21, 2013, www.defensie.nl/actueel/nieuws/2013/11/21/defensie-kiest-reaper-als-onbemand-vliegtuig

Defense Update, "Netherlands to Field Four MQ-9 Reaper Drones by 2017," February 8, 2015, http://defense-update.com/20150208_dutch_reapers.html

Official Governmental Documents

France

Governmental Report to Parliament on the Conditions of Military Intervention on Domestic Soil to Protect the Population, 2016 [translated from French "Conditions d'emploi des armées lorsqu'elles interviennent sur le territoire national pour protéger la population"].

White Paper on Defense, Livre Blanc sur la Défense et la Sécurité Nationale, 2013, www.livreblancdefenseetsecurite.gouv.fr/pdf/le_livre_blanc_de_la_defense_2013.pdf

Strategic Defense Review, Revue stratégique de défense et de sécurité nationale, 2017, www.defense.gouv.fr/dgris/presentation/evenements/revue-strategique-de-defense-et-de-securite-nationale-2017

United States

War Powers Resolution

War Powers Resolution 6-Month Reports of June 15, 2012, December 14, 2012, and June 14, 2013, www.whitehouse.gov/the-press-office/2012/06/15/presidential-letter-2012-war-powers-resolution-6-month-report

War Powers Resolution 6-Month Reports of December 14, 2012, https://obamawhitehouse.archives.gov/the-press-office/2012/12/14/letter-president-war-powers-resolution

War Powers Resolution 6-Month Reports of June 14, 2013, www.whitehouse.gov/the-press-office/2013/06/14/letter-president-regarding-war-powers-resolution

Letter from the President Barack Obama, War Powers Resolution Regarding Iraq, To the Speaker of the House of Representatives and the President Pro Tempore of the Senate, September 23, 2014, www.whitehouse.gov/the-press-office/2014/09/23/letter-president-war-powers-resolution-regarding-iraq

Letter from the President, "Six Month Consolidated War Powers Resolution Report," June 11, 2015, https://obamawhitehouse.archives.gov/the-press-office/2015/06/11/letter-president-six-month-consolidated-war-powers-resolution-report

Other

Communication of the US regarding the Killing of Harithi al-Yemeni, May 4, 2006, A/HRC/4/20/Add.1

Presidential Policy Guidance, May 22, 2013 – Released only in 2016, "Procedures for Approving Direct Action against Terrorist Targets Located outside the United States and Areas of Active Hostilities."

"Fact Sheet: The President's May 23 Speech on Counterterrorism," 2013, www.whitehouse.gov/the-press-office/2013/05/23/fact-sheet-president-s-may-23-speech-counterterrorism

"Fact Sheet: U.S. Policy Standards and Procedures for the Use of Force in Counterterrorism Operations outside the United States and Areas of Active Hostilities," May 23, 2013, www.whitehouse.gov/the-press-office/2013/05/23/fact-sheet-us-policy-standards-and-procedures-use-force-counterterrorism

French Ministry of Armed Forces, Presentation of the Serval Operation in Mali 2013–14, "Présentation de l'Opération," www.defense.gouv.fr/english/operations/missionsachevees/operation-serval-2013-2014/dossier/presentation-de-l-operation

Letter Dated 23 September 2014 from the Permanent Representative of the United States of America to the United Nations Addressed to the Secretary-General, UN Doc. S/2014/695, September 23, 2014.

US Department of Defense, "Obama, Hagel Mark End of Operation Enduring Freedom," DoD News, Defense Media Activity, Washington, December 28, 2014, www.defense.gov/News-Article-View/Article/603860/obama-hagel-mark-end-of-operation-enduring-freedom

Office of the Coordinator for the Counterterrorism, National Consortium for the Study of Terrorism and Responses to Terrorism: Annex of Statistical Information, June 2016, www.state.gov/j/ct/rls/crt/2015/257526.htm

Executive Order, July 2016, "Releasing Aggregate Data on Strikes Undertaken by the U.S. Government against Terrorist Targets outside Areas of Active Hostilities."

The White House, Executive Order, "United States Policy on Pre- and Post-Strike Measures to Address Civilian Casualties in U.S. Operations Involving the Use of Force," July 1, 2016, www.whitehouse.gov/the-press-office/2016/07/01/executive-order-united-states-policy-pre-and-post-strike-measures

Bureau of Counterterrorism and Countering Violent Extremism, Country Reports on Terrorism 2016, Released July 2017, www.state.gov/documents/organization/272488.pdf

President Donald Trump, National Security and Defense, Executive Order on Revocation of Reporting Requirement, March 6, 2019, www.whitehouse.gov/presidential-actions/executive-order-revocation-reporting-requirement/

Agreement for Bringing Peace to Afghanistan between the Islamic Emirate of Afghanistan Which Is Not Recognized by the United States as a State and Is Known as the Taliban and the United States of America, February 29, 2020, www.state.gov/wp-content/uploads/2020/02/Agreement-For-Bringing-Peace-to-Afghanistan-02.29.20.pdf

Joint Statement on the Signing of the US–Taliban Agreement, by Special Envoys and Special Representatives of the European Union, France, Germany, Italy, Norway, the United Kingdom, the United Nations and the United States of America on the Occasion of the Signing of the US–Taliban Agreement on February 29 in Qatar, March 9, 2020, www.state.gov/joint-statement-on-the-signing-of-the-u-s-taliban-agreement-2/

United Kingdom

UK Ministry of Defence, Joint Doctrine Note 2/11, "The UK Approach to Unmanned Aircraft Systems," March 30, 2011.

UK Ministry of Defence, "Update: Air Strikes in Iraq," October 6, 2014, www.gov.uk/government/news/latest-iraq-air-strikes

Government Legal Department, Leigh Day, "Proposed Application for Judicial Review by Caroline Lucas MP and Baroness Jones of Moulescoomb," October 23, 2015.

UK Ministry of Defence, Joint Doctrine Publication 0-30.2, "Unmanned Aircraft Systems," August 2017.

UK Ministry of Defence and the Rt. Hon. Ben Wallace MP, "Update: Air Strikes against Daesh," May 29, 2020, www.gov.uk/government/news/update-air-strikes-against-daesh

Parliamentary Investigations

France

French National Assembly, Statement of French Former Minister of Defense, Déclaration de M. Jean-Yves Le Drian, Ministre de la Défense, en réponse à une question sur les frappes aériennes françaises en Syrie, à l'Assemblée nationale le 30 septembre 2015, Questions d'actualité à l'Assemblée nationale, September 30, 2015.

French Parliament, Committee of Inquiry on the Means Used by the State to Counter Terrorism, Commission d'enquête parlementaire relative aux moyens mis en œuvre par l'Etat pour lutter contre le terrorisme depuis le 7 janvier 2015, Reports, Comptes rendus, www2.assemblee-nationale.fr/14/autres-commissions/commissions-d-enquete/moyens-pour-lutter-contre-le-terrorisme/(block)/ComptesRendusCommission/(instance_leg)/14/(init)/0-14

French Parliament, Committee of Inquiry on the Means Used by the State to Counter Terrorism, Commission d'enquête parlementaire relative aux moyens mis en œuvre par l'Etat pour lutter contre le terrorisme depuis le 7 janvier 2015, Hearing Transcripts, www.assemblee-nationale.fr/14/cr-cemoyter/15-16/c1516032.asp

Commission d'enquête parlementaire relative aux moyens mis en œuvre par l'Etat pour lutter contre le terrorisme, Audition, à Huis Clos du Général Pierre de Villiers, Chef D'état-Major Des Armées Compte Rendu de L'audition, May 9, 2016.

Rapport d'enquête relative aux moyens mis en œuvre par l'Etat pour lutter contre le terrorisme depuis le 7 Janvier 2015, Assemblée Nationale, July 2016.

Among other interventions, see in particular:

Hearing of Général Bruno Le Ray, gouverneur militaire de Paris, and of Colonel Marc Boileau, chef de cabinet, March 21, 2016.

Hearing of M. Marc Trévidic, Premier vice-président du TGI de Lille, April 6, 2016.

Hearing of Général Pierre de Villiers, Chef d'état-major des armées, May 9, 2016, www.assemblee-nationale.fr/14/cr-cemoyter/15-16/c1516020.asp#P324_120754

Hearing of Pierre Razoux, directeur de recherche à l'Institut de recherche stratégique de l'École militaire (IRSEM), May 19, 2016.

Jean-Yves Le Drian, Minister of Defense, June 1, 2016, www.assemblee-nationale.fr/14/cr-cemoyter/15-16/c1516032.asp

French Senate, "Drones d'observation et drones armés: un enjeu de souveraineté," Rapport d'information de MM. Cédric PERRIN, co-président, Gilbert ROGER, co-président, Jean-Marie BOCKEL et Raymond VALL, fait au nom de la commission des affaires étrangères, de la défense et des forces armées, no. 559 (2016–2017), May 23, 2017, www.senat.fr/espace_presse/actualites/201705/les_drones_dans_les_forces_armees.html, 14, 18, 77.

United Kingdom

UK House of Commons, Louisa Brooke-Holland, "Overview of Military Drones Used by the UK Armed Forces," Briefing Paper, No. 06493, October 8, 2015.

UK House of Commons Debate, Prime Minister David Cameron, November 25, 2015, column 1491.

Prime Minister David Cameron, Memorandum to the Foreign Affairs Select Committee, Prime Minister's Response to the Foreign Affairs Select Committee's Second Report of Session 2015–16: The Extension of Offensive British Military Operations to Syria, November 2015.

UK Parliament Joint Committee on Human Rights (JCHR), "Report on the Government's Policy on the Use of Drones for Targeted Killings," May 10, 2016.

UK Parliament Intelligence and Security Committee, Report on UK Lethal Drone Strikes in Syria, April 26, 2017.

United States

CIA Director George Tenet, "Written Statement for the Record of the Director of Central Intelligence before the National Commission on Terrorist Attacks upon the United States," March 24, 2004, 16, http://govinfo.library.unt.edu/911/hearings/hearing8/tenet_statement.pdf

Parliamentary Debates

France

French Parliament, Debated Law on Military Programming for 2019–2025, Transcripts, Full Legislative File Available Here: www.senat.fr/dossier-legislatif/pjl17-383.html

Among other interventions, see in particular:

First Session of Tuesday 20 March 2018, Minister of Armed Forces Florence Parly, Assemblée nationale, XVe législature, Session ordinaire de 2017–2018, www.assemblee-nationale.fr/15/cri/2017-2018/20180160.asp#P1204140

Session of 23 May 2019, Communist Party Amendment Proposal no. 52, www.senat.fr/seances/s201805/s20180523/s20180523011.html

United Kingdom

UK Parliament, "Commons Recalled to Debate Iraq: Coalition against ISIL," September 26, 2014, www.parliament.uk/business/news/2014/september/house-of-commons-debate-uk-government-response-to-isil/

UK Parliament Joint Committee on Human Rights (JCHR), Report on the Government's Policy on the Use of Drones for Targeted Killings, May 10, 2016.

UK Parliament Intelligence and Security Committee, Report on UK Lethal Drone Strikes in Syria, April 26, 2017.

Reports and Databases

Databases

Database of The Bureau of Investigative Journalism on Drone Warfare, www.thebureauinvestigates.com/projects/drone-war

TBIJ, "Civilians Killed," https://docs.google.com/spreadsheets/d/1NAfjFonM-Tn7fziqiv33HlGt09wgLZDSCP-BQaux51w/edit#gid=1976356146

TBIJ, "Drone Strikes in Afghanistan," www.thebureauinvestigates.com/projects/drone-war/afghanistan

TBIJ, "Drone Strikes in Yemen," www.thebureauinvestigates.com/projects/drone-war/yemen

TBIJ, "Afghanistan: Reported US Covert Actions 2019," www.thebureauinvestigates.com/drone-war/data/afghanistan-reported-us-covert-actions-2019

TBIJ, Case no. AFG4236Ci, March 24, 2020, www.thebureauinvestigates.com/drone-war/data/afghanistan-reported-us-covert-actions-2020#strike-47179

TBIJ, "CIA and US Military Drone Strikes in Pakistan, 2004 to Present," www.thebureauinvestigates.com/projects/drone-war/charts?show_casualties=1&show_injuries=1&show_strikes=1&location=pakistan&from=2004-1-1&to=now

TBIJ, "US Strikes in Yemen, 2002 to Present," www.thebureauinvestigates.com/projects/drone-war/charts?show_casualties=1&show_injuries=1&show_strikes=1&location=yemen&from=2002-1-1&to=now

TBIJ, "Yemen: Reported US Covert Action," www.thebureauinvestigates.com/drone-war/data/yemen-reported-us-covert-actions-2016#YEM224

TBIJ, "Pakistan 2004 onwards CIA Drone Strikes," www.thebureauinvestigates.com/projects/drone-war/charts?show_casualties=1&show_injuries=1&show_strikes=1&location=pakistan&from=2004-1-1&to=now

TBIJ, "US Drone Strikes in Pakistan," www.thebureauinvestigates.com/projects/drone-war/charts?show_casualties=1&show_injuries=1&show_strikes=1&location=pakistan&from=2004-1-1&to=now

TBIJ, "Pakistan: Reported US Strikes 2010," www.thebureauinvestigates.com/drone-war/data/obama-2010-pakistan-strikes

TBIJ, "Pakistan: Reported US Strikes 2018," www.thebureauinvestigates.com/drone-war/data/pakistan-reported-us-strikes-2018#strike-19510

The Bureau of Investigative Journalism, "US Strikes in Somalia, 2007 to Present," https://docs.google.com/spreadsheets/d/1-LT5TVBMy1Rj2WH30xQG9nqr8-RXFVvzJE_47NlpeSY/edit#gid=1110953463

TBIJ, Covert War on Terror, The Data, www.thebureauinvestigates.com/2011/08/10/the-bush-years-2004-2009/

Chris Woods and Christina Lamb, "CIA Tactics in Pakistan Include Targeting Rescuers and Funerals," The Bureau of Investigative Journalism, February 4, 2012, www.thebureauinvestigates.com/stories/2012-02-04/cia-tactics-in-pakistan-include-targeting-rescuers-and-funerals

Jack Serle, "Comment: If Drone Strikes Continue in Afghanistan, the Lack of Transparency Must Not," October 16, 2014, www.thebureauinvestigates.com/2014/10/16/comment-if-drone-strikes-continue-in-afghanistan-the-lack-of-transparency-must-not/

The Bureau of Investigative Journalism, "Afghanistan: US Air and Drone Strikes, 2015 to Present," www.thebureauinvestigates.com/projects/drone-war/afghanistan

Jack Serle, "Trump's 100 Days: US Air Campaign Hammers Yemen with Almost a Strike a Day," April 27, 2017.

Drone Wars, https://dronewars.net/

Chris Cole, "Drone in Iraq and Syria: What We Know and What We Don't," Drone Wars UK, November 7, 2014, https://dronewars.net/2014/11/07/drones-in-iraq-and-syria-what-we-know-and-what-we-dont/

Chris Cole, "Information Tribunal Dismisses Drone Wars Appeal over British Drone Secrecy," Drone Wars UK, August 17, 2017, https://dronewars.net/2017/08/17/information-tribunal-dismisses-drone-wars-appeal-over-british-drone-secrecy/

"Interview of Air Marshall Greg Bagwell by Chris Cole," Drone Wars UK, January 2018, https://dronewars.net/interview-of-air-marshall-greg-bagwell-drone-wars-uk

The Intercept, The Drone Papers, September 2015, https://theintercept.com/drone-papers/

The Intercept, The Drone Papers, "The Kill Chain," https://theintercept.com/drone-papers/the-kill-chain/

The Intercept, The Drone Papers, "The Assassination Complex" (2015), https://theintercept.com/drone-papers/the-assassination-complex/

Nick Turse, "Target Africa: America's Expanding Drone Network," in The Intercept, The Drone Papers, Article no. 8 of 8, October 15, 2015.

The Intercept, Nick Turse, Henrik Moltke, and Alice Speri, "Secret War: The US Has Conducted 550 Drone Strikes in Libya Since 2011 – More Than in Somalia, Yemen, or Pakistan," The Intercept in partnership with La Repubblica, June 21, 2018, https://theintercept.com/2018/06/20/libya-us-drone-strikes/

Forensic Architecture, The Drone Strikes Platform, https://forensic-architecture.org/investigation/the-drone-strikes-platform

Forensic Architecture, "Case Study No. 1: Datta Khel, North Waziristan, March 16–17, 2011," www.forensic-architecture.org/case/drone-strikes/

Forensic Architecture, "Airstrikes on the Al-Jinah Mosque," https://forensic-architecture.org/investigation/airstrikes-on-the-al-jinah-mosque

Uppsala Conflict Data Program, http://ucdp.uu.se/#/encyclopedia

Center for International Security and Cooperation (CISAC), https://cisac.fsi.stanford.edu/mappingmilitants

"Al Qaeda in the Arabian Peninsula," Stanford Center for International Security and Cooperation, https://cisac.fsi.stanford.edu/mappingmilitants/profiles/al-qaeda-arabian-peninsula#text_block_18748

"Al Qaeda," Stanford Center for International Security and Cooperation, https://cisac.fsi.stanford.edu/mappingmilitants/profiles/al-qaeda#text_block_18733

"Timeline: Al-Qaeda," BBC News Special Reports http://news.bbc.co.uk/2/hi/7546355.stm

"A Wedding That Became a Funeral | US Drone Attack on Marriage Procession in Yemen," Human Rights Watch, February 19, 2014, www.hrw.org/report/2014/02/19/wedding-became-funeral/us-drone-attack-marriage-procession-yemen

Reports and Resolutions

UN Security Council

UN Security Council, Resolution 1970 (2011), February 26, 2011, S/RES/1970, www.undocs.org/S/RES/1970%20(2011)

UN Security Council, Resolution 1973 (2011), March 17, 2011, S/RES/1973, www.undocs.org/S/RES/1973%20(2011)

UN SC 6526th Meeting, May 2, 2011, UN Press Release SC/10239.

UN Security Council, Resolution 2178 (2014), September 24, 2014, S/RES/2178, www.un.org/en/sc/ctc/docs/2015/SCR%202178_2014_EN.pdf

UN Security Council, Resolution 2249 (2015), Adopted by the Security Council at Its 7565th Meeting, on November 20, 2015, S/RES/2249 (2015).

UN Security Council, Resolution 2359 (2017), Adopted by the Security Council at Its 7979th Meeting, on June 21, 2017, http://unscr.com/en/resolutions/doc/2359

UN Security Council, Resolution 2372 (2017), August 30, 2017, SC/12972, www.un.org/press/en/2017/sc12972.doc.htm

UN Human Rights Council

Human Rights Council, Report of the Special Rapporteur on Extra Judicial, Summary or Arbitrary Executions, Philip Alston, May 28, 2010, A/HRC/14/24/Add.6.

Report of the International Commission of Inquiry on Libya to Investigate All Alleged Violations of International Human Rights Law in the Libyan Arab Jamahiriya, June 1, 2011, A/HRC/17/44.

Human Rights Council, "Report of the Special Rapporteur on Extrajudicial, Summary or Arbitrary Executions," Christof Heyns, Submitted in Accordance with Assembly Resolution 67/168, September 13, 2013, A/68/382.

Human Rights Council, "Ensuring Use of Remotely Piloted Aircraft or Armed Drones in Counter-terrorism and Military Operations in Accordance with

International Law, including International Human Rights and Humanitarian Law," Resolution (A/HRC/25/L.32), March 24, 2014.

Human Rights Council, "Report of the Special Rapporteur on Extrajudicial, Summary or Arbitrary Executions," Christof Heyns, April 24, 2015, A/HRC/29/37.

Human Rights Council, "Report of the Independent International Commission of Inquiry on the Syrian Arab Republic," August 8, 2017, A/HRC/36/55.

Human Rights Council, "Report of the Special Rapporteur on Extrajudicial, Summary or Arbitrary Executions," UN Special Rapporteur Agnes Callamard, June 29, 2020, A/HRC/44/3.

UN High Commissioner

"Pillay Calls for International Inquiry into Libyan Violence and Justice for Victims," Office of the High Commissioner for Human Rights, February 22, 2011, www.ohchr.org/en/NewsEvents/Pages/DisplayNews.aspx?NewsID=10743&LangID=E

"Report of the United Nations High Commissioner for Human Rights on the Situation of Human Rights in Afghanistan and on the Achievements of Technical Assistance in the Field of Human Rights in 2013," January 10, 2014, A/HRC/25/41.

UN General Assembly

Secretariat Memorandum on the Régime of the High Seas (July 14, 1950), United Nations (General Assembly) Doc. A/CN. 4/32.

Other

ICRC, "Interpretive Guidance on the Notion of Direct Participation in Hostilities," 2009. HCJ 769/02 Public Committee against Torture in Israel v. Gov't. of Israel, PD 62(1) 507 [2006] (Isr.).

ICRC, International Humanitarian Law and the Challenges of Contemporary Armed Conflicts, Report of the 31st Conference of the International Red Cross and Red Crescent, Report, 2011, https://www.icrc.org/en/doc/resources/documents/report/31-international-conference-ihl-challenges-report-2011-10-31.htm

North Atlantic Treaty Organization, "NATO and Afghanistan," last updated August 2022, www.nato.int/cps/en/natohq/topics_8189.htm

"Libya Security Forces Kill 84 over Three Days," Human Rights Watch, February 19, 2011, www.hrw.org/en/news/2011/02/18/libya-security-forces-kill-84-over-three-days

"Popular Protest in North African and the Middle East (V): Making Sense of Libya," International Crisis Group Middle East/North Africa Report No. 107, June 6, 2011.

International Human Rights and Conflict Resolution Clinic (Stanford Law School) and Global Justice Clinic (NYU School of Law), "Living Under Drones: Death, Injury, and Trauma to Civilians from US Drone Practices in Pakistan," September 2012, www-cdn.law.stanford.edu/wp-content/uploads/2015/07/Stanford-NYU-Living-Under-Drones.pdf

Cora Currier and Justin Elliott, "Drone Warfare 'Signature Strikes'," *Global Research*, February 27, 2013, www.globalresearch.ca/drone-warfare-signature-strikes/5324491

Barry D. Watts, "The Evolution of Precision Strike, Centre for Strategic and Budgetary Assessments," August 6, 2013, https://csbaonline.org/uploads/documents/Evolution-of-Precision-Strike-final-v15.pdf

Amnesty International, "'Will I Be Next?' US Drone Strikes in Pakistan," October 2013, www.amnesty.org/download/Documents/12000/asa330132013en.pdf

Human Rights Watch, "Between a Drone and Al Qaeda, The Civilian Cost of US Targeted Killings in Yemen," October 22, 2013, www.hrw.org/report/2013/10/22/between-drone-and-al-qaeda/civilian-cost-us-targeted-killings-yemen

Open Society Foundations, "After the Dead Are Counted: U.S. and Pakistani Responsibilities to Victims of Drone Strikes," November 2014, www.opensocietyfoundations.org/publications/after-dead-are-counted-us-and-pakistani-responsibilities-victims-drone-strikes

Fiona Nelson, "Litigating Drone Attacks: ECCHR's Expert Workshop and Public Forum in Review," in Report "Litigating Drone Strikes," ECCHR, 2017, 22, www.ecchr.eu/fileadmin/Publikationen/Litigating_Drone_Strikes_PDF.pdf

Rosalind Comyn, "Rights Watch (UK) Taking UK Government to Court over Refusal to Disclose Legal Basis for Targeted Killings," *Rights Watch UK*, July 20, 2017, www.rwuk.org/rights-watch-uk-taking-uk-government-to-court-over-refusal-to-disclose-legal-basis-for-targeted-killings/

Azmat Khan and Anand Gopal, "The Uncounted," *The New York Times*, November 16, 2017, www.nytimes.com/interactive/2017/11/16/magazine/uncounted-civilian-casualties-iraq-airstrikes.html?_r=0

"Making Sense of the Sahel in Recent Years, the Region Has Become a Base for Violent Extremists and Those Fighting Them," *ADF*, July 7, 2020, https://adf-magazine.com/2020/05/making-sense-of-the-sahel/

United Nations, Multidimensional Integrated Stabilization Mission in Mali (MINUSMA), "Report on the Bounty Strike" ["Rapport sur l'incident de Bounty du 3 janvier 2021"], March 2021, https://minusma.unmissions.org/sites/default/files/rapport_final_bounty_bounty9.pdf

United Nations, UN SRCT Drone Inquiry, "Case 1 – Datta Khel," http://unsrct-drones.com/report/159

ICJ

ICJ, Independent International Fact-Finding Mission on the Conflict in Georgia, Report, September 2009.

Online Media Sources

"Musharraf Makes His Case for Helping U.S.," CNN World, September 19, 2001, https://edition.cnn.com/2001/WORLD/asiapcf/south/09/19/pakistan.address/index.html

"'Reaper' Moniker Given to MQ-9 Unmanned Aerial Vehicle," US Air Force, September 14, 2006, www.af.mil/News/Article-Display/Article/129780/reaper-moniker-given-to-mq-9-unmanned-aerial-vehicle/

"Most Bajaur Victims Were under 20," *The News*, November 4, 2006 www.thenews.com.pk/archive/print/646502-'most-bajaur-victims-were-under-20

Salman Masood and Pir Zubair Shah, "C.I.A. Drones Kill Civilians in Pakistan," *The New York Times*, March 17, 2011, www.nytimes.com/2011/03/18/world/asia/18pakistan.html

Tom Wright and Rehmat Mehsud, "Pakistan Slams U.S. Drone Strike," *The Wall Street Journal*, March 18, 2011.

Scott Shane, "Contrasting Reports of Drone Strikes," *The New York Times*, August 11, 2011, www.nytimes.com/2011/08/12/world/asia/12droneside.html?ref=asia&mtrref=undefined&gwh=AA5BB874ECB05EFD4B4F0EFBA50C0835&gwt=pay

Julian E. Barnes, "U.S. Expands Drone Flights to Take Aim at East Africa," *The Wall Street Journal*, September 21, 2011.

CNN, "Al-Shabaab Joining al Qaeda, Monitor Group Says," February 9, 2012.

"Predator Drones and Unmanned Aerial Vehicles (UAVs)," *The New York Times*, March 5, 2012, http://topics.nytimes.com/top/reference/timestopics/subjects/u/unmanned_aerial_vehicles/index.html

David Cenciotti, "The Dawn of the Robot Age: US Air Force Testing Air-Launched UCAVs Capable to Fire Maverick and Shrike Missiles in 1972," *The Aviationist*, March 14, 2012, http://theaviationist.com/2012/03/14/the-dawn-of-the-robot-age/

Jo Becker and Scott Shane, "Secret 'Kill List' Proves a Test of Obama's Principles and Will," *The New York Times*, May 29, 2012, www.nytimes.com/2012/05/29/world/obamas-leadership-in-war-on-al-qaeda.html?_r=0

"10 Killed in Two South Waziristan Drone Attacks," *The News*, June 3, 2012 www.thenews.com.pk/archive/print/622794-10-killed-in-two-south-waziristan-drone-attacks

David D. Kirkpatrick and Steven Lee Myers, "Libya Attack Brings Challenges for U.S.," *The New York Times*, September 12, 2012, www.nytimes.com/2012/09/13/world/middleeast/us-envoy-to-libya-is-reported-killed.html

Greg Miller, "In interview, Yemeni President Acknowledges Approving U.S. Drone Strikes," *The Washington Post*, September 29, 2012, www.washingtonpost.com/world/national-security/yemeni-president-acknowledges-approving-us-drone-strikes/2012/09/29/09bec2ae-0a56-11e2-afff-d6c7f20a83bf_story.html

"Plan for Hunting Terrorists Signals U.S. Intends to Keep Adding Names to Kill Lists," *The Washington Post*, October 23, 2012, www.washingtonpost.com/world/national-security/plan-for-hunting-terrorists-signals-us-intends-to-keep-adding-names-to-kill-lists/2012/10/23/4789b2ae-18b3-11e2-a55c-39408fbe6a4b_story.html?hpid=z1&utm_term=.1143e2137871

Craig Whitlock, "Remote US Base at Core of Secret Operations," *The Washington Post*, October 25, 2012.

Tara McKelvey, "A Former Ambassador to Pakistan Speaks Out," *The Daily Beast*, November 20, 2012, www.thedailybeast.com/a-former-ambassador-to-pakistan-speaks-out

Ben Hartman, "Ya'alon: IDF Cuts Revolutionary, Will Recreate Army," July 11, 2013, *The Jerusalem Post*, www.jpost.com/defense/yaalon-idf-cuts-revolutionary-will-produce-new-army-319510.

"Ground Unit," *ESD ARTeMIS*, April 30, 2014, https://esdartemis.wordpress.com/

Greg Miller, "White House Mistakenly Identifies CIA Chief in Afghanistan," *The Washington Post*, May 25, 2014, www.washingtonpost.com/world/national-security/white-house-mistakenly-identifies-cia-chief-in-afghanistan/2014/05/25/ac8e80cc-e444-11e3-8f90-73e071f3d637_story.html

"Dealing with Boko Haram," *The New York Times*, May 30, 2014, www.nytimes.com/2014/05/31/opinion/dealing-with-boko-haram.html

"Fin de Serval au Mali, lancement de l'opération 'Barkhane' au Sahel," France 24, July 13, 2014, www.france24.com/fr/20140713-operation-serval-mali-france-barkhane-le-drian-defense-militaire-terroriste

Jean Guisnel, "Le Drian et Hollande installent l'opération Barkhane," *Le Point*, July 16, 2014, www.lepoint.fr/editos-du-point/jean-guisnel/le-drian-et-hollande-installent-l-operation-barkhane-16-07-2014-1846497_53.php

Craig Whitlock, "Pentagon Set to Open Second Drone Base in Niger as It Expands Operations in Africa," *The Washington Post*, September 1, 2014.

Yara Bayoumy, "ISIS Urges More Attacks on Western 'Disbelievers'," *The Independent*, September 22, 2014, www.independent.co.uk/news/world/middle-east/isis-urges-more-attacks-on-western-disbelievers-9749512.html

Andrew Sparrow and Claire Philipps, "UK Parliament Approves Air Strikes against ISIS in Iraq – As It Happened," *The Guardian*, September 26, 2014, www.theguardian.com/politics/blog/live/2014/sep/26/mps-debate-and-vote-on-air-strikes-against-islamic-state-politics-live-blog

Louise Arimatsu and Michael Schmitt, "The Legal Basis for the War against ISIS Remains Contentious," October 6, 2014, *The Guardian*, www.theguardian.com/commentisfree/2014/oct/06/legal-basis-war-isis-syria-islamic-state

State of Israel, "The 2014 Gaza Conflict: Factual and Legal Aspects (2015)" [2014 Gaza Conflict Report], http://mfa.gov.il/ProtectiveEdge/Documents/2014GazaConflictFullReport.pdf

"Charlie Hebdo Attack: Three Days of Terror," *BBC News*, January 14, 2015, Section Europe, www.bbc.com/news/world-europe-30708237

"Seven Killed in Shawal Drone Strike," *The News*, January 20, 2015, www.thenews.com.pk/print/10388-seven-killed-in-shawal-drone-strike

Robert Windrem, "Only One of Six Al-Qaeda-Linked Americans Killed by Drone on Purpose," NBC News, April 23, 2015, www.nbcnews.com/news/us-news/only-one-six-al-qaeda-linked-americans-killed-drone-purpose-n347046

Eli Lake and Josh Rogin, "How the U.S. Tracked Down Al-Qaeda's Yemen Chief," Bloomberg View, June 16, 2015, http://goo.gl/kk526Q

"Yemen al-Qaeda Chief al-Wuhayshi Killed in US Strike," *BBC News*, June 16, 2015, www.bbc.com/news/world-middle-east-33143259

Greg Miller, "CIA Didn't Know Strike Would Hit al-Qaeda Leader," *The Washington Post*, June 17, 2015, http://goo.gl/RCUSut

Ewen MacAskill and Richard Norton-Taylor, "How UK Government Decided to Kill Reyaad Khan," *The Guardian*, September 8, 2015, www.theguardian.com/world/2015/sep/08/how-did-britain-decide-to-assassinate-uk-isis-fighter-reyaad-khan-drone-strike

"MQ-9 Reaper," September 23, 2015, www.af.mil/About-Us/Fact-Sheets/Display/Article/104470/mq-9-reaper/

CNN, "Operation Enduring Freedom Fast Facts," Regularly Updated until September 30, 2015, http://edition.cnn.com/2013/10/28/world/operation-enduring-freedom-fast-facts/

Andrea Shalal, "U.S. Government Approves Italy's Request to Arm Its Drones," Reuters, November 4, 2015, www.reuters.com/article/italy-usa-drones-idUSL1N12Z05620151104

Eleanor Steafel, "Paris Terror Attack: Everything We Know on Saturday Afternoon," *Telegraph*, November 21, 2015, www.telegraph.co.uk/news/worldnews/europe/france/11995246/Paris-shooting-What-we-know-so-far.html

Gordon Lubold and Julian E. Barnes, "Italy Quietly Agrees to Armed US Drone Missions over Libya," February 22, 2016, www.wsj.com/articles/italy-quietly-agrees-to-armed-u-s-drone-missions-over-libya-1456163730

Sarah D. Wire, "Essential Politics May Archives: U.S. House Rejects Rep. Barbara Lee's Push to End War Authorization," *The Los Angeles Times*, May 2016, www.latimes.com/politics/essential/la-pol-sac-essential-politics-20160501-htmlstory.html#u-s-house-rejects-rep-barbara-lees-push-to-end-war-authorization

Spencer Ackerman, "US to Continue 'Signature Strikes' on People Suspected of Terrorist Links," *The Guardian*, July 1, 2016.

Thomas Gibbons-Neff, "Britain Set to Purchase $1 Billion in Advanced U.S. Predator Drones," *The Washington Post*, November 17, 2016, Section Checkpoint, www.washingtonpost.com/news/checkpoint/wp/2016/11/17/britain-set-to-purchase-1-billion-in-advanced-u-s-predator-drones/

Eric Adams, "A Stronger, Faster Predator Drone Is Headed for European Airspace," *Wired*, December 12, 2016.

Tim Lester, Ray Sanchez, Mark Bixler, Sean O'Key, Michael Hogenmiller, and Mohammed Tawfeeq, "ISIS Goes Global: 143 Attacks in 29 Countries Have Killed 2,043," CNN, Last Update February 13, 2017, http://edition.cnn.com/2015/12/17/world/mapping-isis-attacks-around-the-world/index.html

The Editorial Board, "Preventing a Free-for-All with Drone Strikes," *The New York Times*, March 16, 2017.

Thomas Gibbons-Neff, "U.S. Finds that March Airstrike that Struck Building Described as Mosque Was Legal," *The Washington Post*, June 7, 2017, www.washingtonpost.com/news/checkpoint/wp/2017/06/07/u-s-finds-that-march-airstrike-that-struck-building-described-as-mosque-was-legal-and-resulted-in-one-civilian-casualty/

Thomas Gibbons-Neff, "ISIS Drones Are Attacking U.S. Troops and Disrupting Airstrikes in Raqqa, Officials Say," *The Washington Post*, June 14, 2017, Section Checkpoint www.washingtonpost.com/news/checkpoint/wp/2017/06/14/isis-drones-are-attacking-u-s-troops-and-disrupting-airstrikes-in-raqqa-officials-say/

Michelle Nichols, "France Softens Proposed U.N. Backing for Sahel Force to Appease U.S.," Reuters, June 20, 2017, www.reuters.com/article/us-africa-security-sahel-un/france-softens-proposed-u-n-backing-for-sahel-force-to-appease-u-s-idUSKBN19B321

Jonathan Watts, "Battle for the Mother Land: Indigenous People of Colombia Fighting for Their Lands," *The Guardian*, October 29, 2017, www.theguardian.com/environment/2017/oct/28/nasa-colombia-cauca-valley-battle-mother-land

Jack Khoury and Yaniv Kubovich, "Gaza-Based Islamic Jihad Drops Claim of Israeli Drone Strike," *Haaretz*, December 12, 2017, www.haaretz.com/israel-news/gaza-based-islamic-jihad-drops-claim-of-israeli-drone-strike-1.5628454

EFAD Country Profile on the Netherlands, 2017, www.efadrones.org/wp-content/uploads/2017/12/The-Netherlands.pdf

Alex Liautaud, "More Bombs, More Boots, More Casualties," Vice News, January 15, 2018.

Samuel Osborne, "Does ISISs Really 'Claim Every Terror Attack'? How Do We Know If a Claim Is True?," *The Independent*, March 23, 2018, www.inde

pendent.co.uk/news/world/middle-east/isis-terror-attack-claim-real-true-legitimate-fake-false-how-to-know-a8270116.html

Declan Walsh and Eric Schmitt, "U.S. Strikes Qaeda Target in Southern Libya, Expanding Shadow War There," *The New York Times*, March 25, 2018.

Shuaib Almosawa and Maryam Saleh, "A 13-Year-Old Boy and Other Yemeni Civilians Were Killed in U.S. Drone Strikes This Month," The Intercept, March 26, 2018, https://theintercept.com/2018/03/26/yemen-drone-strike-civilians-war-on-terror/.

Linda Schlegel, "Interview: Rising Drone Capabilities of Non-state Actors," *Global Risk Insights*, April 17, 2018, https://globalriskinsights.com/2018/04/interview-risk-non-state-actor-drone-capabilities/

"President Macron on Relations with the US, Syria and Russia," Fox News, April 22, 2018, www.foxnews.com/transcript/president-macron-on-relations-with-the-us-syria-and-russia

Adam Rawnsley, "Family Says They're Innocent Victims of Trump's Drone War," *The Daily Beast*, May 7, 2018, www.thedailybeast.com/family-says-theyre-innocent-victims-of-trumps-drone-war

Joe Penney, Eric Schmitt, Rukmini Callimachi, and Christoph Koettl, "CIA Drone Mission, Curtailed by Obama, Is Expanded in Africa under Trump," *The New York Times*, September 9, 2018, www.nytimes.com/2018/09/09/world/africa/cia-drones-africa-military.html

Spencer Ackerman, "Trump Ramped Up Drone Strikes in America's Shadow Wars," *The Daily Beast*, November 15, 2018, www.thedailybeast.com/trump-ramped-up-drone-strikes-in-americas-shadow-wars

"ISIS Not Defeated in Syria Despite Trump Claim, Says UK," *The Guardian*, December 19, 2018, www.theguardian.com/politics/2018/dec/19/isis-not-defeated-in-syria-despite-trump-claim-says-uk

Mark Landler, Helene Cooper, and Eric Schmitt, "Trump to Withdraw U.S. Forces from Syria, Declaring 'We Have Won against ISIS'," *The New York Times*, December 19, 2018, www.nytimes.com/2018/12/19/us/politics/trump-syria-turkey-troop-withdrawal.html

Charlie Savage, "Trump Revokes Obama-Era Rule on Disclosing Civilian Casualties from US Airstrikes outside War Zones," *The New York Times*, March 6, 2019, www.nytimes.com/2019/03/06/us/politics/trump-civilian-casualties-rule-revoked.html

Nathalie Guibert, "La France entre dans l'ère des drones armés," *Le Monde*, March 21, 2019, www.lemonde.fr/international/article/2019/03/21/la-france-entre-dans-l-ere-des-drones-armes_5439209_3210.html

"U.S. Drone Strike Kills 30 Pine Nut Farm Workers in Afghanistan," Reuters, September 20, 2019, www.reuters.com/article/us-afghanistan-attack-drones-idUSKBN1W40NW

Héni Nsaibia and Caleb Weiss, "The End of the Sahelian Anomaly: How the Global Conflict between the Islamic State and Al Qaida Finally Came to West Africa," CTC, July 2020, https://ctc.usma.edu/the-end-of-the-sahelian-anomaly-how-the-global-conflict-between-the-islamic-state-and-al-qaida-finally-came-to-west-africa/

"Mali: le doute subsiste après une intervention de l'armée française," TV5Monde, January 6, 2021, https://information.tv5monde.com/afrique/mali-le-doute-subsiste-apres-une-intervention-de-l-armee-francaise-390514

M. Drevet, L. Mieusset, R. Mignot-Mahdavi, C. Pinel, and A. Yehiel, "Testimony of a French Drone Operator: Anticipatory Strikes in the Sahel," European Forum on Armed Drones (EFAD), February 16, 2022, www.efadrones.org/testimony-of-a-french-drone-operator-anticipatory-strikes-in-the-sahel/

"Mali: France Has Lost 'Legal Basis' for Military Operations," *Africanews*, May 4, 2022, www.africanews.com/2022/05/04/mali-france-has-lost-legal-basis-for-military-operations/

Documents and Media of Jihadist Groups

Jamaat Nusrat al-Islam wal Muslimeen, *Az-Zallaqa Foundation Journal*, no. 152, March 8, 2020.

Case Law

International Court of Justice

ICJ, Fisheries Case (United Kingdom v. Norway), Pleadings, ICJ Reports, 1951, Vol. IV, p. 605.

ICJ, Military and Paramilitary Activities in and against Nicaragua v. US, Judgment, 1986 ICJ Reports 1986, p. 14 and Separate Opinions of Judge Ago and President Singh.

ICJ, Elettronica Sicula S.p.A. (ELSI), Judgment, ICJ Reports 1989, p. 15.

ICJ, Legality of the Threat or Use of Nuclear Weapons, Advisory Opinion, July 8, 1996, ICJ Reports 1996, p. 226.

ICJ, Oil Platforms (Islamic Republic of Iran v. United States of America), Judgment of November 6, 2003, ICJ Reports 2003, p. 161, and dissenting opinions of Judge Elaraby and Judge Simma.

ICJ, Legal Consequences of the Construction of a Wall in the Occupied Palestinian Territory, Advisory Opinion, July 9, 2004, ICJ Reports 2004, p. 136.

ICJ, Professor M. Brownlie, Audience Publique en l'affaire des activités armées sur le territoire du Congo, Translation, CR 2005/7, April 18, 2005, p. 31.

ICJ, Armed Activities on the Territory of the Congo (Democratic Republic of the Congo v. Uganda), Judgment of December 19, 2005, ICJ Reports 2005, p. 168.

ICJ, Application of the Convention on the Prevention and Punishment of the Crime of Genocide (Bosnia and Herzegovina v. Serbia and Montenegro), Judgment, ICJ Reports 2007, p. 43; Dissenting Opinion Judge Al-Khasawneh (dissenting opinion, [36]–[39]) and Judge ad hoc Mahiou (dissenting opinion, [113]–[117]).

International Criminal Tribunal for the Former Yugoslavia

ICTY, Prosecutor v. Dusko Tadić a/k/a "Dule," Decision on the Defence Motion for Interlocutory Appeal on Jurisdiction, Appeals Chamber, IT-94-1-I, October 2, 1995.

ICTY, Trial Chamber, Prosecutor v. Tadic, Trial Judgment, Case No. IT-94-1-T, May 7, 1997. ICTY, Prosecutor v. Mucić et al. (IT-96-21), Trial Judgment, November 16, 1998.

ICTY, Prosecutor v. Tadić (Judgment), Case No. IT-94-1-A. 38 ILM 1518 (1999), Appeals Chamber, July 15, 1999.

ICTY, The Prosecutor v. Dragoljub Kunarac, Radomir Kovač and Zoran Vuković, Case No. IT-96–23 & IT-96–23/1-A, Judgment, June 12, 2002.

ICTY, Trial Chamber, Prosecutor v. Slobodan Milošević (IT-02-54), Rule 98 bis Decision, February 5, 2004.

ICTY, Trial Chamber, Prosecutor v. Halilović (IT-01-48), November 16, 2005.

ICTY, Trial Chamber, Prosecutor v. Limaj et al. (IT-03-66), November 30, 2005.

ICTY, Trial Judgment, Prosecutor v. Hadžihasanović & Kubura (IT-01-47), March 15, 2006.

ICTY, Trial Chamber, Prosecutor v. Martić (IT-95-11), Judgment, June 12, 2007.

ICTY, Trial Chamber, Prosecutor v. Mrkšić et al. (IT-95-13/1), Judgment, September 27, 2007.

ICTY, Trial Chamber, Prosecutor v. Haradinaj et al. (IT-04-84), April 3, 2008.

European Court of Human Rights

ECtHR, Cyprus v. Turkey [GC], Appl. No. 25781/94, May 10, 2001.

ECtHR, Banković and Others v. Belgium, Appl. No. 52207/99, December 12, 2001.

ECtHR, Al-Saadoon and Mufdhi v. the United Kingdom, Appl. No. 61498108, June 30, 2009.

ECtHR, Al Skeini and Others v. United Kingdom, Appl. No. 55721/07, July 7, 2011.

United States Courts

US Supreme Court, Salim A. Hamdan v. Donald H. Rumsfeld et al., No. 05-184, June 29, 2006.

US Court of Appeals DC, Belkacem Bensayah v. Barack Obama et al., No. 08-5537, June 28, 2010.

US Court of Appeals DC, Mohammed Al-Adahi v. Barack Obama et al., No. 09-5333, July 13, 2010.

US District Court for the District of Columbia, Moath Hamza Ahmed Al-Alwi v. Barack Obama et al., No. 09-5125, July 22, 2011.

US District Court for the District of Columbia, Nasser al-Aulaqi v. Leon Panetta, US Motion to Dismiss, US District Court for the District of Columbia, December 14, 2012, www.aclu.org/files/assets/tk_govt_motion_to_dismiss.pdf

US Court of Appeals for the District of Columbia, Abdul Razak Ali v. Barack Obama, No. 11-5102, December 3, 2013.

UK Courts

First-Tier Tribunal, General Regulatory Chamber, Chris Cole v. The Information Commissioner and the Ministry of Defence, July 11, 2017, No. EA/2016/0290, https://dronewarsuk.files.wordpress.com/2017/08/023-150817-open-decision.pdf

Norms and Legislation

International

Article 2(4) of the United Nations Charter, 26 June 1945, entered into force on October 24, 1945.

Article 38(1)(b), ICJ Statute (part of the United Nations Charter).

Official Records, Diplomatic Conference on the Reaffirmation and Development of International Humanitarian Law Applicable in Armed Conflicts, O.R. IV, p. 12, CDDHII/79.

Geneva Conventions and Their Additional Protocols:

Convention (I) for the Amelioration of the Condition of the Wounded and Sick in Armed Forces in the Field. Geneva, August 12, 1949.

Convention (II) for the Amelioration of the Condition of Wounded, Sick and Shipwrecked Members of Armed Forces at Sea. Geneva, August 12, 1949.

Convention (III) Relative to the Treatment of Prisoners of War. Geneva, August 12, 1949.

Convention (IV) Relative to the Protection of Civilian Persons in Time of War. Geneva, August 12, 1949.

Article 2 Common to the 1949 Geneva Conventions, https://ihl-databases.icrc.org/ihl/WebART/365-570005

Article 3 Common to the Four Geneva Conventions of 1949.

Protocol Additional to the Geneva Conventions of August 12, 1949, and Relating to the Protection of Victims of International Armed Conflicts (Protocol I), June 8, 1977.

Protocol Additional to the Geneva Conventions of 12 August 1949, and relating to the Protection of Victims of Non-International Armed Conflicts (Protocol II), June 8, 1977.

Commentaries of the Geneva Conventions and Additional Protocols

ICRC, Commentary on the Geneva Convention for the Amelioration of the Wounded and Sick in Armed Forces in the Field (Jean S. Pictet, ed., 1952).

ICRC, Commentary on the Additional Protocols of 8 June 1977 to the Geneva Conventions of August 12, 1949 (Yves Sandoz, Christophe Swinarski, and Bruno Zimmerman, eds., 1987).

Frederic Siordet and Jean S. Pictet, Geneva Conventions, Commentary (Four Volume Set): For the Amelioration of the Condition of the Wounded and Sick in Armed Forces in the Field – The Geneva Conventions of August 12, 1949 (International Committee of the Red Cross, 1995).

ICRC, Commentary of 2016, para. 223, https://ihl-databases.icrc.org/applic/ihl/ihl.nsf/Comment.xsp?action=openDocument&documentId=BE2D518CF5DE54EAC1257F7D0036B518#51_B

International Committee of the Red Cross, Commentary on the First Geneva Convention (Cambridge University Press, 2017).

Domestic

Constitution of the French Fifth Republic, October 4, 1958, Article 15, www.conseil-constitutionnel.fr/sites/default/files/as/root/bank_mm/anglais/constiution_anglais_oct2009.pdf

US Congress 2001, Authorization for the Use of Military Force (AUMF), Public Law 107–40, September 18, 2001, www.gpo.gov/fdsys/pkg/PLAW-107publ40/pdf/PLAW-107publ40.pdf

(French Statute Reference) Loi no. 2018-607 du 13 juillet 2018 relative à la programmation militaire pour les années 2019 à 2025 et portant diverses dispositions intéressant la défense, www.legifrance.gouv.fr/eli/loi/2018/7/13/ARMX1800503L/jo/texte

Annexed Report to the French Law on Military Programming (it should be noted that it also has legislative value), Rapport annexé (appears at the end of the legislation), www.legifrance.gouv.fr/affichTexte.do?cidTexte=JORFTEXT000037192797&dateTexte=20181122

INDEX

CAMBRIDGE STUDIES IN INTERNATIONAL AND COMPARATIVE LAW

Books in the Series

180 *Drones and International Law: A Techno-Legal Machinery*
Mignot-Mahdavi

179 *The Necessity of Nature: God, Science and Money in 17th Century English Law of Nature*
Mónica García-Salmones

178 *Making the World Safe for Investment: The Protection of Foreign Property 1922–1959*
Andrea Leiter

177 *National Governance and Investment Treaties*
Josef Ostřanský and Facundo Pérez Aznar

176 *Who Owns Outer Space? International Law, Astrophysics, and the Sustainable Development of Space*
Michael Byers and Aaron Boley

175 *Intervening in International Justice: Third States before Courts and Tribunals*
Brian McGarry

174 *Reciprocity in Public International Law*
Arianna Whelan

173 *When Environmental Protection and Human Rights Collide*
Marie-Catherine Petersmann

172 *The International Law of Sovereign Debt Dispute Settlement*
Kei Nakajima

171 *The Everyday Makers of International Law: From Great Halls to Back Rooms*
Tommaso Soave

170 *Virtue in Global Governance: Judgment and Discretion*
Jan Klabbers

169 *The Effects of Armed Conflict on Investment Treaties*
Tobias Ackermann

168 *Investment Law's Alibis: Colonialism, Imperialism, Debt and Development*
David Schneiderman

167 *Negative Comparative Law: A Strong Programme for Weak Thought*
Pierre Legrand

166 *Detention by Non-State Armed Groups under International Law*
Ezequiel Heffes

165 *Rebellions and Civil Wars: State Responsibility for the Conduct of Insurgents*
Patrick Dumberry

164 *The International Law of Energy*
Jorge Viñuales

163 *The Three Ages of International Commercial Arbitration*
Mikaël Schinazi

162 *Repetition and International Law*
Wouter Werner

161 *State Responsibility and Rebels: The History and Legacy of Protecting Investment Against Revolution*
Kathryn Greenman

160 *Rewriting Histories of the Use of Force: The Narrative of 'Indifference'*
Agatha Verdebout

159 *The League of Nations and the Protection of the Environment*
Omer Aloni

158 *International Investment Law and Legal Theory: Expropriation and the Fragmentation of Sources*
Jörg Kammerhofer

157 *Legal Barbarians: Identity, Modern Comparative Law and the Global South*
Daniel Bonilla Maldonado

156 *International Human Rights Law Beyond State Territorial Control*
Antal Berkes

155 *The Crime of Aggression under the Rome Statute of the International Criminal Court*
Carrie McDougall

154 *Minorities and the Making of Postcolonial States in International Law*
Mohammad Shahabuddin

153 *Preclassical Conflict of Laws*
Nikitas E. Hatzimihail

152 *International Law and History: Modern Interfaces*
Ignacio de la Rasilla

151 *Marketing Global Justice: The Political Economy of International Criminal Law*
Christine Schwöbel-Patel

150 *International Status in the Shadow of Empire*
Cait Storr

149 *Treaties in Motion: The Evolution of Treaties from Formation to Termination*
Edited by Malgosia Fitzmaurice and Panos Merkouris

148 *Humanitarian Disarmament: An Historical Enquiry*
Treasa Dunworth

147 *Complementarity, Catalysts, Compliance: The International Criminal Court in Uganda, Kenya, and the Democratic Republic of Congo*
Christian M. De Vos

146 *Cyber Operations and International Law*
François Delerue

145 *Comparative Reasoning in International Courts and Tribunals*
Daniel Peat

144 *Maritime Delimitation as a Judicial Process*
Massimo Lando

143 *Prosecuting Sexual and Gender-Based Crimes at the International Criminal Court: Practice, Progress and Potential*
Rosemary Grey

142 *Capitalism As Civilisation: A History of International Law*
Ntina Tzouvala

141 *Sovereignty in China: A Genealogy of a Concept Since 1840*
Adele Carrai

140 *Narratives of Hunger in International Law: Feeding the World in Times of Climate Change*
Anne Saab

139 *Victim Reparation under the Ius Post Bellum: An Historical and Normative Perspective*
Shavana Musa

138 *The Analogy between States and International Organizations*
Fernando Lusa Bordin

137 *The Process of International Legal Reproduction: Inequality, Historiography, Resistance*
Rose Parfitt

136 *State Responsibility for Breaches of Investment Contracts*
Jean Ho

135 *Coalitions of the Willing and International Law: The Interplay between Formality and Informality*
Alejandro Rodiles

134 *Self-Determination in Disputed Colonial Territories*
Jamie Trinidad

133 *International Law as a Belief System*
Jean d'Aspremont

132 *Legal Consequences of Peremptory Norms in International Law*
Daniel Costelloe

131 *Third-Party Countermeasures in International Law*
Martin Dawidowicz

130 *Justification and Excuse in International Law: Concept and Theory of General Defences*
Federica Paddeu

129 *Exclusion from Public Space: A Comparative Constitutional Analysis*
Daniel Moeckli

128 *Provisional Measures before International Courts and Tribunals*
Cameron A. Miles

127 *Humanity at Sea: Maritime Migration and the Foundations of International Law*
Itamar Mann

126 *Beyond Human Rights: The Legal Status of the Individual in International Law*
Anne Peters

125 *The Doctrine of Odious Debt in International Law: A Restatement*
Jeff King

124 *Static and Evolutive Treaty Interpretation: A Functional Reconstruction*
Christian Djeffal

123 *Civil Liability in Europe for Terrorism-Related Risk*
Lucas Bergkamp, Michael Faure, Monika Hinteregger and Niels Philipsen

122 *Proportionality and Deference in Investor-State Arbitration: Balancing Investment Protection and Regulatory Autonomy*
Caroline Henckels

121 *International Law and Governance of Natural Resources in Conflict and Post-Conflict Situations*
Daniëlla Dam-de Jong

120 *Proof of Causation in Tort Law*
Sandy Steel

119 *The Formation and Identification of Rules of Customary International Law in International Investment Law*
Patrick Dumberry

118 *Religious Hatred and International Law: The Prohibition of Incitement to Violence or Discrimination*
Jeroen Temperman

117 *Taking Economic, Social and Cultural Rights Seriously in International Criminal Law*
Evelyne Schmid

116 *Climate Change Litigation: Regulatory Pathways to Cleaner Energy*
Jacqueline Peel and Hari M. Osofsky

115 *Mestizo International Law: A Global Intellectual History 1842–1933*
Arnulf Becker Lorca

114 *Sugar and the Making of International Trade Law*
Michael Fakhri

113 *Strategically Created Treaty Conflicts and the Politics of International Law*
Surabhi Ranganathan

112 *Investment Treaty Arbitration As Public International Law: Procedural Aspects and Implications*
Eric De Brabandere

111 *The New Entrants Problem in International Fisheries Law*
Andrew Serdy

110 *Substantive Protection under Investment Treaties: A Legal and Economic Analysis*
Jonathan Bonnitcha

109 *Popular Governance of Post-Conflict Reconstruction: The Role of International Law*
Matthew Saul

108 *Evolution of International Environmental Regimes: The Case of Climate Change*
Simone Schiele

107 *Judges, Law and War: The Judicial Development of International Humanitarian Law*
Shane Darcy

106 *Religious Offence and Human Rights: The Implications of Defamation of Religions*
Lorenz Langer

105 *Forum Shopping in International Adjudication: The Role of Preliminary Objections*
Luiz Eduardo Salles

104 *Domestic Politics and International Human Rights Tribunals: The Problem of Compliance*
Courtney Hillebrecht

103 *International Law and the Arctic*
Michael Byers

102 *Cooperation in the Law of Transboundary Water Resources*
Christina Leb

101 *Underwater Cultural Heritage and International Law*
Sarah Dromgoole

100 *State Responsibility: The General Part*
James Crawford

99 *The Origins of International Investment Law: Empire, Environment and the Safeguarding of Capital*
Kate Miles

98 *The Crime of Aggression under the Rome Statute of the International Criminal Court*
Carrie McDougall

97 *'Crimes against Peace' and International Law*
Kirsten Sellars

96 *Non-Legality in International Law: Unruly Law*
Fleur Johns

95 *Armed Conflict and Displacement: The Protection of Refugees and Displaced Persons under International Humanitarian Law*
Mélanie Jacques

94 *Foreign Investment and the Environment in International Law*
Jorge E. Viñuales

93 *The Human Rights Treaty Obligations of Peacekeepers*
Kjetil Mujezinović Larsen

92 *Cyber Warfare and the Laws of War*
Heather Harrison Dinniss

91 *The Right to Reparation in International Law for Victims of Armed Conflict*
Christine Evans

90 *Global Public Interest in International Investment Law*
Andreas Kulick

89 *State Immunity in International Law*
Xiaodong Yang

88 *Reparations and Victim Support in the International Criminal Court*
Conor McCarthy

87 *Reducing Genocide to Law: Definition, Meaning, and the Ultimate Crime*
Payam Akhavan

86 *Decolonising International Law: Development, Economic Growth and the Politics of Universality*
Sundhya Pahuja

85 *Complicity and the Law of State Responsibility*
Helmut Philipp Aust

84 *State Control over Private Military and Security Companies in Armed Conflict*
Hannah Tonkin

83 *'Fair and Equitable Treatment' in International Investment Law*
Roland Kläger

82 *The UN and Human Rights: Who Guards the Guardians?*
Guglielmo Verdirame

81 *Sovereign Defaults before International Courts and Tribunals*
Michael Waibel

80 *Making the Law of the Sea: A Study in the Development of International Law*
James Harrison

79 *Science and the Precautionary Principle in International Courts and Tribunals: Expert Evidence, Burden of Proof and Finality*
Caroline E. Foster

78 *Transition from Illegal Regimes under International Law*
Yaël Ronen

77 *Access to Asylum: International Refugee Law and the Globalisation of Migration Control*
Thomas Gammeltoft-Hansen

76 *Trading Fish, Saving Fish: The Interaction between Regimes in International Law*
Margaret A. Young

75 *The Individual in the International Legal System: Continuity and Change in International Law*
Kate Parlett

74 *'Armed Attack' and Article 51 of the UN Charter: Evolutions in Customary Law and Practice*
Tom Ruys

73 *Theatre of the Rule of Law: Transnational Legal Intervention in Theory and Practice*
Stephen Humphreys

72 *Science and Risk Regulation in International Law*
Jacqueline Peel

71 *The Participation of States in International Organisations: The Role of Human Rights and Democracy*
Alison Duxbury

70 *Legal Personality in International Law*
Roland Portmann

69 *Vicarious Liability in Tort: A Comparative Perspective*
Paula Giliker

68 *The Public International Law Theory of Hans Kelsen: Believing in Universal Law*
Jochen von Bernstorff

67 *Legitimacy and Legality in International Law: An Interactional Account*
Jutta Brunnée and Stephen J. Toope

66 *The Concept of Non-International Armed Conflict in International Humanitarian Law*
Anthony Cullen

65 *The Principle of Legality in International and Comparative Criminal Law*
Kenneth S. Gallant

64 *The Challenge of Child Labour in International Law*
Franziska Humbert

63 *Shipping Interdiction and the Law of the Sea*
Douglas Guilfoyle

62 *International Courts and Environmental Protection*
Tim Stephens

61 *Legal Principles in WTO Disputes*
Andrew D. Mitchell

60 *War Crimes in Internal Armed Conflicts*
Eve La Haye

59 *Humanitarian Occupation*
Gregory H. Fox

58 *The International Law of Environmental Impact Assessment: Process, Substance and Integration*
Neil Craik

57 *The Law and Practice of International Territorial Administration: Versailles to Iraq and Beyond*
Carsten Stahn

56 *United Nations Sanctions and the Rule of Law*
Jeremy Matam Farrall

55 *National Law in WTO Law: Effectiveness and Good Governance in the World Trading System*
Sharif Bhuiyan

54 *Cultural Products and the World Trade Organization*
Tania Voon

53 *The Threat of Force in International Law*
Nikolas Stürchler

52 *Indigenous Rights and United Nations Standards: Self-Determination, Culture and Land*
Alexandra Xanthaki

51 *International Refugee Law and Socio-Economic Rights: Refuge from Deprivation*
Michelle Foster

50 *The Protection of Cultural Property in Armed Conflict*
Roger O'Keefe

49 *Interpretation and Revision of International Boundary Decisions*
Kaiyan Homi Kaikobad

48 *Multinationals and Corporate Social Responsibility: Limitations and Opportunities in International Law*
Jennifer A. Zerk

47 *Judiciaries within Europe: A Comparative Review*
John Bell

46 *Law in Times of Crisis: Emergency Powers in Theory and Practice*
Oren Gross and Fionnuala Ní Aoláin

45 *Vessel-Source Marine Pollution: The Law and Politics of International Regulation*
Alan Khee-Jin Tan

44 *Enforcing Obligations* Erga Omnes *in International Law*
Christian J. Tams

43 *Non-Governmental Organisations in International Law*
Anna-Karin Lindblom

42 *Democracy, Minorities and International Law*
Steven Wheatley

41 *Prosecuting International Crimes: Selectivity and the International Criminal Law Regime*
Robert Cryer

40 *Compensation for Personal Injury in English, German and Italian Law: A Comparative Outline*
Basil Markesinis, Michael Coester, Guido Alpa and Augustus Ullstein

39 *Dispute Settlement in the UN Convention on the Law of the Sea*
Natalie Klein

38 *The International Protection of Internally Displaced Persons*
Catherine Phuong

37 *Imperialism, Sovereignty and the Making of International Law*
Antony Anghie

36 *Principles of the Institutional Law of International Organizations*
C. F. Amerasinghe

35 *Necessity, Proportionality and the Use of Force by States*
Judith Gardam

34 *International Legal Argument in the Permanent Court of International Justice: The Rise of the International Judiciary*
Ole Spiermann

33 –

32 *Great Powers and Outlaw States: Unequal Sovereigns in the International Legal Order*
Gerry Simpson

31 *Local Remedies in International Law (second edition)*
Chittharanjan Felix Amerasinghe

30 *Reading Humanitarian Intervention: Human Rights and the Use of Force in International Law*
Anne Orford

29 *Conflict of Norms in Public International Law: How WTO Law Relates to Other Rules of International Law*
Joost Pauwelyn

28 –

27 *Transboundary Damage in International Law*
Hanqin Xue

26 –

25 *European Criminal Procedures*
Edited by Mireille Delmas-Marty and J. R. Spencer

24 *Accountability of Armed Opposition Groups in International Law*
Liesbeth Zegveld

23 *Sharing Transboundary Resources: International Law and Optimal Resource Use*
Eyal Benvenisti

22 *International Human Rights and Humanitarian Law*
René Provost

21 *Remedies against International Organisations*
Karel Wellens

20 *Diversity and Self-Determination in International Law*
Karen Knop

19 *The Law of Internal Armed Conflict*
Lindsay Moir

18 *International Commercial Arbitration and African States: Practice, Participation and Institutional Development*
Amazu A. Asouzu

17 *The Enforceability of Promises in European Contract Law*
James Gordley

16 *International Law in Antiquity*
David J. Bederman

15 *Money Laundering: A New International Law Enforcement Model*
Guy Stessens

14 *Good Faith in European Contract Law*
Reinhard Zimmermann and Simon Whittaker

13 *On Civil Procedure*
J. A. Jolowicz

12 *Trusts: A Comparative Study*
Maurizio Lupoi and Simon Dix

11 *The Right to Property in Commonwealth Constitutions*
Tom Allen

10 *International Organizations before National Courts*
August Reinisch

9 *The Changing International Law of High Seas Fisheries*
Francisco Orrego Vicuña

8 *Trade and the Environment: A Comparative Study of EC and US Law*
Damien Geradin

7 *Unjust Enrichment: A Study of Private Law and Public Values*
Hanoch Dagan

6 *Religious Liberty and International Law in Europe*
Malcolm D. Evans

5 *Ethics and Authority in International Law*
Alfred P. Rubin

4 *Sovereignty over Natural Resources: Balancing Rights and Duties*
Nico Schrijver

3 *The Polar Regions and the Development of International Law*
Donald R. Rothwell

2 *Fragmentation and the International Relations of Micro-States: Self-Determination and Statehood*
Jorri C. Duursma

1 *Principles of the Institutional Law of International Organizations*
C. F. Amerasinghe